A History of Early Film

A History of Early Film

Volume 2

Stephen Herbert

Routledge
Taylor & Francis Group

LONDON AND NEW YORK

First published 2000 by Routledge
4 Park Square, Milton Park, Abingdon, Oxon, OX14 4RN

and by Routledge
605 Third Avenue, New York, NY 10158

Routledge is an imprint of the Taylor & Francis Group, an informa business

First issued in hardback 2019

Typeset in Times by Keystroke, Jacaranda Lodge, Wolverhampton

British Library Cataloguing in Publication Data
A catalogue record for this book is available from the British Library

Library of Congress Cataloging in Publication Data
A catalogue record for this book has been requested

ISBN 978-0-415-21151-2 (set)
ISBN 978-0-415-21153-6 (Volume 2) (hbk)
ISBN 978-1-032-51274-7 (Volume 2) (pbk)

Publisher's note
The publisher has gone to great lengths to ensure the quality of this reprint, but points
out that some imperfections in the original material may be apparent.

Our First Kinematograph Show.

By Sylvanus.

It was clear to any one passing through our pretty little village that something unusual was on foot that summer evening. All the inhabitants of the cosy little cottages seemed out of doors, and there was a general air of expectation all over the place. It was so very seldom that anything occurred to disturb the serenity of the little village, for it was quite out of the beaten track, and not on the highway to any of the large cities, consequently it seldom saw a motor or any of the latest marvels of science. And to-day it was to see its first kinematograph show!

There, on the village green, was the large white tent, dazzlingly bright in the sun. Around the door was to be seen a group of rustics, gazing open-mouthed at the preparations within. What *were* those queer-shaped things like great iron bottles, and what *could* be inside that square-looking box. Altogether, curiosity and excitement ran high. The bills exhibited outside the tent announced "A Kinematograph Living Picture Show," admission 6d. and 3d. "Kinematograph"—what did the word mean? It was a foreign language to them. "Living pictures"—well, they knew something about "pictures"; did not their own rector's son, every Christmas, give them a lantern picture show, an event looked forward to by one and all the whole year round? Anyhow, whatever it all meant, they were nearly all going, and as soon as the doors were opened in they flocked, till nearly every seat was taken.

And now the lights are extinguished and all eyes turned towards the screen. Suddenly a picture appears—but what is this? The figures are moving, trees are waving in the wind, and everywhere is to be seen life and motion. It was a comic film that was being presented to our eyes, and intensely amusing, but there was no roar of irresistible laughter to be heard; all was utter silence for a few minutes, then awe found relief in a long-drawn exclamation of wonderment. Presently a sound of laughter was heard, but it was of a very subdued nature, for to the ignorant country mind there was a touch of the uncanny about it all. But as the evening wore on, and picture after picture followed in quick succession, enjoyment began to take the place of wonderment. It was a never to be forgotten evening to them all. They were taken to places and lands where they saw wonders and sights never dreamt of, and there was opened up to the more intelligent of the audience new fields of thought, and the knowledge that right away from this quiet little village there was a "delectable land"—a knowledge that bore fruit in after years to many there.

Presently there came upon the screen a picture of their own Queen Victoria, but this, I must confess, was a big disappointment to many of them. It was a complete disillusionment, and one little maid expressed the thoughts of many when she was heard to exclaim audibly, "Why, she's just like my Granny! Where's her crown?" It took them some time to recover from the knowledge that their Queen was apparently like any other old lady.

But the "pièce de resistance" was yet to come. Earlier in the week the village had been visited by two men, carrying a queer looking box on three legs, which at intervals they placed on the ground, whilst they appeared to be busily engaged turning a handle. This had been an object of great interest to the villagers, but had been forgotten in the greater excitement of the Kinematograph Show. Timothy Collins had been heard to express his opinion that it was a new-fangled scarecrow, for "he'd seen 'em up in Lunnon.' He had once been on a day's excursion to London, and this unique fact alone had made him the oracle of the village.

And now the last picture was announced, "A few familiar faces," and there on the screen before them is their own village street, and surely that imposing figure parading in great style is their own "arm of the law," whose services were called into requisition once a year at the most. Now the village tavern comes into view, and there to be seen is old Matthew, the village veteran, smoking his long pipe and holding forth to a group of old cronies tales of the good old times. It is natural to the very life, and again the feeling of awe takes hold of the audience.

Then a village mother is to be seen busy with her washtub outside her cottage door, but who, seeing a neighbour over the garden hedge, succumbs to the temptation of a gossip. A cluster of small children are seen playing in the road, making themselves as grubby as possible, in the way they have. Presently a quarrel ensues, and we are treated to a "battle royal" for a few minutes, the ultimate end of which is reached by the babies all scurrying home in different directions with their tales of woe. Not particularly elevating, perhaps, but highly amusing. But not more so than the very audible remarks from those mothers present who owned the various babies. These were very diverting, and it is a temptation to give them for the benefit of our readers, but we will refrain from doing so. And now in the distance, slowly wending their way through the meadows, come Farmer White's cows, driven by a sweet-faced maiden, who presently is joined by a youth whose face tells its own tale.

This brings the entertainment to a close, and the audience breaks up, not to go away and forget in a few days what they have seen, but to talk and wonder about it all for many a long day.

Notes on Current Topics.

Looking at some recent topical films, I could not help reflecting on the ease with which future generations will be enabled to form a conception of the habits and manners of our time, by means of the hundreds of films, representing practically every phase of our every-day life, which are in existence, as compared with the difficulty we experience in arriving at the condition of life in, say, the Elizabethan period. Few, if any, of these subjects have been taken with the actual purpose of informing our grandchildren in this way, but they rather gain than lose from the fact that they were primarily intended for our own amusement, just as a snapshot of a royal personage in a moment of relaxation may be more true to life than an elaborate painting by a flattering artist.

History on Tap.

Just think for a moment of the events of absorbing interest which our fortunate posterity will be enabled to see reproduced to the very life, by means of the motion picture film! The King's Coronation procession; the troups leaving for the South African war, their return through streets filled with cheering crowds; Kitchener's reception at Southampton; innumerable records of foreign royal visits; pictures of the sports of the day. All these, in conjunction with the written accounts of the various functions, will go to present an almost complete picture of the habits and happenings of our time. Of even greater value will be the incidental pictures given of present habits, methods of dress, etc., which will probably become obsolete in the course of the years. One has only to look round to see that even in our time objects which were once the commonest are now rare, and will shortly have disappeared. The "growler" is giving way to the taxicab, and will soon no longer add a picturesque appearance to our streets, while a horse-drawn tram is already an anachronism, and the "four-wheeler" and the tram are both recorded for the amazement and amusement of the people of the 23rd century. What would we not give to have similar records of the sedan chair and old mail coach?

Comics in A.D. 2200

There is also an amusing side to this matter. Of course we cannot guess in what direction future generations will develop, whether universal education will make them all preternaturally wise and serious, or whether class distinctions will tend to become more marked, so that one half of the population obtains to an abnormal cleverness at the expense of the degradation of the other half, as H. G. Wells suggests in one of his books. Whichever of these turns out to be true, one can easily imagine that our "comics" will be an object of the deepest interest to future students of history. Just as the students of our own day discourse learnedly on the character and intelligence of past ages from what evidences there are of their amusements, we may surely expect those of 2200 to form their opinion largely from our film subjects. Will their judgment be flattering or the reverse? On the whole, surely, not unfavourable, for with very few exceptions, the fun of our films is wholesome, and the pathos in the best of taste, while the films of scenery, industries, pageants, etc., must all speak well for us.

The Kinematograph a Political Power.

At times of political excitement—election times particularly—party organisers have occasionally risen to the height of showing slides of well known newspaper cartoons at their meetings, and during the recent L.C.C. elections in London, when money flowed so freely, we also saw, probably for the first time in this country, the kinematograph given an opportunity of showing its power in the same direction. It was used, but it was used in such an unenterprising manner that it is obvious that the parties in question were unaware of the fact that a living picture film, carefully prepared, has powers of caricature which almost overshadow those of the many clever men who employ their pencils as cartoonists on either side. I am not merely arguing for the employment of the kinematograph in electioneering. The amount of business to be done in this direction is so small that it would not be worth while for a manufacturer to cultivate it. I should like to see development of its powers of caricature both for electioneering purposes and in other directions which arise practically every day.

The Growth of Taste.

The difficulty of securing "plots" is, as we pointed out in our last issue, much less than is generally supposed, and no manufacturer need fear a fall in custom while he retains the ability to develop the dozens of suggestions which must reach him in one way or another. But it cannot be denied that we are appealing to a more critical public each year. The very fact that the pictures which he sees are continually improving, both in subject matter and in technique, gives rise to the expectation, in the breast of the average member of an audience, that they should still further improve. Friends of living pictures will not be completely satisfied if future developments take place on the lines of the plot, or "comic" subject, of to-day, though the humour and interest of the new subjects may be of a higher class than that of any which have gone before. There is a demand among the more critical section of the public—and that is the section worth cultivating—for development on slightly different lines. The chronophone and cinematophone are in a sense due to a realisation of that fact, at all events the abundant appreciation with which they have been received points to the fact that the public appreciates a new departure. The ambitious expeditions which have recently been launched for kinematograph purposes (all from England, be it noted in passing), point in the same direction.

Animated Cartoons.

The powers of caricature alluded to would seem to provide one direction for development. Instead of projecting F.C.G.'s or G.R.H.'s pictures by means of slides one might take a film founded on some of the best of them, in the manner advised last week, in respect to the *Leader's* "Humours of History." There was a cartoon in the *Westminster* last week, admirably suited to this purpose. Lord Robert Cecil and Mr. Alfred Lyttleton were represented as sportsmen armed with rifles labelled respectively "free trade" and "preference." They are in argument about a rabbit at their feet, which bears the features of Mr. Balfour, and of course the allusion is to the fact that while Mr. Lyttleton has been claiming Mr. B. as a tariff reformer, Lord Robert has been equally certain of his adherence to Free Trade principles. The *Punch* cartoon, on the same subject, also strikes us as suited to kinematographic illustration. Here the two gentlemen previously alluded to are rival shoe blacks. Each has firm hold of one of Mr. Balfour's legs and they seem likely to upset him between them. On the other side another *Punch* cartoon represented Sir Henry Campbell-Bannerman in the guise of a shop walker, directing everybody who comes in to the "Royal Commission Dept.," a hit as his undeniable tendency to dispose of questions in this manner at the beginning of his administration. A good film subject could be worked up from this.

Social Film Skits.

The foregoing are purely political subjects, and would be, of course, quite impossible in a music hall program, but they suggest others which are not open to the same objection. An Urban film, which illustrates Seymour Hicks editing the *Tatler* for a day, is the only subject which approaches the class we mean, which would take off the peculiarities of social notabilities—actors, etc.,—just as those already sketched take off political big wigs. For instance, we all know Mr. Algernon Ashton, almost as well as we know the king, and his two habits of putting people to rights and showing up the neglect of famous burial places, have often enough been made the subject of good-natured jokes in the newspapers. Why should not the kinematograph take a hand? "Mr. Ashton at home," Mr. Ashton writing to the papers," and "Mr. Ashton pointing out his errors to a sculptor," suggests humorous possibilities.   W.H.B.

THE AMATEUR PHOTOGRAPHER
&₂ ₅ PHOTOGRAPHIC NEWS

Cinema Notes

THE SCIENCE AND ART OF THE CINEMATOGRAPH.

THE ARTISTIC AND EDUCATIONAL VALUE OF THE MOVING PICTURE.

AS we have previously stated, the amateur photographer should be able to derive much benefit from an occasional visit to the cinematograph theatre. The artistic merit of the average film is by no means inconsiderable; in fact, in many pictures it is easy to see that the producers are experts in photographic technique as well as in theatrical production. The cinematograph provides a constant and permanent means of seizing and delineating the most subtle and transitory beauties of Nature; its power of seizing fleeting effects, of interpreting the subleties of light and shadow, give to cinematography a character of its own that is entirely unique. A knowledge of correct composition, of the laws governing the distribution of light and shade, and an ability to distinguish "values" can be acquired by paying occasional visits to the best picture theatres. The compositions that form on the screen are frequently the result of unposed grouping, and are therefore far finer in effect—when the effect is noted—than the deliberately posed group. It is the difference between dynamic and static art, as Mr. Haldane Macfall has pointed out.

Teaching by Film.

We have also, in previous notes, referred to the value of cinematography in general, and the remarkable Kinemacolor process in particular, as a great factor in modern education. For natural history teaching the Kinemacolor film is exceptional in its "forcefulness." Everyone knows that (even allowing for a little poetic license from lecturers upon the subject) the amount of time and patience required to get photographs of insects, birds, and other small game is something prodigious. One can take school children into the lanes and fields and show them buttercups and snails and arum-lilies, and such things; and one can call it "nature study." But, after all, it is an exceedingly superficial aspect of the subject. To understand the history of one insignificant creature often requires years of study on the part of a highly-trained specialist, involving days and nights of incessant labour and observation. And yet the whole of this toil can be condensed on to a small roll of film and its results exhibited with a minimum amount of trouble to an unlimited number of scholars.

Horticulture, farming, bee-keeping, and a host of similar subjects can be demonstrated with equal facility. Kinemacolor become the most potential enemy of the objectionable house-fly, inasmuch as by its aid we are able to show the history of the creature, its filthy habits, and also the most approved methods of destroying it. This film has been used by the U.S. authorities for the past three years in their crusade against the fly pest.

Municipal Cinematograph Shows.

A remarkable campaign has been inaugurated in some of the towns of Germany and France, so we learn from the *Photo Revue*, with the object of moralising the cinematograph. The mayors of several towns, together with other interested people, have combined in a public effort to emphasise the value of the film as an "educateur-moralisateur," and as a source of instruction in schools and barracks. It is regrettable, says one leader of this movement, M. Coissac, that the intellectual possibilities of cinematography should have been neglected owing to the speculative rush which has followed upon its popularisation. It is time to increase the number of definitely instructive films, to guide the invention to nobler ends, to make it a translator of the superb spectacles of Nature, the thrilling pageant of history, as well as a recorder of the travels and discoveries of men. One town in Alsace-Lorraine has actually opened a cinematograph exhibition which serves almost entirely the purposes of instruction. Another municipality, that of Altona, in Holstein, has taken an old theatre, and installed it as a cinematograph hall, under civic management, the idea being that this model establishment will exercise a pressure on private cinematographic enterprise in a healthy direction. Another burgomaster, in an official publication, asks what communal administrations have already had experience of cinematograph displays, and suggests that towns which have anything in the nature of municipal "cinemas" should exchange their films.

Teaching the Old Idea to Shoot.

Among the many applications of the cinematograph towards the acquisition of knowledge by the general public, the series of films prepared for the London General Omnibus Company last week will rank high. The great number of accidents to pedestrians that have been recorded lately in the papers—mostly stated to be the fault of careless or reckless driving of motor omnibuses—are undoubtedly due in part to the thoughtlessness or ignorance of the pedestrians themselves. The series of films that have been taken are intended to demonstrate not only the skill with which a good driver deals with unforeseen accidents and incidents, but will make a useful object lesson for the other users of the roadways as well. The right way to cross a road crowded with traffic is, unfortunately, one of those things that most men and women think need no learning.

Speed and the Cinematograph.

The cinematograph operator is a great power in our midst, but we hope he will realise his responsibilities, and not too lightly upset our cherished convictions. We all have an idea, for instance, that the Dutch are a slow-moving folk, leisurely and deliberate in all that they do. Do we not recollect how a Photographic Conventioner last July begged the Dutch waiter to let him have his "Pilsner" before the winter came on? Yet some excellent films we saw recently, illustrative of life in Holland, showed the worthy people infected with a mania for hustle. Bicyclists were scorching along the canal banks, the sails of the windmills were going round at a furious pace, and even the fishermen, like the Skegness variety, found it bracing. The secret, of course, was a disregard of the rule of sixteen pictures per second, but we confess that our hearts fail us when we think of the cinematograph bringing to nought the traditional picture of a certain type of British labourer.

Perhaps it is too much to say that in order to get a still picture one must make extraordinary haste, and in order to get a moving picture take ample leisure. But the elementary mistake of the beginner in cinematography is to take his pictures too rapidly. The idea that rapid action is necessary is one that only bitter experience can eradicate. Two workers—both of them amateurs in cinematography, one having applied the method to natural history, and the other to travel—recently avowed this to be their trouble. Wiser and more experienced was the professional cinematographer who deposited himself leisurely one Saturday afternoon in the busiest part of a London suburb, and was content to give every now and then a slight turn to his instrument. The film, which must have occupied an hour or two in the taking, was shown at the local theatre the same night, and revealed how great a variety of different phases of life is packed apparently in but five minutes of High Street. Can the reader, by the way, say how it is that the wheels of a wagon in a cinematograph picture often appear to be moving in the opposite direction to that in which the wagon itself is travelling? Mathematical wits, please set to work! Now, who spoke?

All the World a Stage.

The cinematograph as an illustrator of travel will assuredly have a great future. Every week the evidence of its value in this respect accumulates. The other night Mr. Harry de Windt was assisted by the cinematograph when he lectured at the Royal Society of British Artists on the subject of the Balkan people. Doubtless he wished that he had been accompanied by such an instrument when he was making his famous journeys in Persia, Siberia, and the gold-fields of Alaska. We should not be surprised if the cinematograph as an illustrator of other customs and countries eclipses for a time its use for specially staged subjects. The latter, however, as reproduced by the film, still have a tremendous popularity, and in France, which is their home, they are gathering around them a literature. We have before us a brochure, recently published in Paris (118, Rue d'Assas), called "La Prise de Vues Cinématographiques," which gives information as to the scenery most suitable for cinematograph plays, the decoration, the costumes of the actors, even the composition of their paint and powder.

663

3

Representative Kinematograph Shows.

SINGING PICTURES AT THE HIPPODROME.

A well known writer once remarked on the "individuality" of the leading music halls in London, by which he meant not only that each of the "West End" halls gave different programs, but gave them in a style peculiarly their own. You might go from a suburban "Empire" to a neighbouring "Palace," he said, and though a different set of artistes would be performing, you might be looking at a repetition of the show which you had just left, so closely do the two resemble each other in essential points. But in the case of the halls within the magic circle of which Charing Cross is the centre, the matter is different. Each hall has a character of its own—a personality one might almost call it, for it is usually the reflection of the manager's personality. Thus, the Palace program will be met with at the Palace and nowhere else, an Oxford show would be out of place if presented at the Empire, and the Alhambra clientèle would be astonished if the Tivoli caste were transferred to that house in a lump, as it were. The Palace, for instance, is the place for musical comedy or "legit" artistes converted temporarily to variety, and the best class singers, if they tread the music hall boards at all, will probably tread them at this hall. And so on.

The London Hippodrome not only possesses the individuality of which we have spoken, but possesses it in a most marked degree. It, in fact, possesses the virtue of being Itself, of imitating no other hall's program, and putting it out of the power of other halls to imitate its own, in a stronger degree than probably any of the halls we have mentioned. If the Alhambra is the home of the ballet, the Hippodrome is the home of Novelty and, in its best sense, of Sensation. The Hippodrome itself was something of a sensation when it opened, and so perhaps it is natural that practically all the really unique turns which have been introduced to the London public should have made their bow under its auspices. If there is a giant or a dwarf, a man with two heads or a man with none in London, a letter addressed to the Hippodrome would probably find him. In their continual search for the new the Hippodrome management have introduced, among others, Chung Ling Soo, Consul (the man monkey), the Ituri Pigmies, Maknow, the Russian giantess, and Lindsay (the whip expert), to the public. Above all, they have had the privilege of first staging the turn which is indicated in the title to this article, Gaumont's Chronophone.

Probably even the Hippodrome has presented nothing more completely novel than the Gaumont Singing Pictures, which they are showing at the present time by means of the same firm's "Chronomegaphone." The Chronophone (the more impressive title Chronomegaphone is used to indicate a specially loud model for use in large halls) was the first practical attempt made to combine the kinematograph and the talking machine, and during the two or three years it has been on the market it has gradually progressed towards perfection. The fact that it was booked for the Hippodrome, and still more that it has continued there for eight months, seems to indicate that, if it has not yet reached the ideal, it is sufficiently far on the road for all practical purposes of the showman. Indeed, many fine showmen have done sound and good business with the instrument, and the proprietors of the Hippodrome, apart from the show at that hall, have bought an instrument and sent it round the Moss-Stoll circuit.

The principle of the Chronophone is by this time fairly well known; it is the comparatively simple one of showing an artiste on the screen, while a talking machine reproduces one of his,

or her, songs. The difficulty lies, of course, in securing exact synchronisation between the movements of the artiste's lips and the said reproduction, right through the performance. One can best appreciate the importance of accomplishing this to a fraction of a second by getting the Gaumont people to put on one of their earliest productions, before the machine had been perfected. The life-like illusion is completely destroyed by the most momentary departure from exact synchronism. The difficulty of avoiding this is evidently a considerable one, calling for much care in the taking; but in projection synchronism is secured by most simple means for which Gaumonts' have a patent.

The "Illusion of Life" at the Hippodrome was particularly good on the occasion of our visit, Harry Lauder's voice being one admirably suited to the Singing Pictures. Half the effect of Harry Lauder's songs are due to his interpolations, and sudden pauses, which are very difficult to synchronise. These were rendered with a most laughable exactitude. Lauder stayed on the Hippodrome bill for 16 weeks. This was a special turn, and probably a record for singing pictures.

Lauder's engagement inaugurated an entirely new departure in the singing picture business, which the Gaumont Co. are continuing—and that is the exclusive engagement of celebrated artistes to be filmed and "recorded" in their leading numbers. Among the other artistes who have been fixed up besides the famous Harry are Will Evans, Victoria Monks, R. G. Knowles, Clarice Mayne, etc.

The first type of Chronophone was a comparatively heavy instrument, consisting of a Professional Chrono Bioscope, a cyclophone, or talking machine, and a separate controlling mechanism, and this model is still recommended for large halls, but for the travelling showman, or for use in private shows, a "hand Chronophone" has been introduced, which can be fitted to an existing Chrono Bioscope installation, and in which the synchronism is effected by the man at the projector, who has only to keep a pointing needle in the centre of an indicator to ensure that the two reproductions coincide, thus controlling complete synchronisation.

As to the Chronophone program of the Gaumont Co., it may be described as an ambitious one. They have already a series of records and films for the complete opera of "Faust," "Carmen," and other operas, and in the future it is not unlikely that we shall be able to see a complete dramatic performance by means of the instrument. The suggestion gives one an interesting idea of the possibilities of the Chronophone, and it would be a rash man who should prophesy the final position of Singing Pictures in the entertaining world.

(This series to be continued.)

Another "Walturdaw" Success!

The
"Cinematophone"
(Patented in all Countries).

The Greatest Wonder
of Modern Science !

The man who turns
the Handle controls
the
whole mechanism.

We have pleasure in introducing to our customers an entirely new invention, which has proved an immediate phenomenal success, and which is admitted by all to be the most perfect

Singing Picture Machine

in existence. It can be fitted instantly to any existing Animated Picture Machine—any operator can work it after five minutes practice—and singing and talking pictures can be presented with unerring fidelity and **absolute syncronism.**

Price Complete,

£72 nett.

rand Repertoire of Films at
10d. per Foot,
including the Sound Record.

CALL AND SEE IT WORKING!!!

THE
WALTURDAW CO., LTD.,
3 & 4, Dean Street,
High Holborn, W.C.

THE TRIUMPH OF COLOUR.

Since the last "Machinery and Export Number" of THE BIOSCOPE was published a year ago, it is not too much to say that the lines of development of the cinematograph industry have undergone a very considerable change, by reason of a phenomenon which may be summed up in the phrase, "The Coming of Colour." Within the year—almost within the last six months—Mr. Charles Urban's Kinemacolor process has come right to the front, and has become a formative influence upon the future of the business, the importance of which cannot be over-estimated. " Colour " has now become a *sine qua non* of the picture theatre programme, and one cannot pass along the streets without seeing from the announcements of exhibitors that they are fully alive to this, and, if they have not a Kinemacolor licence, they are making a special feature of tinted or coloured films in order to cope with the public demand.

The recent progress of Kinemacolor has been quite one of the romances of industry ; in fact, no one who saw the early examples shown at the Palace Theatre, Shaftesbury Avenue, W., could fail to realise that sooner or later the new process must become a force to be reckoned with, although few, we imagine, foresaw the surprising developments of the last few months. It is interesting to look back upon the various stages of this recent development. " There is nothing like ocular demonstration "—a maxim to which everyone in the film trade ought to heartily subscribe—and Mr. Urban's success, we think, has been largely due to his realising this. On Tuesday, April 11th, he inaugurated his bold policy of showing, at the Scala Theatre, the possibilities of Kinemacolor as an attractive, interesting, and unique entertainment. The prophets of doom could reel off any number of reasons why the scheme could not succeed, but all their prophecies have been falsified. It is clear that if Kinemacolor had specialised on a particular class of subject it must have failed. Obviously a producer of Western drama, and nothing else, or of travel subjects and nothing else, could not have succeeded, however attractive his pictures might be as colour studies. Kinemacolor, thanks to Mr. Urban's knowledge of men and things, has reproduced life in every aspect : its own inherent magic has enabled it to show us life as it really is—growing beneath the tropic sun or subdued to neutral tones in the frozen North.

" Coronation year " was, of course, an important factor in bringing about the recent almost sensational advance of Kinemacolor. It is in reproductions of State ceremonies and military pageantry that monotone photography is weakest, and Kinemacolor strongest. As a process able to show the wonderful events of the year in all their brilliance and majesty, Kinemacolor has attracted the especial attention of the Royal House, whose members have been greatly interested, naturally enough, in seeing from a spectator's point of view the gorgeous ceremonies in which they took so prominent a part. Consequently Mr. Urban has been honoured with commands to give special performances, first before Her Majesty Queen Alexandra, at Sandringham, and next before Their Majesties the King and Queen, at Balmoral.

Meantime, the success of the Scala Theatre has been one of the events of the entertainment world. All through the heat wave the theatre was crowded. West-End society folk have become regular patrons of the entertainment, and, by clever advertising, the initial drawback of a theatre unknown to the pleasure-seeking public has been overcome. Displays have been given for two months or longer without the slightest change, to crowded houses. Side by side with the success at the Scala, the development of Kinemacolor in the country and the world at large has proceeded rapidly. Important foreign rights have been disposed of, and exclusive exhibition licences for the whole of this country have been taken up. Handsome theatres have been opened with Kinemacolor in the United States, Canada, India, and the Continent of Europe. Camera experts have been touring the world, reproducing life in the infinite charm of Nature's varied hues.

It is necessary to be very cautious in drawing lessons from the rise of Kinemacolor and applying them to the cinematograph industry as a whole. It seems more than likely that the new process will develop as an entirely separate branch of the motion picture business. Because at the Scala Theatre the policy of a weekly or twice-weekly change of programme has been disregarded, and programmes have run for two months or more, it does not follow that all moving picture exhibitors would be safe in following this plan. Similarly, because high prices are being obtained at the Scala, it would not do to counsel exhibitors everywhere to raise their charges of admission by some hundreds per cent. It will be generally admitted that Mr. Urban has inaugurated what is practically a new phase of cinematography, and one which will reach the highest development without necessarily interfering in any way with the scope of the black-and-white film industry.

ARRIVAL OF THE CINEMATOGRAPH BILL.—Consternation amongst Penny Showmen.

MARKET MOVEMENTS.

The rapidly increasing numbers of registered Companies connected with the Bioscope business, and the surprising claims made by some of the more or less irresponsible promoters, have suggested to our Artist possibilities which he depicts above.

A Lady Kinematograph Operator.

SOME FACTS ABOUT SENORA SPENCER.

Ladies, have, on occasions, shown themselves to be specially interested in kinematograph work, and we know of at least one member of the gentler sex who has done much laborious work in the securing of some plant-life records. Others there are who have actually operated on special occasions; but we know of no lady who has devoted so much time and thought to the work as the subject of our sketch.

Senora Spencer, who is at present in London for medical treatment, was born in Edinburgh. When she was but three years of age, she was taken to Bilbao—(Kipling's Bilbao) on the north coast of Spain and situated near the Pyrenees mountain range.

About eight years ago Senora Spencer visited America and here she met Mr. Spencer. Since their marriage both Mr. and Senora Spencer have been engaged in providing the public (chiefly in Australia) with refined exhibitions of living pictures; in which the work of operating the projecting machine is entirely conducted by Senora Spencer. Her husband claims that she is the only lady operator in the world. "It is very delicate work," he says—"to turn the handle and I claim that my wife is a better manipulator of the machine than any man. Not only that, but she takes a keen interest in the work.'

This lady operator has travelled to many parts of the Commonwealth with her exhibition, including Adelaide, Broken Hill and to the West, but Sydney has been the chief place of exhibition where, in Pitt Street, at the Lyceum Hall, earlier known as the Lyceum Theatre the shows have met with unusual appreciation and praise. The cause of the popularity of the Spencer exhibitions is not far to seek. Both Mr. and Senora Spencer are artists. When new subjects arrive from the manufacturers, they are each in turn passed through the projector and criticised most severely. Any unnecessary padding is at once cut out, and without in any way upsetting the plot depicted, the duration of subjects is modified, so that they fit in with the orchestral program.

Senora Spencer informed us further, that in some instances, the music has been re-written to suit the scenes depicted, each subject being rehearsed a great many times before it was ready for final exhibition upon the screen. A full and highly talented orchestra is provided, and the various mechanical effects that each subject demands are most carefully thought out and secured.

The esteem in which this lady operator is held will be gathered from the following extract from the *Australian Star.*

"The closing night of the Theatrescope season at the Lyceum on Saturday was marked with a little un-rehearsed number, which, however, met with the warmest approval of the large audience.

"Towards the close of the program Mr. H. M. Hawkins, front of the house manager, came forward, and apologising for the break in the program, asked the kind attention of the audience for a minute or so. In a few well-chosen words he referred to the unique record the Theatrescope had achieved in having successfully completed a second eight weeks' run, making a total of sixteen weeks during the last six months. As a memento of the auspicious occasion, and a mark of personal esteem, he asked Signora Spencer to accept from the whole of the house staff, a diamond and ruby brooch, which, together with a choice box of confections, he then handed her.

"Senora Spencer's appearance, together with Mrs. Spencer, on the stage, was received with tumultuous applause from all parts of the house, the gallery and the dress circle joining equally markedly in their tribute of praise. The orchestra caught the spirit of the occasion, and it was not till they had finished the number generally associated with such gatherings that Mr. Spencer could get the opportunity to respond on behalf of his wife. He warmly thanked Mr. Hawkins and his staff for their little memento and gladly paid a tribute to the excellent work the staff had done.

"It was by the hearty co-operation of all concerned that the season had been such a success. He could not reject the opportunity given him to thank the Sydney public for their generous and sustained support. He had tried to give the best. They had appreciated the effort in a practical way. Signora Spencer and himself would take with them many happy memories of Sydney, and in the hope that in coming days he might be with them again, he said, Au revoir, and not good-bye."

Grand Opening of the School for Lady Operators.
(WE DON'T THINK.)

ILLUSTRATED BY OUR ARTIST WHO WASN'T THERE.

It was supposed to be the opening of the school for lady operators, but it turned out to be an exhibition—at least the ladies made exhibitions of themselves. Punctually to time the mere male operator arrived, but, of course, all the ladies were late; in fact, some were so late that they did not get there at all. That sounds a bit Irish, but my last five have been Scotches, so perhaps that accounts for it. At length, sufficient had arrived to form an aquarium (beg pardon, a quorum), and after they had arranged their hair and hats the instructor commenced his lecture. He told them that in order to become efficient operators they must first learn all the theory, which, he said, would take two or three weeks. That did not appear to be to the liking of Isa...b...a P...nk...rst, so she stood on a box, and displaying a purple, green, and white poster, she shouted: "We demand the right to operate *at once.*" So the instructor proceeded to show Miss Flighty how to operate the bioscope, and they got along swimmingly, so much so, that when she left off turning the handle the film caught fire. And the air went blue for miles—that is, of course, when you add what the in-

structor said to what the ladies shrieked. Order had only been partially restored when in walked the assistant-instructor, carrying a cylinder of oxygen, and enquiring: "Does any lady require more gas." You *should* have seen the looks they gave him, and the gas they expended on him. To make matters worse, a small mouse waltzed across the class-room. Thereupon there arose shrieks, screams, and uproar. The ladies rushed pell-mell to safety—on forms and desks, inside the stand of the machine—anywhere to be safe from the dangerous rodent. Mrs. Arabella Jones was awfully frightened at the various pieces of apparatus, and refused to switch over the resistance with her hands. When last seen she was endeavouring to poke it into the next notch with her umbrella. At length, the lesson was at an end, and amid sighs of relief from the ladies the class was brought to an abrupt conclusion. The ladies then formed up into small groups and talked harder than ever—all at once. It was noticeable that the lady who, a few minutes earlier had demanded the right to operate at once, did not want to do so at all after the first few minutes. Fickle woman!

Fatal Accident at a Picture Show.

PANIC AMONG AUDIENCE CAUSES DISASTER.

We regret to report that as a result of a panic among the audience attending a film entertainment at the Town Hall, Newmarket, on Saturday last, which turned what might have proved a slight mishap into a catastrophe, a number of persons were more or less severely burned, while one unfortunate woman succumbed to her injuries on Sunday morning. Our readers will probably have already read the accounts appearing in the daily papers, which reported the affair in detail, but in many cases with some incorrectness and a great deal of exaggeration. Our own account is founded on information supplied us by the Assistant Manager of the Gaumont Co., Mr. Welsh, after he had paid a visit to the scene of the accident and had interviewed the operator and manager and many of those present in the hall, and it will be found to correct that appearing in other places in several important particulars.

Mr. Welsh was first informed of the accident by a paper which he glanced at in a friend's house on Sunday, and he instantly came up to the Gaumont offices to interview the operators on their return.

Cause of the Mishap.

The entertainment had been arranged by Mr. C. H. Nunn, and consisted of pictures of the various pageants in different parts of the country which have been photographed by the Gaumont Co., and Mr. E. Court had charge of the arrangements.

The interval had been reached, and a slide bearing an announcement to that effect was placed in the instrument, with the result that numbers of the audience made for the door before the gas had been turned up. In the darkness several of them, making for the exit at the rear of the projector, and not exercising over much care in their anxiety to get outside, came into rough contact with the apparatus, with the result, as stated by the dailies, that the rubber tube connecting a cylinder of coal gas to the jet was pulled off, the gas ignited, and, in its turn, ignited the film in the machine. The sheet of flame, of course, immediately illumined the room, and a cry of "fire" being raised, the efforts made by Mr. Greenwood, the operator, and his wife, who acted as pianist, to convince the people that there was no danger, were ineffectual, and a desperate rush was made for the doors. Mr. Court had already pluckily carried the burning film into the street, and there is not the slightest doubt that, but for the fact that the audience lost their heads, the flames would have been extinguished in a few minutes.

A Struggle for the Doors.

As it was, the press of people at the door pushed several people into contact with the flames, several being burned; one, Hannah Starling, a young married woman, so severely that she died from shock in the Rous Memorial Hospital, while many others were injured in the frenzied fight for the exits. The death which occurred was undoubtedly due wholly and solely to the unreasonable panic which seized the audience, and can no more be legitimately ascribed to the comparatively simple accident which had occurred than the latter could be blamed on to the operator.

Small Damage to the Hall.

The smallness of the actual accident is to be adduced from the fact that the fire was extinguished and the hall cleared in less than fifteen minutes, while the hall is practically undamaged. Captain Frank Simpson, of the Newmarket Fire Brigade, happened to be in the hall and to the efforts of this gentleman and those of Mr Court is largely due the fact that the accident was not still more serious. Mr. Simpson quickly brought the Town Hall hose into play and the flames, which had spread to one of the folding doors and to an adjacent cupboard were soon put out. Police Sergeant Gorham and Constable Wright also did good work, the latter dragging women and children from the hall and passing them out to Gorham, who passed them outside to the street in his turn.

The floor was littered with articles of clothing, jewellery, hats, etc., most of which have since been claimed.

Newspaper Exaggerations.

Mr. Welsh drew our representative's attention to a statement in several papers to the effect that the audience was about 700 in number, and that of these quite 300 were more or less injured by burns or shock. As a matter of fact, the size of the hall was only 44 × 31 ft., and the actual number of persons present was 333. Before the start of the entertainment, Mr. Court had had to refuse admission to several persons, owing to the fact that every seat was occupied.

Questioned as to the non-use of an operating chamber, Mr. Welsh explained that the operators always carried such a chamber with them, but that its use was impossible owing to the size of the hall. So far from thinking that the use of the box under the circumstances would have in any way prevented the accident, Mr. Welsh is of opinion that so great was the rush that the only difference would have been that it would have been turned over with the operator inside, and have led to his certain death, besides making the extinguishing of the flames a more difficult matter.

The Hall appears to be a somewhat inconvenient chamber and by no means up to date in its equipment. As already explained, the principal exit was at the rear of the projector.

The Inquest

on the body of Mrs. Starling, held on Monday, revealed no new facts concerning the accident, and was adjourned until Wednesday next.

The Injured.

Of those injured, few appear to have suffered serious harm. Clara Ashby, a domestic servant, was, however, we regret to say, reported to be in a critical state on Monday, but no further news of her condition has reached us. A similar report is given of another girl, named Martha Draflin, and Henry Jellis, a jockey, is detained in Hospital.

The Gaumont Co.'s loss amounts to several hundred pounds.

The Press and the Barnsley Accident.

No lengthy account of the sad accident at Barnsley is necessary here, most of our readers having already probably become acquainted with the details through the accounts published in the daily papers. The catastrophe occurred while the Harvey Institute was occupied by a travelling picture show, and it is owing to this fact and to the further circumstance that one or two newspapers saw fit to at once jump to the conclusion that the terrible death roll was due to the kinematograph that we desire to allude briefly to the accident here.

We have, through the kindness of a Dewsbury reader, been put in possession of a *Yorkshire Daily Observer* placard of Monday last. The whole of the bill is occupied by the following announcement in the largest and blackest type of which space allows :

BARNSLEY
CINEMATOGRAPH
DISASTER
16 CHILDREN
CRUSHED TO DEATH
ROYAL MESSAGES.

We need not say what impression is produced on the mind of the man in the street by a bill of this sort. He naturally believes what the bill tells him, that the kinematograph was responsible for the deaths of 16 children. Now the facts as regards Barnsley are that a special entertainment was being given for children, that the gallery had been filled, and that a large number of little ones who had climbed the stairs to secure admission were informed of the fact and told that they would be accommodated in another part of the hall.

Unhappily, it seems that instead of the children at the *bottom* of the stairs being first directed to their seats those at the *top* were told to descend, and in doing so met with resistance from those still trying to ascend, with the awful results with which everybody is acquainted. To call this a kinematograph accident is to produce an entirely erroneous impression, and as an illustration of the tendency of hurried pressmen to jump to the conclusion that every accident which occurs where a picture machine is installed is due to that machine, we suggest that this poster calls for the serious consideration of everyone interested in living pictures. This is by no means an isolated instance. A short time ago a fused wire caused a trifling fire at a picture show in a London suburb. The accident, trifling though it was, and though it had no connection whatever with the projector or films, was promptly billed as " Another Kinematograph Accident." Instances of this nature could be multiplied indefinitely. Misrepresentation has become so common that it threatens to harm the living picture showman's business seriously, and some method of combating it on the part of the trade as a whole seems desirable. We commend the finding of the method to the new Exhibitors' Association, when it comes into being.

The Barnsley accident is not without its lessons to exhibitors, however. We have when visiting picture shows frequently noticed the comparatively little care lavished on the management of the front of the house, even in places where the projection, effects, music, and all the details of the actual entertainment are first class. In many cases it is a matter of paying your shilling—or twopence, as the case may be—and finding your way to your seat, and, at the conclusion of the show, your way out. Sometimes there is only one woman in charge of some hundreds of people. This is noticeable not only in picture shows, but in other classes of entertainment.

It is obvious that a certain amount of blame attaches to the showman when accidents occur through the lack of a sufficiently large front-of-the house staff, or when the accident becomes more serious from that cause. The most serious accidents in connection with living picture shows have resulted, not from the film catching fire, but from the panic ensuing from such a fire. That was the case at Newmarket, it was the case at nine-nine per cent. of the accidents which have occurred for years past. The wisdom of having a sufficiently large staff of attendants to convince the audience of their safety is therefore obvious.

We have from the inception of our journal tried to make exhibitors, manufacturers and everyone interested in the trade use every endeavour to convince both press and public that the danger from kinematograph shows is small when taken in comparison with other forms of entertainment. The scare of the first disaster in Paris gave food for the penny a liner of the future.

We, as the representative organ of the trade, shall do our utmost to prove to the alarmists and those who are led away by them what little foundation they have for their scares. Unless this is done our trade is ruined, as kinematograph shows will be barred on every hand.

Only last evening at the meeting of the Holborn Guardians, the City Road Workhouse Committee reported that they had accepted the offer of Major M. Archer Shee, D.S.O., of Park Street, W., to give the inmates a kinematograph entertainment on Jan. 27th. Mr. William Howes, the chairman of the Board, said that in view of the terrible disaster in America he did not think it wold be advisable to accept the offer. The workhouse master was fearful about having the entertainment, as there would be 1,080 persons present, and in case of anything happening there would be great difficulty in getting them out. It was decided that Major Archer Shee be invited to give some other form of entertainment.

This is but of the many instances in which business has been lost to the trade by fright and alarm, and some very decided steps must now be taken to combat such a loss to the showman, or the trade will suffer severely.

THE FAULTS OF NON-INFLAMMABLE FILM.

A well-known exhibitor writing upon the subject of non-inflammable films, says:—

"In the first place, until we can get accustomed to it most of us will be fooled at the length of the film, because the non-inflammable is much thicker than the inflammable and therefore what would appear to be a full reel of the new goods is in reality several fractions shy—a fact which too many of us discover only after we have thrown it on our screens.

"Again, the photography is bad in the new film. That is to say, the photographer either has not mastered the secret of focussing or else the new film is not susceptible to proper focus. The figures in the foreground of any picture will be excellent while the foilage or mountain scenery in outdoor views is blurred almost beyond recognition.

"Again, the new film, which is perforated before developing and printing, shrinks in the latter processes, and in consequence does not register perfectly in the sprockets of the machine. Moreover, the new film scratches very readily, and in my own experience I have found that it will be more rainy and scratched after three weeks' use than the old film would be in three months. It lacks pliability and in long reels will pile up in such a stiff manner as to be in the way of the operator.

"Aside from failing to perfect the non-inflammable film, the manufacturers have also failed to produce a satisfactory cement. Of the cements now on the market, one may be known as the 'quick' and the other as the 'slow.' The quick cement binds the film so quickly that the chances are the operator in a hurry will bind the film break in a crooked manner so as to compel the next operator to repeat the operation, whereas the slow cement goes to pieces almost as soon as the lamp heat strikes it."

George Eastman, president, and Mr. Lovejoy, manager, of the Eastman Kodak Company, of Rochester, N.Y., visited New York City recently, for the purpose of examining the complaints of some film manufacturers regarding non-inflammable film.

After hearing and considering the points at issue, Messrs. Eastman and Lovejoy assured the gentlemen present that they could easily overcome the situation and promised to deliver non-inflammable film that will render perfect service and give satisfaction both to manufacturers and Exchange men. The evident zealous interest evinced by them to bring the non-inflammable product to a standard of perfection, where adverse criticism will fail to reach, impressed convincingly all who had gathered to discuss the mooted points.

STANDARDISATION.

THE REASON FOR THE PRESENT GAUGE.
By Arthur S. Newman.

The moving picture, having passed through the successive stages of being at first, merely a seemingly impossible scheme; than an accomplished fact only attained by the overcoming of many difficulties; and, subsequently, a commercial enterprise in the hands of a select few, has finally developed into an important and world-wide industry, providing employment for many thousands of workers, and one engaging the attention of a vast army of actors, authors, operators, and managers. The factories for the production of film have attained colossal proportions and the demand for what may be called raw material (perforated film) is continually on the increase. It is rather surprising that with an industry of such importance demanding so large an amount of raw material, and that always of one size; that no precise statement of that size—no definite standard has been universally agreed to. The photographic trade has its accepted sizes for plates and materials, the engineering and other allied trades have their definite sizes for sundries of all kinds. Metals, wood, cotton, paper, can all be obtained to definite measurements, and as the uses to which such materials are applied are so numerous, the sizes are consequently numerous; but perforated film being used for only one purpose, and all the machines in commercial use being built to take one size only, it is most important that the exact width of the film should be settled once for all, and also that the size and shape of the perforated holes and their distance apart should also be absolutely determined. To an extent these measurements have been settled and agreed to all round, but so far this has not been completely and scientifically done. Our English system of measurement is responsible for some of the difficulties, but it is, nevertheless, not fair to blame the system. The real trouble is due to the fact that a different unit of measurement obtains on the Continent from that which is generally in use in England, the Colonies and America. For fine work at home, a decimal system, having for its unit the inch, is becoming general among engineers and scientific instrument makers, while on the Continent the millimeter and its multiples and decimal divisions; is in use, and has been for many years past. Only during recent years has the decimally divided inch come into favour here. The introduction of the standard wire gauge, the sizes of which are all dependent upon the decimal-inch, has done much to familiarise the men in the mechanical trades with decimal measurements. Many congresses and committees have spent much time trying to get all countries to agree to an universal unit of measurement, but, partly owing to conservatism and vested interests, and partly because it is impossible to make different nations see the same things from the same point of view, no agreement has yet been arrived at. In the moving picture industry, an unfortunate history has done much to cause the present confusion. Edison, the first to adopt a definite standard size for perforated film, chose the proportions which are usually acknowledged to be the bases of the present sizes. Whether they are the most suitable that could have been used, is for us, quite beside the subject. We must look at things as they are, and, doing so, we shall find that, owing to the tremendous number of machines in use, and the quantity of capital invested in film subjects, any great deviation from any of the existing patterns of width of film and size of perforation cannot be tolerated. Edison originated his gauge for use in the Kinetoscope, for which instrument it was eminently suitable. Its measurements are simple, viz., width of film, 1 3/8th in.; pictures per foot, 16; perforations per picture 4. The shape of the hole was that of a parallelogram with rounded corners.

The pin machine of Lumière may be fairly considered as having been the first practical and commercial apparatus for the exhibition of moving pictures. So great a success was the result of its exhibition that in a short time many mechanicians designed and made apparatus for the same purpose, and sales were quickly effected at quite fabulous prices. Many of these first machines were quite crude productions, but in spite of this they had a ready sale, and a show of even so small a number as six subjects, each 75 feet in length, would command money. Then a great difficulty was presented to the showmen. Machines there were in plenty, but film subjects were few. The disused films designed for the Kinetoscope were eagerly bought up, although their having been originally photographed at a speed varying from 30 to 40 pictures per second, made them anything but suitable for projection in heavy running machines such as most of these first ones were; but the public were mad for moving pictures, good, bad, or indifferent. Lumières' first style of perforation had only one pair of holes to each picture, and the size of the picture was slightly different from that of the Edison films, so the machines constructed to take one gauge would not work the other. By the time the Kinetograph films were worn out, several people had made taking and printing-machines; and as, by that time, the number of machines for working the Edison gauge was far in excess of those for Lumière gauge, the people who started to manufacture film subjects naturally chose the system which presented to them the probability of the largest market for their productions. Thus the gauge introduced by Edison (or I should say, an approximation to that gauge) became general—for many of the first productions were very crude imitations so far as the gauge was concerned. Lumières' gauge also suffered from the fact that it was built on the millimeter unit, and could not easily be originated or verified by English measurement. By the time Continental firms began to seriously manufacture film subjects, the number of Edison gauge machines was so large that the Edison gauge had become the standard—and so it remains to the present day.

(To be continued.)

MR. M. A. PYKE'S LATEST.

MAGNIFICENT PICTURE THEATRE AT EALING.

It would be difficult to convey to our readers any adequate idea of the sumptuous scale on which Mr. M. A. Pyke's latest picture theatre — the Ealing Cinematograph Theatre — has been arranged. In going over it we could only think of Byron's lines :—

> " What the eye has not seen
> Words cannot paint.
> What the eye has seen
> Words seem faint."

The Ealing Cinematograph Theatre is a veritable palace of luxury, and admitted by those who have seen it and are in a position to compare it with others, to be the finest the world has yet seen. The whole arrangement of the interior and the decorations are magnificent, yet in good taste, and any display of adjectives in describing the building will be pardonable. This will give our readers the keynote of the Ealing Cinematograph Theatre, which was opened on Wednesday of last week ; and a description of it was crowded out of our last issue. By the courtesy of Mr. Pyke, however, we are enabled to give an extended notice of this most interesting moving picture exhibition and to illustrate it from actual photographs. It will

INTERIOR OF HALL

be of considerable interest to showmen all over the country, particularly to those who are not above taking a leaf out of the notebook of a successful contemporary showman.

The building is in a very central position in the Broadway, Ealing, being next door to the Ealing Hippodrome. Entering the handsome vestibule, with its galaxy of beautiful indigenous and exotic plants, which are also conspicuous in the hall, we are at once struck by the lavish scheme of decoration, the marble floor, and the thick pile carpet. The hall speaks comfort and luxury, and the numerous chairs which are there for the use of patrons, and the cheery looking fire, make us feel at once that here is ease and rest. From the hall, there is a grand staircase leading to the balcony, manager's office and other rooms at present unoccupied, the balcony being reserved for the highest-priced seats, and from this position a splendid view of the pictures is obtained as we sit in a luxurious arm-chair. Straight through the hall we enter the auditorium, and are at once attracted by the splendid decorations from floor

TEA-ROOM AND LOUNGE.

to ceiling and everything strikes the eye with pleasing effect. There is a thick carpet covering the whole floor space, and comfortable upholstered seats throughout. The front seats are priced at 3d., the back seats 6d., and those in the balcony are 1s. The hall is interspersed with red-shaded lamps of the old-English style.

We must not omit the lounges. There are three of these, two of which are entered from the auditorium, one being reserved for threepenny seat-holders, and the other two for sixpenny and shilling patrons. The first we may describe as that leading off the entrance hall. Here are to be found all the leading daily and weekly papers; the room is profusely set with chairs and sofas, and patrons can sit down and read the papers by the side of a cheerful fire. The whole room is redolent of luxury, and we can only compare it to the drawing-room of a first-class hotel. The two lounges inside the auditorium are similarly furnished, but, so far as we could see, are not supplied with papers. We venture to state that no such conveniences and aids to the comfort of patrons on

ENTRANCE HALL FROM BALCONY.

SMOKING LOUNGE.

the part of an entertainment caterer have yet been attempted in this or any other country. It cannot, therefore, any longer be a reproach to Great Britain that she is behind in looking after the comfort of her entertainment patrons. On the contrary, she leads the way.

Accommodation is provided for from 450 to 500. The hall is about 60 ft. high, with a fine arched stucco-plaster ceiling, and is 68 ft. long by about 40 ft. broad. The operating room is delightfully cool, having walls of brick and cement 14 in. thick, and is fitted with two of Gaumont's famous Chrono machines. The voltage is 105 alternating current, and a Cooper-Hewitt transformer has been installed, with two small resistance frames to steady the arc. In addition to the ordinary requirements, a complete set of tools, stocks, dies, etc., has been provided, by which the operators can effect ordinary repairs to the machines.

There is no lack of music by which appropriate accompaniments are obtained to the pictures.

Piano and organ are provided, and on the occasion of our visit the music was tastefully and skilfully rendered in keeping with the subject of the pictures. In addition one of Messrs. Keith, Prowse's splendid automatic pianos, which gives high-class selections, one of Messrs. Hepworth's wonderful singing picture machines — the Vivaphone — has been installed.

The pictures themselves are steady and well projected. The screen is 14 ft. by 12 ft., and is set in a beautifully finished proscenium.

The premises were previously known as the Lyric Rooms, and a rather pleasing coincidence is that the main hall was previously known as the Montague Room, which fact, no doubt, commended itself to Mr. Montagu A. Pyke. It will be interesting to know the use to which Mr. Pyke will put the unoccupied rooms upstairs. Will it be a miniature "White City," we wonder?

ENTRANCE HALL AND GRAND STAIRCASE.

The films were supplied by the Cinematograph Film Hiring Company, Limited, who are also supplying Mr. M. A. Pyke's other first-class theatres.

The manager is Mr. George Leybourne, son of the late well-known music-hall star. The operator is Mr. V. Bond, and the assistant operator Mr. R. D. Longmuir.

TEA-ROOM.

The complete electrical heating and lighting arrangements, and the operating room work, were carried out by Messrs. Cathcart & Company, under the supervision of Mr. J. C. Kingdom, one of the partners. The furnishing was carried out by Messrs. Hamptons, the seating by Messrs. H. Lazarus & Son, 21, Great Eastern Street, E.C., and the attendants' uniforms were supplied by Messrs. Landy & Berlin, 417, Brixton Road, S.W.

We congratulate Mr. Pyke on his enterprise, and hope it will be rewarded to the extent that it deserves.

Bioscope Theatres in Vienna.
(From a Correspondent.)

During a brief visit to Vienna recently I was introduced to a few of the bioscope theatres in the Austrian capital, and although it was impossible to see all the 70 theatres where bioscope entertainments are given, I brought away with me an impression of prosperity and hard work. The best are very good, and there are not, I was assured, any really bad ones. Some of the halls in the lower quarters of the city present films of a highly sensational order, it is true, but police regulations, as all who have travelled on the Continent know, must be observed very carefully where questions of public morality are concerned.

Two of the best Vienna bioscope theatres are managed on American lines. Mr. Joseph Quester runs the American Bio, and makes a speciality of his orchestra. Only first-class Viennese music is played, and the theatre, being homely, and, as the German says, " of the people," it has a sound middle-class clientèle. The American Kino in Neubaugürtel is managed by Mr. Joseph Stiller, an energetic manager, who gives his patrons all the novelties.

Herr Rady-Maller, who controls four of the bioscope theatres, is perhaps the most prominent man in the trade in Vienna, and he is also director of a film-hiring firm. He is a very keen censor of films, and his programmes are invariably such as can be set before " the young person."

A large number of the Viennese houses are managed and owned by ladies. Perhaps one of the daintiest of these is the Grand in the Mariahilfer Strasse, which is built on the lines of a regular theatre with boxes, stalls, and dress-circle. It is upholstered in old tapestry, and the decorative scheme is red, white, and gold most tastefully displayed. Electric lighting is used throughout the theatre, and Frau Mizzi Schäfer, the owner, has installed a full set of voice imitators and noise-producing machinery.

Frau Eckstein manages two houses—the Vienna Bio and the Graben Kino, which are both fitted up in identical fashion, the only difference being that the attendants at the one house are dressed in dark red, at the other in violet. Frau Irma Handel is another lady bioscope theatre manager who is well known in Vienna. Her houses are in the Alser Strasse and the Mariahilfer Strasse, and are both famous for novelty and up-to-date films.

Foreign News.

France.

The growth of bioscope entertainments in France is quite as remarkable as it is in England. The extension of the moving picture show in the last twelve months has been more rapid than ever, and at the present moment in Paris and the provinces the bioscope is far and away the most popular spectacle presented to the masses. In far-off mountain towns, in tiny sea ports—everywhere, in fact, that fifty people can be gathered together to patronise an entertainment—bioscope shows are given, and in Paris at every few yards along the boulevards there is a hall which has been expressly built as an electric theatre or has been converted into a bioscope show. The bioscope even has brought success to bigger establishments which had failed in their original purpose as circuses and hippodromes. They are now running vast pictorial exhibitions, and are financially successful for the first time in their existence.

Of the preparation of pictures for these shows the Paris correspondent of *The Globe* has given some interesting details recently :—" One of the numerous ' authors ' whose ingenuity devises the episodes depicted, has prepared a scenario. The stage manager holds the manuscript of the play in his hand. At his direction the scene is set. It represents the interior of a French cottage, for ' La Poupée de Jeannettee ' is to be photographed to-day in pantomime. There are a score of actors, some of them players out of work, more of them regularly employed to pose for these pictures, just as they might be engaged to act in a theatre. Over and over they are drilled to go through the first scene, until they can run it off smoothly, with some show of naturalness. The scene represents a wedding. Although they have no use for dialogue in a bioscope play, the natural instinct for speech is too strong to be repressed, and the actors salute one another with ' Bon jour ' as they enter. With the canvas scenery, the paper flowers, the litter of the ' studio ' on all sides, the scene looks anything but realistic. But there is a string tacked on the carpet, which the players never overstep. If you peep through the ' finder ' of the camera, you will see why—that string marks the edge of of the lens. Within its compass, seen through the camera, the picture becomes as lifelike as any stage setting ever can. When the actors have been drilled for one or two hours till they know exactly what to do, the lights are turned on, the film is set whirring through the camera, and the picture is taken.

" Next day, perhaps, the actors and heavy camera machine are carted down to some isolated farm, an hour's ride from Paris, and the second scene is rehearsed till it, too, is duly photographed on the next one hundred feet of film. Perhaps the third episode of the story takes place on a city street. To avoid attracting crowds the actors are taken to some sleepy suburb and there, often with the aid of natives pressed into service as supers, go through the antics which later cause mirth in a thousand moving picture theatres. Many of the marvellous adventures that befall these characters are, of course, but tricks of the camera. I walked into a ' studio ' one day and saw an actor prone on his stomach, wriggling across the floor. But the carpet was painted to represent a wall, and over the actor's head,

suspended from the ceiling, was the camera. When that film was run through the projecting lantern, the audience saw a fugitive come to a high stone wall, scale it with marvellous ease, and from the summit look down in triumph at his baffled pursuers. The ingenuity of these moving picture artists is endless. Recently I saw a horse and cart and driver roll head over heels down a cliff into the sea, while the avenging husband stood gloating on the summit. The entire episode was, I was assured, constructed from a fake photograph in the ' studio.' Yet I know that sometimes the bioscope man, with a desire to be faithful to nature, does not stop at downright barbarism and cruelty. Not long ago two men in the employment of a moving picture agency goaded a poor horse until it rushed headlong over a precipice in Brittany, dragging a cart with it, so that the dramatic incident might furnish films for a realistic bioscope display. They were both heavily fined. Some time ago I attended a rehearsal for a picture representing a Christian being sacrificed in the arena. Nero sat in his tribune, with his beautiful but cruel favourites, and real lions prowled about the arena, behind a strong wire grille. The Christian was represented by the silhouette of a man, behind which pieces of flesh, recently dipped in blood, were hung on hooks. The stage setting was highly picturesque, but though the lions ultimately discovered the meat, they did not attack the silhouetted Christian as eagerly as the photographer would have liked. Now the great ones of France have succumbed to the golden lure. Rostand has written a play for moving pictures, an automobile pantomime with the scene laid on Olympus ; and so have Capus and Lavedan. Bernhardt and Réjane have acted before the camera and talked into the phonograph, and moving pictures have even been used in Paris in a performance of the ' Götterdämmerung,' to depict the fall of Valhalla."

The article is incorrect in one detail. The men who drove the poor horse over the cliff were not heavily fined. The maximum penalty allowed by the French law was imposed, but as that was a fine of only 12s. the punishment certainly did not fit the crime.

The Guillotine.

" If the guillotine," said M. Claretie in the Paris *Temps*, " continues to operate it will have to do so behind closed doors, and this will not be over easy in an age of snapshots and bioscopes."

" I do not despair," he added, ironically, " of seeing a bioscope execution, just as we seen the bioscope life-saving at Messina and the destruction of the walls of Reggio."

The Minister of the Interior has issued a circular pointing out that special precautions were taken to prevent the taking of bioscope pictures of the quadruple execution at Béthune, but that it was reported that, either by subterfuge or by surprise, clichés had, notwithstanding, been taken. Even it this were not the case, faked films might possibly be exhibited.

The circular points out that the mayors have full powers to prevent these representations, and they are instructed to act in the interests of public order.

FOREIGN NEWS

The Latest Film News from all Parts of the World.

AMERICA.

An ordinance has been introduced in San Francisco prohibiting picture houses from including vaudeville acts in their performances.

The Princess is a new house in Milwaukee, and seats 900 people. The floor is made of cork to deaden the sound of persons entering and leaving.

If reports—that the Shuberts have offered Daly's Theatre on Broadway to the Loew Enterprises (People's Vaudeville Company)—are borne out by future developments, the spectacle of the house made famous by the great and late Augustin Daly presenting moving pictures, perhaps of the Shakespearian plays that producer staged so well, will be presented. What the spirits of the departed will do when this occurs is a matter for the imagination !

Walter Rosenberg has opened a season of " pop." vaudeville and moving pictures on the New York Theatre Roof at an admission scale of 10 to 25 cents. A lease of the roof at $15,000 a year has been obtained for five years, but the roof has to be vacated from June 1st to September 1st.

The building inspector at Cincinnati has notified all the local film exchanges that they must move their stock to locations in neighborhoods and buildings where the public is excluded and where no other business of any sort is conducted.

The Johnson-Jeffries Moving Picture Company, which will handle the big fight pictures, estimates that the pictures will clear $250,000.

The galleries of the legitimate, burlesque and vaudeville houses in Washington are suffering severely in patronage from the swarm of moving picture places which have lately sprung up here. Washington already has sixty of such theatres in operation, and twelve more are in process of building or remodelling for that purpose.

Rev. John R. Mason, pastor of the Methodist Church in Milville, New Jersey "believing that the bad effect of the average moving picture show must be counteracted," has issued invitations to his congregation to come to his picture show, which is to be held in the church building, and for which 1 cent admission will be charged.

Henry Hemleb, proprietor of a moving picture show in Atlantic Avenue, Brooklyn, was fined $50 in Special Sessions last week for allowing children under sixteen years of age to attend the show without the company of parents and guardians. The authorities in this section are watching picture places closely to prevent this breach of the penal code.

The Boadway, heretofore given over to legitimate attractions, on Christmas Day started a new policy of moving pictures and vaudeville, to be presented whenever there are open nights with no legitimate shows booked. The Broadway will be only one of several legitimate theatres in New England to be operated along these lines.

Work has begun on a building which will give Louisville the finest picture house in the South. It is expected to be completed by March 1st, and the approximate cost is about $50,000.

On June 1st, Wm. Bradstreet, a New England moving picture magnate, will take possession of Cook's Opera House, on a long term lease, just consummated with James H. Moore, its owner and until recently its manager. " Pop" vaudeville and moving pictures will be presented.

Edwin Sanborn, the photographer at the Bronx (New York) Zoo, received a good hugging while photographing a Russian bear. The brute evinced a sudden dislike for the photographer when the latter prodded Bruin to secure action for the moving pictures being taken. Mr. Bear grabbed Sanborn and hugged him tight. Sanborn struggled, but the bear seemed only to mind when he yelled for help. At each yell the hug became stronger, until Sanborn struggled silently, finally escaping with many bruises and little clothing.

AUSTRALIA.

Despite the strike amongst the coal miners business at Spencer's Theatrescope, Sydney, remains good. Included in the program are a fine series of New Zealand views, shown by special arrangement with the New Zealand Government, in praise of which the press are very eulogistic with regard to their intrinsic value as an educational factor for the people. Mr. Spencer has been highly complimented upon his projection of these films. A private invitation view was given by the Government previous to their being exhibited to the public, when about 1,000 persons were present, amongst them being the leading lights of society. These films are now drawing big business. The Hiring and Sales Departments are kept pretty busy, and all other departments in this great enterprise have no cause to complain of lack of business generally.

The Australian correspondent of *The Performer* writes : " In reviewing vaudeville for the past year in Australia, it is advisable that consideration be given to a careful survey of what the biograph has done to mitigate the all-round success of variety.

" In 1908 and during the early portion of 1909 the opposition from the picture machine was particularly strenuous. In Sydney alone—that is the metropolis—there were four picture houses to every one of vaudeville, and as each of these shows was doing satisfactory business, it must be understood that the damage done to vaudeville was considerable. On the outskirts of the city picture machines were particularly numerous, though, for the greater part, these were of the mushroom variety, and after a time sank into oblivion. However, sufficient were left to attract a regular *clientèle*, which previously had supported the city shows. Of late the class of material served up by these "two-eight" shows has consisted, for the bulk of the programs, of well-worn subjects, and this, added to the fact that many inexperienced operators were responsible for badly displayed films, has helped to kill the biograph in many places. In the country the picture show has been worked almost to death. The class of program submitted is even worse than that of the suburban showman. Consequently, at this time, the cry is for vaudeville, and many little houses are beginning to make good again. It must not be forgotten, though, that in the various centres the high-class picture show will continue in public favor so long as the present system of high-grade programs is maintained."

CANADA.

John Griffin & Son, of Toronto, declare an intention of establishing a chain of small theatres reaching almost across the Continent. The firm has been in operation only four years. Before that, father and son were in the circus business. They control or own fifty houses, and have booking offices or connections in Toronto, Montreal, Detroit, and Buffalo. The firm also manufactures the moving pictures which are used in its theatres, operating a plant here for that purpose.

At the Bijou, Montreal, never in the history of the theatre has the management failed to get a most creditable production for Christmas week, and, though there was nothing absolutely exciting and sensational in the bill, the program was as cramful of fun and real live interest as it could possibly be.

CHINA.

The American Cinematograph Company are continuing to draw large houses at their cosy house, where they are showing the latest native and foreign pictures. At present an unusually good film depicting scenes in Pekin, including the funeral of the late Empress-Dowager, is being nightly exhibited, and this picture should prove interesting wherever shown, in London or elsewhere.

FRANCE.

A French manufacturer, nameless for the present, having paid a visit to the United States, sends a very gloomy report to his colleagues in France on the outlook of the independent firms supplying the American market, and urges his friends to immediately make a decision on the question of grouping themselves in order to offset the manœuvres of the Moving Pictures Patent Company. In a recent letter, published in the French trade organs, he sums up the situation in the following strain :—

There are fully 10,000 picture shows in the United States, of which about 4,000 could be supplied by the independents at once, provided the exporters were properly organised so as to furnish a constant change of program of well-chosen films. One of the reasons why many renters would willingly patronise the independents is that the Trust sends them all the same subjects, so that it frequently happens four or five moving picture theatres in the same street are giving the identical pictures at the same time. This state of affairs will probably be remedied in the near future, but it behoves the independents to step in and secure their orders before the Moving Picture Patent Company.

Consequently, many renters would be only too happy to march under a new banner if they were sure of a constant change of program which would be different to his neighbor.

The writer then gives warning that if the importers of independent films do not pay strict attention to the present crisis, it is certain the Trust will assume control of the whole market.

An appeal is then made that all interested parties will bury the hatchet, forget their personal quarrels, and go hand in hand after the American market if they wish to make a profit on those transactions. Otherwise, they will be shut out for another four and a half years, or can only do business at a loss.

INDIA.

The Excelsior Company are showing a capital selection of films at Bombay. Comics, dramatics, and historical pictures combine to make a program that wants beating, whilst the excellent travel subjects enable the native, in imagination, to visit fields far away, and to study the conditions under which the inhabitants of other climes live.

NEW ZEALAND.

Spencer's Theatrescope Company commenced a season at the Theatre Royal, Christchurch. Included in the program was the series of Shackleton films, which, as may be expected, aroused the keenest interest. All the features of the enterprise were fully dealt with, and the different branch expeditions, including the final and almost successful dash for the Pole, found a complete pictorial representation. As usual with Mr. Spencer, everything was done in first-class style.

The Large Coliseum Building at Christchurch has been filled nightly, the attraction being Fuller's pictures.

Pathé's pictures at His Majesty's, Christchurch, continue to draw large crowds.

SOUTH AFRICA.

The previous visit of Beetar's Excelsior Bioscope to East London met with such a good reception that it was prophesied that a return visit would prove successful, and this prophecy was fulfilled when the return visit was paid. The pictures were clearly shown, and were free from flicker, being evidently carefully selected.

Those who like the new popular " Picture" entertainment will be well catered for on the Rand, for in addition to the Bijou Theatre, which has been running biograph and vaudeville for some time, a new house, styled " The Vaudette and Lounge Tea Rooms," opened recently in Pritchard Street—an excellent position. At this establishment there are comfortable tea rooms opening on to a balcony, beyond which is a cosy little theatre with seating accommodation for some 300 persons. Here picture shows and vaudeville are given at intervals during the afternoon and evening, while arrangements are being made for the installation of automatic attractions to be placed in the tea rooms. This venture has done well and raked in the shekels during the holidays.

Then we are to have the Tivoli Theatre, with its promised pictures and variety turns; but this structure is still to be erected.

With the foregoing and the two theatres running it will be seen that visitors to the Hub of South Africa had plenty of amusement during the holidays, especially as a circus or two found its way here, and some of the travelling bioscopes drifted this way. Let them all come !

known French firm with a proposition to prepare for them productions of 'Hamlet,' 'Macbeth,' and other Shakespearean plays for cinematographic purposes.

" Business reasons only prevented the arrangement going further than the mere preliminaries, but the fact that the men behind the moving picture business are going for assistance directly to the centre of thought in the theatre to-day leads one to the conclusion that they are continuing to raise the artistic standard of their work to a level on which they can more successfully compete with the flesh and blood drama."

THE BIOSCOPE IN INDIA.

AN INTERESTING LETTER FROM OUR SPECIAL CORRESPONDENT IN CALCUTTA.

Dwellers in India, as in other countries across the seas, have much to thank the bioscope for—much more, indeed, than the average stay-at-home Englishman realises. By its agency, the exile can gaze once more upon old and familiar places; can see his fellow-countrymen moving about on business or pleasure bent; and can, for the moment, at any rate, forget the 7,000 miles that separate him from his kith and kin, and feel that, after all, home is not so very far away. It is not surprising, therefore, although the picture theatre—as the term is understood in England and America—has not yet "arrived" in India, that in every city in the country in which there is a moderately large European population there is to be found a bioscope show. In some cases these entertainments are housed in public halls or theatres, while in others special tents are built for them. To take Calcutta as an example. Here, in the cold weather season, a Parsee gentleman runs a bioscope in a huge marquee erected on the Maidan. His tent season opens in October and concludes in April, and this year he is trying the experiment of giving shows during the hot weather in one of the theatres. Thus far, however, the experiment has not proved altogether a success, owing to a variety of causes. The chief of these is the weather. Just now the heat is very trying, and few people care to venture out after dinner unless they are absolutely obliged to. Again, experience has proved that an entertainment in a theatre does not attract the native population. They will go to the Elphinstone Bioscope—as the Calcutta picture show is called—when it is located in a tent; but they will not visit it when it is shown in a European theatre. Thus it comes about that the audience is restricted to Europeans, the majority of whom, as has been said, prefer to spend their hot weather nights at home rather than in the theatre. In Rangoon, a similar state of affairs prevails, but in Bombay there are, at the time of writing, four companies running picture shows, and they are all doing well. It is difficult to explain why there should be this great difference between cities like Calcutta and Bombay, but perhaps the fact that there is a large floating population in Bombay has something to do with it. Another reason may be that while in Calcutta full two and a half hour shows are given, in Bombay they are much shorter; on Saturdays four one-hour exhibitions are given.

Mr. Madan, the proprietor of the Elphinstone Bioscope in Calcutta, is an enterprising man. He believes in avoiding competition, and to that end gives his patrons plenty of value for their money. During the last cold weather he had a complete change of program every three days, and as, at each performance, 5,000 ft. of film

were shown, the expense incurred was considerable. Next cold season other companies are expected to open out in the capital, and it is Mr. Madan's intention then to change the program every second day, which means that each week 15,000 ft. of film will be shown.

The great drawback to bioscopic enterprise in India to-day is the cost of the films. These have to be bought outright, and at 4d. a ft. the cost of a show becomes quite a formidable item, especially when it is remembered that after they have been shown for a few days the films are of no further use, and have to be sold at half-price or even less, usually to men who tour the smaller towns and villages with little tip-up tents, and who can only afford to buy one film at long intervals. The experiment has been tried of sending new films to Madras, Bangalore, and other places, but it has not been particularly successful. If there were an agency in the country which hired out films, as is done in England, the bioscope showman would find his expenses greatly diminished, he would be able to put on new shows every night, and would be tempted to exploit the smaller towns, in which, owing to the entire lack of amusements, there must be a big field which is at present practically untouched. The only films that can be hired in India to-day are those depicting art subjects, and particularly French plays, which have had a great vogue in Calcutta during the season just ended. Pathé Frères—from whom the Calcutta Bioscope obtain their films, except special topical subjects such as the Boat Race, and the Opening of Parliament, which are taken direct from the manufacturers—lend these on hire.

With the European portion of the audiences who packed the tent during the season the topical pictures were, of course, most popular, but with the natives, the comic pictures appeared to be most appreciated. The programs, however, are always well varied, and include at least one dramatic and one open-air subject, with a plentiful leaven of humorous pictures.

As has been pointed out, the expenses are heavy, and this is not only the case with regard to films, but also in the matter of rent, lights, advertising, etc. Then, too, the operator costs money, for a European—a Frenchman in the case of the Elphinstone—has to be employed. The native, Mr. Madan has found, is not a success as an operator. He can be trained to turn the handle and work the show when everything goes smoothly, but he cannot be trusted to keep his head when anything untoward happens. Therefore, a careful man, knowing that one scare is sufficient to ruin a whole season, has to employ a properly trained European, in order to be on the safe side. With regard to

the future of the bioscope in this country, those
connected with it are optimistic. They think that
it will be some years yet before the picture theatre
—by which is meant a theatre specially built and
adapted for a bioscope show—becomes an institution in the land; but they are firmly convinced
that if the cost of films could be reduced, either by
the formation of an agency to hire them out, or by
any other means, this type of entertainment must
continue to grow in favor; a belief one can
readily subscribe to, for pictures do not need the
spoken word to explain them—a factor of considerable importance in a country in which scores of
different languages are spoken.

The Progress of Cinematography in Japan.

BY S. KURIMOTO.

It was in 1896 that cinematography was first introduced into Japan by Mr. Prancini, an Italian engineer attached to the Japanese Arsenal. Mr. Prancini exhibited a projector, together with some films, but at that time no one knew how to operate them. He thereupon sold the rights to Messrs. Yoshizawa and Co., importers of lanterns and slides, who were interested in the new invention, and after many and varied experiences, the firm acquired a good, all-round knowledge of what might surely be termed "early cinematography."

The following year the Edison Kinetoscope was imported by a company acting in co-operation with Messrs. Yoshizawa and Co., and thus, for the first time in Japan, cinematograph pictures, or "moving photographs," as they were termed, were shown to the public at the theatres in Tokio and Yokohama. In those days films were projected from the inner side of the screen, as the present method of operating was not fully understood. In order to project sharp pictures, the screen was sprayed with water each time a film was shown. The length of the films was, at most, about 50 ft., and the subjects were very simple, such as "Flying Birds," "School Children at Exercise," "Sea Waves," etc. The admission then charged was from 1s. to 5s.; thus easily breaking the record of prices hitherto charged for admittance to any entertainment in Japan; yet, in spite of this, the theatres were crowded at each performance, which was given once nightly: and even the Europeans and Americans resident in Japan were frequently known to request the management to have special shows provided for them. It is interesting to note that the prices now charged at the best Japanese picture theatres range from about 1¼d. to 6d.

Messrs. Yoshizawa soon realised the necessity of appointing a lecturer to explain the subjects, as they were not familiar to many, and the lecturer also described, to the best of his ability, the details of the new invention, as well as the construction and operating of the machine. Messrs. Yoshizawa's initial attempt was very successful, and was prolonged for three months.

Soon after the Russo-Japanese war, films illustrating the various battle scenes were produced with great success, appealing very forcibly to the nation's patriotic feelings. The films showed marked improvement in quality, and were of increased length. At this period, by the command of the Crown Prince of Japan, a gala cinematograph performance was held at Aoyama Villa, Tokio.

A little later saw the opening of the first special cinematograph theatre, "Denki-Kan" (electric theatre) being established, under the management of Messrs. Yoshizawa and Co., at Asakusa Park, the most famous amusement place in Tokio, and the new venture was attended with considerable success. From that time onward picture theatres became popular throughout Japan, and they have proved a most formidable rival to the legitimate theatre as well as to the music-hall.

At that time most of the films were imported from Messrs. Pathé, Urban, Warwick, and Gaumont, while two new firms sprang into existence, namely, Messrs. Yokota and Messrs. Umeya. With the ever-increasing popularity of moving pictures the public became very anxious to see original Japanese plays reproduced by the cinematograph, and as a result, the above firms provided studios for that purpose.

In 1908 Messrs. Yoshizawa sent a representative to London, in the person of Mr. K. Tateshima, who founded a branch of the firm at 32, Victoria Street, S.W. He remained in London until quite recently, when he was succeeded by Mr. S. Kurimoto. Mr. Tateshima was the first Japanese gentleman to come to this country for the express purpose of exporting the films, projectors, accessories, etc.

In 1910 another firm commenced operations in Tokio, under the title of Goshi Kwaisha Fukuhodo, whose representative, Mr. A. Suzuki, is now managing the company's branch at 7, Bera Street, Leicester Square, W.C. Both the managers of these firms are endeavouring to introduce into Japan American, Italian, and other films, which hitherto have not been largely imported.

It is important to state that the cinematograph industry in Japan has grown to such an extent that genuine Japanese films will be introduced to the European market before long. European films now arrive in Japan in such a short space of time that they are exhibited, in many cases, a fortnight after release date. Especially is the quickness of transit noticeable in the cae of important topical subjects, and as an example it may be mentioned that the films of the Coronation and subsequent processions were shown to the Japanese public on July 9th, that is to say, thirteen days after the event took place in London.

Practically all classes of films are equally well appreciated, be they classical, dramatic, or comic, although—such is the modesty of the Japanese maiden—that any picture depicting a passionate love scene, or in which the ardent lover is seen embracing the girl of his heart, would have little chance of success. And the reverence for the guardians of law and order would subject the proprietor exhibiting a comic film showing a policeman receiving the knock-out blow so familiar to us a severe reprimand.

CINEMATOGRAPHY IN ITALY.

BY THE EDITOR OF "LA CINEMATOGRAFIA ITALIANA ED ESTERA."

Italy was one of the last countries to produce films, and almost the last to invent new machinery for this purpose. Until a short while ago, France, America, England, and Germany were long in the field, but now quite a number of Italian manufacturers help to keep up the high standard of film now produced. Amongst the best-known Italian manufacturers are the following:—Itala, Milano, Aquila, Ambrosio, Cines, Pasquali, Latium, Helios, Vesuvio, Unitas, Partenope, Dora Correrio, and Treos, all of whom produce a good number of films, and the quality of which leaves little to be desired. In the North the most promising firms are Saffii, Auriteium, Cinema Brixia Docet, Lavonia, and finally Psiche and Giovanni Pettine, which includes the trade mark A. Croie, of Milan, and the film D'Arte Italiana. We are shortly expecting the Roman branch of the French house Bonne Bresse to bring out some instructive and religious films, which we are promised will be amongst the best in the world. Of course, it is easy to criticise the productions of most of these firms, as the historical subjects are not always true, the dramatic subjects are sometimes slightly *risqué*, and the scientific often impossible. The comic films, again, are often of a type of humour which does not appeal to other temperaments besides those of the Italians themselves; but, just as it is always easier to criticise than to produce something which is absolutely perfect, so it is to be hoped that, after the existing obstacles of administrative troubles have been successfully overcome, the Italian productions will be second to none in the world. As it is, we claim to be already far and away superior, from every point of view, to the average product of any other country, and we only have to watch the productions of Itala, Milano, Aquila, Pasquali, Ambrosio, and Cines to feel sure that we shall shortly be beyond the necessity of making apologies. There are many representatives of foreign houses in Italy, but they are all attempting to put too much fuel on the fire at once. These proceedings are dangerous, both to the producer and the agent.

The first agents in Italy were Marzetto e Baronetto and Co., of Bologna; G. Barattolo, of Rome; and Frieda Klug, of Turin. We cannot say much of the other agents, except that they do not appear to be progressing very favourably, from what we have seen of the subjects they have put on the market.

As regards the renting houses, we now come to the weakest branch of the cinematograph business in this country. There are plenty of hiring firms, and their stock is large and various, but it is mainly "junk," and quite unworthy of being shown on the screen. They hire their programmes out at a very low price, and have many sub-agents and sub-representatives, especially in the Centre and South of Italy, but they appear like mushrooms and disappear as rapidly.

With respect to the Italian picture theatres, there are several thousand, but the really good theatres can easily be enumerated. Generally it is just a big room, not very well furnished, and without any comfort whatever. Some of them are underground, with all the attendant dangers in case of fire, and right in the city of Turin there are already four of these, one of which is very large, and would be the seat of a terrible catastrophy in the event of a panic. There are, of course, a few the memory of which makes us proud that they are to be found in this country. Amongst these we might mention La Splendour, La Borsa (in Turin), Le Centrale, Le Cinema Palace, and the Santa Radegonda, of Milan, and several others belonging to Signor Cav. L. Roatto, of Venice. The prices are exceedingly low, the highest price for arm-chairs being about 6½d., and the others ranging from 4d. to 1d. At Verona, in the Cinema San Sebastino, "Notre Dame de Paris" has been shown to-day, at an entrance price of less than an English ½d. What luxury! But, of course, the performance only lasts for about twenty-five to thirty minutes. The posters are many and varied, and nearly always artistic and elegant. The illumination is always good, as is the music. The operators are now licensed—and that is saying a great deal—but there is no doubt that the better operators suffer from having to accept 3s. 6d. to 4s. 6d. per day, which is the average rate of pay. The managers are well educated, kind, and attentive, but very badly paid. The porters at the doors can be heard two streets away proclaiming the wonders to be seen in their theatre, and they also give away thousands of advertising hand-bills, which are well written, but do not add to the cleanliness of the pavements. The programmes are not censored, and children of any age are admitted to any performance, whether accompanied by adults or not. The theatres are not closed on Sundays, and it is then that they do their best business.

These remarks will suffice to show that the utmost liberty is allowed to the cinematographer in this country.

The journals relating to the trade are the following:—*La Cinematografia Italian ed Estera*, of Turin (one of the oldest), and *La Cine Tono*, of Naples, also of good repute, and well established in Italy. *Il Films* and *Il Cinema* are two new papers, published at Naples, and Turin is now printing a new paper, called *La Vita Cinematografica*.

There are many inventors in this country, foremost amongst whom is Signor F. Poggi, who is the inventor of the "Cinema Clock and Journal of the Cinematographer"; Mr. Vittorio Benagili, the inventor of the plasticscope; and Signor Carlo Rossi, the inventor of the much-discussed, but not yet on sale , duplex films; Messrs. Cremonese and Rizzi, inventors of the cinema for the school and family; while the firm of Fumagalli and Co., of Milan, are the only ones who make projectors, machines which bear favourable comparison with the most celebrated makes in the world.

This is a short pen sketch of Italian cinematography, and we would only add that Italy produces actors and actresses of most uncommon value, plot writers and stage managers of the highest technique, and scenery unsurpassed by any country in the two hemispheres. In short, there is every prospect of Italy becoming one of the first, if not *the* first, country in this Trade, provided that the great disadvantage of the low rate of pay at present existing be once removed.

PROF. GUALTIERO I. FABBRI.

THE FRENCH CINEMATOGRAPH TRADE.

BY THE EDITOR OF "CINEMA-REVUE."

Every industry which develops rapidly knows at one time or another certain moments of temporary lull, during which it seems to find its level and to take its bearings. Cinematography, whose beginning was rather a difficult one, but which reigns to-day in uncontested mastery everywhere, attaining in a few years a development which its inventors had not dared to look forward to, has not escaped this common law. Indeed, scarcely two or three years ago the moving picture industry in France experienced a slackening off which was a serious cause of alarm for the future; this slump arose, to tell the truth, from a real coldness on the part of the public, who, wearied by the many senseless comedies and melodramas extensively composing the programmes of cinematograph theatres, wanted something more natural, more realistic, and more in conformity with actual life. As a result of having tried the nerves of their audiences by making them pass from the wildest merriment to the extreme limits of woe and horror, the managers of cinematograph shows saw their halls deserted by a public who could not find there the sane entertainment they had come to seek.

Happily, however, our film manufacturers immediately understood in what quarter the danger lay, and they at once grasped the remedy. Guided by the experience they had acquired, drawing their inspiration from the preference of the public, they treated the matter in an entirely new light. If comic pictures still intervene from time to time to cheer up the audience, the programme of the picture theatre to-day includes everywhere educational and artistic films, in which dramas and comedies are acted with perfect art by well-known players. But undoubtedly it is the educational film which has contributed most towards the raising up of the picture theatre—travel subjects, subjects borrowed from the industrial arts, and subjects dealing with natural history and geography all receive to-day the heartiest welcome from the public, with the result that the bioscope has done more in two years to raise the standard of education amongst the masses than the books and lectures of the most learned men have done in fifty years. Very few people frequent the public libraries or attend lectures, whilst all the world goes to the picture theatre.

Amongst educational films, those which particularly interest the public are subjects dealing with the life and manners of insects—a world practically unknown to the majority of spectators. It should be mentioned, however, that a form of censorship is maintained over films showing the ferocity of certain insects; these films, which are of the deepest interest to the etymologist, produce in the ordinary member of the public a rather painful and unpleasant impression, which may be harmful to the success of the natural history film in general.

Thus we see that the programmes of cinematograph theatres to-day, although sufficiently varied, have artistic and educational films as *pieces de resistance*. The comic film, however, has not ceased to please; far from that. But the public is showing itself increasingly eclectic; it wants a more restrained form of comedy, and it would be difficult to-day to make pass the clumsy farces which, nevertheless, were very successful at the beginning and, as recently as a few years ago, still had a sufficient popularity.

While film manufacturers have been making really serious efforts, which have resulted in the raising of their productions to an altogether higher level, an equally successful progress has been made in projection apparatus; but there still remains much to be done in this department, and mechanics, like physiologists, may still take heart of joy, if only to secure the total suppression of flickering, at a normal speed.

It is doubtless a matter of interest to those on the other side of the channel to know what sort of welcome has been accorded in France to the "Talking picture." For some years now the conditions necessary for the synchronism of the phonograph and the cinematograph have been realised, but it is rare to come across a set of synchronising apparatus actually in use at a public picture show. The reason for this doubtless lies with the delicacy of regulation and control of the apparatus, and also, perhaps, with the lack of practice amongst the operators who would have to manage the machines. However this may be, one hears with interest that Messrs. Gaumont intend to open certain picture theatres, where a speciality will be made of "talking pictures," and one can foresee that in a few months the public, having shown their preference for such a programme, managers generally will be bound to follow the movement and to take into serious consideration this invention, which up till now has remained rather "in the shadows," but which certainly deserves a better fate.

Apart from the difficulties which result from the monopolisation of cinematographic business by a few big firms, there is in France another trouble with which every new invention has to contest, —namely, the inexperience of operators. In France, despite the strict police regulations as regards the actual building of the picture theatre, no preliminary examination is required to ascertain whether the operator possesses the necessary technical knowledge and the requisite coolness and decision to be equal to any danger in cases of alarm. But it is not only from the point of view of the public safety that this is a great drawback, for, as a result of so few operators having any knowledge of optics, or mechanics, or electricity, every idea and every new invention penetrates only with the utmost difficulty into the circle which should be interested therein.

It is none the less true that the position of the cinematograph business was never better in France than it is at the present day, and there is no reason to suppose that its popularity will do otherwise than continue to increase. The public loves quick and varied entertainments; the cinematograph gives it full satisfaction in this respect, and, in fact, proves a very real rival to the "legitimate" theatre.

If film manufacturers have done much for the popularisation of the cinematograph, and if they have contributed most greatly to its development, the showmen must not be forgotten, for they have succeeded, by clever advertising, in drawing all classes of society, without exception, to the picture theatre. One of the most original and most effective methods of advertisement, especially in industrial centres and neighbourhoods, is that which consists in taking cinematograph pictures of the employées coming out of a large factory, or even of the principal thoroughfares at the busier times of the day. The theatre where these films are subsequently shown is sure of being packed to overflowing, and the public, having once taken the road to the picture show, returns willingly time after time.

Activity and progress are the best warrants for the long life of an industry. The activity which we find in every branch of the cinematograph industry in France, and the progress which is made daily with photographic material, allows us to have the greatest confidence in the future of the cinematograph.

CHARLES-MENDEL, FILS.

CINEMATOGRAPHY IN INDIA.

SPECIAL TO "THE BIOSCOPE."

Practically the sole topic of conversation in India just now is the coming Royal visit, the Durbar at Delhi, and the festivities at Bombay and Calcutta, which will mark the presence in these cities of their Majesties the King and Queen. The visit of the ruling Sovereign of the British Empire to his great Indian dependency is an event unique in the history of the nation, and the Durbar and other functions will no doubt be as interesting to people at home as the visit itself is to us out here, and to the millions of His Majesty's Indian subjects.

Exactly what arrangements have been made by the Durbar authorities for the proper filming of the great event, no one in Calcutta, where I am at the time of writing, can say. All these matters are in the hands of the Durbar Committee at Simla, and all the satisfaction, one can get in reply to written requests for information is that everything has been arranged satisfactorily. One hears, however, that, in addition to the operators who always travel with the King, Mr. Charles Urban is himself coming out with assistants to "take" the functions for Kinemacolor.

That the films will be much sought after is certain. The Durbar will be a magnificent spectacle, even though the elephant procession, which was one of the features of Lord Curzon's Durbar in 1903, has been cut out of the programme, and the number of troops assembled will be considerably smaller than was at first arranged for. In the "Gorgeous East" the show is the thing, and the pomp and pageantry, the brilliant colouring, the glow and the glitter inseparable from ceremonial functions in India, will make the Durbar a spectacle such as has never before been seen through the medium of the cinematograph. At the time of the last Durbar, in 1903, cinematography was in its infancy, and if any animated pictures were taken of that event they must have been very inferior to the ones that will be taken

now. An Indian Durbar, especially one on an Imperial scale, such as this will be, is one of the sights of the world, and can be seen nowhere else in the world than in India; and, as it will lend itself naturally to reproduction, the resultant films will take a high place amongst the great scenes, enacted thousands of miles away, which the bioscope has enabled stay-at-home Britons to witness.

In addition to the Durbar and connected functions at Delhi, there will be great doings at Bombay, when the King arrives in India, and later in Calcutta, when His Majesty pays a week's visit to the capital. In both these cities local firms are making arrangements in order to secure moving pictures of the proceedings, and efforts are to be made to emulate the enterprise of the people at home, and show the pictures the same night. Whether the firms concerned will or will not succeed in their endeavours remains to be seen. There are many difficulties to be overcome which the home operator does not experience—skilled labour cannot be easily obtained, and properly equipped workshops for turning out "rush" work do not exist—but the effort is to be made, and one can only hope that the enterprise shown by the people concerned will meet with its due reward.

The great event of the Royal visit in Calcutta is to be a pageant representing Indian history from the very earliest times down to the present day, and this promises to provide pictures second only in magnificence to those of the Durbar itself. The pageant will include a procession of gorgeously caparisoned elephants, some fifty-six in number, native dances, and other purely spectacular features, that must show up well on the screen, and Mr. Frank Lascelles, organiser of the "Festival of Empire" last year, who has come out to act as Master, hopes to make the pageant the biggest and best ever held in the world. Some fine pictures can, therefore, be expected from Calcutta, as well as from Delhi.

A Visit to a German Picture Theatre.

BY J. OJIJATEKHA BRANT-SERO.

The average German picture theatre is comparatively small, its holding capacity ranging from 300 upwards to 500. It is not difficult for a stranger to see that the theatre had once done service for a store of some sort, and may possibly, at the end of half a year or a year, again become an ordinary refuge for small retailers of wares. At the door one meets a uniformed official sporting a low tone of voice, drawing heavy plush curtains to one side as the patrons pass in. He is also the check-taker and programme distributor. The programmes are free, but if you are well acquainted with the needs of polite service rendered in German, it is a consolation to the gentleman in question that you give him a trifle for luck. On doing so, he tears off the coupon of your ticket, and calls out the *platz* your ticket demands. Another official, probably the proprietor, carrying an electric torch, calls out at the entrance of another curtained doorway in reply. Before entering further, you notice a regular bar, with cigars, cigarettes, sweets, and substantial eatables on the counter and shelves. As you enter, following the usher-proprietor, you are likely to encounter a white-jacketed waiter, who gravely gives you a polite welcome with a sweep of the hand and a slight side nod of the head. You pass up the aisle in perfect silence, save for the music from a piano or organ, a violin, and violoncello, go up three steps and take your seat in the middle of the hall. This is *eorste platz*, just behind a Continental hat worn by a fresh-looking giantess. For a time you dodge about behind the solemn damsel, trying to see the passing pictures with some degree of enjoyment, regardless of your comfort. The picture ends, and you feel a sense of sensation almost equal to the wave of relief in a church after an extempore prayer. The lights go up, and you find right behind, above your head, is an overhanging operating room of respectable dimensions. The walls are decorated with scenes showing considerable artistic skill and painting. In panels one may see a country scene in all its richness of outdoor life, or it may be your fortune to become acquainted with the mysteries of the Germanic sense of humour. A careful supply of couplets, proverbs of the people, find a place everywhere on the walls. One must know German to appreciate their real significance. Along the walls of the *erste platz* are several hooks for cloaks and hats, and over them notices in large type, the prices of things to be had. Nothing is given preference to, apparently, unless it be that you are reminded of the qualities of certain brands of beer. A glass of beer costs a penny—the ordinary price everywhere. Tea or coffee costs twopence half-

penny—specially made for you. Polite notices are displayed, reminding ladies with hats of large dimensions that they are requested to remove their headgear, for the comfort of others. If they should forget, they are asked to do so with painful politeness, either directly or through the medium of its officials, when it is usually done, the lady apologising through her cavalier escort for her oversight, even for a moment. There are also notices issued by the police for the safety of the public, in which are included warnings for ladies to be careful of the long, unprotected hat-pins. Lastly, but not least, in some theatres there is the imperative notice that the police forbid smoking on the premises most strictly. In some of the theatres a row or two is reserved in the *erste platz*, at a slight advance in price, rarely going beyond a shilling, and here, for some reason or other, the ladies are not required to remove their headgear at all. It is purely voluntary if they do so, which is very seldom. The jolly-looking, healthy giantess in front of me, having removed her tremendous hat, smiled in a guilty-blushing sort of way. I, after the German fashion, quickly rose to my feet and graciously acknowledged the compliment, in full view of the audience. Nobody paid the slightest attention to this international display of everyday courtesy in a picture theatre. The waiter came rushing up the aisle with a tray full of orders, his moustache tilted up at the ends, almost reaching his cheek-bones. The little orchestra, after playing a lively popular American air, proceeded with a favourite selection from the German musical classics.

The music has ceased. All is very quiet. Suddenly the lights go out. An extremely comical situation is presented on the screen. The music is equal to the occasion. The waiter comes along, and, having forgotten who ordered the coffee, calls out, " *Ein kaffee!*" duly delivers it. The comical picture goes on, and the silent experiences of comedy on the screen are only equalled in stoical silence by the church-like silence of the audience. Earlier in the evening the same picture would occasionally evoke a muffled snicker from a child in the front seat. However, it being past 9 o'clock, the children having all departed for home, according to police regulations, the grown-ups have free scope. The star film is put on, dealing with the eternal " human triangle," in which the military element is present. This film is shown in three parts. A crowded audience gave not the slightest sign of pleasure or displeasure: their presence was sufficient to prove their love of the German Army, while perhaps sympathising with the woman as a secondary matter.

SOME RHODESIAN THEATRES.

(BY OUR SPECIAL CORRESPONDENT.)

Bulawayo is well catered for by the two handsome bioscope theatres now open there, namely, the "Empire" and "Paterson's Popular Picture Palace." The Empire, situate on Main Street, and managed by Mr. Lago Clifford, well known in South African theatrical circles, is leased from the proprietors by Messrs. Clifford, Assersohn, and Co., and is a thoroughly up-to-date and well-equipped theatre. With a handsome vestibule, off which are situated the bar, restaurant, and cloakrooms, the theatre, both by day and night, is inviting and cosy in appearance, but particularly so when the glow of the numerous electric lights casts its glamour over it. The red-upholstered seats contrast richly with the blue and gold drapings of the private boxes and various doorways, and it is not surprising that the 500 seating capacity is often severely taxed; but, no matter how crowded, cool comfort is assured by the sliding roof.

The electric current is provided by a private generating set, and a "Saxonia" machine projects a fine picture over a 95 ft. throw. Except when the boards are occupied by a theatrical company, picture shows are given every night, including Sunday, and a matinee on Saturday afternoons.

In addition to the theatre, a roller rink alongside enables Mr. Clifford to meet the more strenuous wishes of his patrons, and, all round, the Bulawayo public can have no cause for complaint that amusements are lacking while the "Empire" stands.

Mr. W. R. Paterson, at the "Popular Picture Palace," provides that zest of keen competition for public patronage which stimulates continuous improvement, and ensures the provision of "the best" —to the public benefit. Larger than the Empire, the Palace can seat 800, and is equally well equipped to meet all the requirements of a full theatrical company. The 110-volt generators provide an abundance of light, and a "Butcher No. 12" throws a 20 ft. picture over the 85 ft. from lens to screen. In addition to pictures, Mr. Paterson constantly supplies attractive vaudeville turns, and full companies, as occasion permits. At the time of my visit, various improvements were under weigh, and others being considered, while arrangements were being made for an entire change of pictures every evening of the week, a project which, if effected, would undoubtedly tax the resources of all the film-hiring agencies of the Rand. In addition to the Bulawayo Palace, Mr. Paterson is proprietor of the Palace in Salisbury, where competition is of the keenest, and he deserves and receives a full measure of public support at both places.

Gatooma, a small town of some 400-500 people, on the Bulawayo-Salisbury railway line, has also its bioscope theatre, and I was fortunate in meeting the proprietor, Mr. Dixon, in the train. The "Rose Bioscope," despite many difficulties, is reported on cheerfully as doing "very good business." The town residents afford a liberal support during the week, and at week-ends the influx from the mining properties in the district crowds the little theatre to the doors. Once again an "Empire No. 12" holds sway, and electric current is provided from a generator on the adjacent premises of an engineering firm.

Umtali, 170 miles down the Salisbury-Beira line, has a show provided at the Cecil Hotel, at present worked by a gas plant, pending the arrival and installation of an electrical equipment, which, I understand, is now *en route*. Here, also, Messrs. Butcher's installed their machine, and there can be no doubt that it must pay manufacturers to have "live" agents in South Africa.

At Penhalonga, Mr. H. Perrem has closed down his show, pending the arrival of his electric outfit, which he anticipates will be working early in December.

For North, in the heart of what, but a few years ago, was "Darkest Africa," Mr. N. George exhibits 8,000 ft. of film per week to the residents of Elizabethville, Karanga, Belgian Congo, and, I am advised, has no cause to regret his enterprise.

Salisbury the capital of Rhodesia, with a population of about 4,000, has no less than four bioscope shows in keen competition for public support. Chief among them is the Palace Theatre, not yet fully completed, the property of Mr. Paterson, of Bulawayo. With a seating capacity of 800, and, as at Bulawayo, fully equipped for the accommodation of full theatrical companies, and with a bar and tea lounge attached, Mr. Paterson can boast that it is Salisbury's only "theatre." A Pathé machine, and the silver screen, are here preferred, and shows—unless a company occupies the boards —are given every night. While incomplete, it is hardly wise to criticise the appointments, for the leather-upholstered seats on order, which will oust the present wooden chairs, will in themselves make a vast difference to the cosy appearance of the theatre.

The Market Hall Bioscope is also in a transition stage, the work of redecoration having just begun, but the proprietary syndicate pins its faith to showing the finest pictures in the town, and the public largely endorses the view.

The Posada Rink and Bioscope is under canvas which has seen its best days, and was, I am informed, the first show in the town, when fancy prices were obtainable, and handsome profits could be made. The "Empire No. 12" here again holds sway, and a very clear, bright picture is provided, the evening being divided between rinking and pictures. The probability is that the advent of the rainy season will necessitate closing down.

Living Pictures and Advertisements.

By an Advertising Agent.

How far is the use of the bioscope for the purposes of advertisement justified ?

The question is prompted by the remark of a gentleman, overheard at a West-End music hall last week, where a sort of moving picture show was given at the beginning of the evening. He objected strongly to this "entertainment."

" I didn't come here to be told to go to Hash's Restaurant or to take Kilmee's Kough Kapsules. I want entertainment," he said, and as I sat near him I could not help hearing the remark. It set me thinking, but curiously enough it was the last three words he said which really impressed me.

Can bioscope advertisements be made interesting and entertaining ?

I see no reason why they should not, and the perfection to which "trick" films have now been carried makes it easier than it would otherwise be.

For instance, it should be possible to prepare a very amusing film to advertise a furniture polish. The furniture could be shown at first very dull, and the servant and the mistress busy polishing. Gradually a magnificent gloss would come over all the tables and sideboards, and to raise a laugh the glasses and vases could be shown sliding about on the highly-polished surface.

We are all familiar with the picture of the boy who cried because he could not get the chocolate he wanted. This could be elaborated very easily into a short moving picture for advertisement purposes.

"You Dirty Boy," one of the most famous of advertisements, has been transferred to the bioscope, and was found very successful. Messrs. Pears still have the film. It might be worth while putting it forward again now there is a boom in bioscopes.

It need hardly be pointed out that any moving picture advertisement should contain a recognisable feature. Almost every widely-advertised article is associated in the public mind with some picture or some trade mark. Bovril is a good example, and I can imagine that the picture " Say, Guard, am I right for Bovril ? " would be extremely effective as a living picture if it could be staged. Something has already been done by means of lantern slides, parts of the picture being put in one at a time and gradually building up the picture. I have seen some that were very amusing, but I feel certain that ways and means could be found to make them much more effective.

The old prejudice that advertising is not an art has surely died out by this time. There is no country (not even excepting America) which can show better display in the advertisement pages of its periodicals than our own. It is a commonplace, in fact, to say that the advertisements are more interesting than the literary matter. It seems to me that there is a very extensive field for artistic advertisement in the bioscope theatres, and if at the same time the films for this purpose can be made entertaining as well as useful, there should be no serious opposition to their introduction.

Of their acceptance by theatre managers there could not, I think, be much doubt.

THE BIOSCOPE

Incorporating
"The Amusement World" & "The Novelty News"
Published by the Bioscope Press,
8 Cecil Court, Charing Cross Road, London, W.C

FEBRUARY 25, 1909.

NOTICES.

Publishing.

"The Bioscope" is published every Thursday at **8 Cecil Court, Charing Cross Road, London, W.C.** Telegrams: "Biolesque," London.

Telephone: 2421 City.

Subscription.

"The Bioscope" will be sent regularly by post to any address for Four Shillings a year, payable in advance.

Editorial.

All Editorial communications and matter for insertion should be addressed to the Editor, and must reach the offices not later than first post Tuesday morning. All articles, paragraphs and drawings published in "The Bioscope" are the copyright of the publishers, from whom alone authority to re-publish or reproduce can be obtained.

Articles are invited only from writers who are experts in their subjects. Writers are advised to lay their ideas before the Editor before sending in contributions. No responsibility can be undertaken for the safety of MSS submitted, but endeavour will be made to return promptly in case of rejection.

Advertisements.

All copy for advertisements and instructions for alterations must reach the offices not later than first post Monday morning to ensure attention in the current week's issue.

Small paragraph advertisements are inserted at the rate of one shilling for the first 20 words, and one penny for each word in excess of 20. All words in name and address are charged for. Groups of initial letters or figures not exceeding six count as one word. Terms: Cash with order.

Advertisers wishing to have replies addressed to a box-number may do so without extra charge if they send for the replies. If replies are required to be sent by post, sufficient stamps must be enclosed to cover cost of postage. In counting the words of an advertisement using a box-number, nine words must be allowed for the address, thus: A101, c/o "The Bioscope," 8, Cecil Court, London, W.C.

Scale of Charges for displayed advertisements may be obtained on application to the Manager.

Explaining the Pictures.

Audiences are strange things, as the showman finds often to his cost. There is no crowd so fickle as the crowd that has gathered together to be amused, and strangely enough there is no crowd that is quite so lazy in the matter of using its commonsense. Each member of the audience seems to have said to himself as he approached the pay box: "I have come here to be amused; I am not going to tire myself thinking about the entertainment." And as a result in many a bioscope theatre, films that are really dramatic and films that are really interesting are watched without a glimmer of intelligence and frequently with complete boredom. The question of industrial subjects may be left for the moment on one side, with a remark in parenthesis that in a continuous show the appearance of an industrial subject is generally the signal for a certain proportion of the audience to terminate their visit. But anyone with a long experience of picture halls knows that the stories of many dramatic pictures are quite incomprehensible to many of the people who watch the events that transpire on the screen.

We have thrown this out as a reproach to the audience, but the train of thought thus started must bring the reader ultimately to the question:—Is it all the fault of the audience? And when he has reached that stage he may well begin to cast about for ways in which to remove the trouble. There are, of course, two primary ways—by means of a lecturer and by means of a written explanation on the lantern slide. There is much to be said in favour of the lecturer if he is competent, if speaking to pictures is with him more of a hobby than a duty, and if he has a sympathetic voice. But there are plenty of lecturers who are calculated to make any audience feel very ill in bed, and the supply of good men is by no means equal to the demand. We come then to the explanation by lantern slide, and country managers will be well advised to give the matter consideration, because they are showing to audiences whose experience of the world is less, and whose knowledge is therefore less than that of the visitors to picture palaces in large towns. Comic films as a rule require no explanation; it is in the dramatic and historical pictures that the need for some brief synopsis is most felt.

The first question to be decided is how much of the story the audience should be told. We are inclined to the belief that one hundred words outlining the opening scenes, and stating the order in which the events follow one another would be enough. It is necessary to avoid "giving away" too much of the plot, for otherwise there are no thrills, and the charm of the unexpected has gone. But there can be no thrill if the meaning of the opening scene has not been grasped, and we have in mind one particularly fine dramatic film now showing one criticism of which that we overheard in a bioscope theatre was: "Well, what's it all about?" The question could have been answered in a few words, but the lack of those few words spoiled the enjoyment of the film for that person, and for many others like him. It may be urged, and very justly, that in part the manufacturer is to blame if the story of a film is not instantly apparent. The plot may be too complicated, or, in the case of the film we have in mind, the stage-management may be somewhat at fault. But, generally speaking, manufacturers have gauged very nicely the capacity of the average mind. It is for the theatre manager to see that those whose intellectual powers are deficient are helped and not sent empty away. One patron dissatisfied generally means five prospective patrons warned off.

"Telling the Tale."

By T. W. KINGSTON, Manager (England) "West's Pictures."

Being very interested in the article in THE BIOSCOPE recently, entitled "Explaining the Pictures," and as I have had considerable experience in this same department of the picture showman's art, perhaps a few words from me might serve as a sort of appendix to the before-mentioned ably-written digest. Personally, up to as recent a date as the beginning of 1908, I had done very little in this particular line, but I had been for the better part of my life singer, actor, stage-manager; and producer, so that in a measure I was well qualified to start out in this new direction. Accident gave me the opportunity. I had been touring Scotland with a new musical comedy, which should have been a financial success, but wasn't. We were accordingly paid off in Edinburgh, and, like Othello, "My occupation was gone." However, in a roundabout way I heard a great sacred painting—to wit, Joseph Weneker's "Come unto Me "—was about to be exhibited at the Albert Hall, and a lecturer was wanted; I put in for the job, and got it. I had already heard my predecessor in another city, and I had the syllabus of the lecture, but I thought I saw flaws in it and remodelled the tale to my own ideas. Now comes a point I wish to emphasise, i.e., a straight lecture, such as the one I am now speaking of, can be made by one happy phrase; this I was lucky enough to do. I described it as "a sermon in oils painted by an inspired brush." The General Assembly of the National Church of Scotland was in conference at this period, and when the discussion came on as to the proper way of preaching a sermon, my poor little lecture was cited as an example. For the next six weeks my six or seven lectures a day were attended by parsons of all denominations, ranging from Roman Catholic Priests down to "meenisters of the Wee Free," and many of them actually came to me for notes for their Sunday sermons on the text which gave the title to the painting. As a general rule, I do not believe in too much talkee, talkee, but at the same time, there are many films which are helped by a little explanation. Cut out at once dramatic and humorous sections, these are unworthy of their definitions if the situations in the one and the humour in the other have to be explained. I always introduce each subject in a few words, and with my comics generally manage to get a laugh before the picture is flashed on to the screen. Sometimes the title itself is humorous, and then a mere inflexion of the voice does it—a mock tragic, or a bantering tone will ensure the film a mirthful reception. To attempt to describe in words what is palpably told in pictures is an insult to the intelligence of your audience, and they are quick to resent this. I once heard a man, wishing to emphasise some feminine attribute to a character, gravely inform his hearers: "She is not only a woman, but, mark you, a female "—of course, with the inevitable result a voice from the darkest corner of the "gods," retorted: "Show us a woman what's a male, guv'nor." But of all classes

of raconteurs, save us from those of the ponderous and would-be learned order. Now, forty-nine out of every fifty persons who come to a picture show come to be amused, not to be instructed, although, of course, in a properly organised programme, the medicine of instruction is artfully concealed in the jam of amusement; but they don't want it thrust down their throats. Now, a rock this last class of orator splits upon is that sort of film which may be described as scientific—cheese mites, microbes, and such like, he crams up the proper names of these, and reels them off, and is generally very pleased when he has finished. The chances are that in the audience there are a great many people who know far more about these creatures than he, whilst to the majority his harangue has been merely gibberish. I find in these instances a patter-lecture is the best method. To point the moral with a tale. I had a film called "Pond Life," a splendid subject, but, of course, the syllabus was simply a list of Latin names, and a description of the animals' habits, etc. I gave their various proper nomenclature, but I introduced them something after this fashion (a writhing furry looking thing, I have long since forgotten its awful name): "No! ladies, this is not what you imagine, that lovely feather boa, marked 5s. 6d., which was in the window at So-and-So's sale to-day, this is the, etc., etc.," and so on.

In the mixing of a lecturial pudding, I have often found "soft soap," or, in other words, a neatly-turned compliment paid to one's auditors a most useful ingredient. My meaning will be clearer perhaps if, ex professo, I give a couple of illustrations. I was spouting in Edinburgh on "The Destruction of San Francisco." It was just the season of the year (early summer) when the modern Athens is full of American tourists, who are taking a preliminary canter through the British Isles before migrating to the Continent. Naturally, the subject interested them, and they usually provided a fair proportion of the audience. In June and July, the theatres in Auld Reekie are closed down, so I used to get in my shot thus:—When I came to the ruins of the Opera House, I described it as "All that remains of the once beautiful building wherein the world's greatest tenor, Caruso, was singing the night before the catastrophe, looking under its present aspect as if it would require a lot of renovation before it re-opened for the autumn season. Ah! I see you smile; you think that a wild assertion; let me tell you it is a prophecy, for the American with his undoubted energy, his business grip, and patriotic zeal, will soon build up a new 'Frisco to rise phœnix-like from the ashes of her predecessor, even fairer than before." The result of this peroration was that parties of unmistakable Yankees would wait behind with a little address of this sort: "Shake, Mr. Lecturer, shake, and allow us to thank you for the handsome things you said about our country, sir; we are Americans—shake." Now, we haven't always American tourists with us, but we do have the ladies in our midst (bless 'em) at all times, so here comes the second sample. Quite recently I was giving some explanatory notes upon a classical picture in a certain Southern seaside resort, which is, moreover, famous for its pretty women. I had to indicate a lovely mortal, and told them: "She was so beautiful that had she not been a Grecian maiden, she might have been mistaken for a lady of so and so." This line always got the reward of a round of gentle pit-pats from daintily-gloved hands, and I could positively her the darlings "purr."

Mind you, there are times when you can break in with a fine dramatic line, and get a good round. There are times when a little eloquence is useful in covering up defects; let me finish with a yarn to illustrate this. Two springs back, between my own seasons, I took on the office of chief lecturer to a company, now wound up, and my duty was to describe journeys through distant lands. One day they sent us "A trip through the Arctic Circle." Now, this was in parts a shockingly blurred and dull film. The manager was in despair, and said to me: "We had better send this back." I said: "What? the best film we have shown for some time." He got quite wrath. I said: "All right, come in and hear me tell the tale." We arrived at the bad portion. "Now, ladies and gentlemen," said I, in solemn tones, "I want you to notice particularly this portion of our journey, for we are now in the midst of that wonderous arctic night, that night without light of moon or stars to guide, simply those mystic—nay, one might call them, holy—lights, which scientific men term the Aurora Borealis. To me this has seemed one of those fascinations which lured the old explorers farther and farther north, in search of the great Unknown. God knows, some of them may have found it, but *they*, THEY have not returned to tell us." When my chief saw dear old ladies with tears in their eyes thanking me for my beautiful words, and old gents stuffing cigars into my pocket, and taking me around the corner to have one, he understood there was more in films—than films.

Random Flickers.

By OBSERVER.

What is the hep worth if it begins to pall?

The latest farce is "A Trip to Paris." The best English comedians are in it.

Good films are Lux-urious, and unrestricted.

A good story is being told of a certain picture-hall proprietor, whose knowledge of his subject was elementary. He was showing the local reporter round on the second night the hall was opened, and among his films was one of Italian Cavalry jumping.

'Here's a fine jump for you," he remarked, as the horse flitted across the screen. "Not so bad," said

the journalist, without enthusiasm. "Ah! my boy!" retorted the proprietor; "you should have seen that horse jump last night. He did it much better!"

My remarks on the music-man have brought me the following interesting remarks from a correspondent. He writes:—"The music-man in the picture-hall is not usually a genius, but that is hardly to be expected at the prices that are offered. A weekly wage of 30s. was offered me recently by the proprietor of a continuous performance hall, where the profits are probably over £20 a week. For this sum I was to play from 2 p.m. to 11 p.m. I am an L.R.A.M., and a good hand at improvising.

"If I may offer a word of advice, I would say to the picture-palace proprietor: 'Get a man who can improvise and pay him well.' In your Flickers you indicate some ways in which a thoughtful pianist can help the pictures. But the man who can improvise a little, who can blend one or two familiar refrains into a little tune of his own to illustrate the story that is going on is a pearl of great price, and if only managers would try to deal justly by such men they would find it a good investment."

There is also to be considered the value of high-class incidental music as an adjunct to picture shows. The following paragraph from the "Illustrated Sporting and Dramatic News," published in Sydney, February 4th, alluding to the famous orchestra conducted by Louis de Groen (known as the Australian Sousa) which accompanies Mr. T. J. West's great show in Sydney, is worth repeating:—

"Everyone who goes to West's pictures at the Glaci., sits in amazement at the size of the orchestra. Some of the music played during the passing of the Oriental films is so wild and bizarre in character that it compels one to come again. There is nothing like music to envelop a foreign film with atmosphere, and the Glaci. is the only picture show in town that begins to realise the importance of this."

This is a hint worth taking by some of our English showmen.

There is another new word in the film trade—bio-Röntgenography. Naturally it comes from Germany.

What they say in America:—That the initials M.P.-P.C. stand for Modern Pocket Picking Coterie. The English equivalent has no initials as yet. Being still born it could not be baptised.

Apropos my remarks the other week on topical films, I see that Mr. Hilton Fox, the operator at the Opera House, Workington, has got into his bill for this week "The King's Favourite Watering Place—Beautiful Biarritz." Perhaps Brighton might object to the first five words, but the idea is excellent. Everybody knows the King has gone to Biarritz, and everybody is interested to see what sort of a place it is.

Music in Picture Theatres.

To the Editor of THE BIOSCOPE.

SIR,—As a regular reader of your paper, I have been greatly interested in some recent remarks I have seen in it, on the subject of music in picture-halls. Now, I can fairly claim to have had a good all-round experience, both in town and on tour, and the conclusion I am forced to is that it is not altogether a matter of pounds, shillings, and pence ; the human element is, in these days, often overlooked. The really good picture pianist is born, not made. He must possess brilliant technique, an excellent memory, be able to play *without music*, to extemporise, and, above all, must be gifted with imagination and romance, and be well educated.

Now, take my own case. I am a public school man. I cannot honestly remember when I was unable to play ; I certainly used to play at the age of five. I have the Heaven-sent gift of extemporising on the spur of the moment, and a memory that enables me to play such pieces as Rachmaninoff's " Prelude in C Sharp Minor," Dvorak's " Humoresque," and—as a contrast— " Down South." Now, at first, I did management and advance work, under Mr. Alfred West, of " Our Navy," and to that gentleman, and his late musical director, Julian Fredericks, I owe a lot. The latter is, in my opinion—and I am not alone —the finest of all picture pianists, and, in addition, a composer who can hold his own in any company where popular music is concerned.

I used to attend the theatre I now play at, and often, on leaving, made caustic comments on the music A young lady used to make feeble attempts at " Faust " and other like selections that had no earthly relations to the pictures on the screen, with the result that the whole show was spoiled for me. Then one day I was sent for, and told

that an application on my part for the post would probably be successful. I made it, took the post, and have never regretted it. I found I had a magnificent Steinway grand to play on, and was surprised to find it there at all. It had simply been half-used.

Now came my problem. I could have no preliminary view of the pictures I had to play to ; the show was a continuous one, and the programme changed twice a week. Well, I found I had, on the spot, to invent two completely new programmes of music every week, for even now, after a year, I only know—at the start of the show on Monday and Thursday evenings—the names, lengths, and character of the pictures. How on earth, under these conditions, could anyone run an orchestra ? And I maintain that, to follow the pictures properly, one has to watch them continually, play first to this character, then to that one, and generally try to convey to the audience in music the meaning of every scene which appears. Our operator backs me up splendidly, and is an artist in making a dance or march past of troops run dead to time ; and let me say at once that, unless there is a perfect sympathy between the pianist and the operator, much is lost.

I quickly found that I had an audience that appreciated really good music. I have often, when a really good classical drama is on the screen, and I am playing, perhaps, the middle movement of Beethoven's " Kreutzer " Sonata, or " Tannhauser," been thrilled by the rapt hush that comes over the hall. One could hear a pin drop. I often get requests for such pieces as Mendelssohn's " Spring Song," and always oblige, if the pictures permit.

I had an amusing experience not long ago. On coming to the hall, my manager told me that two of the regular patrons had a five shilling bet as to whether we had a pianolo or not, and the loser was not satisfied until he had actually seen the piano ! The fact was that, in playing Chopin's " Marche Funebre," for a funeral picture, I had produced a tremolo effect in octaves in the beautiful trio for which this piece is famous, and the gentleman in question declined to believe that anyone could play in this manner. I had a similar experience with two ladies over the pace at which I played Rachmaninoff's " Prelude." These are only a few of many instances that have shown me how people love good music, and if picture-hall proprietors will only engage really good players, who are, at a trial, able to sit down to the piano with a strange picture on the screen, and satisfactorily play to it, then they need not worry about orchestras, except when they are running a one show a night programme for a week ; even then, the result is rarely satisfactory. Of course, my remarks are meant to apply to the ordinary picture palace, and not to shows like " Our Navy " and " Kinemacolor "—which are in a different category (musically) altogether.

To proprietors, therefore, I would say : " Get the best man you can ; treat him well ; don't try to teach him his job; pay *him* well; and stand by for results that will pay *you* well." And if the artist in question happens, as I am, to be well known in the town the show is in, so much the better, for his friends will—as mine do—back the show up by attending (*and paying*) frequently.

I am fortunate in having for employers gentlemen who treat me with every possible kindness and consideration, and I venture to think that they have, in some measure, been repaid for their policy.

I must apologise for the length of this letter, Mr. Editor, but this question of music is one that has a most important bearing on the success of a hall; even the organist of Westminster Abbey might be helpless if planted in front of a picture-hall piano and asked to play a "Wild West" film of 1,000 ft. at sight, as I often have to do; but the fact is that playing to pictures is a branch of the musical profession by itself, and if proprietors will only stop the short-sighted policy of engaging young women at 15s. a week to attempt work that should be done by trained men for at least twice that sum, they will reap the benefit of their enterprise.

I hope I shan't be accused of egotism. This letter is not written as an advertisement, but in the interests of music as allied to the cinematograph.—Yours, etc.,

A PIANIST.

Southsea,
    November 3rd, 1911.

"The Bioscope" Parliament.

Readers are invited to express their Opinions upon any subject of General Interest,

Correspondence submitted for publication must be accompanied by the full name and address of the writer, not necessarily for publication but as an evidence of good faith. Anonymous letters will be promptly consigned to the Waste Paper Basket. Publication of a letter must not be taken to imply that the views expressed are endorsed by the Editor.

The Picture Pianist.

To the Editor of THE BIOSCOPE.

SIR,—For consummate conceit, the letter from PIANIST, Southsea, in your issue of November 9th beats everything. PIANIST's " gifts " of being able to extemporise to any picture do not seem to lead him in the right path, otherwise, why does he want to boast of his ability to play the Prelude in C sharp " Minor," Dvorak's Humoresque," and—wonderful!—" Down South " ? This is not extemporising, and, after all, it is not such a marvellous feat to perform these particular pieces from memory.

He says he obtained his first and present engagement by making caustic comments on the music provided by the lady then playing. He evidently has a grudge against " young women," as he is pleased to designate us, but I shall say something about this later on. If PIANIST has no rehearsal of pictures, surely he can use his gifts and his brains to study the weekly supplement of THE BIOSCOPE, and read the synopsis provided of each picture. I notice he says that he has often heard a pin drop when playing " Tannhauser." Does he mean a rolling pin? I thought " Tannhauser " was a brilliant selection. Anyway, very few passages arranged for piano would admit of a pin-drop being heard.

Apparently PIANIST has his own ideas of adding music to standard works. Imagine everyone doing this! I cannot find any tremolo movement in octaves in " March Funébre," neither does the " Prelude " have to be played at the rate of 100 notes per second, as your correspondent seems to suggest ; but of course he has his own tempo for these pieces!

Now we come to the advice to proprietors: " Get the best *man* you can, pay *him* well, and all *his* friends will back up your show by attending and *paying* frequently! Dear me! And how about the pictures ? They don't count, I suppose! Why should PIANIST think only *men* can play to pictures? I have been a picture pianist for six years, and have seen a few so-called trained men, and I know a few ladies who could hold their own any time with PIANIST, or any other " mere man." These ladies can earn 30s. to £3 10s weekly, and play to a 1,000 ft. Wild West picture at sight.

The music for pictures should be an accompaniment, sufficiently interesting to show patrons what the film is about, but not predominant. No one goes to hear pianoforte recitals at picture theatres. People cannot enjoy the pictures if the music is overpowering and from what I can

see, PIANIST is the only person of importance in his show, although he does acknowledge the operator!

Having played here for nearly two years, the audience being one of the most critical in London, I think I must have given satisfaction, even though a mere " woman."—Yours, etc.,

MADGE CLEMENTS.

Kilburn Palace,
  Belsize Road, N.W.,
    November 20, 1911.

To the Editor of THE BIOSCOPE.

SIR,—I was much interested in the article headed " Music in the Picture Theatres," in your paper of the 9th inst. I am only seventeen, but have been brought up in the picture business and, like PIANIST, of Southsea, played the piano at the age of five.

I can extemporise, but am not sure if it is " Heaven sent," " have an excellent memory," am " gifted with imagination and romance " (I hope, as I'm a girl), " my memory enables me to play such pieces as ' The Prelude to Robert le Diable,'. standard overtures, and other classics," and, as a contrast, " The Monkey's Serenade." I have no " preliminary view of the pictures," and we change every night. Our operator is upstairs in a sound-proof box, therefore I must keep time to him in dances and marches. I believe the majority of the audience does appreciate really good music, as I, too, have noticed, when playing " Tannhauser " or the like to a classical drama, " the rapt hush! which comes over the hall." I also have had requests for Mendelssohn's " Spring Song," and played it, but am sorry to say the uninitiated often mistake it for a popular comic song!

I do not happen to be of the town I am playing in, so my friends cannot " back up the show " for the benefit of my proprietor; and I do not visit other picture shows, " and on leaving make caustic comments " on the abilities of a person I should feel I am manœuvring, and eventually succeed in supplanting.

This letter is not from the " Lady of the Feeble ' Faust,' " and it is intended merely to intimate that PIANIST, of Southsea, is not the " only pebble on the beach."—Yours, etc.,

PIANISTE.

Portsmouth,
  November 14, 1911.

THE MUSIC OF THE PICTURE THEATRE.

BY "SOUFFLEUR."

From some recent utterances of pianists in the columns of THE BIOSCOPE, it would appear that the audiences of picture theatres appreciate good music, and in particular that good music that those particular pianists play. The question of the music of the picture theatre is one that, though considerable, is growing to be one of more importance every day.

The orchestra of the regular theatre is employed to while away the *entr'actes* of the farce or comedy. It occasionally plays the *melos* in a melodrama, and during the intervals of a musical comedy it takes a much-needed rest—appreciated by the instrumentalists and frequently by the audience.

The orchestra (or its substitute) in the picture theatre was instituted, I take it, in the first instance, to liven things up a bit, when the silent picture was found to need something in the way of support. It was not necessary for a genius to be born to make the discovery that music could be found that was more or less appropriate to the picture.

That the ideal picture-pianist is born and not made is only a half truth. The ideal picture-pianist should be born, and then reconstructed, and when completed he would be so valuable that no proprietor could possibly pay his salary and leave any profit for himself. Gilbert's recipe for a heavy dragoon applies—with variations.

This picture-pianist of the future would be, as some profess to be, heaven-born (out of the head of the mighty Jove himself); he would be able to improvise, read anything and everything from sight, would possess a wide and far-reaching memory and a sense of humour, and a rapid grasp of the situation. Very few ordinary pianists can really improvise, for improvisation should be a capacity to compose at a moment's notice, to picture emotions and phases of action by musical sounds arranged in an orderly and scholarly manner. If a pianist cannot improvise satisfactorily he should possess a considerable *répertoire* of varied works, and it is unfair to expect a good result from such an artist unless he is allowed to see the pictures beforehand, or is provided with an adequate synopses of their plots or stories.

The music of the old melodramas would be well worth the study of the would-be pianist. The "slow music," the "hurry," etc., are just what is required for pictures. Such collections of themes assist the picture without interrupting the action by attracting too much attention to the music. This is what so many people fail to realise: that the music, whatever it may be produced by—piano, organ, orchestra, jew's harp, or dulcimer—should never be so conspicuous as to take away from the interest of the picture.

The method should be that of the expert accompanist and the uneven singer. When an accompanist accompanies well it is not because he is a good executant, but it is because he knows the weak points of the singer besides knowing the strong ones. He assists the former and emphasises the latter. He effaces himself, so that the singer may be in the centre of the stage.

It is difficult to set a hard and fast rule as to what instrument or instruments are best suited to a picture theatre. The piano is the most common, and is, therefore, the most convenient, but an adroit player of the American organ can produce sounds and effects of which a piano is incapable. It has been known for one individual to play the two instruments at the same time with astonishingly successful results. At some of the large theatres "converted" to pictures, a full orchestra of twelve to fourteen instrumentalists may be heard; but they, as a rule, make no attempt, and wisely so, to play *to* the picture except travel subjects. But, on the other hand, there do exist one or two small orchestral combinations of four or five instruments who take the matter so seriously that they do, in effect, *illustrate* the picture, and, moreover, they manage to convey the impression that the complete assembly of instruments are improvising simultaneously. Such an ensemble cannot be organised in a moment. It is a question of time and whole-hearted devotion to his work on the part of the musical director. There is a vast difference between musical "allusion" and musical "illustration" which will be at once apparent when the point is duly considered.

To obtain something like an adequate illustration to a picture, it should first of all be seen—or, as I have said before, a detailed synopsis of the story should be obtained. While it is being run through careful notes should be made of the various emotions displayed by the actors, and the changes in the scenes. Then selection should be made from the library or repertory of those numbers or portions of numbers or movements or themes that are considered to illustrate such phases and emotions. Adroitly dovetailed, "coda-ed," and there you are! your picture is illustrated! But pause before you conclude that one solitary "piece," prelude, nocturne, chanson, rhapsodie, or opus is suitable or illustrative in or by itself to one particular picture play. The intention may be honourable, but the strenuous moments of picture and music may not coincide, and then possibly the *morceau* is shorter than the duration of the picture, and then what happens? Is it proposed to play the same thing all over again? It is done sometimes in some halls of repute, but I need not say that the result is the reverse of artistic.

HOW MOVING PICTURES HELP ACTRESSES.

Woman's chances of making a living have been increased by the rise of the biograph machines. Many a young actress anxiously awaiting an engagement will agree to this. Every year there has been an increased demand for women to pose, and indications are that the demand will go on increasing.

"I need these in my business," explained a young woman who was surprised in her bed-room by a visit from a friend. She was working on what looked like a very full pair of bloomers made of coarse, inexpensive grey flannel, with blouse to match.

"When do you expect to need anything so ugly?" asked the other in surprise.

"Next Monday morning, when I shall jump into the water, strike out for a rowing-boat, clamber in, and row off."

"Mercy!" gasped the listener. "What sort of a play are you booked for now? I thought you were not expecting an engagement for two months to come."

Then the other confessed. She was posing for moving pictures, and her ability to swim and manage a rowing-boat had got her the job. These talents had not so far been of any particular use to her in her stage career, but, supplemented with her stage experience, they made her eligible for a moving-picture model at a time when a pound or two looked like a fortune to her. In doing her feat, she explained, after she and the photographer and his assistants had journeyed to an isolated suburban spot, the young woman would wear the grey flannel suit—the full bloomers easily passing for a skirt, especially when water-soaked. In scene number two of the same series she beaches her boat, supposedly ½ mile away, although in reality she only goes a few yards down the shore, jumps out, and runs away. In fact at this juncture she does make a beeline to a house near by, where dry wearing apparel awaits her. The succeeding scenes of the same series may not be made until the next day, and in quite a different part of the country, the length of time required depending a good deal on the cleverness of the posers. This is another way of saying that the average amateur, no matter how accomplished she thinks she is in aquatic exercises, or how much at home she may be in a boat, is not likely to be favorably regarded by managers for the *rôle* of a moving-picture model.

"We haven't time to coach the inexperienced," explained the head of one moving-picture concern. "Moving pictures are pantomime, and to give good pantomime requires clever actors."

As a matter of fact so tremendously varied is the present output of moving pictures that every possible variety of talent can be and is used in their manufacture. Women who have never had a chance to do more behind the footlights than move about gracefully, and actresses who earn £20 a week when lucky enough to get an engagement, are alike registered at the office of the several concerns which make and keep the pictures moving, as well as women who have learned the business of the stage without getting a chance to put it all in practice.

All these, and in the aggregate there are several hundreds of them, jot down by advice of managers in the line under their name any speciality they imagine they have, whether it is falling downstairs, fainting, giving a knock-out blow, weeping real tears, running, swimming, playing ball, firing a gun, climbing ladders, or jumping out of a window.

There is an adage that no woman can be taught how to run or to throw anything straight; therefore the woman who registers as a good runner or ball-player usually finds herself as much in demand as the woman who records that her speciality is Shakespearian *rôles*. What is more to the point, her pay will be equally good. A sovereign a day is the usual remuneration received by a moving picture model, and often it takes many days to complete a series of pictures, particularly if the scenes are made out of doors and photographers and models must travel to some distant spot.

Women engaged by a biograph manufacturer need give no attention to wardrobe or properties of any sort. Every company sets up a property room which includes a collection of wearing apparel, draperies, sporting goods, musical instruments, and other things which would make any second-hand dealer the world over turn green with envy.

Tram and railway fares, carriage and motor-car hire are all paid by the manager. Thus the sovereign handed to each actress is subject to no deductions for expenses, and none is asked to wait for her pay until the end of the week or until the series of pictures is finished.

"Do you really succeed in getting actresses who have played leads in Shakespearian *rôles* to pose for moving pictures?" a manager was asked.

"Certainly we do. They are not to be had every day, of course, but at the off seasons, when there is nothing doing in their line and no revenue is in sight, women who when playing an engagement draw their little £20 or £30 a week are perfectly willing to register with us. And at any time when we are short of a certain style of woman to pose for dramatic pictures of a high class, all we have to do is to advertise the fact, and we have more applicants than can be taken care of.

"We have no graded scale of pay, and the woman with a beautiful face gets no more than the plainer woman. Action, not looks, is what recommends a woman for employment with us, and the more experienced the applicant the better chance she has. *Ingenues* are not popular with biograph managers, and novices with no stage experience have no show at all."—*Bristol Times.*

PHANTOM PLAYERS

Cinema Actors and Actresses whose faces are familiar to an enormous public which they never see.

MISS DAPHNE WAYNE.

Miss Daphne Wayne, of the American Biograph Co., was an actress on the legitimate stage, but during the last year she has become one of the most popular "Phantom Players."

She took the leading part in "The Battle," a cinema drama which has created immense excitement on account of the terrific storm it depicts. It has proved a great success in all parts of the world, including China, Russia, and Persia.

MISS CHRISSIE WHITE.

Miss Chrissie White has been in one of the Hepworth stock companies since she was eleven years old. Though she is now only seventeen, she has already scored many conspicuous successes.

Of the stage proper she has had little or no experience, for she feels that in picture work her talent has a chance for freer development.

JUDSON MELFORD.

>>>→

Judson Melford is the son of George Melford, producer to the Kalem Co.

Though only ten years old, little Judson is already a great favourite with Picture Palace audiences.

He rides splendidly, and has played in many Western films both in drama and comedy.

J. P. McGOWAN.

←‹‹‹

Mr. McGowan is another of the Kalem Co.'s most popular actors; and though up to two years ago he had never attempted dramatic work, he is now earning £30 a week.

He has played the leading part in many of their most successful films.

Born in Australia, he became a Boundary Rider, and afterwards volunteered for service in South Africa and went through the Boer War.

MISS GLADYS SYLVANI.

Miss Gladys Sylvani, of the Hepworth Company, can justly claim a place in the very front rank of English picture artistes. She has had a wealth of experience upon the theatrical stage, both in musical comedy and serious drama, and it is only within the last year or two that she decided to abandon the footlights for the camera.

MISS ALICE JOYCE.

←‹‹‹

Miss Joyce, of the Kalem Co., is well known to English audiences as a "cow-girl," and has appeared in all the most popular Western films.

She was an artist's model before she took up Cinema work, but finds the latter far more interesting and remunerative—she now earns £30 a week all the year round.

MISTINGUETTE.

›››→

Mistinguette is the idol of Paris.

Both on the stage proper and on the screen she is well known, and her appearance invariably calls forth the utmost enthusiasm.

She has proved invaluable to Messrs. Pathé Frères, both as an actress and producer—for she has arranged many of the dramas in which she has appeared.

Photo.   Boullinger.

MISS FLORENCE LAWRENCE.

Miss Lawrence, of the Lubin Co., draws a larger salary than any other cinema actress. Born at St. Louis, Missouri, she went on the stage as a child, and when the bioscope craze began was selected on account of her pantomimic powers. She has been tremendously successful in this work, and is now very popular indeed.

"LIEUTENANT DARING, R.N."

>>>→

When "Lieutenant Daring" joined the British and Colonial Company, he had already had considerable experience as an actor.

To the Cinema world he has become famous as the intrepid hero by whose name he is always known.

In private life he is Percy Moran, an Irishman.

MISS GENE GAUNTIER.

←<<

Miss Gauntier is not only one of the cleverest actresses in the Kalem Co., she writes and produces plays as well!

Born in Kansas City, she took to the stage as a child, and was one of the first actresses who attempted moving picture work.

She now draws a salary of £40 a week for fifty-two weeks in the year.

At present Miss Gauntier is in the Holy Land, taking Bible stories—the first time a Film Company has played there.

ARTHUR V. JOHNSON.

←‹‹‹

Mr. Johnson, of the Lubin Co., is the "Lewis Waller" of the Picture Palaces. Every night some 1500 audiences follow his adventures with breathless interest, for his *forte* is strong dramatic work.

Mr. Johnson was the first actor to forsake the stage proper for the Cinema, and his success has been unqualified.

"GLADYS."

›››→

Not everyone can boast of earning £10 a week at nine years old, but The American Biograph Company is only too glad to pay that amount to "Gladys" for her services.

This clever little girl is best in heavy drama; one of the most popular films for which she played a leading part being entitled "What Drink Did."

THE ONE-EYED MACHINE

By Margaret Chute.

Every day nearly a million people in this country watch "moving pictures" and marvel at the ingenuity and skill which have made such things possible. The following article gives an extraordinarily interesting peep behind the scenes of the Cinema theatre.

In 1895 there was not a single Cinema theatre in the world. To-day there are 50,000 scattered over various continents, of which England can claim 4,000 for her own, or one for every 10,000 people.

And the manufacture of cinematograph films is providing an income for thousands of actors and actresses, operators and mechanics, managers, and shareholders, in addition to giving education and amusement to millions daily.

Picture films are divided into two great branches—Topical and Dramatic. The cry for "topical" films never ceases. Something is always happening; and at a wreck, coronation, smart wedding, earthquake, or football match, the alert figure of the operator perched on a pair of steps has become a recognised part of the scene. Intrepid operators carry their machines far and wide; and in the security of a Cinema house, the man in the street watches a programme that represents an outlay of thousands of pounds, and risk to life and limb of daring Cinema men.

Our great actors have bowed to the supremacy of the film fiend; and Sir Herbert Tree, Mr. H. B. Irving, and Mr. F. R. Benson have already made successful records, which are now being shown from Australia to Cape Horn. Before the English stage awoke, French actors realised the power of the cinematograph, and excellent films have been made by leading players of the Vaudeville, Comédie Française, and other theatres. The latest convert is Madame Réjane, who has consented to hand a complete record of her marvellous Madame Sans-Gêne down to posterity, *via* the cinematograph. M. Le Bargy is also playing for film reproduction; and by the time these lines appear Sarah Bernhardt herself may have bowed to the inevitable !

The production of topical films is, of course, expensive, involving journeys of thousands of miles, with the chance of failure at the end. The "one-eyed machine" is greatly dependent on the weather; and many a topical film is ruined through fog and rain. In connection with the *Pathé Gazette*, the great firm of Pathé Frères have operators all over the world watching their interests. They had no fewer than four picked men at the Durbar; and when that unique ceremony was over a rush across ocean and continent began among an army of Cinema men to be first in the London field with their spoils.

There is a good story about an operator working for a well-known firm, in connection with King George's first public appearance after his accession. The King opened a new wing of a hospital, and every film firm and illustrated paper had operators on the scene. It was a rainy day, and at such times an operator, while waiting, always stuffs a handkerchief into the front of his machine, to prevent the lens getting spotted and spoiling the film. The man in question waited patiently with the others, casting a cute eye around in order to discover a better position than the one he occupied, his firm having offered £5 for the best film forthcoming.

Just as the Royal party arrived, he spied a large flower bed a few feet from the path along which the King would come. Seizing his camera, he fled, and planted himself and the machine in the centre of the flowers. Several officials, bursting with wrath, shouted at him, but it was too late for anything to be done, as the Royal party was in sight.

Chuckling, the operator began "turning," and to his unbounded joy the King noticed him in his isolated position, and graciously turned facing his machine, bowing and smiling. The operator realised that he had scored a veritable triumph, tore back to the office, announced that he had made the scoop of his life, and proceeded to develop the

film. This done, he discovered that a blank strip of celluloid was his only possession, as he had forgotten to remove the handkerchief from the eye of the machine. Such are the tragedies of the film trade !

A most striking example of bravery in the face of huge risks, was displayed by the operator who accompanied Captain Scott's South Pole expedition. This man faced death in a hundred ways to secure a lasting representation of the dash to the Pole. His most daring exploit was securing pictures of the prow of the *Terra Nova* cutting its way, inch by inch, through the ice.

This was impossible from the deck; but, determined not to be outdone, the operator had a small, fragile platform constructed, which was slung over the side of the vessel, as near the prow as was practicable. He was lowered, with his precious machine, by ropes; and there he remained, swaying against the ship, for three hours, "turning" whenever he could, and securing a film that is absolutely without equal in history.

The whole time he remained on that tiny platform he was in perpetual danger of being crushed by the moving ice, or swept overboard into the freezing water below when a particularly large piece of ice was dislodged. Such feats of bravery are being performed the world over by cinematograph operators; and it is to their daring that half the success of the Cinema may be ascribed.

The dramatic side of cinematograph work is as important as the topical. It embraces scenes and incidents that would appal ordinary stage producers; but nothing baffles the one-eyed machine. £1,000 has been spent before now on producing a picture play that lasts for twenty minutes ! To acquire the dramatic story of "Rory O'Moore" for the Cinema, ten actors and actresses were sent from New York to Ireland. Their passages were paid each way; they stayed at an Irish hotel for a fortnight, and were paid full salary all the time. Of course, the "letting" value of good films is great, and ultimately repays the big outlay; but it sometimes happens that films costing a small fortune are never used.

Breakages run into a good deal of money, many things being specially manufactured for destruction in photographing a play. For instance, a series of "drama stories" came to an incident in which a torpedo-boat had to be blown to smithereens. Determined that the explosion should be no canvas and plaster affair, the firm set out to buy a *real* torpedo-boat ! They ended by purchasing

A film that is absolutely without equal was secured by the operator who accompanied Captain Scott's South Pole expedition. He had a small platform constructed, which was slung over the side of the vessel; and there he remained for hours, "turning," though in constant danger of being crushed by the moving ice.

an obsolete boat suiting their purpose admirably, from the Government, and paid £500 for it. They risked all that money on the chance that *one* explosion would result in a good film ; for, naturally, no rehearsal was possible !

The fatal deed occurred in mid-Channel, and was recorded by eight or ten cameras in case of accidents, The operators encircled the doomed vessel, at a safe distance, needless to say; and the explosion was completely successful.

Many times motor-cars have been driven over parapets, or into rivers, on purpose, the machines being completely wrecked. Old railway carriages are often purchased solely for destruction, for the edification of the one-eyed machine. When a film picture of a mining disaster was taken, a colliery company in the north, being approached in the matter, kindly handed over their mine and workings to the Cinema people for a substantial cheque.

Costumes are always an expensive item, though actors in modern comedy or drama generally provide their own. But for any character play the firm hires costumes, and when 2,500 people are engaged, as in the case of the " Siege of Calais," done by Pathé Freres, the hiring of the costumes is no small consideration.

Choice of locality in exterior subjects is often difficult and expensive. A little while ago a large company was whisked off to Westward Ho! in order to act a fishing village drama in suitable surroundings. They stayed a fortnight, waiting for a particular sunset that was desirable, and got it in the end.

In the play a death struggle was arranged to take place at sea between the hero and the villain. On the day appointed, with the sea comparatively calm, the actors and operators embarked, sailed out some distance, anchored, and waited for a favourable moment. Alas ! it was long in coming; and the actors, who had found the motion while sailing not particularly to their liking, discovered that to be anchored was torture. They grew greener and greener, until, with a groan, the fierce and daring villain curled up, helpless, in the bottom of the boat.

An effect of a man hanging from a rope, suspended from a balloon, cutting it, and dropping into the sea, was cleverly obtained by means of a plank extended from the end of a pier, with a rope attached. Down this the actor climbed, knife in hand, the operator focussing his machine so that only the man and the rope were visible. At the crucial moment the man cut the rope, and dropped several feet into the sea. The effect gained, by stopping and refocussing the machine, was that he had fallen a long way ; and he was next shown struggling landwards. All went well until he had nearly reached the beach, which he should have done all alone. To the operator's horror, as the man neared the shore, a crowd of excited people were seen rushing with boats and ropes to the rescue. They had been officiously roused by a well-meaning pedestrian, who was convinced that the struggles to seaward were those of a drowning man !

One of the most remarkable and interesting films yet taken is the Barker Motion Photography Co.'s record of Sir Herbert Tree's production of Henry VIII. This marked the first appearance on the screen of a leading English actor ; and guaranteed the handing down to posterity of one of the finest theatrical productions of our time.

At first Sir Herbert was dubious, but persuasion won the day. Mr. Barker paid him £1,000 for the privilege of making the film, and on the day he handed Sir Herbert a cheque for that amount he was able to dispose of the Australian rights for exactly the same sum. So before a single picture had been taken £2,000 had changed hands and the firm's speculation had not meant the loss of a penny.

Two unsuccessful trials were made to take the pictures, the entire company turning up at 9.30 in the morning, in full costume, only to find that thick fog prevented any "turning. Special scenery reproducing the stage effects in black and white (and in miniature) had to be made, and carried, with hundreds of costumes, out to Ealing and back to His Majesty's before the evening. The third try was a brilliant success and resulted in the wonderful film which was shown throughout England for six weeks last year.

At the end of that time, according to a previous agreement, the twenty-four sets of film in circulation were " called in," and burnt on Mr. Barker's huge field at Ealing.

On a double sheet of corrugated iron, about six feet square, and placed in the centre of a ten-acre field, the films were unrolled. There were twenty-four of them, each containing something like five miles of coloured celluloid. At a fair distance five or six operators stood behind their machines, ready to take a record of the unique event. Two men remained by the glistening mound,

matches in hand; and striking them, applied them to the films at the same instant.

One match went out. There was a breathless pause: then, with a roar like cannon exploding, the heap caught fire. Suddenly the wind caught the flaming mass and blew it across the grass. The watchers ran for their lives; but the operators, ready for any emergency, caught up their machines and ran *backwards*, "turning" ceaselessly even in that moment of danger.

On lifting the iron sheets, the grass below was found burnt to a cinder, literally frizzled to death through two thicknesses of iron.

Studio acting is quite as interesting as any that takes place out of doors. In Paris, Pathé Frères have a large studio for

The burning of the films recording Sir Herbert Tree's production of *Henry VIII*. took place in a large field. Suddenly the wind caught the flaming mass and blew it across the grass. The crowd fled, but the Cinema men who were there to record the unique event, caught up their machines and ran *backwards*, "turning" ceaselessly even in that moment of danger.

indoor work; and in London their operating theatre in Great Portland Street is one of the best of its kind, fitted with a marvellous light instalment. This firm believes in doing all exterior pictures *out of doors*, and not by means of scenery; but many clever dramas are acted in their studios.

The first step is the choice of subject. When this is made, the setting of the different scenes, exterior and interior, is arranged. Scenery is procured, and special arrangements made regarding open-air sets.

An exhaustive synopsis of each "scene" is then prepared, and when the actors assemble the story of each scene is read to them in detail. This tells them exactly what

they are to do, to think, and to *say*. For actors always *speak* when playing to the one-eyed machine, although not a word of their parts is heard by their subsequent audiences. If they did not, the effect would be unreal.

When the "producer" thinks that a scene is thoroughly understood by the players, he tells them to start acting it. Sitting where the camera will stand, he watches them, correcting here and improving there. When the scene is arranged as he wishes, it is rehearsed straight through five or six times, till it seems that it can be played to the camera without a mistake.

Being satisfied, the producer says, "Now turn!" and the scene is played through again, with two cameras, having practically the same focus, recording it at once. It is then repeated with the machine still working; two complete records of every scene being made by each camera. This means that the final choice of film can be made from two reproductions, the cameras working for England and the "World's Edition" respectively.

It often happens that the first "turning" is the best, or parts of the second may fit into the first of other scenes. One complete edition of each film is developed in London, being the British edition, while the other—the "World's Edition"—is sent to Paris.

THE WONDERS OF KINEMACOLOR.

Colour cinematography has made great strides recently, but at present the Kinemacolor process of the Natural Colour Kinematograph Co. is practically unrivalled. The wonderful part of this invention is that any scene is shown in the natural colours, and yet only two colours, red and green, are used.

The cover design of this number gives a good idea of the Kinemacolor system. This is the way the film is prepared:

The pictures are taken at the rate of forty a second instead of the usual sixteen, on a specially prepared film sensitive to colours. The first exposure is made through a red screen, and the second through a green screen, and so on, alternately, to the end of the film.

When the film is shown, the pictures are projected through red and green screens in the same order as they were taken. The result is an effect to the eye of natural colours, though only two are used, and it is remarkable that blue, yellow, and every colour are seen by the audience.

The cover design

shows first the green picture, taken and shown through a green screen, and second the red picture, taken and shown **through a** red screen. The third section is the picture in natural colours, as it appears to the spectator. The cover is printed in two colours, and does not give so true an effect as Kinemacolor, which shows every shade as it appeared in the actual scene.

It is impossible to explain the Kinemacolor process more fully than this in an article, as a whole volume might be written about it.

Acting for the cinematograph is a new profession for men and women, and offer increasing openings. Many legitimate actors and actresses have taken it up; but it often happens that stage actors make bad studio actors, for fine delivery or subtle expression counts but little to the one-eyed machine. A capacity for "make-up" and "character" work is more useful, and breadth of style is imperative.

Well-known Cinema players, whose voices have never been heard by the millions to whom they act daily, owe their fortunes to their faces. Miss Florence Lawrence, the brilliant leading lady of the Lubin Company, is credited with an income of £2,000 a year drawn from Cinema work. Mr. McGowan, once a boundary rider in Australia, now draws £30 a week from an American film company, scoring through his expert horsemanship. A little boy of seven, Herbert Smith, is a perfect hero to audiences in Cinema theatres, and is paid £10 a week for his services.

Many cinematograph tragedies have been turned into real ones through accidents. A man was killed in France a short time ago on the

A scene in the Ealing studio of the Barker Motion Photography Co., during the acting of a film play, showing the stage-manager, actors, scene-shifters, and the Cinema man with his camera.

railway, while acting in a mimic train wreck. Last December a party of Swedish players hired a steamer, to produce a fictitious shipwreck, including stranding of the vessel and rescue after great dangers. While cruising about, to enable pictures of ordinary life at sea to be taken, a terrific storm arose as if in mockery, and for ten hours the steamer drifted at the mercy of wind and waves. She was on the point of foundering in reality when help arrived, and the players were rescued in the nick of time, the steamer sinking fifteen minutes after they left her.

In the United States, the educational facilities afforded by the cinematograph have been made the most of. A popular American film is called "Boil your water," and depicts the germs in a glass of water, much magnified. Another illustrates the life of the house-fly, showing him proceeding direct from the dust-bin to the dinner-table, carrying infection with him. The New York Milk Committee also prepared a film illustrating the dangers of insanitary cow-sheds. And, last but not least, an American battleship has been provided with a cinematograph outfit.

TRICK FILMS.

The preparation of trick films is a very wonderful part of bioscope work. Extraordinary and impossible effects are obtained solely through clever "faking." One of the best firms for trick films is the Hepworth Company, which has also turned out some of the finest all-British drama films on the market. Mr. Hepworth has produced some remarkable "ghost" films, and the explanation of the "ghost" is rather interesting.

The only dogs in England which have been trained to act in Cinema dramas belong to the Hepworth Company. They will "worry" a victim in the most realistic manner, without really hurting him in the least. This scene is taken from a film called "The Lost Will."

A double exposure of the same negative takes place in this work, the background being first taken, together with any figures —apart from the ghost—who appear in the scene; but these figures must be perfectly still or the effect is lost. Then the *same piece of film* is passed through the camera again, this time with the "ghost" acting his part. The result is a film in which the background has had a *full* exposure, and the ghost only a partial exposure, with the effect that the background is seen *through* the ghost's figure.

One of the best Hepworth trick films is called the Perils of Invisibility, and demonstrates the fatal result of drinking a potion which makes a man's body invisible, but not his clothes. The clothes appear on the film without the man—and proceed to take themselves off till only the shoes are left, and the presence of these shoes throughout the story is the sole indication of the "invisible" man's presence.

The trick is done in this way: the man appears as himself up to a certain point, acting in a scene which has a partly black background—a passage, for instance. The film is stopped, and the man's head, neck, arms, and hands swathed in black tights; he stands against the black background, and when the film begins again his clothes appear to be standing up without anybody to support them, and the undressing process seems miraculous.

During the remainder of the film the shoes are manipulated by means of wires from behind or above. This film needed, of course, very careful rehearsal.

A POCKET PICTURE-PALACE.

CLOSE upon the heels of the Cinematograph follows the Biofix, which bids fair to revolutionise modern portrait photography, for the advantages of the new invention are legion.

In the old days one entered the studio in a state of nervous panic, had one's head screwed into an iron vice, spent a breathless time trying to "keep still and look pleasant," and eventually received a photograph which—well, suffice it to say it was the one expression we did not wish to perpetuate.

He who would be Biofixed has a very different experience.

"Don't try to pose," says the cheery young man at the wheel, "just be natural."

In a moment the victim finds himself laughing and talking —and lo! in less than a quarter of an hour he is transfixed within the pages of a neat little book. He has only to apply his thumb to this, and the pictures leap into life, showing him smiling and waving—or he can purchase a little round machine and make himself "live" by the mere turning of a handle.

Of course, the Biofix is the ideal form of photography for children —think of the joy given in after life by so fascinating a record of Baby's first step, and his pretty childish ways.

Similar memories of family pets—dogs or cats or other animals — are equally delightful.

From a scientific point of view the possibilities of the Biofix are endless. Already it has led to the arrest of criminals in connection with a large jewel robbery, for, though an ordinary photograph may not even resemble the sitter, the Biofix cannot lie.

Every little characteristic, every possible expression is faithfully reproduced, and the result is literally a living likeness.

And the cost of it all is nominal. For as little as a shilling one can purchase a small book of oneself, the price increasing according to the length of film required.

The joy of being Biofixed will not long be within the reach only of dwellers in or near London. Branches are being opened everywhere; moreover, the inventor is now busy preparing a special camera with the aid of which the amateur will be able to Biofix his friends.

It is not likely to become a very cheap hobby as yet, but it has the merit of being not in the least tedious. The professional Biofixer can print the photographs at the rate of a hundred a minute.

The pictures of Miss Phyllis Dare which adorn this number, give a good idea of a Biofix booklet.

How it is done—a scene in the Biofix studio. Note the victim's contented expression! On the table are two of the little machines for showing the booklets.

—

THE HANDBOOK OF KINEMATOGRAPHY

THE HISTORY, THEORY, AND PRACTICE OF MOTION PHOTOGRAPHY AND PRO- - - - JECTION. - - -

BY

COLIN N. BENNETT, F.C.S.,

AND COLLABORATORS.

1913.

Published by
THE KINEMATOGRAPH WEEKLY
Tottenham Street, LONDON, W.

THE HANDBOOK OF KINEMATOGRAPHY

COLIN N. BENNETT

PUBLISHERS' FOREWORD.

In 1905 *we converted* THE MAGIC LANTERN JOURNAL, *for thirteen years successfully conducted by Mr. J. Hay Taylor, into* THE OPTICAL LANTERN AND CINEMATOGRAPH JOURNAL. *For two years this monthly publication met the exigencies of the growing trade, and on May 16th, 1907, we launched a sixteen-page weekly entitled* THE KINEMATOGRAPH AND LANTERN WEEKLY. *This has grown until at the present time it has become a bulky periodical with a circulation of considerably over* 10,000 *weekly and nearly two hundred pages in each issue.*

Notwithstanding these enormous strides, which have developed in ratio to the wonderfully increasing popularity of Motion Pictures, there had not been produced a standard handbook containing information on every department of kinematography, that could be utilised by those desiring to enter the profession, or could be referred to with confidence by those anxious to perfect their knowledge in the science until we published the first edition of this work in 1911. *That the time was ripe for such a work is proved by the numerous technical, legal and varied questions which we have answered from time to time in our pages, and by the very many applications we have received for such a book—applications which quickly exhausted the first edition.*

The varied knowledge—photography, electricity, stage managership, legal and local necessities and what not—made the production no easy task. We arranged for Mr. Colin N. Bennett, F.C.S., an expert in photography and kinematography, and a well-known writer on scientific

3

matters, to collaborate with experts in the legal, business and other cognate branches of the subject, and to produce an exhaustive book worthy of what has now become a gigantic industry.

In this second edition much has been entirely re-written and revised, so that the book may be increasingly valuable as an up-to-date reference work and one which may be depended upon for helpful knowledge in every department of the science of kinematography.

Naturally, certain sections which are subsidiary to the actual practice of kinematography have had to be somewhat curtailed, but those worthy of more space than we can command have been issued as separate publications, such as "Playing to Pictures," and "How to Manage a Picture Show."

No book on kinematography can be called exhaustive— new ideas and inventions seem hourly to add improvements to the subject—but in this second edition will be found carefully compiled data and useful information, much of it the result of original investigation, while the bulk of the information comprised in Part I. is to be obtained from no other written source.

We anticipate that this edition, like the first, will soon become exhausted, so that another revised edition may become necessary. We shall be gratified if any reader discovers an error, either of commission or omission, in the present work, if he will acquaint us with particulars.

E. T. HERON & CO.

TOTTENHAM STREET, LONDON. W.

AN ACKNOWLEDGMENT.

———

First and foremost, my acknowledgments and thanks are due to MR. E. T. HERON, *the existence of this volume being a result of his initiative, created from a genuine and ceaseless endeavour to improve the conditions and prospects of the kinematograph industry.* Mr. *Heron has taken an untiring interest in the present* HANDBOOK OF KINEMATOGRAPHY *from its inception onwards, and the author is indebted to him for countless facts and helpful suggestions contained within its pages.* Acknowledgments are further *due, and are herewith tendered to* MR. HENRY MORRELL, *of His Majesty's Theatre, Haymarket, for the chapter contributed by him on " Acting before the Kinematograph," to the* KINEMATOGRAPH WEEKLY *for the important chapter on "The Law and the Kinematograph," to* MR. THEODORE BROWN *for the original drawings, and lastly, to the numerous firms in the trade, including* MESSRS. R. R. BEARD, R. AND J. BECK, LTD., F. J. BROCKLISS, W. BUTCHER AND SONS, LTD., EMIL BUSCH, J. H. DALLMEYER, LTD., THE GAUMONT CO., LTD., L. KAMM AND CO., KINETO, LTD., INFALLIBLE METER EXPOSURE CO., PATHE FRERES, VOIGTLANDER AND CO., THE WALTURDAW CO., LTD., WATKINS AND CO., WILLIAMSON KINEMATOGRAPH CO., LTD., WRENCH AND CO., CARL ZEISS, LTD., *etc.*

COLIN N. BENNETT.

AUTHOR'S HISTORICAL PREFACE.

—

The history of the kinematograph is long, complex, and infinitely stodgy. It is long because it reaches back from now till at least the year 65 B.C., at which date Lucretius, in his work " De Rerum Natura," made certain pertinent remarks relative to persistence of vision—the rock upon which the whole theory of motion photography is built. It is complex by reason of the way in which evolution of the kinematograph proper has in its latter days been crossed and re-crossed by inventions and patents partly, yet not fully, relevant to the moving photograph machine. It is stodgy as cheap plum duff is stodgy, with many an interesting spot here and there, but oceans of plainness between.

Let us leave the full history of the subject for those who like it. It would fill the whole of our book were we to let it do so. As a matter of fact it has filled the whole of a very excellent historical work—" Hopwood's Living Pictures," published 1899—and though the volume in question is long since hopelessly out-of-date from the practical point of view, its retrospect of kinematograph invention prior to 1897 is none the less sound and interesting to the man of antiquarian tendencies.

The endeavour of this preface is solely to set forth in condensed form a few of the most salient facts connected with the infancy and growth of motion pictures.

Let us begin with Ptolemy Lucretius has already had his turn. Ptolemy was a Greek philosopher who wrote a book, or rather a series of books, on optics, about the year A.D. 130. In one of these he not only took note of the fact of " persistence of vision," which is the scientific way of setting down the truth that the sensation of light coming from an object remains in the brain for the tenth to the twentieth part of a second after the object's actual disappearance, but Ptolemy also described a simple piece of apparatus in the form of a revolving disc with spots on it wherewith this phenomenon might be demonstrated. Like many other valuable principles, Ptolemy's was duly conserved and handed down from age to age and from sage to sage, never being entirely forgotten, never being made the slightest use of till the year 1825, which saw the birth of that modest yet amazing optical toy, the Thaumatrope.

What is the Thaumatrope? Perhaps the name is not familiar ; at any rate, the instrument is almost certain to be. It is neither more nor less than the well known oblong piece of card with a picture on either side and a piece of string run through it in such a way as to facilitate its being turned rapidly round and round on its axis. When this is done the two pictures are seen to unite by the agency of the same persistence of vision commented upon by Lucretius and first exampled by Ptolemy. The present price of the Thaumatrope ranges from a halfpenny downwards. Marvellous it is to read in Hopwood's book " Living Pictures, 1899," that in the year of its inception there was something in the nature of a controversy between two eminent scientists as to which of them was the true inventor. Dr. Paris claimed it and even went further and placed it on the market at the price of seven and sixpence, but there seems to be the strong probability that the Thaumatrope is really due to the brain of Dr. Fitton, his contemporary. Be that as it may, our halfpenny spinning card remains the solitary practical 'moving picture machine' from thence onward till the year 1832. Work upon the subject of optical synthesis was done in the meantime, notably by Doctors Roget and Faraday, but only in the latter year was the Thaumatrope finally supplanted in popular estimation.

The lucky rival came into the world under somewhat strange circumstances, being invented at one and the same time by two distinct and quite independent scientists, Stampfer and Plateau. Dr. Plateau called the contrivance by the name of 'Phenakistoscope,' and by this simple and expressive cognomen it has thenceforward been known to the world. Since the Phenakistoscope marks something like a recognisable step towards our goal, it is worthy of a short description. Briefly, it consisted of a circular card around which were painted a series of figures or other devices illustrating to the best of the artist's ability the several phases of a given movement. The card was arranged to rotate upon a central shaft, and was backed by a second larger card, also rotating upon the same centre and at the same rate as the one bearing upon it the painted figures. Around the area of the larger card were cut equidistant slits corresponding in number with the figures on the smaller disc. Such is the somewhat complicated description of the Phenakistoscope, but its manner of working is at least correspondingly simple. On revolving the contrivance in front of a mirror with the eye placed behind the slotted area of the larger disc, the reflected figures were seen as though in motion. Since the present sketch is purely historical, there will be no pause here to explain the why and wherefore of the optical illusion. Such will become clear in the course of the description of the modern kinematograph projector as found later on in the body of this book.

Once again after 1832 we have to record a lengthy interval without any very notable advance in the synthesis of the motion picture, an interval broken at last by the introduction of the Zoetrope, or Wheel of Life.

The Zoetrope belongs to the year 1860. It was in effect a cylindrical form of the Phenakistoscope with, however, this striking difference, that instead of a mirror image being viewed, the apparently animated figures themselves were watched through slits placed around the edge of the canister in which they revolved. And still, though by now the problem of obtaining the illusion of motion in a diagram or drawn device may be said to have been solved, it would be almost as difficult as ever to recognise in the solution a single point of resemblance to the action of a modern kinematograph.

This resemblance first became distinct in a little invention due to Mr. Beale—the Choreutoscope. But by now, history is moving apace. We have arrived at the year 1884. In the Choreutoscope we have, barring the flexible photographic film, practically every essential of the modern maltese cross machine, and this notwithstanding that the whole contrivance was designed to fit into the stage of an ordinary magic lantern. The Choreutoscope consisted of a wooden slide fitted with a ratchet arrangement in which ran a notched frame bearing a glass panel painted with designs representing the several phases—or supposed phases—of a simple movement. The turning of the ratchet handle imparted to the slide intermittent movement through the notches on its periphery, while each shift was covered during projection by the automatic rising and falling of a small drop shutter.

On placing the little instrument on the stage of the optical lantern and turning the handle, there was therefrom projected on the screen an effect somewhat similar to that previously obtained by direct vision of the original image in the Zoetrope or by the observation of the mirror image of a succession of movement phases cast by the Phenakistoscope. But still we are dealing with the creation of apparent animation in drawn or painted designs, whereas the essence of the kinematograph is that it goes to nature as revealed by means of photography for its movement analyses.

And now in order to understand the trend of events, it must be recorded that during the latter years, from the early seventies onwards, while one batch of inventors had been hard at work trying to perfect the synthesis of imaginary movement phases, such as might be culled from drawings or time-exposed photographs of models, another class of inventors had been engaged upon what must be looked upon as the totally different subject of true movement analysis. The earlier attempts in this latter direction were made through the means of photography upon glass plates, and the records of movement were obtained not as a series of single pictures but as a superposed jumble of black and white guide streaks, which might tell those in the know a great deal, but would certainly tell the average man in the street nothing whatever.

It was a great advance—something of a minor revolution in the nature of things—when in 1872 Muybridge, an American, rigged up a series of separate cameras so arranged that the shutters were released one by one upon the passage in front of them of a trotting horse. The result of the departure was a number of photographs of consecutive true movement phases which, when combined in the Phenakistoscope or Zoetrope, gave something approaching a complete rendering of actual motion. Thus was the first elementary success in motion photography attained. Very soon, however, the use of a series of cameras for general work was found to be impracticable for a number of reasons, and the Muybridge system accordingly came to be supplanted by the Marey system, wherein one lens only was made use of. The Marey Photographic Gun of 1876 is a case in point. It was shaped something after the style of a monster revolver and took twelve quickly successive images of a moving object, recording them upon a circular sensitive surface. Later, in 1888, appeared the first printed work upon the then newly discovered sheet celluloid as a vehicle for carrying photographic emulsions, and the year afterwards, 1889, saw the filing by Messrs. W. Friese Greene and M. Evans of the specification of their machine for taking and projecting moving photographs—the admitted father of all true kinematographs.

The Friese Greene kinematograph camera and projector utilised photographically coated strip celluloid just as do those of the present day. It was fitted with a shutter, also with an intermittent movement actuated by a spring cam, and the results obtained with it were both creditable and practical. From this point onwards, the principle of kinematography must be looked upon as solved.

The history of the subject now becomes more one of improvements than of new ideas. For this reason, as also for the sake of brevity, only two other machines will be touched upon in the present historical preface. One of them is the kinematograph of Donisthorpe and Crofts, patented August 1889, and worthy of special mention as being the earliest representative of the loopless camera.

The last camera of all to be mentioned here among the antiques is the 'Lumiere Cinematographe,' introduced in 1895. This was a pin or claw camera and projector. So accurate and reliable did its performance prove that very soon it found its way to a London music hall as a star attraction, and thereupon was inaugurated the living picture craze, a craze which seems as far from dying down as ever it did—perhaps farther, as instance the following, written by Mr. Cecil M. Hepworth in the year 1897:

"That the kinematograph has contributed much to the "gaiety of nations can hardly be denied, but that it will con-"tinue to do so to anything like the same extent for much "longer is most improbable."

The above is an excellent instance of the futility of prophecy in the kinematograph world. But of the 'Lumiere Cinematographe'? How has that particular machine fared in the melting pot of time? Well, how should it fare? It has gone, of course, like all its contemporaries.

But a few months since, the writer had occasion to invest in a kinematograph camera of the very latest type. It was an excellent and an expensive instrument, so new in design that the very patent

specification on which it was built was hardly emerged from the government printing press. *And on opening the front panel and looking
at the newly patented works, they were found to be in all essentials identical with those of the defunct Lumiere machine.*

Thus, briefly, we have the history of the kinematograph—a
history of development and improvement which has ultimately resulted in a scientific entertainment, the like of which has never been
enjoyed and witnessed by the people of the whole world, the possibilities of which we can barely imagine, which gives employment to
thousands and enjoyment to millions daily, and which amuses, edu-
cates, and brings into closer relationship the inhabitants of every
quarter of the globe.

[THE DANCER.

THE COCK FIGHT.

SOME OF THE FIRST SUBJECTS
EVER PHOTOGRAPHED FOR
LIVING PICTURES:

THE BLACKSMITH.

THE WHEELWRIGHT.

PART I

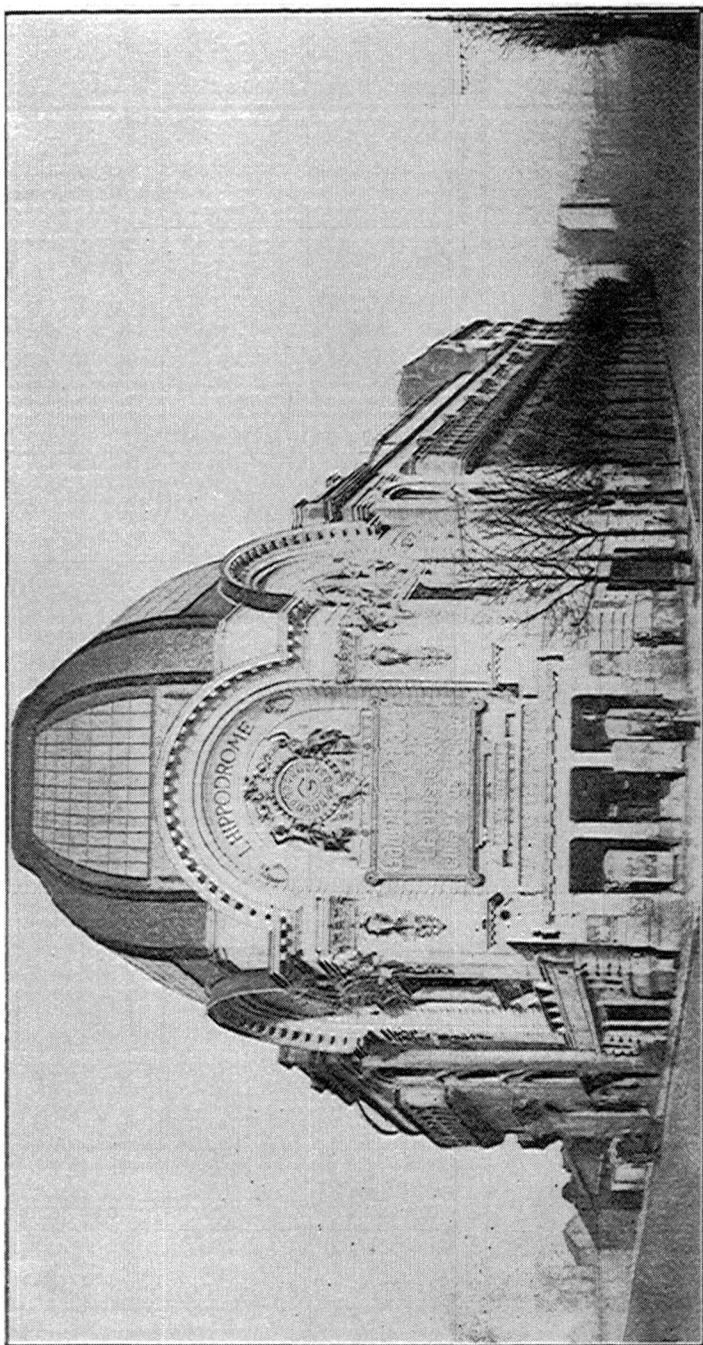

The Largest Cinema in Europe. A Unique Building in one of the busiest parts of Paris which is crowded daily with over 5,000 Picture Theatre Enthusiasts.

KINEMATOGRAPHY

CHAPTER I.

———

THE PHOTOGRAPHIC PRINCIPLE.

Kinematographic photography is best led up to by a brief survey of the principles of photographic picture making in general. Indeed, between it and ordinary snap-shot work there is but one small difference, that whereas the latter takes a single instantaneous photograph at a time and has done with it, the former takes a succession of them at such quick intervals, one after the other, that each second suffices for the making of roughly sixteen complete photographic records.

For the purpose of subsequent projection upon a screen by means of a moving picture projector, it has, moreover, been found necessary that the kinematograph camera should make its multiple records upon a long roll of emulsion-coated celluloid ribbon, while the hand camera makes its single one upon either a glass plate (the technical term for an oblong piece of photographically coated glass) or else upon a comparatively short length of wide celluloid sheet of a like shape. Thus we early arrive at the conclusion that the only vital difference between the moving picture recording machine and the ordinary snap-shot camera is in the quantity and speed with which the views are taken.

Let us then first turn to the consideration of the principle of cameras in general.

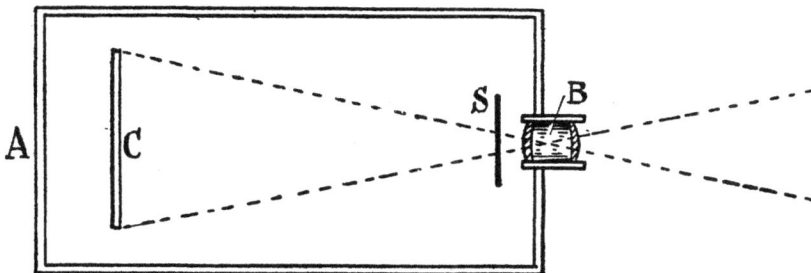

FIG. I.

Fig. I represents a diagrammatic view of the arrangement of an ordinary hand camera. A, A, A are the sides of the familiar box in which the photographic plate is enclosed. This box is made light

tight except for the hole occupied by the lens B, through the glass of
which light may be admitted upon the surface of the prepared plate
C, or may be shut off by the interposition of a shutter S at the will
of the photographer.   Normally, this shutter is in its light stopping
position as represented.   Only when the photograph is to be taken
is a spring set in motion by which the shutter is switched out of the
way of the lens for the small part of a second, during which time light
is consequently allowed to stream in through B upon the sensitive
surface at C.   Such is a brief sketch of the working of a hand camera.

Let us next turn to the consideration of the nature of the sensitive coating upon the plate C, the function of which is to become
affected, or as it is called ' exposed,' by the light action.   Briefly,
C is a piece of sheet glass which has been coated in the dark with gelatine containing in it the chemical known as silver bromide.   This
sensitive coating or ' emulsion ' has before exposure to daylight a
pale milky yellow appearance, and the same is not altered even by
exposing the plate to daylight for a minute or more at a time.   Even
a very short exposure has, however, the effect of bringing about in
the emulsion a sort of secret change, which, although not discernible
in itself, becomes evident enough on treating the plate with a special
chemical solution known as a ' developer.'   Suppose a photographic
plate to have been taken out of its light tight box in which it is supplied by the makers and to have been put into the camera in darkness
(or by a special red ' dark room light,' so called because a deep shade
of this colour is without the action about to be ascribed to daylight) ;
suppose the camera has been thus ' loaded,' and that it is now taken
out into the open and the shutter S allowed to flick for a moment out
of the way of the lens so that light may stream for a brief instant upon
the plate.   Now we will take the camera back to the same ' dark
room,' withdraw the ' exposed ' plate and place it in a dish filled with
' developer.'   What will happen ?

Very soon we shall notice a strange change come over the milky
whiteness of the ' emulsion.'   It will turn darker and darker in degree
as the lens has cast more or less light upon it.   If we go on long enough,
and supposing the exposure has been sufficient, we shall end by getting
the plate quite black in parts.

This blackness is caused by the developer having ' reduced'
the silver bromide to a deposit of finely divided metallic silver, which
remains held to the glass in its matrix of gelatine.

Suppose that our developed plate is in fact what it should be—
a satisfactory photographic negative, we shall also notice that the
blackness produced upon it by the developer is not of equal degree
all over its face.   Some parts may even still be of the old milky white
hue.   We now rinse off the developing solution and apply another one
known as the ' fixer.'   Here the remaining whiteness entirely leaves
the gelatine.   The negative is from this moment complete, except for
the need of a good washing under the tap to free it of chemicals.
Suppose we take it out into daylight, to which it has by this time

ceased to be in any way responsive, it will be found that where the milkiness remained to the last before fixing, there will be nothing left afterwards but colourless gelatine. Over other parts of the glass surface will be a cloud of varying opacity, consisting of the metallic silver deposited by development, and the finely divided state of which causes it to appear without any metallic lustre, and merely as a grey-black dull veil upon the plate.

But we shall notice something more also, provided the camera lens was in focus. It will be seen that the silver deposit has formed itself into a sort of replica in black and white of the scene toward which the lens was pointed at the moment when the shutter was released.' Why is that?

This brings us to the consideration of the one remaining important part of the single picture camera—the lens. The lens is the camera's eye and as such performs for it much the same function as our own eyes do in our heads. Long ago it was discovered that a piece of glass ground to a sphere, or portion of a sphere, would throw some sort of a reflection or 'image' of real objects before it. Doubtless the first of these images to be formed in practice was the sun's disc. The spot of light formed by the mischievous boy's burning glass is in reality nothing more or less than a well shaped 'focussed' image of the sun thrown upon a suitably combustible substance with the avowed intention of utilising the heat rays concentrated together with the light rays for the purpose of bringing about a conflagration. But though the sun is the easiest object to get a visible image of by means of a lens, since it is so bright that such can be seen and focussed in full daylight, yet all other objects throw images in precisely the same way if the light reflected from their surfaces is similarly 'brought to a focus.' Moreover, these images are made visible at once by the simple process of screening off extraneous light, which would otherwise obscure the comparatively dim evidence of their formation.

Hence we arrive at the general arrangement of the hand camera as shown in fig. 1.

The surface of the plate actually gets thrown upon it at the moment of exposure a real picture or 'image' of the actual objects in front of the camera. Since some of these outside objects are naturally darker than others, it will follow that subsequent development of the plate will bring about a silver deposit of variable density according to whether the amount of light action has been great or little at any particular point. So do we produce the 'negative,' or black and white record upon glass, of the object photographed, upon which record the whole basis of practical photography rests, and from which 'negative' the 'positive' or regular photograph is obtained by a process known as 'printing,' of which more in a later chapter.

That the image thrown by a lens upon the sensitive surface is in fact a real one is very easily proved by removing the back of the camera and substituting in place of the sensitive plate a piece of finely ground glass. If, then, the shutter be opened so as not to impede the light, a picture of all objects before the camera will be seen upon the ground glass in the form of a coloured and inverted image. The inversion of the picture is got over in practice by the extremely simple expedient of righting the negative when using. There is no simple way, however, of obtaining a record of the colours thrown by the lens. For present purposes, therefore, these must be neglected.

A brief semi-technical description of the action of a lens appears in the appendix to this part.

We have now mentioned the three fundamental parts of a still picture camera, namely, the sensitive plate, the light tight box surrounding it, and the lens. Let us hope that from the consideration of these, we have also grasped something at least of the underlying principle of photography as such. It remains for us to go a step further and examine the one additional contrivance by which what would otherwise be a still picture camera is turned into a moving picture recorder. This contrivance may take various forms, all of them intended to accomplish the same purpose—the moving onward, jerk by jerk, behind the lens, of a band of photographically coated celluloid so that this same coated band may play the part of a rapidly replaced succession of ' plates,' for the quick recording of negative after negative at the rate of approximately sixteen pictures per second.

The contrivance which imparts to the film band its above mentioned jerky movement, and which is possessed only by kinematograph cameras, thereby differentiating them from those of the single ' still picture ' variety, is known as the ' escapement,' or intermittent mechanism.

A PICTURE SHOW PROPRIETOR IN THE FAR EAST.

CHAPTER II.

THE KINEMATOGRAPH CAMERA.

Granted we have contained in our kinematograph camera a sufficient length of the ribbon-like film to be photographed upon, there are two main problems to be faced in the manner of applying the required intermittent motion to it. First, we must provide the motion with a satisfactory grip upon the film stock. Then there will be the matter of arranging the mechanism of the camera so as to pull down an amount of film corresponding with the height of one picture sixteen times a second for so long as it is in operation. The way of making film stock capable of being easily gripped is by 'perforating,' or punching small holes in its edges at intervals.

Unperforated film stock looks like a plain milky white coated length of celluloid ribbon, whereas when perforated, the apertures are plainly seen running along its edges as in fig. 2. Once these perforations have been made, it is easy

Perforated film stock

FIG. 2.

to see that the task of getting a grip upon the film for its intermittent movement is immensely simplified. Neither is it difficult for the mind to conceive that such is probably accomplished by a species of hooking action.

The form of hook actually employed in the intermittent movement or escapement of kinematograph cameras is called by the various names of 'pin' or 'claw.' They both really mean the same thing, except, perhaps, to the straw-splitting mind. The following diagram is intended at one and the same time to give the reader a fair idea of the internal arrangement of a motion picture camera and to explain simply the hook, pin, or claw action upon which in some form the mechanism almost always depends.

Fig. 3 shows an excellent and simple type of present day motion picture camera with the film threaded as it would be during use. This film will be seen to emerge through a light trap in the outer bottom corner of the upper film box. From thence it passes between an upper 'sprocket' (a 'sprocket' or sprocket wheel being a wheel cut with a double row of blunt spurs or teeth to fit into the film's perforations) and an 'idler,' B. The function of the idler is merely to keep the film fed against the top sprocket, which moves at

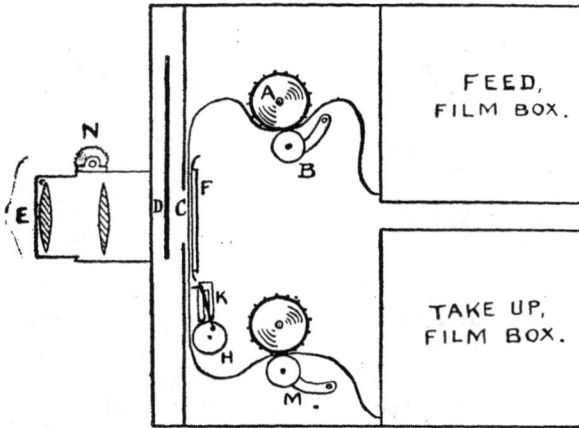

FIG. 3.

a constant rate on turning the camera handle (not shown in the diagram), and so causes the sensitive stock to move from the upper film box.

A moment's thought will show that if this were the only moving part in the camera, the result of it would be merely to wind the whole of the sensitive film out of the film box into the body of the instrument without accomplishing anything else. As a matter of fact, nothing of the sort happens. And that brings us to the consideration of the escapement itself.

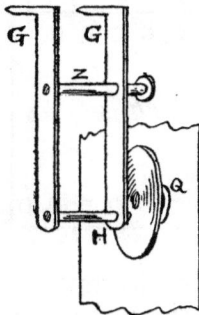

FIG. 4.

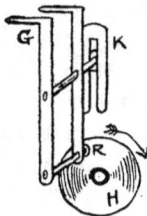

FIG. 5.

This will be found figured just below the gate runners F. G is a double bar made of finely tempered steel (see fig. 4). It is pivoted eccentrically upon the revolving skeleton drum H (fig. 3), also shown larger in fig. 4. This skeleton drum, is like the sprocket wheel, caused to turn at a uniform rate by operating the camera handle. But as it revolves, it will have the effect of turning the double hook arms G not round and round with it but more or less up and down in a track which is further governed and made definite by the cam K, shown in fig. 5. This cam has in it a groove of just the right size to accommodate the roller-encased bar Z (fig. 4).

But to go into this last more carefully: Look at fig. 5 once again and we will ask ourselves what is the effect of revolving the drum H in the direction of the arrow. It will be plain that such rotation would have the effect of pulling the pivot R of the arm G to the right and downwards. This would throw the hooks on the end of G toward the film stock, since the roller bar held in the cam is converting G into a lever. Imagine that the amount of sideways throw is just sufficient to cause the hooks to become firmly engaged with the nearest perforations before such motion is counterbalanced by the downward thrust brought about by the continued rotation of H. We now have the film firmly gripped by its perforations and in a state of being pulled rapidly downward. Such movement will be continued until the movement of R to the left again, as it nears the lowermost extent of its travel, causes G to swing to the right, leaving the film free. Once that phase has come about, the film's movement naturally stops dead and remains so for approximately one half a revolution of H, by which time the point R has come up again, and into position for the repetition of the whole cycle.

Here then we have practically realised the required intermittent motion required by the exigencies of kinematography. All that now remains to be done is to take up the slack film as it is passed through the gate C, behind the camera lens E, and shutter D. This taking up of slack is accomplished by the second sprocket and idler LM which are like the top ones geared to move continuously. The final winding up of the exposed film is accomplished by leading it through a light trap into the take-up box, where a spring attachment holds it to a revolving bobbin.

So much for the description of one of the typical modern camera escapements. It may fairly be said that once the above action has been grasped, the numerous variations of the claw or pin movement found in cameras of different makes should furnish no real difficulty to the mechanically minded photographer. But still, there are several points about the motion picture camera which have so far been undescribed, notably the camera shutter, the take-up mechanism, the arrangement of the gate, and the gearing whereby the necessary motion is imparted to the whole mechanism on turning the camera handle.

The ' gate ' of a motion picture camera consists fundamentally of two parts ; the picture mask proper and a spring plate so arranged as to press the film upon it, thus holding it firm and flat after each period of travel. Camera gates look different in various instruments. They may have their own ways of opening and closing when film has to be ' threaded.' Also the pressure springs and ' runners ' by which the film is kept tight against the mask may be differently arranged and have different modes of adjustment. But all gates are the same in principle and fulfil exactly the same purpose. They all need most careful attention by the camera man at frequent intervals, and all give speedy evidence of neglect by a host of imperfections arising in the negatives taken with their help. Chief among such defects are scratches and breakages, to say nothing of unsteady pictures, all of which follow as the necessary result of a dirty gate mask or runners, or of wrong adjustment of spring tension. In fact, without going too far, it may well be said that nine-tenths of the difficulties encountered by the camera man in connection with his apparatus will be mixed up with the gate. Camera gate springs, runners, and mask are best kept clean by rubbing with the end of a clean oblong piece of typewriting eraser, after which the cleaned parts should be carefully wiped with a very slightly oily rag.

Let us now to the shutter and its mechanism.

The shutter of a kinematograph camera is of a gratifyingly simple kind. It consists of a sector of a circle of light metal placed upon the end of a shaft so geared as to cause the metal blade to revolve one whole turn for each picture shift. The blade is timed to come in the track of the lens, thus intercepting the light rays, whenever the escapement comes into operation to shift the film downwards. At other times, the image thrown by the lens is allowed to reach the film unobscured.

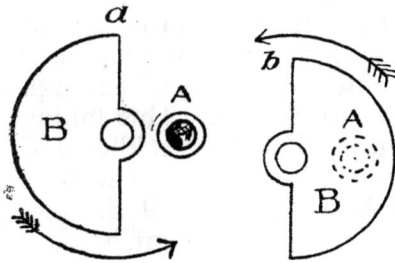

Fig. 6 gives a diagrammatic idea of the relative position of lens and shutter as seen from a point of view in front of a skeleton camera: A the lens, B the shutter; (a) represents the position of the sector during exposure of the film in the gate, while (b) represents the position of shutter at time of picture shift. For the sake of clearness, arrows are included showing the plane of rotation of the shutter.

FIG. 6.

In practice, the shutter of a motion picture camera instead of being made solid as represented in fig. 6, is generally composed of two pieces which can be set to overlap one another till they assume the same form as that already depicted, or may be drawn apart, so as to narrow down the cut-away portion of the metallic light obscuring circle as in fig. 7, thus giving the photographer an additional power over his instrument. How this power is taken advantage of in practice will be gone into later on. In looking after the shutter of a motion picture camera, the great thing is to see that the gearing which drives the shaft is kept well oiled with not too thin an oil, that the shutter blades themselves remain dead black and do

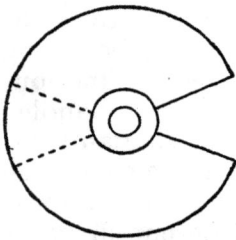

FIG. 7.

do not become bent, and that the sectors are quite firm in their bush. A tin of some high quality photographic dead black should always be kept handy for going over the shutter blades and front of the picture mask. The reason of the presence of the shutter in a kinematograph camera is one which will be apparent to every photographer. Were it not for its function of ' capping the lens ' during each picture change, the movement of the film would cause the sky portion of each negative to fog the foreground, while all bright objects of small size would appear on the film negative with comet-like tails of fog proceeding upwards and downwards from them.

The reason of the ' take-up ' has already been explained. It only remains to make clear how its effect is brought about. Each film box is provided in its interior with a revolving bobbin connected through a light-tight bushing with a rotating plate on the outside of the back of the box. The face of this plate is provided with studs to engage with an independent bar connected with a friction-clutch driven by the camera handle. All that is necessary, therefore, when using a film box as a take-up is to pass the end of the film (previously threaded through the gate and lower sprocket unit) through the light trap in the box's corner, and then connect it firmly with the bobbin by means of a suitable spring clip. The constantly rotating bar driving through the friction clutch in the camera's mechanism does the rest.

And now to the nature of that mechanism itself. In most cameras of ordinary type it is to be got at by opening a door on the right hand or opposite side of the camera to that giving access to the film and escapement. Broadly speaking, it will be found to include a main gear wheel mounted on a suitable frame and capable of being expeditiously connected with the moveable camera handle. This main wheel transmits power to the five principal camera motions either through a train of spur wheels or by a mixture of spur wheel and chain drive. Spring bands are often employed for connecting the take-up. Power has to be transmitted somehow to top sprocket, shutter, escapement, bottom sprocket and take-up, and it is important that the camera man should not content himself merely with mastering his machine as revealed through the left-hand door, but should also make himself thoroughly acquainted with the nature and function of every wheel and piece of gearing hidden behind the right-hand one as well. This will have to be done principally by the use of his own common sense, since in hardly any two cameras is the arrangement for the driving gear of the various motions exactly similar. At the same time, it is only by mastering the meaning of each chain and spur wheel that the photographer is in a position to guess the meaning of any suspicious ' grind,' which may from time to time strike upon his ear, and to know how to put it right forthwith.

Such then is a brief dissertation on the bare bones of the moving picture camera. There are, of course, several important parts of the instrument which have been never so much as touched upon in the foregoing. For instance, nothing so far has been said upon the arrangements for, or methods of focussing. Then again, motion picture cameras are fitted with various quite important, though subsidiary, devices without which their use would be very much a matter of hit and miss. Under such heads might be classed film recorders for registering the number of feet of sensitive film stock consumed when taking any given subject, view finders, and the like. But the place of such may well come in the next and succeeding chapters. The tripod is also a most important feature of the kinematograph photographer's kit which will be dealt with hereafter.

What we have tried to do for the present is to describe the essentials of motion picture taking apparatus just sufficiently to enable the reader to bring an intelligent mind to bear upon the more particular descriptions of different makers' instruments which follow.

CHAPTER III.

────

THE CHOICE OF CAMERA KIT.

Before we can go to the practical side of handling motion picture apparatus, it will be necessary to see about purchasing the apparatus itself.   Only when we decide on the particular camera, tripod, or whatever it may be, we contemplate using, shall we be in a position to thrash out the many minor details of manipulation which distinguish it from other and slightly differing models on the market.   Thus, to take the motion picture camera as a start, our particular one may be furnished with two sprockets, or it may have only one.   It may possess outside film boxes (though these are now pretty nearly obsolete), or it may be fitted with the more modern inside ones.   It may have focussing from the front or the back of the camera.   In fact, a motion picture camera is, in its way, quite an individuality.   Let us pass from the abstract to the concrete, and examine the individualities of some of those most worthy of our attention.

FIG. 8.—SECTIONAL VIEW OF LOADED CAMERA.

For the extremely moderate sum of £8 10s., Messrs. Butcher and Sons supply their Empire Camera No. 1.   This is a useful little instrument of the single sprocket variety, having inside film boxes of 120 feet capacity. It is fitted with a Voigtlander Collinear lens, and will be found an admirable little instrument for the amateur or learner, as also for the picture theatre manager wishful to turn out his own short length local topicals. Fig. 8 shows the Empire Camera No. 2, put out by the same firm. This is a regular professional instrument. It has film boxes of 165 feet capacity, and a Zeiss Tessar lens working at F6.3. Focussing is from the front and also from the back of camera. There is a film indicator to show number of feet used on any given subject, and altogether the camera is a thoroughly efficient one.

Messrs. Butcher have lately informed us that they are putting on the market a simple yet rigid tripod for use with their No. 1 camera. The price of this tripod will be about £3, so that an unpretentious yet handy moving picture taking outfit will be easily within the reach of the ambitious amateur or the smaller picture show management, where it is required to take occasional local topicals.

THE WALTURDAW

Fig. 9.—A Camera Closed for Use.

Needless to say, where a professional type of instrument is required, cost must always be reckoned as subservient to solidity and accuracy of construction. A camera combining moderation of price with many especially valuable features is supplied by Messrs. Walturdaw, the name of this firm being also a household word in the trade. We append an illustration of this Walturdaw D model patent Bioscope Camera (fig. 9). Though this particular picture does not show the camera's interior, it may be taken for granted by the reader all's well

within as well as without.   The claw movement is of the best, bushings being specially hardened, and the whole tested to the point of
absolute unswerving reliability.   The Walturdaw camera also boasts
a feet film indicator, so essential both in general, and even more particularly in trick work.   The two lower bosses shown on the camera's
side are respectively the handle connections for reversing and speeding
down, both of which matters will be found described further on in
the chapter on trick kinematography.   The lens also possesses accurate
means of focussing, while inspection of the focussed image is through
a tube extending from the camera gate to the back of the instrument.

FIG. 10.—ANOTHER POPULAR CAMERA.

FIG. 11.

THE CAMERA SHUTTER.

Perhaps this focussing tube arrangement will be better understood
by reference to the next illustration, that of the Kineto camera (manufactured under Moy and Bastie's patents).   Here the tube will be seen
to be situate between the two film boxes.   It may be recognised as
that portion of the instrument on which the block maker has engraved
the name 'Kineto.'   Looking carefully at the camera back, one sees
a door partially open, and through which, on looking through the aperture and up the length of this tunnel-shaped tube, sight of the gate

can be obtained for focussing purposes. This same illustration will give us an excellent idea of the mode of threading up the film in a high grade camera. The unexposed roll has been previously placed in the topmost film box. The projecting end will then be seen to pass between the jockey rollers and the topmost or feed sprocket of the camera, down through the gate and back into the take-up box over the sprockets of the take-up sprocket wheel. The whole system of threading is, however, shown much plainer in the illustration than

FIG. 12.—EXTERIOR OF PATHÉ CAMERA.

any verbal description could make it. The Kineto camera, besides being provided with all the advantageous movements and attachments common to high grade picture taking instruments in general, boasts many features quite its own, all of them tending toward the greatest perfection in kinematograph photography. Thus, the shutter is of very light construction, and of very variable aperture (see illustration 11), also the escapement, while conforming in general with the principle of the claw, is exquisitely constructed upon a system reminiscent of the old Lumiere movement, which for sheer unerring accuracy, has never yet been surpassed either in camera or projector. The lens fitted to the Kineto camera (failing contrary orders) is a Zeiss Tessar, working at the extremely wide aperture of F3.5, and supplied in a helicoidal focussing mount, which renders the operation of focussing

FIG. 13.—WORKING PARTS OF PATHÉ CAMERA.

—as also of scaling the lens when so required—one of extreme ease. The Kineto camera is therefore a most perfect instrument, but it is not low in price ; neither is the Pathé camera, illustrated in Figs. 12 and 13.

Fig. 12 gives a general view of the camera as seen by the man in the street. Here we note that a strong point in its favour is its similarity in general appearance to a rather large snap-shot camera. Where ostentation may prove a disadvantage, as is by no means seldom the case, the above points may tell heavily towards the kinematographer's success. The handle, however, must always give away the moving picture man to those even a little in the know. Fig. 13 should set at rest all our doubts as to the Pathé camera being really

FIG. 14.—WRENCH REVOLVING TRIPOD HEAD WITH TILTING TABLE

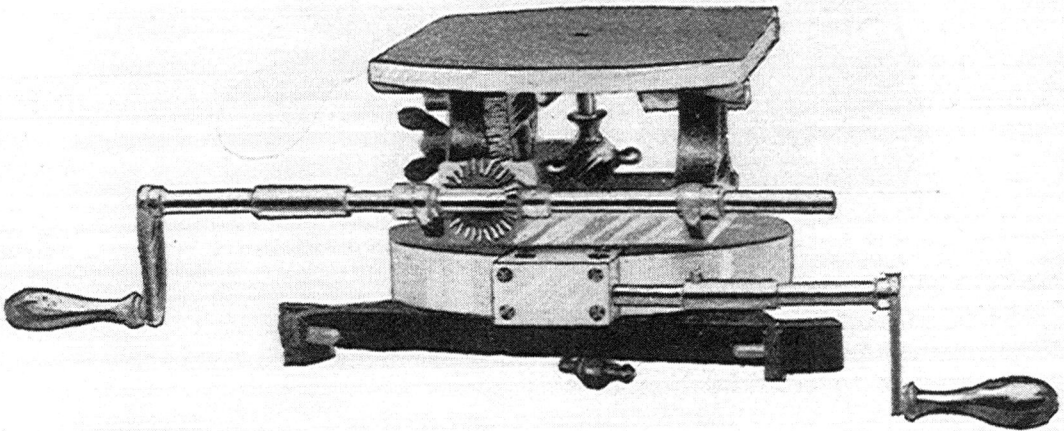

FIG. 15.—A COMPLICATED TRIPOD HEAD.

of the ordinary snap-shot variety. Instead, we see its interior to be fairly seething with machinery, all of it, be it said, of the most accurate and beautifully finished description. Messrs. Pathé's long-lived reputation for having everything of the best should alone be enough guarantee for us in this respect. In the Pathé camera also, the claw movement is modelled largely according to the old Lumiere model, wherein the distinguishing feature is that the pins of the escapement mechanism strike down and up in a rectangular path, their grip or otherwise upon the film perforations being controlled by a second movement which shoots them in and out automatically after the manner of bolts. In common with most other high grade cameras, the Pathé one has film boxes of large capacity, thus admitting of the continuous photographing of incidents extending over upwards of seven minutes at a time. So much then, for kinematograph cameras in general and in particular. We have glanced at models ranging

FIG. 16.—ANOTHER TYPE OF TRIPOD HEAD.

in price from the inside of a ten pound note complete with tripod, to over fifty pounds. And that last remark about the tripod leads on insensibly to consideration of this absolutely indispensable part of the motion picture man's equipment.

Tripods for motion picture work differ from those used in still view photography chiefly on two points, one being their weight—fourteen to sixteen pounds is very moderate for a kinematograph tripod—and the other the presence of mechanical turning movements in the tripod head. Figs. 14 and 15 illustrate two forms of mechanical tripod heads, the first from those excellent makers of apparatus, Wrench and Son, and the other from Pathé Frères. The simpler one, possessing only one handle, is what is known as a ' panoram ' head. In this case, the table top surface upon which the camera is bolted, can be made to revolve slowly round and round in either direction, by virtue of turning the actuating handle to or from the operator.

The more complicated tripod head possesses beyond this panoram action, a second camera tilting device, also worked by a handle-turning attachment, and sometimes referred to as a 'maxim' movement, from the similarity between it and the elevating mechanism of the Maxim gun. The Maxim attachment is very convenient at all times

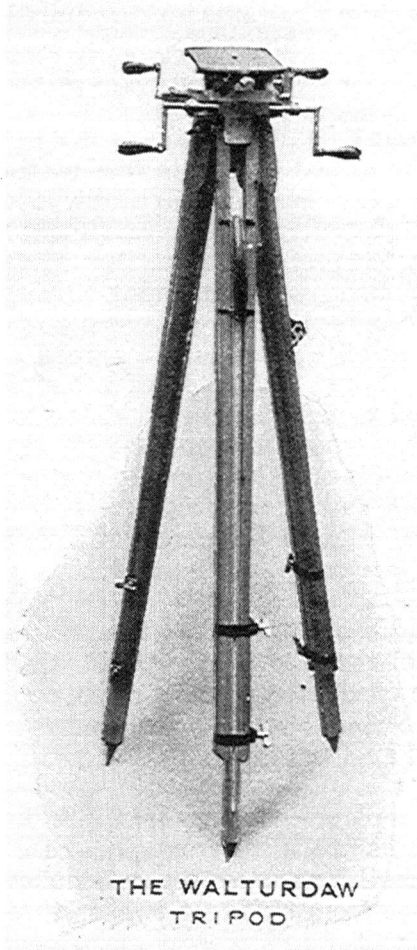

THE WALTURDAW
TRIPOD

FIG. 17.
TRIPOD WITH HEAD ATTACHED.

FIG. 18.
CAMERA HEAD, SHOWING HANDLES
CLOSED.

and especially where it is desired to obtain a wide panorama of objects above or beneath the camera level. In fact, without it, such slanting panoramic attempts are sure to show a tipping of the horizon at some point or other in the resulting picture. Illustration 16 gives another close view of the combined revolving and tilting head as fitted to one of Messrs. Butcher's motion picture tripods.

On page 17, we see the same applied to the Walturdaw tripod. This tripod, it should be added, has the special advantages of lightness (it is not more than fourteen pounds weight all told), portability, and a most reasonable price. It is, moreover, fitted with handles which fold up after use, instead of having to be removed, the latter course often leading to the omission from the working kit of one or other of the tripod handles at a time when it is most required. The writer speaks feelingly on the point, having before now been seriously handicapped through just this catastrophe brought about by a simple failure of memory.

In the matter of the view finder, most field operators will agree that something of the kind should be attached or attachable to the motion picture camera, for use when photographing topicals, fast moving objects, and under conditions of general hurry and excitement. Otherwise, there is great liability for there to be needless waste of film stock by starting the handle too early, and continuing turning after the point is reached when the photographic record ceases to be useful. At the same time, by no means all operators are agreed as to the best form of finder to employ. Some make use of a simple hollow rectangular tube or frame affixed to the camera body in such a position that, by looking through it, a more or less correct idea of the picture field is obtained by simple direct vision, unaided by any form of optical lens system whatever. Probably, the far better course for the budding camera operator will be to make his choice of a view finder from one or two well-known and recognised models. Either let it be a finder of the kind consisting of a rectangular conclave lens, behind which is fixed a central sighting bead, after the manner of a military gun sight, or let it be a finder of the box form type, in which a front convex lens throws a real image of the scene to be taken upon a ground glass screen at the rear of the finder box. View finders of both types are stocked by all makers of and dealers in motion picture cameras.

And now a word as to the motion picture taking lens. It has been said already, kinematograph cameras are usually supplied ready fitted with a suitable lens, but, though this is true, several makers require the purchaser to make his choice from amongst two or three alternative ones specified on their lists. For this reason, we append illustrations of some of those instruments best known and best suited to the work in hand. And here let us say that for ordinary purposes, the focus of a kinematograph lens should be anything between two inches and three and a half inches, the shorter focus being generally most useful for topical filming in restricted situations, and the longer for scenic and artistic work, where there is plenty of elbow room at the camera man's command.

The lenses in most general use are either of 2 in. or 3 in. focal length, but for certain purposes lenses of other focal lengths are of value. Messrs. J. H. Dallmeyer, Ltd., who from a very early period specialised in kinematograph lenses, show in their current list nine

SOME OF THE BEST CAMERA LENSES.

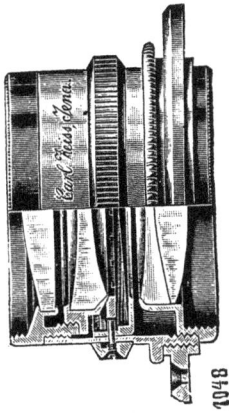

FIG. 19.—ZEISS TESSAR LENS.

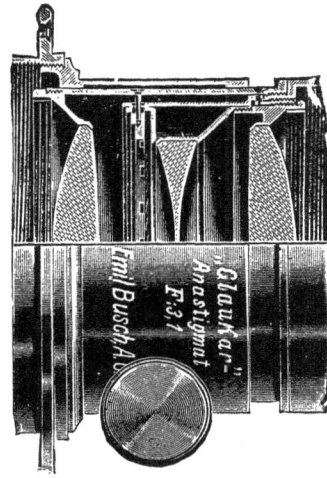

FIG. 20.—BUSCH GLAUKAR LENS.

FIG. 21.—DALLMEYER F/1.9 LENS.

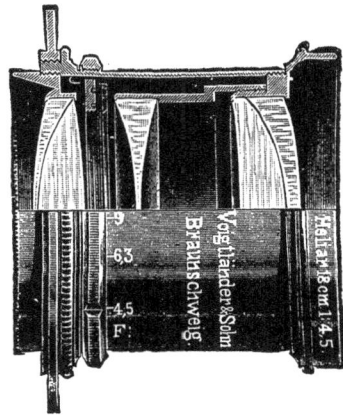

FIG. 22.—VOIGTLANDER HELIAR LENS

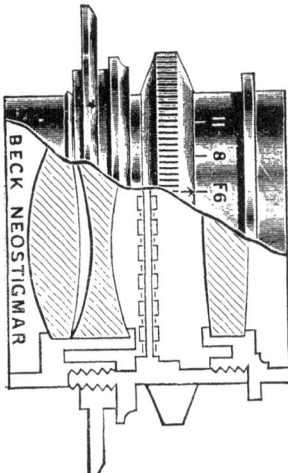

FIG. 23.—BECK NEOSTIGMAR AND ISOSTIGMAR LENSES.

different sizes, starting with a lens of 2 in. focal length, working at the high intensity of F3.8. This is a very generally useful lens and is widely fitted to the leading makes of cameras. They make also a remarkable lens of 3 in. focal length working at the enormous aperture of F1.9, which permits of instantaneous exposures, even under bad conditions of light indoors and late in the day. The remarkable power which this lens places in the hands of kinematograph operators will be understood when it is seen that with it less than one quarter the usual exposure is required. Films may therefore be made under most adverse conditions. (Figure 21.)

The latest introduction of this well-known firm is a tele-photo-kinematograph lens working at F4.5, which gives pictures three times as large as those obtained with the ordinary lens. This means that the operator may be three times the normal distance from his subject and yet get a picture of full size. It is particularly in cases where single figures have to be photographed that such a lens proves its value. See remarks on tele-kinematography (Part 3).

Illustration 19 is of a Zeiss Tessar lens. This lens works at F3.5, at which extra wide aperture it gives critically sharp definition over the whole area of the kinematograph film picture. More than this we need not say of it, for its suitability for the work in question is a matter of universal acceptance.

Illustration 20 shows another lens still newer in design, and wider of aperture (that is to say, more rapid) than the Tessar. This is the Busch Glaukar at F3.1. Although quite a newcomer into the kine-matograph field, the Glaukar is well spoken of, whilst its great rapidity, coupled with the name of the firm producing it—the Emil Busch Optical Company—should assure for it a triumphal future.

To finish up the matter of lenses, we figure two other well known types, namely the Heliar of Messrs. Voigtlander and Sohn, and the Isostigmar of Messrs. Beck. (Illustrations 22 and 23.)

The former of these two lenses has a great popularity both in England and on the Continent as a medium rapid kinematograph lens, rendering pictures of absolutely irreproachable definition and good apparent depth of focus. Its aperture is F4.5. This is also the aperture of the Isostigmar, but here the claim to recognition is somewhat different, inasmuch as the latter lens is notable as being the commercial expression of a completely new idea in optical formulae. Perhaps, however, to the purchaser, another and even more pressing point of excellence in the Isostigmar may be found in its extreme moderation of price. We will only add that it is in all ways every bit as good as any other lens here mentioned.

The present would seem to be the place to touch briefly upon the subject of film perforating machines. As has already been explained, the action of the kinematograph escapement upon the film depends upon its first having been perforated with a series of extremely accurately spaced and sized holes near either edge of the film stock. The making of these holes or perforations will be readily appreciated as a task in-

volving the most precise of mechanical contrivances, since upon absolute freedom from error depends the ultimate steadiness of the projected
moving picture, as seen by the public on the theatre screen. Moreover,
extremely delicate and accurate machinery cannot, of its nature,
be cheap to buy. Below we figure the Williamson perforator known
technically as a 'step by step' machine, the older rotary pattern
perforators being now quite obsolete. For further particulars of the

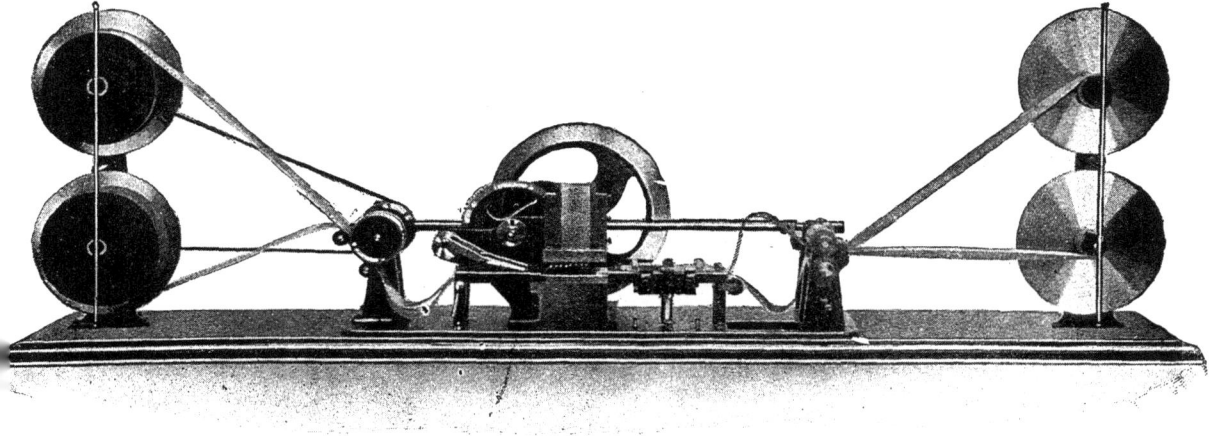

FIG. 24.—WILLIAMSON FILM PERFORATOR.

step by step principle, as applied to kinematograph machinery, see
the chapter on film printers and positive printing.

The Williamson perforator is a beautiful little machine, comparatively inexpensive and highly efficient. It can be driven by hand or
motor power, and perforates two films at a time, face to face. Since
film stock is perforated unexposed, at which time it is highly light-

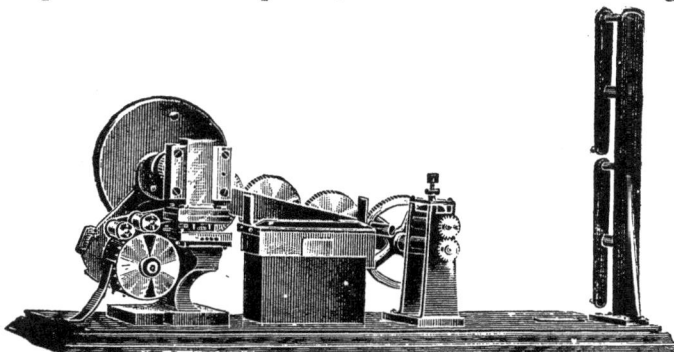

FIG. 25.—EMPIRE FILM PERFORATOR.

sensitive, those with some experience of photographic matters will
at once realise the necessity of perforating under strict 'dark room
conditions.' Others will probably buy their first few rolls of film stock
ready perforated, leaving the business of doing this at home till the time
when they will be a trifle more expert in the handling of the sensitive

film rolls.   Another perforator of excellent accuracy and great moderation of price is the Empire perforator of Messrs. Butcher (Fig. 25). It sells at £30, a lot of money perhaps, but a mere bagatelle compared to the price of some perforators.   The Empire is a splendid little instrument.

Those who are determined to 'hang the expense,' may be interested in the accompanying illustration of the Debrie perforator.

FIG. 26 —DEBRIE FILM PERFORATOR.

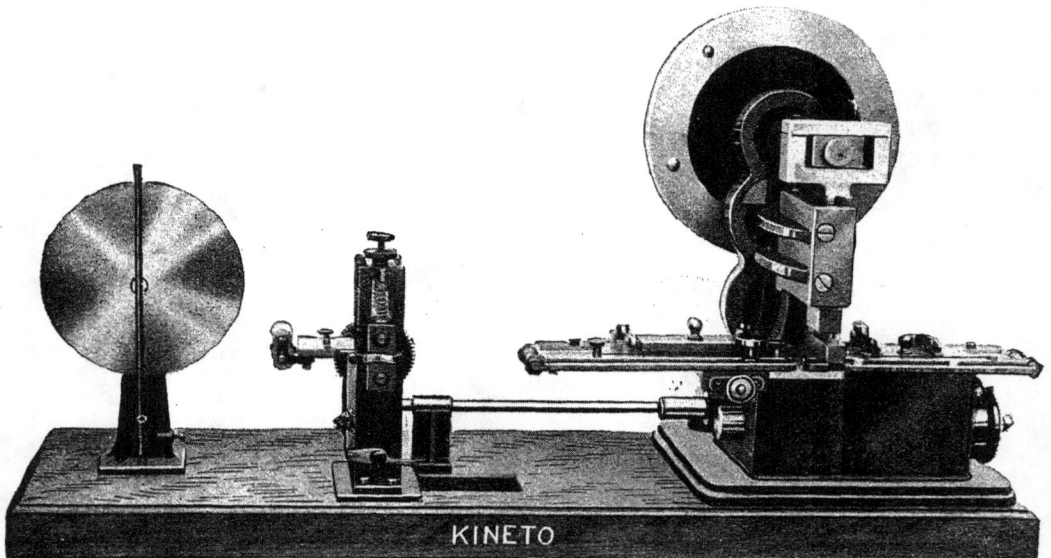

FIG. 27 —KINETO FILM PERFORATOR.

The firm of Debrie, it may be said, has its headquarters in Paris, and has for years led the way in the matter of sumptuous motion picture apparatus of all descriptions.

We complete the list of perforators we can recommend whole-heartedly with an illustration of the Kineto machine. As in all matter connected with the name of the firm, there is nothing of the cheap and nasty about it. On the other hand, it combines elegance with 'doing the work,' and this in the most complete way possible.

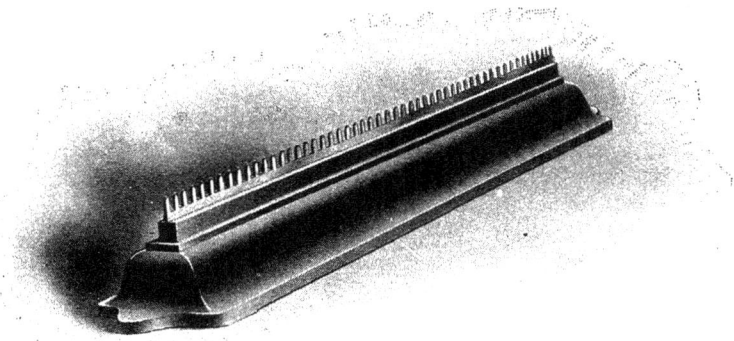

FIG. 28. DEBRIE PERFORATION GAUGE.

Our next illustration (Fig. 28) is of a little film perforation gauge made by the firm of Debrie. It will be seen to consist of a number of accurately cut metal teeth so spaced that by applying them to the perforation holes of a correctly perforated film, complete and perfect registration will result. Another excellent way of testing perforations

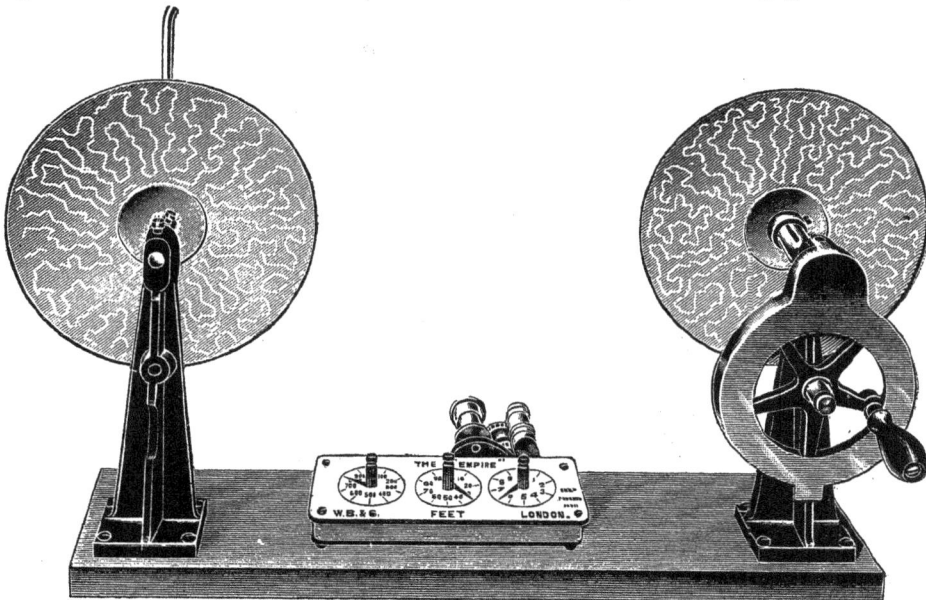

FIG. 29.—A POPULAR FILM MEASURER.

without any special appliance whatever, is to double a length of the film over itself at a point midway between two perforation holes, and lay the doubled up film under pressure between slabs of plate glass.

Observation as to the alteration of register between opposing sprocket holes will soon show whether the film perforator is or is not at fault.

Where there is reason to suspect that rolls of film stock may be of short length—and perhaps also where there may be no definite reason for believing it—common sense would indicate the advisability of installing some check on film lengths, if such can be conveniently done at small outlay. Such an effective check is forthcoming in the little machine known as a film measurer, of which an example (that of Messrs. Butcher) is shown, Fig. 29. Unlike the perforator, the film measurer is a machine of comparatively low price. In the case of shortage of length of film consignments, it will save its cost in no time. It is also of service for checking the length of completed kinematograph positive films intended for projection. Moreover, the particular model here figured may, if desired, be on occasion pressed into general service as an excellent film winder or rewinder.

There is but one item more that need be touched upon in this chapter before bringing it to a close. It is not, strictly speaking, a piece of kinematograph machinery either, for it is just as applicable and almost as useful to the still view photographer. It is the pocket exposure meter, without which no conscientious picture man can ever consider himself fully equipped for his work.

Exposure meters are of various patterns, but most of them work on the same fundamental principal ; that of (A) testing the value of the light by means of a timed exposure of a strip of light sensitive paper, the test time being that in which the exposed sensitive strip occupies in turning the colour of a given painted patch upon the meter's face ; and (B) the ascertaining of the correct exposure by means of printed scales upon the meter, read in conjunction with the figure denoting the time taken by the test strip to darken, the aperture of the lens stop, and the rapidity of the film stock employed in the camera.

The two most used exposure meters are those known respectively as the Watkins, and the Wynne meter. Watkins meters run from 2s. 6d. upwards, Wynne meters from 6s. 6d. Both are at a casual glance much like ordinary watches to look at, in fact, when had in sterling silver cases, they make very sensible and sightly additions to the blank end of a double swivel watch chain. They are figured below.

FIG. 30.—EXPOSURE METERS.

CHAPTER IV.

IN THE FIELD.   SCENIC WORK.

Suppose ourselves ordered to take a series of exposures on some well known home beauty spot. We will try to set forth something of the system of going to work.

First we ascertain the length of film we shall require, and endeavour to obtain possession of stock as fresh as possible. It must be perforated.

Having got hold of the requisite perforated negative film and collected as many spare film boxes as required to hold it, load up and see that this is accomplished the right way. To load a film box, first open it empty in daylight and dust it well inside, after which examine the velvet lining of the light trap. Make sure this velvet is firmly stuck down and not lopping about loose inside the box, as the writer has known it to be before now. Also see to it that the lips of the trap are clean and free from grit. This may be done by carefully passing a slip of cambric between them on the point of a thin-bladed paper knife. Draw the cambric backward and forward till the slit is cleaned. Presuming the box is sound and light tight, it is now ready for loading in the dark room.

The arrangement of this dark room will not be gone into deeply here ; it is to be treated of in a separate chapter. Suffice it to say for the present that when loading film boxes, the room has to be illuminated only by a lamp capable of shedding a pure dull red light, and a by no means strong one at that.

Unfasten the top from the film tin, lift out the paper or foil enclosed roll of stock and remove all wrappings. Now run the fingers of the right hand round the celluloid rim of the roll gently till the end of it is found. The roll is now laid loosely over the bobbin of the film box, but *not* fastened to it by means of the spring clip used when threading a take-up box. The correct way of the loaded-in roll is such that the film unwinds from it parallel to the bottom of the box, as in fig. 8. Loaded in such a way, the tag of film sticking through the out-

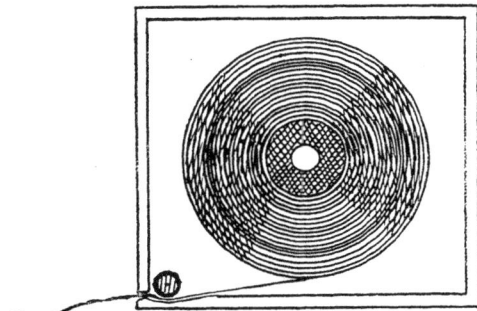

Fig. 31.

let (through which, of course, the end must be passed) will have its emulsion side uppermost. Should the celluloid side be uppermost, it is proof the film roll has been inserted wrong way round. When the film is loaded, and before taking the film box from the dark room, don't forget to put on the door and turn the catch securely.

As to the advice just given, to use a sufficient number of film boxes to contain all the stock for the trip, it will be understood this only applies to flying trips made in the home country, and where the amount of film used is not to be more than one or two thousand feet at most. Under such circumstances, it is a great saving of time and temper to do as suggested, and thus get rid of the annoyance attendant upon having to unload and re-load film in hotel bedrooms, etc.

Now to collect our kit before getting out and about. This should consist of the following camera (with handle), view finder, film boxes, and take-up box, spring bobbins for clipping the film ends in the take-up (the same number of these will be required as there are charged film boxes), tripod with the necessary handle or handles for controlling the automatic gear. Probably, a stiff carrying case will also be included wherein to keep the camera when not in use, while another small piece of apparatus will find a place in the pocket of the really conscientious and up-to-date camera man, though the writer is well aware it is in by no means general use by the members of the motion picture making fraternity. This last adjunct is an exposure meter, the nature and use of which has already been explained on page 24.

Let us now get to the actual filming operations. Artistically speaking, there are a good many more ways than one of going to work. One man will make it an invariable rule before touching the beauty spots of any locality to do a preliminary round of the picture post card shops by way of obtaining inspiration for his work. A hurried trip will then be taken to the scenes thus selected by him for the purpose of arranging with the local cottagers and others any simple effects of movement, such as milking, sheep-driving and the like, which may be possible.

The weak point here would seem to be chiefly the dependence placed upon the picture postcards in the first place. But yet, it must be admitted, the film man would often be at a grave disadvantage without them. Generally he comes to make his films on a strict time limit. He is not able to ramble about at his own sweet will day after day till he has discovered pet scenic effects for himself. What else can he do then but have recourse to previously existing photos of the locality? Let us grant all this. Yet even so, one can at least exercise the privilege of handling a conventional view from a slightly different standpoint to the usual one, and also, if possible, under rather different circumstances of lighting from the stereotyped conditions of the local view maker, and this much, in the writer's opinion, the first rate camera man should and will do.

Now to the technique of exposing a scenic film. Let us suppose we are standing before the subject to be recorded. It may be a waterfall, a mountain path, or such like. The first thing to do is to take the height and direction of the sun. If the day is cloudy or dull, the same must be estimated as well as possible, though a really dull day can never be expected to yield results possessing any great amount of brilliancy and sparkle.

Having got the sun's direction, one notes whether this will be to the front, back or side of the camera when the lens is pointing towards the required view. Roughly speaking, the best position is when the sun is behind but not quite at the back of the camera. Such a standpoint is at least more often useful than any other. With the sun right behind you get a flat result. With the sun quite to the side, shadows thrown by the various objects in the view are apt to become obtrusive, though this is not to say such an effect is always an evil. Sometimes even for special effects, one may photograph with the sun straight in front of the camera, provided it is high in the heavens, and the lens glass is kept well shaded from its rays. That remark has no connection with the making of so-called moonlight effects, where the lens is pointed right at a cloud behind which a low sun is shooting out its rays. Such ' moonlight ' work almost comes under the head of trick photography, whereas the effects obtained with a high sun and well-shaded lens are often highly pleasing and artistic. They are, however, more of the nature of advanced studies for the hardened camera man, and not the sort of thing to learn upon. Let us lay down for a start then that we may have the sun anywhere within a semi-circle of which the middle would point toward the back of the camera, and provided also the objects we want to stand out in the film record are well illuminated. This is giving the lie direct to the superstition that flat back lighting is the right thing to make for, such an idea being absolute bosh.

Having selected view and lighting, which is best done with the aid of a box view finder, the next thing is to carry the camera kit to the point from whence the desired effect is obtained, and fit up. After that, focussing is accomplished either on the threaded film itself, should the general light be good, or on a piece of matt celluloid placed in the gate for the purpose, where lighting conditions are poorer, or the motion picture man's eyes not quite up to the strain of framing a sharp image on the somewhat opaque sensitive film. (Instructions for threading film were given in Chapter 3.) For the purpose of focussing, and supposing a reasonably good lens is being employed, the full aperture is utilised, while the object sharply focussed is invariably to be that which is of most importance in the finished film.

Now re-thread the film in the gate (supposing it has been taken out for focussing on matt celluloid), give a last look at the film and escapement to see all is in place, attach the camera handle and give a half-turn with the left hand door open, watching the while to make sure the escapement and take-up are going right. See that the door of the take-up box is in place, then close camera door securely, and *proceed to take the light value with the aid of the exposure meter.* This is the very best advice the writer can give, and those who follow it from the first will not regret doing so.   There never was a greater absurdity than the idea current among some camera men that one is not a finished photographer until one can tell the light value 'by instinct.'   No one can tell the light value by instinct.   The most they can do is to stumble upon the correct exposure for certain average classes of conditions, which conditions will be for ever deceiving them, and causing them to make howling mistakes right up to the end. *But they won't admit it, and so to themselves they seem to have achieved the impossible.*

'Don't run before you can crawl' is a good motto, but in the present connection, its application is indirect, since no sensible man ever pretends to have got to the stage of perfection as regards judgment of exposure, and those who do pretend to it are not sensible men.

Now to set the stop and shutter aperture.   Here is real scope for a master hand.

In the first place, supposing the light is very good, we shall probably find ourselves placed with the alternative of very small stop or equally small shutter aperture.   If we adopt the former course and stop down tremendously it will have the effect of putting the whole of the view into marvellously sharp focus.   But don't run away with the idea that this is always the best thing to aim for.   For instance, the scene may embrace a waterfall, which can't be too sharp, and which has therefore been focussed upon in the first place so that it will be sharp anyway, and there may also be a range of mountain peaks and hills in the background.   But these latter, especially if tree-clad, might quite possibly be made much too sharp by over-stopping down, in which event the trees upon the hillside would compete with the waterfall for supremacy in the view, so spoiling the effect of each part of the picture.   Here is a simple matter for the camera man's skill and good judgment.   The stopping should be carried to a point where a reasonably harmonious result shows itself on the focussed picture, and the rest of exposure adjustment must now be made by narrowing the shutter aperture.

A word about lens stops or diaphragms.   In the form of lens attached to kinematograph cameras, alteration of diaphragm is effected by the movement of a ring or pin on the lens mount which causes the 'iris' inside to open and close like the iris of a cat's eye, except that the hole in the middle always remains circular in shape.   Around the lens barrel will be found engraved numbers which on English lenses run somewhere as follows : f4., 5.6., 8., 11., 16., 22., 32.   Sometimes the numbers are slightly different to these, such as f3.8., or f11.3., for instance.   Such minor differences need not be very seriously taken into account.

What about the virtue of engraving lenses with these ' F numbers ' ?   The answer is that every lens, no matter how great its size, or ' focal length,' works (theoretically at least) at an identical speed when set at any given aperture. Thus, if the photographer has in his camera set a two and a half inch and a three and a half inch lens, both of them will require the same exposure when both are set at f8, for instance, or f11, or any other similar ' F number.' But these aperture numbers possess another use beyond the above. Each aperture requires double the exposure of the last, thus : if with a lens at f4, the camera man finds the correct exposure would be the eightieth of a second, then the exposure would be the fortieth of a second (approximately the actual kinematograph exposure) at f5.6, or the twentieth of a second (which would be too slow for practical work) at f8. In the latter case the shutter aperture would, if possible, have to be considerably widened in order to avoid under exposure of the kinematograph film. And this brings us to the shutter itself.

Sixteen pictures are taken per second, during which time the shutter is making one revolution at uniform speed for each picture. It follows as a matter of course that with the blades full open (in which case the metallic sector will usually be approximately a semi-circle, the rate of change in kinematograph cameras being about one to one), each effective exposure will be somewhere about the duration of a thirty-second part of a second. To simplify matters, let us say the actual exposure under such conditions is the fortieth part of a second, then by narrowing the cut-away portion of the shutter to a quarter circle, exposure time is reduced to one-eightieth second, while with only one-eighth circle shutter aperture, there will be only the one hundred and sixtieth part of a second allowed for each succeeding exposure.

Nothing but excessive light can justify the narrowing of shutter aperture to such small limits as the last. As to helping the photo-grapher in photographing rapid motion, it does nothing of the kind. In kinematograph work one is not concerned with the freedom from movement blur or otherwise of each single picture. It is true, of course, that given sufficient light and a sufficiently rapid lens coupled with an extremely small shutter aperture wonderfully sharp pictures (sharp, that is to say, in the sense of being free from blur caused by recorded motion) might be obtained of such things as galloping horses, racing motors, etc. *on the film.* They would not project as well even as would a film in which the individual pictures were distinctly blurred through using a comparatively wide shutter aperture. For, whereas in the latter case the eye might see on the screen a somewhat confused impression of the speeding objects, in the former the only result of abnormal closure of the shutter blades would be to produce on the projection screen a double, triple, or multi-outlined image. Hence one has to realise from the start that the shutter of the motion picture camera, like the lens, takes a lot of knowing, for whereas the principal object in a given film should always be sharp as far as its focussing goes, that is not to say the shutter is also to be adjusted so as to elim-inate all movement blur from the record.

As a working basis for the novice at the camera, it might be laid down that generally speaking, and provided the light allows, a stop of about f8 with a shutter opening of one third of a circle is right for most things. If the light varies one way or the other, it is best to make the lens diaphragm anything from f5.6 to f16, according as the exposure meter directs, rather than manipulate the shutter opening. This applies to all scenes where there is a fair amount of movement. Only when the movement to be recorded is very slow, as for instance in panoramic views where practically the whole of the motion is transmitted to the picture by rotation of the tripod head, is it safe to narrow down the shutter greatly rather than lose the effect of atmosphere and softness which would result from over-stopping down to compensate for undue light, or for a flat and over sunny foreground.

The above, at any rate, embodies the writer's general system. Needless to say, there are other, and in some cases, contrary views held by various workers.

But while on this subject, there is another point about lenses which must not go without comment. It is the question of their focal length.

Upon the focal length of a lens—in other words, upon the amount of distance between the optical centre of a given lens and the focussed image of a distant object produced by it upon the kinematograph film—depends a most important quality of the picture: the relative importance of foreground and distance. Figs. 32 and 33 are intended to make the reason of this clearer. In each case, AB represents the focussed kinematograph picture, which is, of course, always of the same external dimensions upon

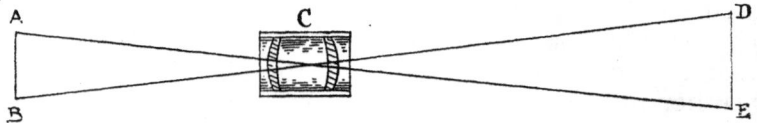

FIG. 32.

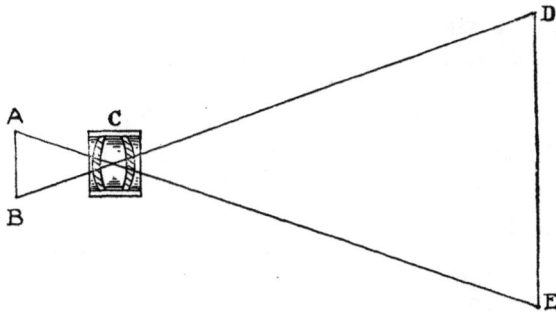

FIG. 33.

the film. CC in the two figs. are two lenses, one of which (C, fig. 32) has a focus three times that of the other. That is to say, its optical centre when it is focussed upon some distant object is three times as far from the film AB, as is the optical centre of the lens in fig. 33. The lines CD, CE show in each case the comparative amounts of view which will be included on the film picture by the two lenses. It will be seen at once that the direct result of the added focal length of the lens in fig. 32 is to cut down its 'angle of view,' so that proportionately less of the foreground is included in the picture thrown by it, while far away objects must, of necessity, be greatly magnified in size so as to fill up the space vacated by their nearer neighbours. The result is therefore as already set forth :—the longer the lens's focal length the more the distance stands out in the picture, and the less of the foreground is included. To return to the practical aspect of the matter. The average 'focus' (the ordinary loose way of referring to focal length) of a taking lens for kinematography, is in the neighbourhood of three inches. It is not usual to go below two and a half inches on the short side, and indeed only a few of the cameras on the market would be able to be fitted with a shorter focus lens than this. On the other hand, long focus lenses may run easily up to four or five inches, while for natural history work, photograph-ing wild animals, birds on their eggs, and some other specialised kinds of kinematography, much longer focus lenses even than the above have been employed with success. It is said that the well-known kinematographer of wild life, Mr. Cherry Kearton, often makes use of lenses of nine inches focus or thereabouts. The longest focal length which will be found of general use by the moving picture man is some-where in the neighbourhood of four inches, while if, as is quite possible, he has to do all his work with one lens, three inches is the 'all round' focus to make for. This point of the kinematograph lens's focus is raised here by way of exemplifying yet another factor in which the scenic photographer may be called to display his skill.

Now we will assume the moment for exposure has arrived. The camera is focussed, the take-up box looked to and closed tight, the camera also closed securely and pointed to the scene to be taken, and we will suppose the finder is in its proper place on the left-hand side of the camera, and as nearly as possible on a level with the lens. There is nothing now to wait for but a satisfactory state of the picture before we let fly upon it.

It may be a waterfall we are taking—the same one we were focuss-ing a while ago—in that case, it is always at work and ready for us. Give a glance upward to make sure there are no clouds drifting to-ward the sun, or if there are, that they will only serve to enhance the general pleasing effect of the picture by the play of light and shade that comes sweeping over the landscape in their train, then all being well, we may turn straight away. Twice a second the handle has to go round with most modern cameras. Each turn accounts for eight kinematograph pictures, and we must see to it the rate of turning is uniform, and that there are no 'dead points' during the twirling of the handle (otherwise, moments when the hand slackens off, and allows a partial drop in speed during the revolution).   While we turn we keep an eye upon the view finder to see that the scenery is all right, and incidentally that the camera is not vibrating unduly.   If it is, or if the tripod legs or head are not screwed up tight, or if the tripod is not widely enough spread, or if it is planted upon a bed of springy heather, one will soon know it by the jerking of the image on the finder glass as soon as work commences.   Stop turning and put matters right before resuming.   Never mind wasting two or three feet of film if by so doing it is possible to convert the rest of the subject from indifferent into good work.   In every case of negative making, unless the length of the subject taken happens to be such as to use up the whole of the roll of stock, its finish is marked on the threaded roll, either by means of the film punch or by opening the camera door and snipping a bit out of the film perforations with a pair of pocket scissors.   See fig. 34.

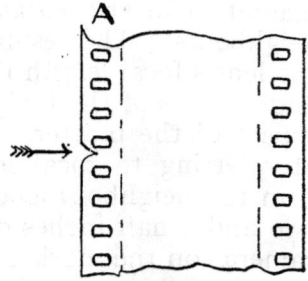

FIG. 34.

Where the view to be taken is a panoramic one, known familiarly as a ' panoram,' there will also be the handle of the tripod head to be turned with the left hand while the camera handle is twirled with the right.   This is not so easy as it sounds, even when the required direction of camera swing makes it possible for both hands to go the same way.   For one thing, the rate at which a panoram is swung depends generally on a much slower motion of the hand controlling the turntable handle than the regulation twice a second which must *always* be given to the camera handle.   With the turntables used by the writer, one revolution of the turntable handle to every two of the camera handle has usually been as fast as it is wise to go for good quality in the results.   Slower rates for the turntable are a matter of the photographer's own judgment, but when it is necessary to swivel the camera round quickly many degrees in the course of taking a picture, even where the tripod mechanism provides for this, such abrupt rotation should never, under any circumstances, be allowed to show in the completed motion picture.

Stop the camera while re-adjusting in such cases, or, if you don't do that, then later on, when making up the negative for printing, just cut out the part where the quick turn comes.   The gap brought about by such procedure will never irritate the audience half as much as would the horrible brain-racking blur occasioned by including the over quickly rotated portion of film with the rest.

But, as has been hinted, the turntable has not invariably to be rotated the way it will go when both hands turn their respective handles in the same direction.   It has also on occasion to go the other way.   This means either that the camera man has to master the art of twirling two handles with his two hands in opposite direc-

FIG. 35.
VARIED
PHASES
IN A
CAMERA
MAN'S
LIFE.

(a)   A LITTLE SPORT IN THE JUNGLE.   (b)   A LAKE IN THE JUNGLE.

(c)   A PERILOUS POSITION.   (d)   A CROWDED PRIZE FIGHT RING.

tions at the same time and at differing though respectively uniform rates—either that, or he must do what many a kinematograph photographer actually does do, and take an assistant with him to manage the turntable according to pre-arranged word of command. The latter is, of course, the easier way, but never forget a man is not real master of his instrument until he can do passable work quite on his own, and manipulate turntable and elevating device as required while still attending to the revolution of the camera handle.

The last sort of scenic subject to be touched upon in this lengthy chapter is even more difficult than the foregoing ones, for while it demands all the knowledge required up to now, it requires in addition something more—the ability to manage live things—men, women, children, and animals. Moreover, to the class of pastoral film calling for such exceptional knowledge, most of the really successful outdoor scenic (to say nothing of topical) work belongs.

It is no light task to mind your camera, see to your turntable and elevation, keep a smiling face for the pretty country girl in the pastoral film, and give the necessary directions to the farmer's boy for the stage management of the ducks and calves, all at the same time. If it looks light work, that only shows that the ' man behind the gun ' knows his business and knows it well. He has learned that if he seems to be working, the joy of what is being regarded by his amateur helpers as a ' piece of fun ' will go from their faces. The smiling girl will smile no more, but only look alarmed or else self-conscious, as so many other country maids have appeared before now in otherwise excellent motion picture films. So our kinematographer smiles the while he surreptitiously flicks away a trickling drop of perspiration from his cheek, and the handle on the right of the camera does its twice a second, and the two other handles on the left of the turntable do their allotted tasks, while the farmer's boy hollows and the live stock wallows, and the farm maiden sorrows, or laughs, as the case may be. And all the while, the film recorder tick-ticks its tal of ' something attempted, something done ' in terms of feet of expose stock.

It is over. The gate goes easy, betokening the end of the film supply, and hence the enforced finish of the subject. At last the motion picture photographer may relax his efforts. He notes particulars of subject and exposure either in his note book against the number denoting the take-up box or else on the ivorine writing tablet upon the box itself, then produces a handkerchief and mops his brow, while the young lady assures him it was ' awful fun being taken,' and the radiant farm lad waits expectant.

' The expected ' has been presented. And now the camera is packed and we are on the homeward march. It doesn't look much. ' So simple,' as the conjurers say, and even the photographer, now it is over and he has taken a final look at his film gate so as to make sure it is still bright (since otherwise, it is next to certain the film would after all have been scratched, and ruined)—even the jaded photographer begins to feel it wasn't so difficult after all, only a bit of nerve strain for the moment. But it is just that expenditure of nerve force which alone can bring success to the picture man.

FIG. 36. CURIOUS POSITIONS FOR THE CAMERA MAN.

(a) A ROUGH SEA.   (b) IN A COAL MINE.

(c) PHOTOGRAPHING THE FALLS.

FIG. 37.   VARIED SCENES FROM A GEOGRAPHICAL STUDY.

CHAPTER V.

———

TOPICALS.

How to get to grips with a topical—that sounds easy. Generally speaking, when it comes to the point it is anything but so. For instance, let us grant we have arranged the catching of trains and other necessary conveyances so as to bring us up with the earliest of the crowd round about the event to be filmed. We then begin to find for a start that any attempt on the part of the camera man to barge his heavy apparatus through a crowded throng of onlookers is not liable to be popular, nor will it probably be successful.

There are three possible ways out of the difficulty.

(1)   Use your own powers of persuasion to cajole the people in your way into moving out of it, or if you have enough and strong enough assistants, set them to ' police ' a way for you.

(2)   Select a pitch as high up as possible (say, on a high pavement or in a house porch) elevate the tripod legs to their fullest extent so that the lens looks over the heads of the bystanders, and proceed to operate, standing on the top of the stiff camera case, which is made specially strong for the purpose.

(3)   Select an eminence right above the crowd, get to it somehow, and operate from there with the camera pointing partially downward.

Where the importance of the occasion warrants it, method 3 is for obvious reasons the soundest way of going to work. Incidentally, it is the one generally in vogue at the present time for obtaining records of state processions and such like.

For all that, and admitting its many advantages, there are still possibilities for things going wrong. For one thing, even supposing a place has been duly rented, it sometimes happens that the camera man will not find himself alone in his position, and the company of a second and unknown motion picture photographer under such conditions, may lead to trouble which was little dreamed of. As a case in point, there comes to the writer's memory the story of how a certain raised platform at Paddington Station was let out to two picture men on the occasion of the funeral of the late King Edward. Each operator was to occupy half the platform, but at the last moment there arose a doubt as to which of the two had the right to the better half. It is not recorded whether on this occasion the rival men came to blows. Certain it is, however, there was some hustling and a hasty appeal to the railway authorities before the matter was finally settled. And all that time, valuable moments of preparation for the filming

109

operations were being wasted.   That is a case where carelessness on
someone's part was responsible.   There are also occasions when difficulties arise through other causes.

At a certain race meeting not so long since, a hopeful camera man
found his view blocked at the last moment by the attentions of his
rival's assistants, who kindly let off smoke rockets in the field of his
lens while the horses were running.   That is a sort of thing there is
no guarding against, and the only moral here is to keep a weather
eye open for such things as may crop up, and take all possible measures
which human nature may forsee to circumvent disappointment.

Lastly, as an unexpected set-back especially likely to affect the
renter of a seemingly ideal position for filming a public ceremony,
may be mentioned a common circumstance for which no one really
is to be blamed.   It follows simply and solely from the natural cussed-
ness of things, yet it is none the less damning to one's results.   It
is the unlooked-for nuisance of decorations at the last moment.

The representative of a speculative film house sees a window to let
from which a perfect view is obtainable of the street down which some
pageant or procession is to come.   He takes it, pays good money for it,
and congratulates himself he has done more than well for his firm.
The great day arrives.   Camera man or men are despatched to their
pitch.   What do they find ?

They find a gaudy flag pole newly painted in such a position as
to cut their view right down the middle, but this is not all.   Across
the important part of the picture runs a line of silly baby flags.   They
are too near to be focussed and made use of in the general scheme of
decoration as depicted in the kinematograph picture, and they bob up
and down in the breeze, not so obtrusively at first, perhaps, but do not
be deceived.   They will not fail when the procession hoves in sight.
And they do not fail.   Just at the critical moment when one holds
one's breath in the expectation of securing the film's vital point, a
long, snaky bunting streamer switches down, down, plop ! and the
whole view is temporarily obscured ; not for long, only just long
enough to spoil the film.

The foregoing is an old tale to the hardened topical man.   The
neophyte will perhaps be better able to steel himself against the future
after reading it.

Sometimes, as in the case of state processions, the preliminary
wait is liable to be on the long rather than on the short side.   Even
so, the very length of the interval brings in its train unexpected pitfalls.   For instance, the light value may be taken, and the lens stop
and shutter set accordingly in the same way as for scenic work, except
that when possible (which is not often) the exposures on topicals should
err rather on the long than the short side.   But suppose after all this,
there is a wait of an hour or more before the actual filming can be
commenced.   In towns, especially, light values alter enormously at
very short intervals with the result that one may as likely as not
be led into bad under-exposure notwithstanding all precautions taken

FIG. 38. SOME CURIOUS PLACES FOR THE CAMERA.

(a) IN CENTRAL AFRICA.   (b) FROM CAPE TO CAIRO ON AN ENGINE.
(c) PHOTOGRAPHING A SHIPWRECKED CREW

Let us turn to the other side of the picture where everything has to be done in a tearing hurry. This is far the most frequent state of things. Here the only chance of coming out well from the ordeal of filming a difficult topical is to have every adjustment that can possibly be made beforehand ready cut and dried by the time one's stand is taken for work. In most cases this will mean that the shutter has been set right, the film threaded, and the take-up adjusted all ready before starting out on the filming expedition, but this is not all. To be smart in topical work there is another adjustment which should on no account be left unmade. Even for scenic studies it is handy enough, though perhaps somewhat liable to lead to slovenliness except in the most expert and conscientious hands, but each and every topical man should have it on his camera. This adjustment is the setting of the lens scale.

Scaling a motion picture lens is really a very simple matter. All it needs is ordinary care to make it accurate, but care must be expended upon the operation, or it will be worse than leaving it undone altogether. It is performed in the following way.

First set the focussing screw or flange-pointer of the lens rack back to its farthest extent ; that is to say, focus the lens back in its jacket as though focussing a distant object, and then continue the motion until the jacket will go no further back. Now pull out the lens bodily from the rack mount. This is, of course, presuming that the instrument is of fairly modern design, where the barrel carrying the lens is separate from the rack mount, and slips in and out of it as do the lenses in kinematograph projectors. Gradually insert the lens barrel more and more back into its mount again, at the same time watching through the focussing tube of the camera to see when some distant object, a far-off tree or chimney-pot, say, becomes sharp. Make certain the distant object is as clear as possible, then scratch a ring on the lens barrel at the exact point where it commences to be covered by its mount. Fig. 39A illustrates the act of scratching

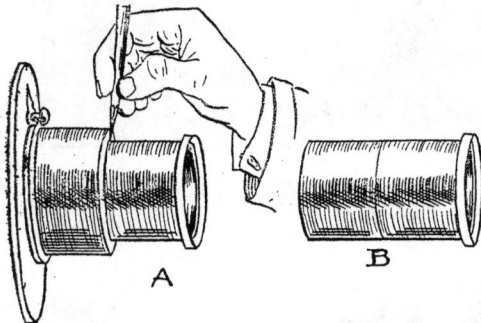

Fig. 39.

the lens tube thus with a sharp-pointed instrument, such as the blade of a knife, while in Fig. 39B, the lens barrel is supposed to have been again withdrawn, showing upon it the scratch so made.

A moment's thought will now convince us that in future, each time the lens setting is put back to its furthest point, and then the barrel pushed in exactly to the point where the scratched line becomes level with the edge of the mount, we shall have a position in which very distant objects, technically spoken of as 'infinity,' will always be sharply focussed. All that now remains to be done is, starting with the above adjustment, rack the lens setting forward till objects at varying known distances (which must be first carefully measured off) are respectively in focus. As each position of the rack mount corresponding with focus for the various distances is determined, we engrave on it the position of adjustment so that it can be again arrived at with certainty. Fig. 40 shows a setting of the focussing flange type with the various 'scale distances' engraved upon the metal plate beneath the movable focussing handle. Where a new camera is being ordered this scaling might be undertaken by the lens makers. Usually it will fall to the lot of the photographer.

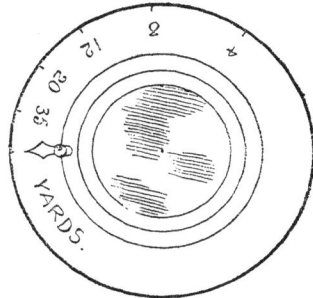

FIG. 40.

For practical purposes, and provided the light is good enough to allow of the use of a stop not larger than f5.6, it is safe for the motion picture man to set his lens at thirty-five yards in lieu of focussing on a topical film, as this will be certain to put any ordinary subject in focus, no matter whether the figures are being taken small or fairly large. Where it becomes a question of working so as to obtain results at very close quarters, say figures three-quarter length, or larger, or where a very large stop has to be used on account of bad weather, the lens scale must be set for nearer objects accordingly, and in this matter the photographer's own judgment is the only criterion. It may be said that the accurate use of the focussing scale, while it may sound simple, is really quite an art in its way. The general rule given as to the medium stop and thirty-five yards setting for all ordinary subjects will, however, be found a real boon to the hurried and worried picture man.

By its means it is possible on numerous occasions to erect the camera, ready threaded and scale focussed, bring the view on to the field of the lens by means of the tripod adjustments and use of the box finder, and begin turning right away, thus often catching a fleeting effect, which would otherwise be entirely missed. The only matter which is here liable to be more or less neglected is the light. But lighting in topical productions is seldom of the best, either as regards direction or exposure. Still, on this matter also, the tied-for-time operator might carry well in his mind the rudiments of the lessons on stop and shutter in their relation to exposure as given in the previous chapter. As to coping with those extra bad lighting conditions which seem to reserve themselves almost exclusively for such occasions as the present, when the film cannot be duplicated, the one and only great way of being ready for the worst is to have the camera fitted with the most rapid lens available. And here, too, the moving picture man has advantages far ahead of his still picture rival.

Considerations of depth of focus (see Appendix) bring it about that the longer the focal length of any lens, the less wide is the largest

aperture at which it will give the required definition in all planes of
a given view. Consequently, it follows that in this matter of wide
aperture—which means rapidity in working—the moving picture
man has things comparatively all his own way. For instance, while
a lens working at f3.5 and having a focus of six inches would be useless
for most things to the still picture photographer on account of the
impossibility of focussing different planes sufficiently well together,
a lens of similar aperture—that is to say, speed—and of just half
the focus is quite feasible in moving picture work, and is indeed
very largely employed. But even this does not sound the limit of
lens rapidity for the kinematograph camera operator. One of the
early moving picture lenses put out by the firm of Dallmeyer had a
working aperture of f2, though its covering capacity might, perhaps,
have been improved upon, while the same firm now supply an instrument working as fast as f1.9. Further particulars of this marvellous lens will be found on page 20. Suffice it to say here
that the actual rapidity of such a lens would be more than four times
that of one working at f4.

Even when a topical has been successfully secured, it must not
be imagined that the battle is over. Having exposed the film, the
next thing—and often a very difficult thing, too—is to get back to
the dark room and place the exposed stock in the hands of the developing staff with the utmost possible speed. This means that in topical
work one must be as careful in making arrangements for the return
journey as for the outward one.

Occasionally, for instance, after a race meeting, it has been known
that taximeter cab drivers have disconnected their taximeters and
flatly refuse to return their fares to their base except at a ruinously
large figure. In such cases it may even be best to pay up and never
wait to haggle ; all depends upon circumstances, as the cab driver
knows only too well. Then, again, return trains may be terribly late
in taking back crowds from the regions where topicals are made,
and the chances of the motion picture man coming in for more or less
bad luck during his experience of such work amount almost to a
certainty. Once again, all the advice that can be given is to set
out with your eyes open, with a just estimate of what may be the
money's worth of an extra hour or half hour gained in getting back
to the developing room, and as a last resource to carry on you an extra
coin or two for unforeseen emergencies. ' Money makes the mare go '
is an ancient proverb which none the less keeps wonderfully fresh
with the years.

And now for a last piece of advice applicable enough in all forms
of outdoor work, but particularly so in the case of the maker of topicals—don't forget to look after the body as well as to attend to the
picture machine. A chilled man can't focus correctly or turn a handle
evenly, leave alone keep all his wits about him for the chances
of the day. Neither can a hungry—or worse still, a thirsty—man
do justice to his work. Never start out on a cold day without a warm

coat and warm gloves. Don't set off upon a long day without food and drink (enough, but not too much of the latter) ready to hand. And if you get wet, change as soon as possible. That last sounds homely, not to say grandmotherly, advice, but a long and varied life teaches that in some respects our grandmothers knew just as much as we do ourselves, and certainly you will come round to that opinion if you find yourself laid up in bed through neglecting the above timely word of warning.

THE KINEMATOGRAPHER ON THE BATTLE FIELD.

ILLUSTRATION 41

"WHILST SHEPHERDS WATCHED THEIR FLOCKS."

FIG. 42.   KALEM'S "FROM MANGER TO CROSS."

Two scenes from the greatest Biblical subject yet produced, taken in the Holy Land at a cost of £20,000.   The careful choice and training of each leading actor and the wonderfully religious feeling pervading the whole story have shown what possibilities exist in producing scripture subjects.

CHRIST AND THE MONEY-CHANGERS.

CHAPTER VI.

————

THE DARK ROOM.

When a length of negative stock has been exposed, the next operation is the development of it. This takes place in a 'dark room,' which is a special workroom fitted with suitable work benches or 'winding tables,' also with the necessary chemical and washing troughs, and having as its sole illumination during development time a suitable number (one or more, according to circumstances) of lamps emitting a feeble pure red light.

First as to this light arrangement. Where work is being conducted on a fairly large scale, nothing can be better than to have suspended from the ceiling, rather high up and over the winding tables and troughs, a number of eight or sixteen candle power electric incandescent lamps, each of them encased in a special ruby glass cover obtainable from the usual trade sources. Before installing the scheme of illumination, it will be necessary to go over the workroom set apart for development and make quite sure that every vestige of extraneous light, as, for instance, daylight, has been prevented from coming into it during film development. Means must also be provided for workers to enter and leave during work hours without light coming in through the open door. This will necessitate the provision of a dark room exit fitted with double doors, having a dark chamber between them to form a light trap. If these doors are set on springs, and the chamber of the light trap be sufficiently long to make sure of the first door closing before the second can be got to and opened, it will be possible for a worker to walk in and out

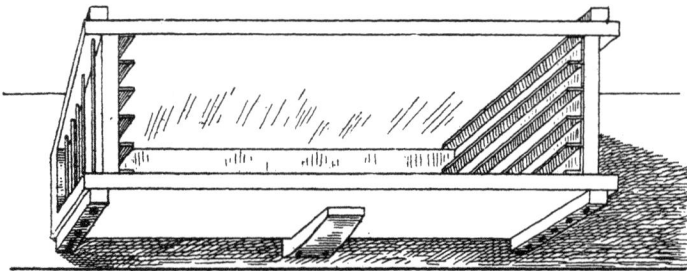

FIG. 43. A TROUGH WITH DIVISIONS.

of the dark room without the least fear of daylight being let in upon any film in course of manipulation.

The troughs necessary for the development of a length of kinematograph film are three in number. They consist of the developing trough proper, a washing trough fitted with syphon arrangement for keeping the water in it constantly changed, and a fixing trough. The usual dimensions of each of these are about thirty inches square by three or four inches deep, varying according to the size of frame used (see later). They are made of glazed earthenware, and are fitted up in a row on brickwork supports at about the height of an ordinary table. The washing trough is the central one, while all three should have water taps over them for purposes of filling, and should also be provided with efficient waste pipes for emptying. In the case of the washing tank, this waste pipe is in addition to the syphon arrangement already referred to, and which latter is used when it is desired to keep the water changed without lowering its level in the trough.

Further, it is absolutely necessary that the developing trough should be provided with means for raising the temperature of its contents in winter time, while the fixing tank may also with advantage be fitted with a similar arrangement. A small gas ring under either

FIG. 44.   IN THE DEVELOPING ROOMS OF A WELL-KNOWN MAKER.

of the two, placed at such a distance from the earthenware as shall introduce no risk of cracking it through too abrupt heating, will answer the purpose, the flame being suitably subdued by placing over the ring such an obvious safeguard as one of the well-known asbestos mats sold for use on stoves and ranges. We also want covers for both the developing and fixing bath. These may be made of wood and fitted with handles for easy rasing. The developer cover, in particular, should fit well and closely, as on this point being observed depends much of the life of the comparatively expensive developing solution.

The above, with the addition of a winding table, gives a fair sketch of the average developing unit of a small commercial concern. Each such unit can tackle one length of negative or positive film at a time, so that the number of them to be installed becomes a matter of simple arithmetic to be decided by the number of hands engaged upon the work of development. Large works will not be in want of any hints on development contained in this book, while for the benefit of the small man (for instance, the picture hall manager who aspires to have his own camera and turn out an occasional local film) there will be further remarks on developing ways and means later on in the chapter.

For the present let us pass on to a fuller description of the winding table, which has already been lightly referred to more than once. We will first proceed to describe the use of this winding table in connection with a well-known system of film development known as the pin-frame system.

In order to develop a roll of exposed film on a ' pin frame,' it is taken out of the take-up box and attached by means of a loop folded in its end to one of the four innermost pins, as figured in illustration 45. A careful look at this illustration, or better still, at the real article, will reveal the fact that the pins are so put into the frame as to admit of a length of film being wound around them spiral fashion, after the manner indicated in Figure 46. This, in fact, is the actual system made use of by the developing hand. The exact manner of going to work to accomplish the winding of the film spiral fashion on the frame will be described presently, but the net result is that once the task is accomplished, the exposed stock is in a state in which it can be handled with comparative ease, for the otherwise limp celluloid is kept practically rigid, so that it is only necessary to immerse the wound frame in any liquid in order that the whole surface of the emulsion may be simultaneously and equally wetted.

In order to wind successfully, the dark room hand must be provided with a suitable amount of clear ' table top ' surface upon which the frames may be laid, and, if necessary, rotated during the process. These wide clear bench spaces are the winding tables alluded to, and they must be of sufficient size and placed

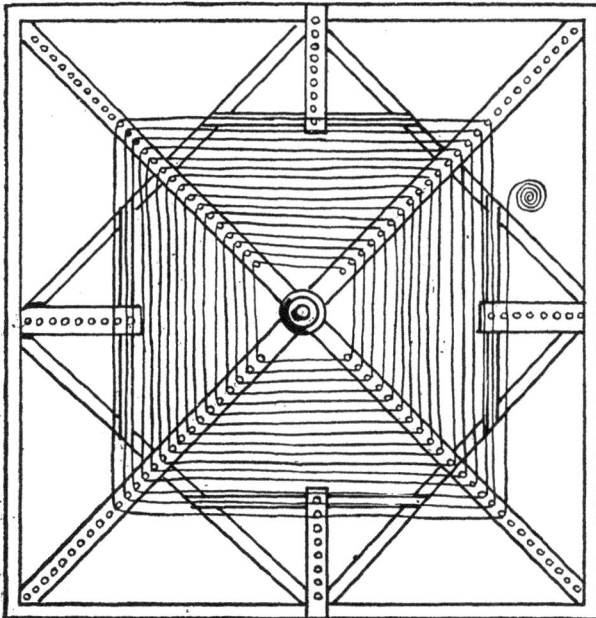

Fig. 45 PIN FRAMES FOR DEVELOPING.

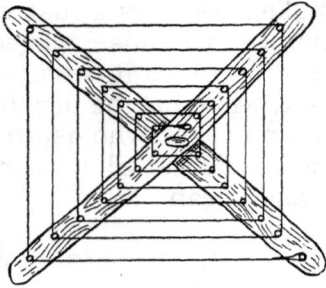

Fig. 46.

at the right height above the floor to accommodate the pin frames employed and also to provide the worker with as much help as possible in what is admittedly a difficult and tedious operation.

The 'pin frames' themselves are usually made of brass, though very soon after use the metal will be found to have become plated over with silver from the developing and fixing baths. A sufficient stock of frames must be laid in to meet all emergencies. Also, provision for storing them when out of use has to be made, and in seeing to this, it is well to remember the pins on them are very delicate and easily bent, while a single bent pin discovered too late, or perhaps not discovered at all, may throw the winding hand out and lead to nasty complications and a messing of the film. Either the wall or ceiling

FIG. 47.

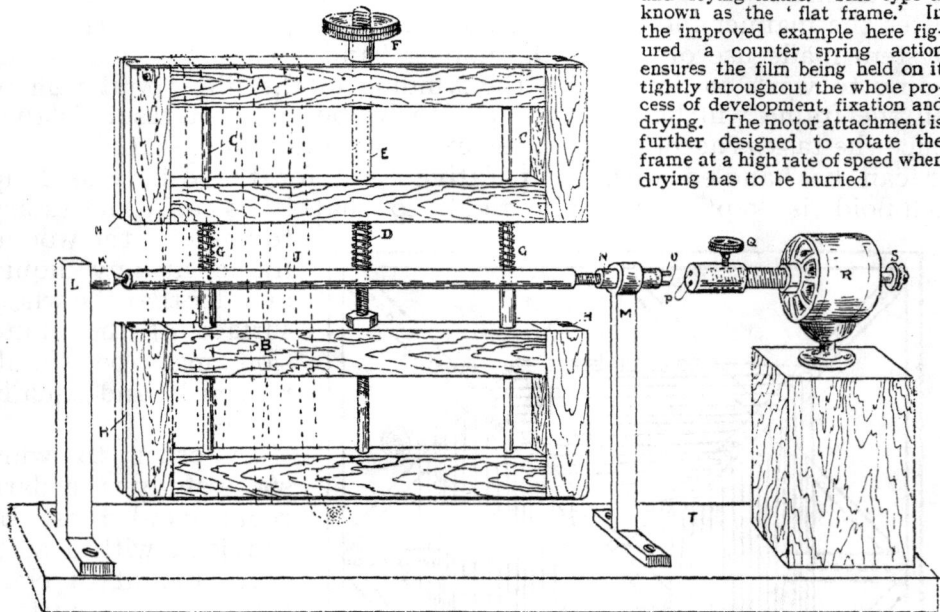

A novel combined developing and drying frame. This type is known as the 'flat frame.' In the improved example here figured a counter spring action ensures the film being held on it tightly throughout the whole process of development, fixation and drying. The motor attachment is further designed to rotate the frame at a high rate of speed when drying has to be hurried.

Action of the frame.—The lowermost portion (as figured) is made firm with the central rod J. The upper portion H slides up and down freely on the guide rods C, B, E, but the wound film (shown in dotted lines) is kept on tension by means of the counter springs G, G, D. The pin attachment connecting the frame with motor screws off during development, which is conducted in a grooved trough. For drying purposes the motor rotates the frame on its axis K, N.

of the dark room are the best places to hang spare frames ; the ceiling only if it is a very high one. Full sized pin frames average somewhat over two feet square and accommodate up to 200 feet of film.

An alternative system is by means of the flat frame, an improved form of which we figure and describe hereunder. Its advantage is in the matter of easy winding, and its disadvantage is its large size for a given capacity of film, as compared with the pin frame.

A short while since, we gave a description of the minimum number of troughs comprising a developing unit. While the three described would be enough for the purpose set forth, it unfortunately happens that more or less often, according to circumstances, the course of development does not run smoothly, in which case after-treatment of the film will have to be resorted to. Consequently there should be at least two other troughs set by themselves, and allocated to such after-treatment methods. Probably the two will do for three or four developing hands to share between them. In fact, they should do, or it means that carelessness in the workroom is becoming the order of the day—unless the business is largely in topicals, in which case anything is to be expected. The place for after-treatment baths is,

FIG. 48. A ROOM OF PRINTING MACHINES.

however, not the dark room, but another workroom arranged so that it may be partially darkened or well lit at will.

Before closing the description of the developing room, it will be necessary to say that the winding tables must be placed well away from all chemical and other baths so as to avoid fear of splashing the dry film. The opposite side of the room is where they should be. Also, at least one clock must be provided, and in order that it shall be of use in the semi-darkness, it is necessary to have a red light burning before its face, or preferably have the face transparent, with a red light burning behind it, and numerals painted so as to show out dark against light, after the manner of an ordinary illuminated street clock. This, and the provision of space for film boxes, completes the dark room fittings as far, at any rate, as necessity is concerned. It is not advised that any portion of this apartment shall be set apart for storage and weighing of chemicals. All that side of the developing business should be kept to a special chemical ' room,' which should be a small one lit by ordinary day or artificial light.

We have treated the developing fittings so far from the ordinary commercial point of view. Let us now say a few words upon the experimental or 'one man' kinematograph dark room, since this aspect of the developing problem is sure to be of service to some, at any rate, of the readers of the present volume.

Perhaps it is safe to suppose for a start that in the case of the small one man show, expense and weight of fittings are both items to be considered. Probably the dark room may not be on the ground floor, in which case the installation in it of brickwork supported earthen troughs would be a difficult, and even dangerous, proceeding. For such, the necessary baths may be fashioned out of zinc, excepting the fixing bath, for which sheet lead is the material to use. Naturally, such troughs will not last one-tenth of the time the other and heavier sort would. Still, they will suffice, and that is the great point. Then take the matter of size. This is important in experimental work.

Where pin-frame development is employed, there is no need for full-sized frames, constructed for winding on whole 165 feet or 200 feet rolls, as the case may be ; 100 feet frames are much smaller (under twenty inches square). Moreover, they can be obtained made so as to take to pieces like the blades of scissors, for the convenience of picture men touring their own developing kit in foreign countries. When using such half-size frames upon a full-length of film, it is, of course, necessary to cut the exposed stock in two. This, however, need cause no noticeable break in the continuity of the picture, provided both halves of the length are similarly developed and afterwards carefully joined together previous to printing. Full details of how to accomplish this joining up will be found elsewhere.

The provision of at least one suitable photographic red light, as also of a winding table and dark room clock which may be seen during development, is still a necessity. Previous remarks also hold on the matter of making provision near the winding table for stacking both full and empty take-up boxes, as well as a small supply of tins of film stock sufficient for present needs. The dark room is not the place to store unexposed film stock in bulk.

The foregoing is a fair description of paraphernalia for film development on a small to medium scale, but before closing the chapter, we feel a warning must be added to the above. Some firms dealing in kinematograph supplies include in their catalogues ' developing drums suitable for the amateur and small worker.' Accompanying this announcement there is generally a cut showing a revolving roller half submerged in a semi-circular trough after the style of the tiny arrangement of the sort actually employed by users of toy hand cameras for the development of their snapshots. However satisfactory such an elementary description of developing drum may be in the hands of the snapshotter, its applicability to kinematograph film only figures as a matter of history. No one in the know uses such an arrangement now for the very best of reasons—it is an inferior system to all others, and one wherein certainty of working is reduced to a minimum. When we see crude kinematograph film developing drums included in the apparatus catalogues of reputable firms, we can only hope they remain listed through mere oversight, and not through any mean attempt to spoof those not in the know out of the ranks of an admittedly comparatively closed profession.

A drum is used in kinematography and a very large one, too, but it is not employed for development. It is a huge unwieldy affair (generally speaking) fashioned in skeleton out of laths of wood, and its purpose is to accommodate film during drying. But this item of the film producer's apparatus will be dealt with further when its turn comes.

FIG. 49.—DRYING ROOM IN THE BRITISH AND COLONIAL CO.'S ESTABLISHMENT.

FIG. 50.—ONE OF THE PRINTING ROOMS AT THE HEPWORTH WORKS

A STRIKING FRONTAGE.

FIG 51.   EXTERIOR AND INTERIOR OF TYPICAL PICTURE THEATRES

A HANDSOME AND ROOMY AUDITORIUM.

CHAPTER VII.

———

DEVELOPMENT AND DEVELOPERS.

Let us start by taking a bird's-eye view of the process upon which we are about to embark.

The first thing to do before developing is to get the baths compounded and brought to working temperature. Development proper then starts upon a test piece or pieces of the particular length of exposed film stock to be taken in hand. This simply means that a few inches of the end of the exposed roll is snipped off with a pair of scissors and plunged into the developer for a given time. Note in connection with the above, the use of the clock in the dark room, and consequent necessity for its installation. When the time fixed upon in the worker's mind as that which shall be allowed for development of this test piece has elapsed, the short film length is fished out of the bath, rinsed in plain water, and transferred to the fixing solution. When fixed, it is again rinsed, and may then be taken out of the dark room and examined by full day or ordinary artificial light. A single glance will be enough to inform a skilled developing hand as to whether the time allowed to the test strip has been right, or whether this must be altered when dealing with the major portion of the subject from which it was snipped. From such information it should be a simple matter to proceed to wind on the remainder of the film roll and develop it correctly. Such is the technique of the dark room, simple, yet tricky, as one's first attempts will soon serve to show. And now to go over the ground again in detail :—

DEVELOPING BATHS FOR NEGATIVE FILM.

Any bath suitable for negative development in still view work will also serve the purposes of kinematography as far as the actual production of a visible image upon the exposed film is concerned. The amount of developer used in the film developing trough being large (often sixty pints or so for a full-sized trough) it becomes a matter of practical importance that the bath shall be so compounded as to be able to be used over and over again at intervals of hours, or even days, until exhausted. Consequently, developing formulae for motion picture work are usually those in which the keeping qualities of the ready compounded bath are of a satisfactory nature. Kinematograph negative developers should, moreover, be so adjusted as to give a fairly plucky result (one in which the pictures show well-marked contrasts) while yet the reducing power is sufficiently great for dealing at a pinch with considerable under exposure. Perhaps he best of all developers, taking everything into consideration, is the well-known Metol Hydroquinone, compounded in single solution form :

METOL HYDROQUINONE DEVELOPER.

Metol	2 ozs.
Hydroquinone	2 ozs.
Soda Sulphite	1½ lbs.
Soda Carbonate	¾ lb.
Pot. Metabisulphite	1½ ozs.
Water	60 pints.

There is a special way of mixing the above ingredients, which must be strictly adhered to, or it may be found difficult to get them all into proper solution. Therefore proceed thus :—

First dissolve the soda carbonate and sulphite in half-a-dozen pints or so of warm water. Crush up the metabisulphite small, and make a solution of it in another pint or two of water. Add this to the dissolved sulphite and carbonate. Lastly, stir into the whole the metol and hydroquinone, dissolved in four or five pints of warm water, and proceed to make up the bath to the required sixty pints.

NORMAL DEVELOPMENT.

The above bath will be found excellent for the general development of any good, clean-working film stock, always provided exposure of the film in the camera has not been over done. The temperature at which to use it is somewhere about 66 F., which temperature should invariably be ascertained by means of a thermometer before commencing development. If the worker should find the developer tends in his hands to give too soft a type of negative, the remedy (except where over-exposure is the cause of the trouble) is to cut down the Metol and increase the amount of Hydroquinone proportionately in future brews. One ounce Metol and three ounces Hydroquinone will tend to greater contrast in the resulting negatives, while at the same time considerably cutting down the expense of the bath.

UNDER EXPOSURE.

Under exposure in the film, showing itself in the production of "soot and whitewash" negative pictures with choked up high lights and empty shadows, is combatted by increasing the metol content. Another way of adjusting matters which does not necessitate meddling with the bath for future batches of stock, is to warm it up to about 75 F., at which temperature it will be found to work both more quickly and much more softly. At the same time the increased temperature will tend to bring out any latent "chemical fog" there may be in the emulsion, and where the film stock is not of the best, this may show itself as a light grey cloud, affecting pictures and perforations alike, and more or less defeating the intention of such " forced development " by clogging the very fine shadow detail it is sought to coax out.

OVER EXPOSURE.

Over exposure of the film is dealt with by treating the developer— be it the above or almost any other formula—in quite a different manner. What we do here is to add to the bath a chemical " restrainer," possessing particular action in the matter of influencing slow and contrasty development.

This chemical is Bromide of Potash. The proportion in which to add it to the sixty pint developing bath may be anything from a couple of drachms to as many ounces, according as a slight " clearing " effect or a strong retarding and contrast increasing action is desired. A very satisfactory way of developing very much over-exposed stock is to treat it in the developing trough usually reserved for print development, and which will be found described in the chapter on developing positive film. Yet another and most excellent way of tackling the difficulty of making the best of widely varying exposure is to have two separate developing troughs in the dark room unit. These are placed side by side, and labelled plainly in such a way as to allow of no mistake in the dim red light. One bath contains a developer of the sort already given, and which will give a satisfactory result in the case of normal or slight under-exposure, while the second trough contains a special contrast producing bath for treating over-exposed stock :—

CONTRAST PRODUCING BATH.

Glycin ...	...	...	...	...	...	8 ozs.
Sod. Sulphite	...	...	...	...	...	$1\frac{1}{2}$ lbs.
Pot. Carbonate	...	...	...	...	...	$2\frac{1}{2}$ lbs.
Pot. Bromide	...	...	...	...	...	1 oz.
Water ...	...	...	...	...	...	60 pints.

The above is also an excellent print developing bath. If found too sluggish in action for the particular brand of film stock in use, the Bromide may be diminished. The converse also applies. Development with Glycin, though slow, produces magnificently clear negatives. For normal to slight over-exposure, use at 66 F. to 70 F ; for great over-exposure, cool down still further. The Glycin bath keeps better than any other, but its first cost is high.

The power of Glycin to produce contrast is heightened, also the time of development greatly diminished, by the addition to the bath of half an ounce of Caustic Soda. The keeping properties of the developer are, however, thereby greatly diminished.

We append a formula for an alternative quick-working negative developer, and which has the advantage of employing the somewhat cheaper developing agent, Eikonogen, in place of Metol, so that it may, therefore, be preferred by some.

EIKONOGEN HYDROQUINONE DEVELOPER.

Soda Sulphite	1 lb.
Potassium Carbonate	1 lb.
Potassium Metabisulphite	1 oz.
Potassium Bromide	½ oz.
Hydroquinone	6 ozs.
Eikonogen	3 ozs.
Water	60 pints.

The same general directions apply to the use of the above developer as to the Metol Hydroquinone bath. So much, then for developing formulae. As has been said before, any single solution bath that will keep, and which is applicable to still view work, may be experimented with by the motion picture worker with every chance of more or less success. But since the inclusion of endless alternative solutions would only serve still further to swell out the all too rapidly growing proportions of the present volume, while anyone on the look out for developer variations can always find them by the score in works on ordinary photography, we will make no attempt at ringing the changes on developing formulae any further than we have already gone.

Fortunately, fixing baths are all much alike. Below is a composition for one which will serve all purposes well.

ACID FIXING BATH.

" Hypo "	20 lbs.
Potassium Metabisulphite	8 ozs.
Water	60 pints.

Use quite hot water for dissolving the " hypo," as this salt has the curious property of cooling water down very rapidly during process of solution. The Metabisulphite should, as before, be dissolved by itself, and added after the other chemical has melted in the water. By the way, some readers may be interested to note, in passing, that " hypo "—short for Hyposulphite of Sodium— is really only a nickname for the chemical to which it usually refers, and is not either in its abbreviated or longer form, a proper chemical designation at all. " Hypo " is actually, and chemically speaking, Sodium Thiosulphate, and the writer has never seen any satisfactory explanation of how it came to be called by the epithet denoting a totally different substance which is never, by any chance, used in photography.

HOW TO MAKE THE TESTS.

We have our baths compounded at last, and it is presumed they are also brought to the requisite temperature of 66 F., and that the washing trough has been allowed to fill with plain water. All is now in readiness for developing the test strips.

THE APPEARANCE OF GOOD AND BAD NEGATIVES.

We have tried by means of these half-tone blocks to give a comprehensive idea of negatives of various descriptions

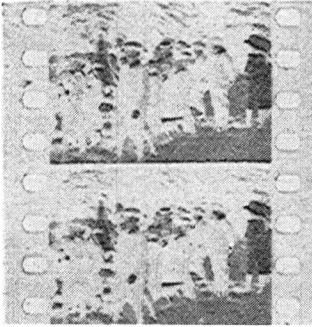

FIG. 52.
Under exposed and under developed.

FIG. 53.
Hopeless under exposure. Note film perforations fogged through forced development.

FIG. 54.
Under exposed and over developed (soot and whitewash).

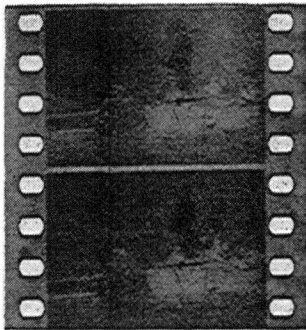

FIG. 55.
Very bad negative, under exposed and scratched by a dirty gate to the camera.

FIG. 56.
Over exposed but correctly developed. Result flat.

FIG. 57.
Correctly exposed. Soft (rather short) development.

FIG. 58.
Exposure correct, but film much over developed.

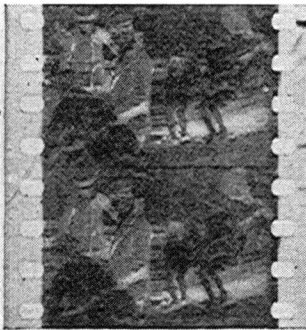

FIG. 59.
Correct exposure. Full (rather long) development.

FIG. 60.
Film fogged by daylight entering film box.

Bring the take-up box, containing its roll of exposed film stock into the dark room, remove the cover in the red light, and pick up the end of the film between finger and thumb without, however, removing the roll bodily from the box. Now snip off two lengths, each of them about six inches, and put back the cover of the film-box in place, so that the bulk of the stock is once again protected from all chance of fogging. Next, raise the cover of the developing bath (where two alternative developers are in use, choose the one believed to be most suited to exposure conditions as noted in the camera man's note book) and immerse both strips bodily, taking the time of so doing, by the dark room clock. If the bath is fairly new, and reasonably quick acting and the conditions generally seem about normal, one of the test pieces may be given ten minutes development, while the next has twenty. Do not let either of them remain long during the process without a gentle stirring of the solution to ensure fair and equal action upon the emulsion. As each test piece comes to the end of its appointed development time, it is rinsed in the washing trough, and transferred to the fixer, where five minutes' immersion should be amply sufficient to complete the necessary chemical treatment. The method of judging whether fixation is complete is, however, as follows :—

Turn the film round and look at the celluloid side. If it is not completely fixed, the emulsion will be seen from the back to retain some at least, of its peculiar milky appearance, characteristic of the original undeveloped film stock. Upon complete fixation all that look goes, and the film takes to itself the usual clear appearance of an ordinary kinematograph positive, except that in a negative film the objects which are light in nature will appear dark, and *vice versa.* Thus a good negative of a snow scene should show both foreground and sky nearly black, while dark tree trunks and such like would appear white. The general and distinctive characteristics of both good and bad negatives will, however, be plainer upon reference to the plate on the previous page giving reproductions of typical developed test strips.

Once the worker knows what a good negative should appear like, it will be but a matter of moments to see whether either of his test pieces approximates to the ideal, and if not, in what way it may be improved. Suppose, for instance, the ten minute piece is not quite " plucky " enough, while the high lights in the twenty minute piece —and which high lights will be rendered dark, remember—are choked, then it follows that a development time between the one and the other is what is needed. Thus fifteen minutes would here be the required development time for the main portion of the given subject. Or again, both test pieces may show over-development, coupled with a want of contrast. In that case over-exposure is the cause, and remedy will lie in the special restrained and alternative developing bath, if such a one is kept handy, or if not, recourse must be had to a liberal dose of Potassium Bromide in the normal working developer. In either of the latter cases further test strips must be developed under the new conditions until the best way of treating the particular film length has been arrived at.

Developing Extreme Under Exposure.

If the twenty minute strip shows want of density, it means one of two things ; either the bath is old and wants renewing, in which case it will be found on examination to have gone brownish in colour or the negative in question has been greatly under-exposed, the treatment then being to warm the bath to at least 75 F., or even higher if the gelatine of the film will stand it (80 F., is the highest one ever dares go to). A test piece is now allowed to remain in the warmed solution for half to three-quarters of an hour, that time being about the longest the emulsion will stand in a warmed quick-acting developer without bad chemical fog. If, on withdrawal, a satisfactory image does not show itself, the subject must be looked upon as well nigh hopeless. A chance for it may still lie in the after treatment known as intensification. Develop up all you can, fix and wash according to the directions about to be given in this chapter, after which turn to the chapter on after treatment wherein intensification methods will be found. This gives an idea, at least, as to how to be guided in the treatment of the film from examination of the test strip. And now comes the question of developing the main portion of the subject according to its revealed requirements.

In the case of pin frame development, the film has first to be wound over the pins. This must be done in order to treat successfully the full length subject in the limited compass of a comparatively small developing trough. The following is a suitable method of setting about it :—

To Wind a Pin Frame.

First, take from a box of them, which should always be handy in the dark room, a couple of steel pins. Don't try to use the common tin ones, as they bend and cause a lot of trouble. Steel ones are on sale at any draper's. These pins should be stuck in the lapel of the coat, where they can easily be got at. Now place a pin frame on the winding table and again remove the door of the charged take-up box, but this time the contained film is bodily drawn out, still in the form of a roll, having for its centre its internal spring hub. Take the roll in the left hand, with the film winding away upwards from the bottom of it, in which position the celluloid side of the unrolled end portion of film will be towards you when this is being drawn upward, as in figure 61. The very top of the film end is now folded down and backward for about an inch, and one of the pins run through the two thicknesses thus forming a loop as in figure 62. It is this loop which is next slipped over one of the four innermost pins of the pin frame, taking care that the way it is placed on and direction of winding are such that the **celluloid and not the emulsion side of the film shall lie against the pins.**

The business now before us consists in getting the film correctly wound on the pins, in spiral form, with due regard to the proper ultilisation of each pin once, and none of them twice over, as we go round and round. Now this winding may be set about in two ways, either the pin frame may be suffered to remain stationary upon the winding table, while the film roll is passed round from hand to hand, or the film may be held more or less stationary in one hand, while the pin frame is rotated with the other. In the latter case it will be necessary to have a spindle of suitable length (a large nail with its head cut off will do) driven into the table so that the central hole in the frame will fit easily over it. If the frame is arranged so that one of its four arms sticks out somewhat from the table top when placed over the spindle, it will be an easy matter to steady its movements as required by allowing the body to come in the way of this projecting

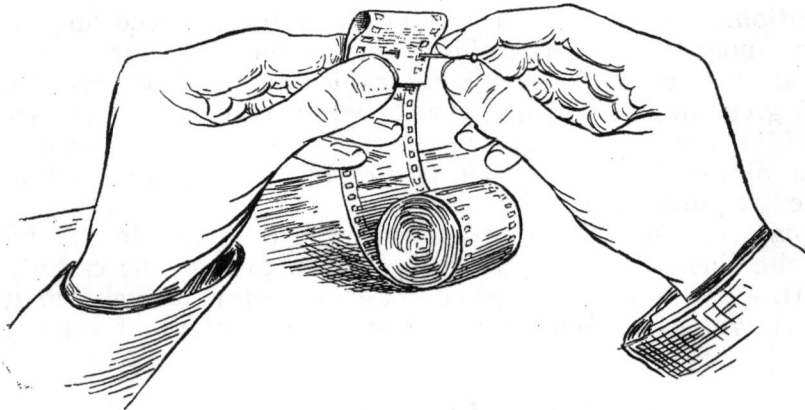

FIG. 62.

FIG. 61.

arm while the film is in the act of being placed over the pins. The body is drawn slightly backward, while the disengaged hand gives the frame a quarter turn. Then, once more the motion is similarly checked for further winding. Such, at any rate, is a simple mode of tackling the winding difficulty, which may otherwise come upon the novice as somewhat formidable. In any case the thing is to remember that what we have to do is to get the frame wound tightly, and with the film right way about, so that the celluloid and not the emulsion side touches the pins. We must learn to do this, and to do it in reasonable time, and for that there is nothing like practice with spoilt or old positive film till skill is acquired.

When the subject length has been wound off, or in the case of two or more subjects being taken on the same length, when the film has been wound to the point where a scissor snip or punched out hole announces the fact of a change of picture, we proceed to complete operations by making a second loop with our second pin, for which purpose we cut the film at the punch mark, if necessary. This second loop is slipped over the nearest pin, making sure that no slackness of film is allowed in the process, and the frame is then wound and ready for immersion in the trough.

EXPERT FRAMING.

Though the foregoing method of framing film is given at length as being the simpler for the beginner at dark room operations, the expert hand usually keeps his pin frame stationary, and standing before him tilted to an angle of 45 deg. upon a winding table constructed so to hold it. After the making of the first film loop and affixing it over one of the innermost four pins, the winding is accomplished by passing the film roll round and round from hand to hand while getting the film on the frame. This latter method, while more difficult of acquirement than the first is favoured in dark room practice on account of the rapidity of framing, which comes of its constant use.

The secret of managing the wound and wetted film from this point is to remember that the agency of the developer and subsequent washing and fixing baths will cause not only the emulsion, but also the celluloid base itself to swell. Hence, even in the case of the tightest wound film, the commencement of development is bound to cause it to become more or less slack upon its supports, and so it must be treated accordingly. For instance, in order to obtain equal development and freedom from the effects of air bells accidentally adhering to the emulsion after its immersion, it will be necessary to keep the frame agitated more or less from the start. On the other hand, too much of this while the gelatine coating is still in an only half saturated and therefore sticky condition will cause the outer turns of film to sag together, producing patches of undeveloped film here and there. The matter is one calling for both care and practice in manipulation.

At the same time a few ideas may be given as to a method of going to work, which meets the case. In the first place, when making up the developer see that there is enough of it in the bath to give a full half an inch depth above the top edge of the immersed film. If this is attended to it will be found that immediately after the first introduction of the frame into the trough one can raise it slightly once or twice, letting it fall back again with a slight bump upon the trough's bottom, and thus detaching all large air bells effectually. Care must be taken when doing this not to lift it to a point at which any portion of the wound film is out of the developer. Nor after the first ten seconds should any further treatment be given the film in the way of such agitation for quite another minute after development starts.

AVOIDING AIR BELLS.

At the end of that time take hold of the frame by its central boss and lift it bodily out of the trough once or twice. plunging it back again each time. This action will deal with all air bells which may happen to be remaining, and at the same time set up currents in the developer which will stir it effectually. By repeating the up and down treatment, say once each five minutes, a successful development should be assured. Upon expiration of the appointed time the frame is finally lifted out and given a similar agitation in the washing trough for a space of about twenty seconds or so, after which it goes into the fixing trough.

Agitate the film again in this, once or twice, leaving it in altogether for ten minutes, after which it will be thoroughly fixed. A final wash in the washing trough, lasting over at least an hour in ordinary cases (a quarter of the time may be made to serve for topicals) completes the cycle through which negative film should normally pass ere it finds its way to the drying drum.

WASHING THE FILM.

Since the object of this last washing is solely to free the wet gelatine of the " hypo " it has absorbed out of the fixing bath, it is of the utmost importance that the water changing arrangement should be properly installed, and of an efficient character. In the case of work on any considerable scale, it will be found necessary, in practice, to build special troughs or tanks for this final washing process, so as to avoid having to hang up the work in the dark room for an hour or more at a time after the fixation of each film length. Extra washing troughs or tanks for this purpose will not have to be placed in the dark room at all Any convenient corner will suit. The syphon arrangement, already

Fig. 63 shows a suitable washing arrangement for a number of pin frames at a time. B is a tank in which the frames can be immersed and held in a sloping position by suitable rails and stops, as illustrated. The water tap A provides the washing water flowing into the top of the tank, while the syphon C removes impure and used water from the bottom. Now were C a simple syphon, one of two things would happen when it started (which takes place automatically by the tank becoming full, since the top bend of C is below the level of the tank walls). Either the syphon would take off less water than the tap supplied (supposing it to be a syphon of small bore) in which case there would be a general

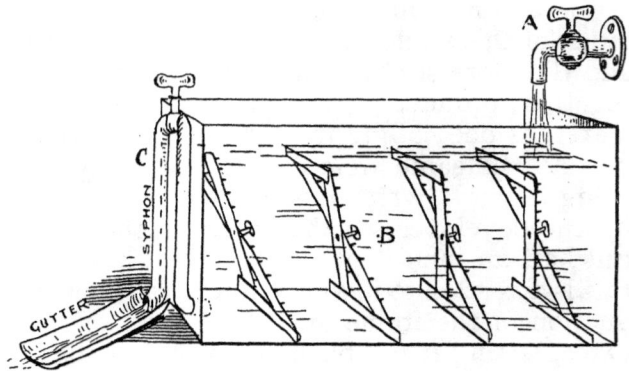

FIG. 63.—SYPHON WASHING TROUGH.

overflow, or else if the syphon were of greater capacity than the delivery the reverse would occur, and the tank would empty itself completely. In practice, both these eventualities are avoided by having a small air inlet at the top of the bend of the syphon tube. This inlet is controlled by a tap and is normally left open.

Under such circumstances the syphon acts as a simple waste water pipe, with the exception that it is fed from the impure water at the bottom of the tank, thus causing efficient circulation of the contents. When, on the contrary, it is required to clean out "B," as should, of course, be done periodically, this is accomplished by closing the trap controlling the air inlet to the syphon and turning on "A" full. "C" now acts its part as a true syphon, and by turning off "A" once again after the overflow has once started, the tank will empty itself completely.

Should "C" show signs of becoming choked with gelatine from the emulsion of the films washed in the tank—as strangely enough does happen occasionally, even though it is only cold water which is used for washing—the treatment is to open the air inlet and insert a small funnel, down which boiling water is poured till the obstruction is cleared away.

referred to, is, however, of the greatest importance in the process of efficient washing. Accordingly, a diagram is here given showing in detail the system employed, and from which it is hoped the reader fitting up negative developing plant will have no difficulty in making his own adaptations to individual requirements.

This completes all that need be said regarding the extremely important item of washing kinematograph film, and be it set down here, neither negative nor positive stock which has been scamped in this particular, can possibly remain in good condition for any length of time. Even when a valuable topical negative has had to be unduly hurried for its first printing a second and thorough washing of it should be undertaken at the earliest opportunity, if it is likely to be of value on a future occasion.

To Ensure Thorough Fixation.

One word, also, on a subject intimately connected with the above since it concerns the other great factor governing permanency in photographic work—the activity of the fixing bath. If the fixing bath is not active, fixing cannot be thorough no matter how much it is prolonged, and no film imperfectly fixed will ever remain permanently clean and free from stain. Therefore, adopt the following rule in the matter of checking the fixing bath, and do not depart from it.

Always give your test strip, by which you find the development period for the film subjects, one definite time in which to complete fixation, and let this time be exactly five minutes. Also see that the strips get an occasional stir up in the bath, which latter should not be below 60 F., at least. While such time suffices completely to clear away all visible milkiness from the short test lengths of film, it may confidently be reckoned that double the period, or ten minutes, will be ample fixation for the regular wound lengths. The moment a test strip shows signs of being under fixed after five minutes' immersion throw the bath away and compound another. Thus can one be certain of keeping on the right side of fixation.

Film drying, though seemingly simple, is considered by the writer worthy of a little chapter to itself, and this it will have in due course.

The formula subjoined immediately underneath is in use by a noted firm of film producers for the production of contrasty negatives, or of somewhat soft prints giving very full detail :

Hydroquinone..	5 oz.
Metol	3 oz.
Soda Carbonate (Cryst.)	2 lbs.
Soda Sulphite (Cryst.)	3 lbs.
Citric Acid	$\frac{1}{2}$ oz.
Potassium Bromide	$\frac{1}{4}$ oz.
Metabisulphite of Potassium	2 oz.
Water	65 pints

Another strong developing bath is given below. This one has the characteristic of developing both negatives and prints to a vigorous density and in a minimum of time. Two to three minutes development at 65 to 70 degrees is usually sufficient in either case. On account of its quickness and handiness for either negatives or positives it is in use for topical work in the developing rooms of a firm whose name were it mentioned would be recognised as a household word :

Metol	3 oz.
Hydroquinone..	1 lb.
Pot. Metabisulphite	2 oz.
Citric Acid	2 oz.
Pot. Bromide	$\frac{1}{4}$ oz.
Soda Sulphite (Cryst.)	4 lbs.
Soda Carbonate	2 lbs.
Water	65 pints

FIG. 64.   AN AWKWARD SCENIC SUBJECT.

CHAPTER VIII.

POSITIVE MAKING OR PRINTING.

So far in this first section of our present work we have dealt with the practical side of taking and developing kinematograph negatives. In the negative the respective values of light and dark are reversed. In order to bring these values back to what they are in nature, it is necessary to " print " a positive from our original negative picture. It is not difficult to follow the reason for the reversal of tones in a kinematograph negative when we remember that the photographic image is formed of a deposit produced by the action of light coming through the camera lens. Naturally such a deposit will form most where the light action is strongest ; in other words, the lightest natural objects will give the darkest deposits on the developed film. Thus the reason of the freakish appearance of the negative is fully explained. At the same time, we all know that in both the still photograph and kinematograph film as exhibited, all this topsy-turvy-dom of tone values has been got over. Also it will be common knowledge that a scene has been photographed only once in order for many copies of it to be easily obtainable.

It is to the process of " printing " that we must look for the explanation of both these latter facts, and thus the art of " printing " or positive making takes rank in all photographic work, whether moving picture or otherwise, as second only in importance to the production of the negative itself.

THE PRINCIPLE DESCRIBED.

The " printing," or production of a positive from a photographic negative can be very simply described. In the first place a sensitive photographic surface has to be provided capable of being acted upon by some suitable light to an extent enough and not too much for convenience sake when worked under printing conditions. Once we have such a sensitive surface of suitably toned down light recording capacity— known technically as a positive printing surface or " positive stock "—the actual *modus operandi* is of the easiest. All that is necessary is to place a negative over the face of the positive emulsion and then expose the latter to light through the former. In this way the image upon the negative will act as a shield of variable density, allowing more or less light to penetrate and act upon the positive stock, according to the opacity of its various parts. Thus, suppose a negative of a target be placed before a piece of positive stock and light then allowed to stream upon the face of it. A target consists in its simplest form of a white outer rim and black bull's eye, so that in the negative these will be the other way about. That is to say, in it the bull's eye will be transparent and the outer rim opaque. Consequently when the light strikes the face of this negative, behind which a piece of positive stock is pressed, the rays will be able to penetrate through the centre or bull's eye portion, while being kept from getting through the black deposit constituting the outer rim. Now suppose the exposed positive to be developed. Naturally, the part which has seen light will be the only part to take a deposit of silver, and that part will now be the area which lay behind the transparent negative image of the bull's eye. The rest of the positive having been shielded from light action by the deposit on the negative will refuse to develop at all. So by process of printing we get once again an accurate reproduction of the target as it was originally, not a negative this time, but a picture showing the black centre and outer rim white as it ought to be, in fact a positive or "print." Further, since by putting the negative to the foregoing use it has not been altered of itself in the least, it follows that we shall be able to repeat the process of making duplicate positives as long as we wish, or as long as the supply of positive stock holds out.

That is just the process we have to embark upon in order to get from our kinematograph negatives useable pictures, showing correct tone values. And now to actual ways and means.

Positive and Negative Film Stock Differentiated.

Positive stock for kinematography is sold in rolls, just as is the similar article used for negative production. Film, whether positive or negative, looks practically speaking identical to the eye. Experts can distinguish unexposed positive from negative film by the fact that the former has a rather more glazed surface to the emulsion. Viewed in daylight undeveloped positive emulsion is of a far fainter cream colour than in the case of negative. This latter test can of course only be applied at the expense of spoiling the length of film so viewed. In reality, positive film is of much less sensitiveness to light than the negative stock. It also has the quality of producing great density in the shadows with comparative ease, while at the same time preserving clearness and purity of high lights far better than would negative stock under like circumstances. In fact, to sum it up in a few words, whereas negative film is suited primarily for negative making, positive film is manufactured solely for use in printing. Both might be used for the process for which they are not intended and both would then work in an inferior manner.

Let us turn to the consideration of how we are going to take in hand the actual printing of a kinematograph positive. Firstly we shall have to contrive some arrangement by which the dry negative film may be held close against the positive stock, while light is allowed to stream through the successive pictures on the former, so as to produce positives accurately spaced and equally exposed upon the latter. Practically speaking, there is only one discovered way of satisfactorily accomplishing this task. That is by employing an arrangement similar in principle to the escapement of a kinematograph camera whereby positive and negative film are pulled face to face through a gate behind the mask of which a light burns, thus effecting exposure. In order to make use of the positive film in this way it is imperative that it shall be perforated as was the negative stock.

Such an apparatus as the above for automatically exposing positive film behind the negative, is known by the name of a " printer." Formerly " printers " on the market were of two kinds—the continuously moving film " printer " (in which negative and positive film were drawn slowly and continuously face to face before an illuminated slit) and the " step by step printer." The step by step system is the one already referred to in which a form of claw movement actuates the two films on an intermittent principle. Now-a-days the latter class of instrument has, by common consent, taken the film as the only really reliable one. It is, therefore, the sole kind we shall trouble to describe in detail. The arrangement of the various parts of a " step by step printer " are shown diagrammatically in Figure 65.

PRINTER MECHANISM.

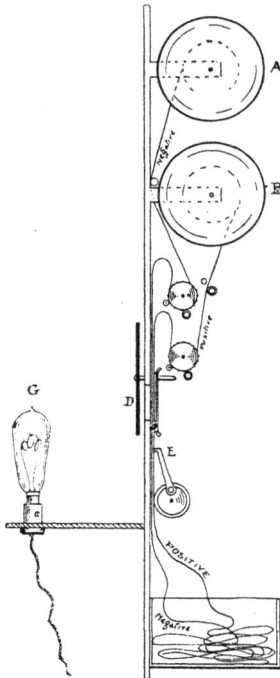

FIG. 65.

Here " A " represents the roll of negative film to be printed from while " B " is the positive stock to be printed upon. Next come sprockets over which the films pass and which give a continuous feed of the faced films to the gate " D," while the claw " E " pulls the films down by means of the now familiar intermittent escapement. " G " is a light source which is in practice suitably enclosed so as not to shine forth broadcast in the dark room where printing is to take place, though here the lamp is represented as open, while there is fitted between it and the gate a revolving shutter exactly similar to and having the precise function of the shutter of a kinematograph camera, namely, to cut off light periodically from the light source and so prevent its striking the film during " change." It will follow that after each pull of the claw " E " as the shutter rotates out of the way of the lamp, light will fall upon the negative behind the gate mask. Passing through the silver negative deposit in ratio to the density of its various parts,

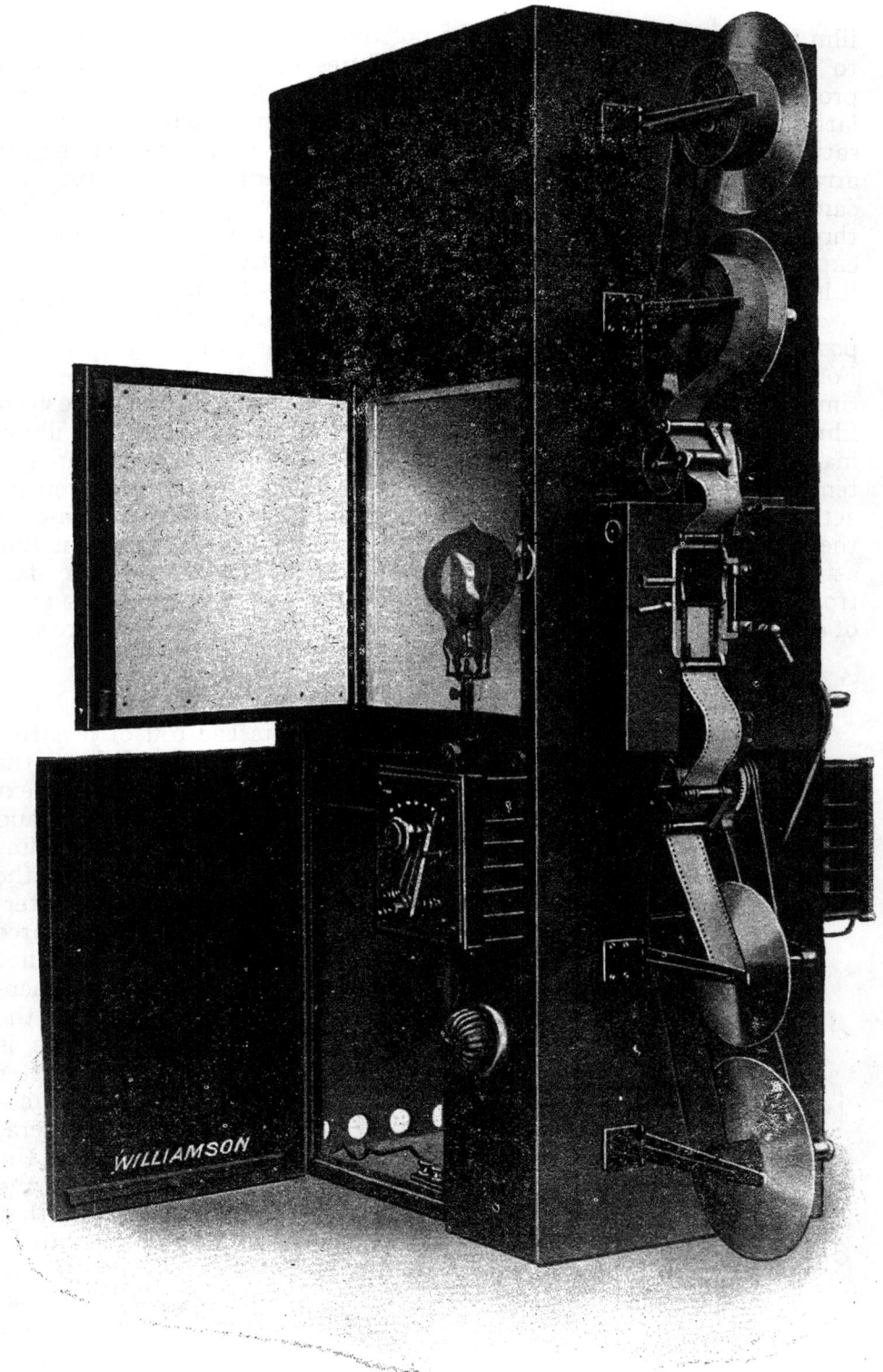

FIG. 66. WILLIAMSON'S MOTOR-DRIVEN PRINTER.

this light will correspondingly affect the sensitive positive film behind and held close against the negative. After exposure lasting a suitable time (say the one-sixteenth or one-twentieth of a second) the continuing action of the mechanism will cause the shutter to cut off the light again, after which the claw " E " once more operates the double thickness of film, so bringing a new negative picture and unexposed positive surface before the mask for exposure.

The annexed plate (Fig. 67) gives an excellent idea of an actual commercial type of " printer " designed to be self-contained and suit-

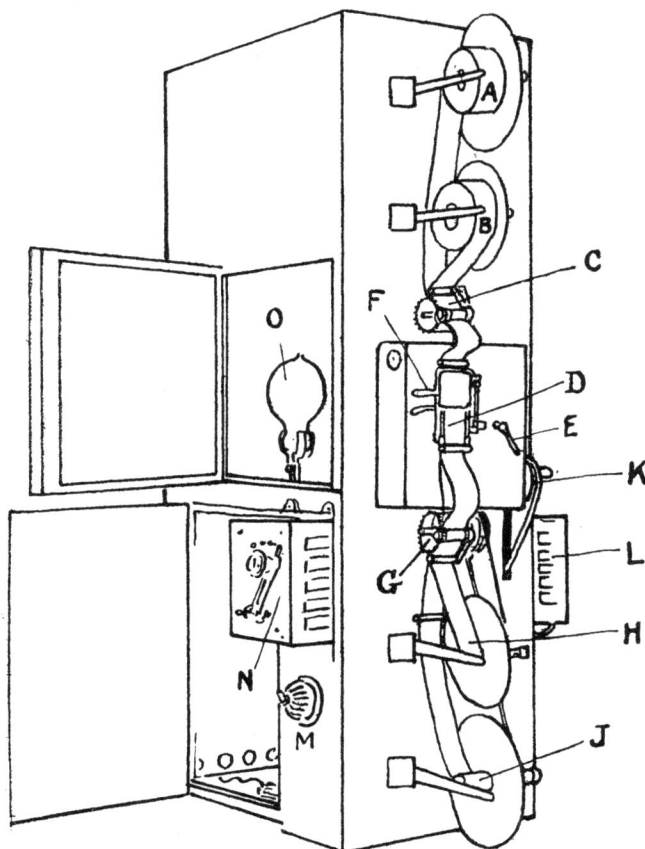

FIG. 67.

KEY TO PHOTOGRAPH OF
WILLIAMSON PRINTER.

Reference Table :

A	Negative Spool.
B	Positive Spool.
C	Top Sprocket.
D	Gate.
E	Lever controlling ruby glass light cut-off.
F	Gate Adjustment.
G	Bottom Sprocket.
H	Positive Take-up.
J	Negative Take-up.
K	Motor Drive.
L	Rheostat controlling same.
M	Switch.
N	Light Dimming Resistance.
O	Printing Lamp (electric).

able for use at high speed and large output when connected up with the electric wiring of the establishment. A few moments spent in explaining this particular commercial printer should put the reader well in possession of the general working details of the whole class of them.

First as to the light source. It will be seen to be an electric lamp of the "focus" type. This is contained in a chamber which is light-tight upon closing the side door at the middle of the printer cabinet. Thus the rays from the printing light are prevented from coming out

into the room (which must, of course, be " dark " in the photographic
sense) and producing general fog upon the roll of positive stock seen
fixed in position upon the spool holder nearest above the gate.   The
actual light allowable in the kinematograph printing room is bright
orange or even a pure yellow (See Safe Lights, Chap. V., part 3). The
topmost spool holder holds the roll of negative which is to be printed,
and in threading the machine, it is of the greatest importance to
make sure the emulsion surface of the downward dangling negative
film end is towards you, whilst that of the positive stock is away from
you when the two rolls are in place.   So spooled, the faces of negative
and positive film stock will be together as the two pass over the sprocket,
figured mmediately above the gate, and the function of which is
to maintain a constant loop of the double film to feed the escapement.

The escapement, invariably some form of the already described
pin or claw action, is in the machine at present under discussion
enclosed in the box to which the gate and mask are fixed, while the
lowermost and next to lowermost spools of all are the rewind or take
up spools for respectively negative film and exposed positive stock.

The lower door of the printer, also shown open in the illustration,
gives access to a small electric motor, controlled by the starting switch
and rheostat, seen attached nearby to the side of the light-tight
cabinet.   The actual mode of working the printer should now be fairly
plain.   For the sake of completeness we will, none the less, give a
brief description of the actual printing of the film length.

PRINTING OFF A LENGTH.

Having first taken careful note of the density of the negative
we are about to print, we adjust the light of the focus lamp accordingly.
This is done in two ways ; either we can push the lamp nearer to or
farther from the gate of the printer by means of an external rack motion,
or we can cause the filament to burn brighter or less brightly, by
altering a variable resistance fixed on the opposite side of the cabinet to
the one shown ; or we may make use of both means of exposure adjustment.   For a normal negative, about three-quarter power of a fifty
candle power focus lamp at a distance of six inches or so will do with
the motor rate so adjusted as to print from five to eight pictures a
second.   Soot and whitewash negatives may be partially corrected
by giving short exposures with a higher printing rate and brightly
burning lamp brought close to the gate, whereas a low printing rate
and dim light pushed well back from the face of the gate will tend
to the production of greater contrast in prints from flat negatives.

The actual threading of the double thickness of film into the gate
is just as when threading a single film into the camera, except that it
is necessary to take a little care over making sure the claw of the
intermittent motion gets grip on the double thickness through superposed perforation holes.   Also in a printer there is an adjustable
printing mask, which is set by means of a rack screw, just as with most

projectors. While adjusting this printing mask and up to the moment of printing, a lever is turned, which lets down a ruby glass light interceptor between the light source and the negative film. All preliminary adjustments can thus be made with ease and accuracy without fogging any film the while. The masking is satisfactory where the whole of one picture and nothing of either of the others appears in the gate between each pull of the claw, which is to say at the " uncover " position of the rotary light shutter.

The film threaded, all that is now necessary is to connect the ends of positive and negative film to their respective take-up spools, after passing them together over the bottom sprocket. The actual printing takes place by first starting the motor to the speed determined upon, and immediately turning the lever that controls the red glass light interceptor, thus throwing the latter out of the way. All being well, the machine will now proceed to print merrily on till the negative length is passed completely through, and rewound upon the take-up spool. The light interceptor is then turned back into place and the positive stock cut off short from the roll of any remaining unexposed film, which may still be on the upper positive spool. The printed positive is boxed in a light-tight case and sent to the developing room. During the actual printing time, white light is prevented from passing out through the gate aperture and into the printing room by the interposition of a second red glass slab, which is fixed permanently in the gate mask at the back of the positive film,—that is to say, between the sensitive film and the printer's eye.

It will be seen from the above that as far as the mechanical side of printing goes, it is simplicity itself. All that is necessary from that point of view is to keep a sharp look out on the take up and sprockets to make sure they are doing their work. It is in the judging of the correct brilliancy and distance of the light source, also the proper speed of motor needed for each negative of varying density, that the real art of high-class printing lies. Nor is it any mean acquirement either to be able to get the best or even something near the best out of each negative that comes along to the printing room. Here, again, as before, the only advice which can be given to the novice is to avail himself of any tips he may be able to get first hand from the actual watching of an expert printer at work, or failing that to practise printing test lengths of positive from various negatives each possessing definitely different characteristics until he has worried out for himself the knowledge of how to gauge results beforehand.

We must not forget that this book has set out to cater not only for the man desirous of going into the kinematograph trade in a fairly large way, but also for the one whose ambitions are more modest ; too modest perhaps for him to run to the expense of a printer such as already illustrated. These more modest aspirants may instal a small hand printer at comparatively trifling cost. A hand printer is simple a printer as described but minus the motor driving arrangement and also such other expensive attachments as can by any means be dispensed with. For instance, both the light-tight cabinet and the rewinding spools with their gearing can be done without. The first economy is effected by affixing the printer to the inner side of the dark room wall, in which is cut a small hole allowing of light coming to the gate from a suitable light source outside the room. The absence of rewinding arrangements for negative and positive film may be compensated for by providing a large clean box into which both films fall after leaving the gate. A hand printer is fitted with a handle for operation, just as is the kinematograph camera itself. The writer has met a man high up in the motion picture trade who boasts that he has turned out as much as eight thousand feet of positive in a day's working, single handed, with such a hand printing

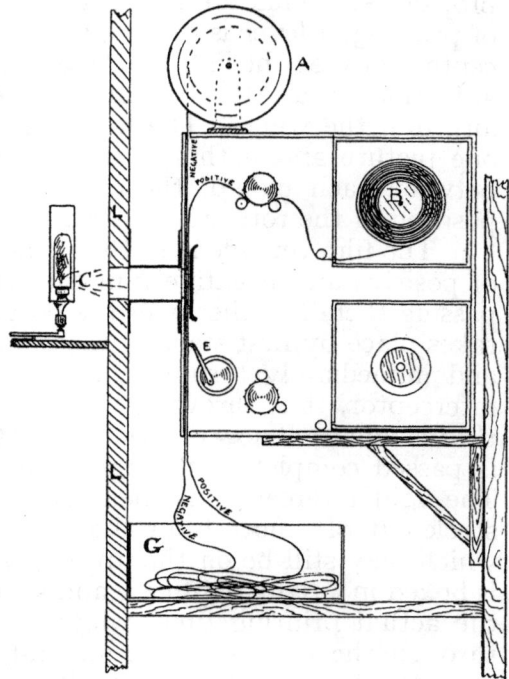

FIG. 68.   A HAND PRINTER.

Camera as arranged for printing. A shows negative film roll feeding through slot in camera top. B box holding positive stock. The positive and negative pass out (after printing) through the slot in bottom of camera and into box G. L, L, wall of dark room through hole in which light reaches film from light source.

arrangement as above described, the cost of which to buy would certainly be well under £20. At a pinch, even, it is not absolutely necessary to possess any printer at all, provided the kinematograph photographer only has need of a small and occasional output of positive from his negative stock, as when he does an occasional print for some local picture hall.

KINEMATOGRAPH CAMERA AS PRINTER.

In this case the camera itself may be utilised for the purpose of positive production. The annexed diagram, figure 68, shows the method of doing this. For the purpose the camera has to be provided with slots both top and bottom. Where it has not got these they can be fitted at small cost without in any way hurting the instrument for its usual work. Needless to say, these slots must be provided with efficient sliding metal light-tight coverings which are only removed for the purpose of printing as about to be described. At all other times they remain firmly closed. To print a positive in the camera the negative film is placed over any simple bobbin support so arranged as to hold it above the top slot, as at the position " A " in the diagram. This negative film is then threaded through the top slot and the gate, and out of the bottom slot through a suitable aperture in the bench supporting the camera, till it falls into the containing box "G." Note that the negative must be threaded with its emulsion side facing the camera back ; also that it is put over neither of the sprockets. The positive stock to be printed upon is enclosed in the top film box " B " from whence it is passed over the top sprocket. It then travels through the gate, and out at the bottom slot, face to face with the negative. Note also, that for printing, neither the bottom camera sprocket nor the take-up box are made use of at all. " L " is the dark room wall, in which has been cut a hole of such a size and in such a position as to admit light from the light source (in this case figured as incandescent gas) straight through the lens jacket to the gate.

The lens itself must be removed when printing.

The diagram does not show the light shutter of the camera, which is, however, in place, fully open, and working as usual.

So arranged the camera will be found to act as an efficient hand printer, and be it understood the work turned out by it, make-shift though it is, need not be distinctly inferior to that produced by the regularly electrically operated machine hitherto described. Of course, camera printing is less quick and convenient than when working with the proper article. Also pains must be taken to turn the handle at an even and uniform rate for any given film if even exposure is to be the result. As before, too great or too little density of the negative is compensated by turning the printing light up and down, or moving it nearer to or farther from the dark room wall ; also by alteration of printing rate. Care must be taken in operating such a contrivance as the above, to see that the printed film and film negative do not stick together at any time when passing through the bottom slot. For this purpose the camera door is kept open, while a bright orange light in the printing room enables one to see the first signs of such sticking, should it occur, and to counteract it by stopping, turning at once and pulling the slack film down into the receptacle " G."

Note.—Camera printing is only possible from negatives taken with the actual camera employed for the positive production, or from other negatives possessing identical " masking." See appendix to this part.

LIGHT FOR THE PRINTING ROOM.

A few definite hints as to safe and useful illumination of the printing and print developing rooms may not be out of place here. Positive film, being much less light sensitive than negative stock, the printing and print developing rooms may safely be illuminated by either pure red or orange red light. Even bright lemon yellow may be employed, provided the yellow is spectroscopically tested and found free from admixture with rays from the " actinic " end of the spectrum, but in practice yellow illumination is usually risky, since samples of commercial glass of this colour invariably pass as well a goodly proportion of the photographically active blue and violet light rays. For further remarks on colour testing, and making of spectroscopically accurate colour filters for dark room purposes, see the end of chapter on Colour Kinematography.

POSITIVE DEVELOPMENT.

Having exposed our positive in the printer, the next thing is to develop it.

The technique of print development is practically the same as that of negative development, except that since the light permissible in the print developing room is comparatively bright, it is relatively easy to judge when the positive image is dense enough by simply taking out the frame from the bath and looking on the face of the wound print. Thus test strips become a needless luxury (not to say time wasted) in positive production. This, of course, applies only to the man with some knowledge of the work. For the novice the more tests he can make for himself to begin with the less good film lengths will he spoil. We have already said in the previous chapter that the developing bath for prints is usually compounded differently to that for negative work. Accordingly we append some formulae for positive development. The first gives fair density and keeps well.

PLAIN HYDROQUINONE.

Hydroquinone	8 ozs.
Soda Sulphite	3 lbs.
Soda Carbonate	3 lbs.
Potassium Bromide	½ oz.
Potassium Metabisulphite	1 oz.
Water	60 pints.

The above bath may be made to work more quickly and give softer results by increasing the amount of Soda Carbonate, or it may be slowed down and at the same time caused to give greater contrast by increasing the proportion of Pot. Bromide.

Another print developing bath which will be found to work more quickly and vigorously than the above, though liable not to keep well is the following :—

HYDROQUINONE WITH CAUSTIC.

Hydroquinone	12 ozs.
Soda Sulphite	3 lbs.
Potassium Bromide	½ oz.
Caustic Soda	6 ozs.
Potassium Metabisulphite	1 oz.
Water	60 pints.

KODAK PRINT DEVELOPERS.

The following is the formula recommended by the makers of Eastman film, for use with their positive stock.

Sodium Sulphite (dry powder)	3 lbs. 5 ozs.
Sodium Carbonate (dry powder)	1 lb. 9 ozs.
Metol	180 grains.
Hydroquinone	8 ozs.
Potassium Bromide	1 oz. 63 grains.
Citric Acid	400 grains.
Potassium Metabisulphite	2 ozs.
Water	8 1-3 gallons.

Use at a temperature of 65 deg. F.

Note.—If crystalised Sod. Carb. and Sulphite are used instead of the dry variety, take double the above-mentioned quantity of each. The above is roughly a 65 pint bath (actually about 67 pints).

The Glycin developer recommended for treatment of over exposed negative stock in the previous chapter is also excellent for positive film. The remarks made in connection with the other formulae regarding adjustment of the respective Carbonate and Bromide contents for varying degrees of vigour in the produced positives apply here as well.

It may further be added for the benefit of those desirous of experimenting in variations of the bath ingredients that the component parts of all ordinary developers may be summed under four heads, thus :—

THE REDUCER.

This is the actual developing agent itself, of which there are legion. Among them may be mentioned such well-known ones as :—

Hydroquinone (syn. : Quinol)
Metol
Eikonogen
Glycin
Pyro
Amidol
Ortol, etc., etc.

The actual developing agent is, in fact, any chemical possessing the property of attacking the silver bromide of the photographic emulsion where the latter has received light action and reducing it to metallic silver. Hence the name. In order to prevent this "reducer" spontaneously decomposing by oxidation when made up in solution, there is added to the bath a

PRESERVATIVE,

which may be

Soda Sulphite
Potassium Metabisulphite
Citric Acid
Dilute Nitric Acid, etc., etc.

This preservative hinders the action of the reducer upon the film's emulsion at the same time as it prevents spontaneous oxidation, which hindering effect is got over and the work of the developer upon the photographic film rendered effective by an

ACCELERATOR.

Accelerators are

Soda Carbonate
Potassium Carbonate
Caustic Soda or Caustic Potash
Formalin, etc., etc.

In the case of the developer Amidol (which gives very fine results upon positive film, though the bath will not keep) Sod. Sulphite acts both as preservative and accelerator combined. Finally, to give the worker control over the rate and character of developing action, as also to avoid tendency to chemical fog production (where the film stock is given to showing signs of it) the bath's chemical contents are completed by the addition of a small quantity of

RESTRAINER.

This is nearly always Potassium Bromide (writen short, Pot. Brom).

Sometimes, for special purposes, other Bromides, such as Ammonium Bromide are employed, as for instance when sepia tones are desired upon positive film by the development of greatly over-exposed stock in a bath strongly restrained with the latter salt. Potassium Citrate is also occasionally used.

With regard to the use of other developers beside those for which suitable formulae have been given, we can only repeat what we said in connection with negative baths. The reader may experiment if he likes, and if so will find untold numbers of alternative formulae for all imaginable processes in connection with photography in, for instance, such a well-informed photographic encyclopaedia as the *British Journal Almanac*, published by the proprietors of the *British Journal of Photography*. For the rest we will only add that sometimes a Metol Hydroquinone positive developer may be useful under certain conditions. Where such is used it may be made up according to the regular negative developer formula given previously, only for positive film this should be of double strength and with the addition of at least an ounce of Pot. Brom. to the working bath.

DEVELOPING POSITIVE FILM.

The actual development of positive film is precisely like that of negative film with the already noted exception that completion of the process is judged by lifting the wound frame out of the bath and examining it before a good bright non-actinic light. Fully developed, but unfixed positive film should show the pictures seemingly over dark, while still the unexposed emulsion around the perforations remains milky white as when first placed in the solution. If further, on holding up the wound pin frame to the light so that a portion of the film can be looked through, the pictures are seen to stand out both dense in the shadows and plucky in the high lights, it may be taken that development is complete, and should be stopped forthwith. But here, as in everything else that has to be learned, practice and nothing else will bring mastery of the secret of correct judgment.

Development ended, the film is rinsed, fixed, and finally washed free from " hypo," just as in the case of negative stock.

The fixing baths for negative and positive film are of the same composition.

A SIMPLE CHEMICAL TABLE FOR KINEMATOGRAPHERS.

Common Name.	Correct Chemical Name.	Solubility in 100 parts of water at ordinary temperature.
Carbolic Acid	Phenol	6½
Citric Acid	Citric Acid	130
Salts of Lemon	Oxalic Acid	10½
Picric Acid	Tri-intro-Phenol	1
Pyrogallic Acid	Tri-Hydroxy-Benzine	44
Alum	Hydrated Ammonium Aluminium Sulphate	12
Chrome Alum	Hydrated Chromium Aluminium Sulphate	16
Ammon. Brom.	Ammonium Bromide	72
Carbonate of Ammonia	Ammonium Carbonate	25
Persulphate of Ammonia	Ammonium Persulphate	65
Chloride of Calcium	Calcium Chloride	400
Slaked Lime	Calcium Hydroxide	$\frac{1}{8}$
Blue Vitriol	Copper Sulphate	40
Eikonogen	Sodium Amido-Betanaphthol-Beta Mono-Sulphate	4$\frac{1}{5}$
Hydroquinone (Quinol)	Para-di-hydroxy-Benzine	6
Iron Chloride	Ferric Chloride	160
Iron Ammonia Citrate	Ferric Ammonium Citrate	25
Nitrate of Lead	Plumbic Nitrate	50
Epsom Salts	Magnesium Sulphate	100
Corrosive Sublimate	Mercuric Chloride	6½
Vermillion	Mercuric Iodide	$\frac{1}{8}$
Bichromate of Potash	Potassium Dichromate	10
Bromide of Potash	Potassium Bromide	65
Carbonate of Potash	Potassium Carbonate	112
Citrate of Potash	Potassium Citrate	166
Red Prussiate of Potash	Potassium Ferricyanide	40
Yellow Prussiate of Potash	Potassium Ferrocyanide	2)
Caustic Potash	Potassium Hydrate	200
Iodide of Potash	Potassium Iodide	140
Permanganate of Potash	Potassium Permanganate	6½
Pyrocatechin	Ortho-dyhydroxy-Benzine	80
Lunar Caustic	Silver Nitrate	227
Borax	Sodium Botate	8
Washing Soda	Sodium Carbonate	63
Salt	Sodium Chloride	35
Hypo	Sodium Thiosulphate	170
Vanadate of Soda	Sodium Vanadate	200
Bromide of Strontia	Strontium Bromide	100
Thiocarbamide	Thiocarbamide	)

FIG. 69. SOME TYPICAL SCENES PRESENTED BY THE KALEM CO. IN PALESTINE.

CHAPTER IX.

TINTING, TONING AND TITLING POSITIVES.

Tinting a kinematograph positive film is in reality not a chemical process at all, but a physical one. It is no more than dipping the film into a bath of dye whereby the high lights of the print become tinted to the colour of the dye bath. The tone of the silver deposit remains absolutely unchanged by such treatment, only where such deposit is light the dye absorbed by the gelatine of the film will show through, thus giving to the whole a semi-toned appearance at the same time as the clear parts of the film take on a more or less strong tint of the dye colour.

We append a table of well-known tinting effects, together with the baths and approximate strengths used in their production. It will be understood that the brand of film and state of the gelatine —due to varying time in the developer, hardening or absence of hardening, etc.—will have a great deal to say as to the amount of dye absorbed in a given time for any given strength of tinting bath, so that only trial on a spare inch or two of the actual film can show what time of immersion will give the correct result aimed at.

TABLE OF TINTING EFFECTS

Moonlight effect	The Positive must be somewhat thin and showing no sharp cut shadows. Tint in quarter per cent. (1 in 400) patent blue dye solution. Strongly printed film. Usually an interior subject.
Candle light and lamplight effects	Tint to a full yellow brown colour in one per cent. Bismarck Brown.
Firelight effect	Tint in one per cent. Eosine solution. Subject must be specially photographed so as to get the light properly concentrated if the effect is to be good.
Weird and murder scenes	These are heightened by tinting the film faintly green in a half per cent. acid green bath.
Early morning	Give the film the faintest pink tint by immersion in a one-eighth per cent. bath of Rose Bengal, followed by washing till colour is very slight.

All the above dyes are easily obtainable, as are also a number of others, ranging through the whole gamut of colours from lemon

yellow to purple, and which may all be employed for producing experimental tinting effects.   Whatever dye is used, and for the production of whatever strength of tint, the rule to follow is firstly,
so to adjust the concentration of the bath that the film may remain
at least five minutes in it without great excess of colour absorption
over what is wanted.   Secondly, after the film is tinted, wash it for
at least thirty seconds—preferably a minute or more—in plain water
(which need not be changed) before setting to dry.   This will discharge
some of the colour, and that must be allowed for when tinting, but
it will also prevent streaks of varying colour intensity in the final
result.   The short wash will also save the drying drum from becoming
unduly charged with various dye colours used in the film tinting.

Recently Messrs. Fuerst of 17 Philpot Lane, E.C. have put upon
the English market a series of " Kine Colours."   These are sold in
100 gram bottles (about 3½ ounces of the dry powder colour) and in
five standard shades :—yellow, orange, carmine, blue and scarlet.
Together with the colours is issued gratis a chart showing actual
kinematograph film tinted to a number of varying hues by means

FIG. 70.   FILM TINTING IN A SMALL WAY.

of the Kine Colours used singly and also in mixtures of definite proportions, these proportions being stated under each specimen tint.
With the set of Kine Colours it is an easy matter to obtain the whole
of the effects described on the preceding page, together with many
other and more unusual ones.

TINTING SHORT LENGTHS.

Probably some small film producers may not wish to go in for
film tinting as far as their subjects are concerned, but may yet wish
to tint their titles as a measure of eye protection for the audience
and by way of enhancing the brilliancy of the pictures which follow
on the screen.   To such it may be interesting to note that short
lengths of title film, up to say twenty feet, can be successfully tinted.

by simply running the film length backwards and forwards in a small dish containing strong dye solution, as shown in figure 70.

"D" is the work bench, which must be clean and free from chemical taint. "C" is the small dish of dye, through which the worker pushes the film backwards and forwards, face upwards. It will be seen that in the process it lops itself alternately in loose folds at "A" and "B" on either side of the dish. If the film is lightly handled and these folds not roughly pulled about, it will be found to take no harm from the seemingly risky performance to which it is thus subjected. The above mode of colouring short title lengths obviates the use of large extra baths, where these are only seldom required. The worker's hands should be protected from dye stains by rubber gloves.

FILM TONING.

This is an entirely different procedure to tinting. Here there is an actual chemical process involved, inasmuch as toning does not consist in altering the high lights of the positive, but in subjecting the silver deposit to the action of chemicals which permanently affect its nature, thereby altering its colour. Thus a sepia-toned film will show no remnant of the black deposit it originally possessed. Every tone will here be sepia of varying density, while the high lights will remain practically as they always were—clear white.

Toning baths are used for reasons similar to those governing the employment of tinting solutions, the chief of these being to break the monotony of a constant black and white exhibition. Also, like tinting methods, they must be employed intelligently if sensible results are aimed at which shall help instead of hinder the audience in following the motive of the picture presented. Thus a discerning film producer would not countenance the toning of a snow scene warm russet brown, any more than he would present the happy *finale* of a drama in such a tone as blue or green.

SEPIA TONING BATH (Two Solutions).

FIRST BATH.

Film **must** be thoroughly washed. Immerse in

Ammonium Bromide	...	...	...	...	1 lb.
Pot. Ferricyanide	...	...	...	...	3 lbs.
Water	...	...	...	...	...	60 pints.

This bath will keep well and may be used over and over again. Film must remain in it till the silver deposit changes to yellowish white. Then wash for one minute in running water and transfer to

SECOND BATH.

Sodium Sulphide (pure)	...	...	...	2½ lbs.
Water	...	...	...	...	60 pints.

Note.—The above chemical is quite different to the Sodium (or Soda) Sulphite, often previously referred to.

Since the success of sepia toning by this " sulphide " process depends entirely upon the Soda Sulphide being absolutely pure and fresh, this chemical should be purchased direct from some good-class chemical works which is willing to issue it with a guarantee not only of its quality at time of manufacture, but also that the manufacturing date is a recent one. The importance of such double guarantee is in the fact that the chemical not only goes off with keeping, but actually changes to another one, which acts as a reducer instead of a toner upon the bleached film.

The effect of a fresh sulphiding bath used after bleaching the film is to turn the deposit in a few seconds to a fine rich sepia, which will at the same time greatly add to the density and contrast of the subject. For this reason sulphide toning is an easy way of correcting under-printing of the positive.

The sulphide bath must be thrown away after each day's work, as it will not keep for long in sufficiently good condition to produce rich, full tones. Its smell is most objectionable, somewhat like that of a rotten egg.

TONING BATH FOR PURPLE BLACK TO RED CHALK TONES.

Copper Sulphate	4 ozs.
Potassium Citrate	3 lbs.
Potassium Ferricyanide...	3½ ozs.
Water	60 pints.

Dissolve the various ingredients separately and mix.

This copper-toning bath is fairly cheap to make up, keeps a day or two at least, and gives a variety of hues, from purple black to bright chalk red (that is to say, reddish brown). Moreover, since the process is a direct one, the alteration of colour in the film may be watched as it proceeds. Perhaps the best tone of all is that produced after half a minute or less of immersion of the film positive. This imparts to the black deposit a warm purplish tinge that carries with it greatly added density for projection.

SPECIAL WARNING.—The projection density of toned film is an entirely different thing to that which film so treated presents to the eye. For instance, with both the sulphide and the copper toning processes the appearance of the film on viewing in the hand would never lead one to expect the great intensification of the image which becomes at once apparent on passing it through the projector.

Needless to say, after any process of after-treatment, kinematograph film should be well washed.

BLUE TONES (with intensification of image).

Ferric Ammonium Citrate	12 ozs.
Potassium Ferricyanide...	12 ozs.
Acetic Acid	10 pints.
Water	50 pints.

Immerse the well-washed film till toned, then wash in water till the high lights are clear and free from stain.

BLUE TONES (without intensification of image).

BATH A.

Potassium Ferricyanide...	...	...	...	3 lbs.
Water	...	...	...	...	...	60 pints.

Immerse film till bleached, then wash very thoroughly in running water (two or three hours) and transfer to

BATH B.

Ferricyanide Chloride	...	...	...	...	4 lbs.
Water	...	...	...	...	...	60 pints.

After five minutes in the above, withdraw the pin frame and plunge straight into a new fixing bath of "hypo," made up plain without metabisulphite, and of strength ten pounds to the sixty pint trough.

The blue colour of the film here completely develops, but may be made stronger by immersion after short washing in a bath of one per cent. Sulphuric Acid, which must be followed by a good final wash.

NOTE.—Strong Sulphuric Acid must be added to water very slowly and with constant stirring, keeping the eyes well back from the mixing receptacle on account of the violence of the reaction which follows. Wherever the worker is unaccustomed to handling strong acids, it is better to have these diluted by a fully qualified chemist. Proportionately larger quantities of such weak acid will then have to be allowed in making up all formulae, according to the dilution.

For further directions on the subject of toning positive images, formulae for other colour toners, etc., the reader is referred to the numerous general photographic text books.

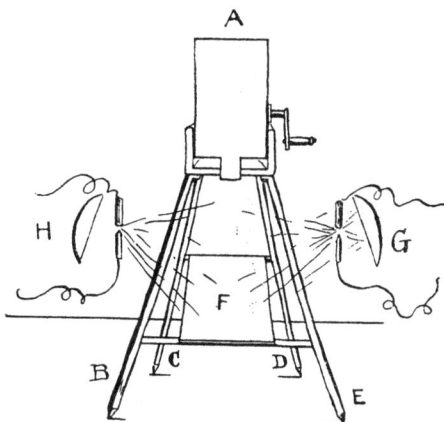

FIG. 71.

TITLE MAKING APPARATUS.

A, downward pointing camera, B, C, D, E, the four legs of its supporting stand, F, the horizontal dead black surface or "copying table," on which the white enamel letters are arranged and supported while photographing. In the present diagram G and H represent two photographic electric arcs, swung on either side of the copying table F, and of such power as to admit of title negatives being expeditiously made independent of daylight conditions.

TITLING FILM SUBJECTS.

A well-known rough and ready method of film title-making is by means of a kinematograph camera supported on a stand so that the lens points vertically downward. Below the lens, near the ground and parallel with it, is a plain dead black surface (usually black velvet) on which may be placed movable white metal or cardboard letters. A diagram of the arrangement is given in figure 71.

In arranging the movable lettering for title making, the greatest care must be expended upon alignment, spacing, and general arrangement of the words, if good-class results are to be obtained. Even then the effect got by the use of such rough and ready movable letters is never up to that achieved when trouble is taken over the preparation of a tastefully decorated black and white title, produced from either a photographic or hand-made negative from the original of an artist properly trained to the work. Such examples of delicate and tasteful design titling are often to be met with commercially, notably in the case of A.B. films, and the worst which can be said against them is that the fine line work deals cruelly with inferior focussing or definition of the projector lens. Where a title is designed on card by the black and white artist, it has only to be laid upon the titling table and photographed, just as would have been a type arrangement. Special title printers for use when film-making in large quantity are also on the market. The one about to be described is typical of the class, which is known by the generic name of " plate titler," since the original title is here first produced upon a photographic plate before its transference to the moving picture film.

DESCRIPTION OF THE PLATE TITLER.

This is in reality a combination of printer and ordinary still view projection lantern. The original title laid out in white letters

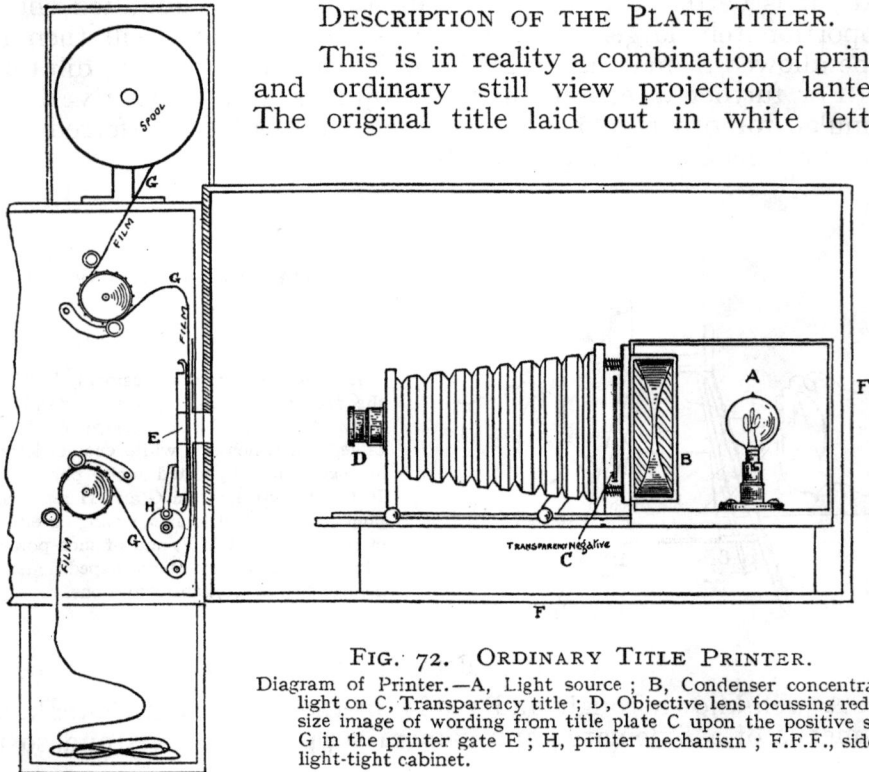

FIG. 72. ORDINARY TITLE PRINTER.

Diagram of Printer.—A, Light source ; B, Condenser concentrating light on C, Transparency title ; D, Objective lens focussing reduced size image of wording from title plate C upon the positive stock G in the printer gate E ; H, printer mechanism ; F.F.F., sides of light-tight cabinet.

on a black velvet ground is first photographed upon a glass plate by means of a downward pointing still view camera. The black letter photographic title transparency so obtained is then centred before the condenser of a projection lantern contained within the printer cabinet. By means of a suitable objective lens, also within the cabinet and situate between the title transparency and the printer gate, a sharp image of the title wording is thrown upon the threaded positive kinematograph stock. Such a form of photographic printing is also known as "reduction titling," as in contradistinction to "contact," where the usual kinematograph negative is employed before the positive stock in the printer. With "reduction titling" it will be seen that only the single thickness of unprinted positive stock is threaded in the gate, the place of the negative film being taken by the projected image of the title borne upon the transparency in the focus of the interior projection unit. The system gives white or black letter titles, according as to the original lettering photographed.

Why Titles have White Letters.

Perhaps this is the place to take note of the reason why titles are usually done in white instead of black lettering. If black letters were used upon a dead white ground the flood of light on the kinematograph screen when the title came to be projected would blind the eyes to the duller picture representations which followed. Hence, wherever black letters are made use of, care is taken to tint the surrounding film deeply enough to take off the glare. With white lettering, however, provided the lines are kept somewhat thin, there is not enough of the screen illuminated to tax the eyes unduly, while at the same time the letters stand out doubly clear and readable on account of the surrounding blackness of the sheet.

Exposing and Developing Titles.

In exposing and developing title lengths, great care must be exercised so as to ensure good contrast in both negatives and positives. Under or over exposure must not be tolerated, and if artificial light be employed from a constant source, at a constant distance, nothing but the most supreme ineptitude on the part of the title maker can possibly bring about such a mistake as wrong exposure after once the correct time has been ascertained. For the making of clear black and white titles, moreover, it is imperative that thickly coated film stock be employed. This is one of the rare cases where positive stock and the positive developing bath may usefully be pressed into the service of negative making, as well as for the actual title printing.

Titling in a Hurry.

The following process is suitable where only a few copies of a given title are required at once. In this case spread white paper on the copying table and arrange black lettering upon it to form the required words. Photograph direct upon positive film, but have it threaded into the camera **wrong way round** ; that is, celluloid side to the lens. The result of developing a film length so exposed will be the production of a correct white letter title reading right way round and produced at one operation. But since the first film has given us a positive right away, there will be no negative available for producing title prints.

TITLING FOR THE OCCASIONAL WORKER.

As before, we give brief instructions for the small man. Get a local letterpress printer to print the title required neatly in the ordinary black letters upon white card. Pin this card up, and photograph upon positive stock threaded in the camera wrong way round. The result will be a correct white letter title at the one operation, just as in the last case. But the method of getting the original in ordinary letterpress type obviates the use of a regular titling arrangement, such as figure 72. Where only the one title is required, with any given wording, the cost of production is cut down 50 per cent through doing without the exposure of an intermediate negative length.

Whether white or black letter titles are produced, they should be well tinted in a suitable tinting bath, save only such title designs as have been artistically executed with very fine white line lettering. These are best left plain.

FIG. 73. LOCAL SCENERY EFFECTIVELY USED IN PICTURE STORIES.

CHAPTER X.

AFTER TREATMENT OF NEGATIVES AND POSITIVES.

Let it be explained at the start that much of the after treatment about to be discussed in the present chapter is not by the nature of things either necessary or even applicable to perfect negatives, prints, or conditions of production. After treatment is, in fact, for the most part, nothing more than cobbling up inferior goods so as to make them passable for the market. An exception must be made in the case of the special after treatment adapted to the purpose of hastening the production of topicals.

Cobbling Bad Negatives.

After treatment of the cobbling variety is called for in the following circumstances : either the film is too thin or too dense. To be accurate, each of these classes should be sub-divided ; thus, of thin films there may be—

(*a*) Thin films which are also flat (wanting in such tone differentiation as might reasonably be expected after due allowance for general want of density). Such specimens are the result of under-development, coupled with more or less over-exposure.

(*b*) Thin films, in which shadow detail is more or less lacking, or only very faintly visible. These are the result of scanty exposure, coupled with under-development.

The two classes of over-dense films are

(*c*) Over-dense flat-looking films, the result of over-exposure and over-development.

(*d*) The well-known strong soot and whitewash effect, which always goes with bad under-exposure and forced development.

Before dealing with failures belonging to the other three classes let us say at the start that Class D is always pretty hopeless. Sometimes a soot and whitewash negative or print can be bettered by careful reduction in a bath of five or six per cent. Ammonium Persulphate until the over-dense parts of the deposit have been pulled down sufficiently, when further action is stopped by plunging without rinsing into ten per cent. Soda Sulphite solution. The treatment is however, erratic, and generally disappointing. When applied to the positive it is apt to spoil its tone, and when applied to the negative it usually spoils that too. On the whole, therefore, it is as well, except in exceptional cases of the kill or cure variety, to regard bad soot and whitewash negatives as past praying for. The other three states of negative imperfection are, however, often quite remediable.

For instance, take the case of films belonging to Class A. The treatment here is immersion in Howard Farmer's reducer (for formula see later in the chapter) till the thinnest shadows become (apparently) clear gelatine. Of course, it will have been understood that the term " thin film " as used a little while ago, applies to the appearance of the silver deposit of the image and not to any mechanical measurement of the thickness of the celluloid base. Well, then, when the thinnest parts of the deposit on this originally thin film have been reduced by the reducer to almost vanishing point, the film is well washed. Next, the wound frame bearing it is immersed in one of the two intensifiers of which the formulae are also about to be given. Either intensifying bath will serve, though the mercuric iodide one usually gives far more strikingly satisfactory results. The treatment sketched out will be found to have the effect of making the heavier deposits of an A type film rather more dense than before, while at the same time taking the flatness out of the lighter portions representing the shadows. The Copper Bromide intensifying bath to be found in Chapter III., Part 3, is excellent for treatment of films belonging to this (*a*) class.

B Class Film Failures.

This is the class which shows striking improvement by after treatment. Where the failure is the simple result of under development or under development coupled with not too great under exposure, the mercuric iodide intensifier will work something approaching a miracle. This may well be taken note of by any film house engaged in topical production, and which may not already be aware of the effect of such intensification. Often and often the iodide bath will be found the means of turning poor, almost unprintable topical negatives into respectable ones. Positives may also be intensified in the same way, though this course is not recommended where not absolutely necessary, since purity of tone and transparency are sure to be more or less impaired by such after treatment of positive films.

C Class Films

are treated simply and solely in the Howard Farmer reducer. The process of reduction must be watched carefully and stopped when gone far enough by transferring the frame carrying the film from the reducing bath to the washing trough.

HOWARD FARMER'S REDUCER.

Water	...	...	...	...	...	6o pints.
" Hypo "	...	...	...	...	...	8 lbs.
Potassium Ferricyanide...		...	...	...	...	4 to 16 ozs.

DIRECTIONS.—Dissolve the " hypo " in a few pints of warm water, make up the bath to volume, adjust temperature as near as possible to 70F, and last of all, stir in the Pot. Ferricyanide (syn. Red Prussiate of Potash) dissolved in a pint or so of water. Then at once plunge in the film to be reduced. The bath keeps very badly, losing all its reducing power within an hour or so of making up. It is at its best for only about ten minutes. The more Pot. Ferricyanide is added the quicker will the reducer work. In cases where it is only required to remove a slight veil from positive or negative film, use a bath containing only 2ozs. of Red Prussiate, instead of the larger amount set down. After the bath slows down, it may be revived once or twice by addition of Red Prussiate, but in any case must soon be thrown away and a new one compounded.

MERCURIC IODIDE INTENSIFIER.

Soda Sulphite ...	...	...	...	...	8 lbs.
Mercuric Iodide		...	...	...	6 czs.
Water ...	...	...	...	...	60 pints

DIRECTIONS.—To make the bath, first dissolve the Soda Sulphite in 20 pints of warm water, cool, and stir in the bright vermilion-coloured Mercuric Iodide powder, till all has gone to form a colourless solution. Lastly, make up the bath to 60 pints by the addition of a further 40 pints of water. This intensifier will keep fairly well in the dark, but goes off quickly in daylight, depositing the mercury as a black powder at the bottom of the trough.

A way of making it up quickly and without the possible delay entailed in procuring the rather out-of-the-way salt—Mercuric Iodide —is the following :—

FIRST SOLUTION.

Dissolve three and a quarter ounces of Mercuric Chloride in four or five pints of hot water, and pour in immediately (with stirring) a solution composed of four ounces of Potassium Iodide, dissolved in a pint of warm water. The effect of making the above mixture will be to throw out a copious precipitate or deposit of the vermilion coloured Mercuric Iodide, which, after well stirring and subsequent standing for a little while in the quiet, will fall down as a sediment at the bottom of the receptacle. When this happens, the clear liquid above is gently tipped off and thrown away. Finally, the red mushy precipitate remaining is stirred into soda sulphite solution precisely as with the dry mercuric iodide in the preceding formula. The quantity of the red salt formed by working to the proportions just given is also as near as possible the six ounces previously stipulated, so that there is no need to dry and weigh it before dissolving. To make the effects of this bath permanent, the intensified film should be washed ten minutes after removal, then plunged for ten minutes into strong developer, and again well washed. Never place film in a fixing bath after any form of after treatment, unless this is definitely recommended.

Chromium Intensifier.

Unlike the baths given up to now, this intensifier works in two stages. Accordingly, two troughs are necessary to hold the solutions that compose it.

Bath I.

Bichromate of Potash ...	...	...	...	1 lb.
Strong Hydrochloric Acid	...	...	...	6 ozs.
Water ...	...	...	...	...	60 pints.

Crush the bichromate, dissolve in five pints of hot water, make up total contents of the bath by addition of cold water to the sixty pints, and finally stir in the Hydrochloric Acid. Well mix.

Bath II.

Any ordinary strong developer. Double strength Metol Hydro-quinone without bromide answers well.

METHOD OF USING CHRONIUM INTENSIFIER. — First immerse film in Bath I., till the black silver deposit has turned to a dull lightish brown. Wash in washing trough till the yellow bichromate stain is totally removed from the clear parts of the film (this may take two or three hours) and lastly plunge into Bath II., till blackening of the image has taken place.

Comparing the characteristics of the two intensifiers above given, the following may be noted :—

Mercuric Iodide Intensifier.

The outstanding feature of this is that it intensifies the lightest deposits strongly, as well as the darker ones. Thus it is especially suitable for the improvement of film in which under-exposure goes with under-development, as in the case of many topicals. Also, the bath allows of intensification being directly watched during con-tinuance of the process.

The Mercuric Iodide bath is rather expensive to make up, and though it may keep fairly well, this is not always the case.

Chromium Intensifier.

This intensifier is exceptionally cheap to compound, and Bath I. keeps for a long time in a stoneware trough. Bath II., being practi-cally speaking an ordinary developer, is usually on hand without the necessity for making it specially.

The Chromium Intensifier differs in characteristics from the Iodide Bath chiefly in that while it intensifies medium and strong densities still more strongly, it is apt to neglect the very lightest deposits. It should, therefore, be of especial service in correcting flatness of image due to over-exposure and under-development, though the writer cannot say he has always found this so in practice. Certainly it is not so good for topicals, etc. Intensification takes place in two stages with the chromium intensifier, going to bring about one set increase of density each time the film is treated successively with Baths I. and II. Moreover, since the result is not capable of being judged by inspection before the end of the whole double process, the amount of intensification with the chromium method cannot be said to be as completely under control as when employing mercuric iodide.

Where one treatment with the chromium intensifier does not prove sufficient, the process may be gone through a second, or even a third time for greater density. No long washing is necessary between removal of a film from the fixing bath and commencing chromium intensification.

Special After Treatment for Time Saving.

The above is called for almost solely when dealing with topical work. The problem here is generally that of cutting down the washing and drying times as far as possible, consistently with safety to the film. This may be done to a large extent by the use of the two following baths :—

"Hypo" Eliminating Bath.

Peroxide of Hydrogen	$\frac{1}{2}$ pint.
Water	60 pints.

Film is taken straight from the fixing tank, rinsed for one minute with constant agitation in the washing trough, then transferred for two minutes to a trough containing the above solution, which has the power of destroying and rendering harmless to the film the remainder of the "hypo" with which it is impregnated. During the time treatment with the peroxide is going on, see to it that the water in the washing trough is completely changed. At the expiration of the two minutes, a further couple of minutes' washing in running water is given (washing in the trough with syphon going and water supply on to the full). We may now safely transfer to a bath, composed as follows :—

Hardening Bath.

Formalin	3 pints.
Water	60 pints.

After ten minutes' immersion in the formalin trough, kinematograph film becomes sufficiently tough to be dried by moderate heat without injury to the emulsion. A device for such forced drying will be found in the next chapter.

With regard to the keeping properties of the two last baths, the peroxide one may be used several times before it is exhausted, while the formalin will serve for weeks or perhaps even months on end, depending on the freedom or otherwise from chemical impregnation of the film immersed in it.

NOTE.—Whenever time is not of paramount importance kinematograph film, both negative and positive, should be allowed to dry spontaneously and without hardening. Hardened and heat-dried film always has a more horny and less pliable and satisfactory surface than the normally produced article.

Where kinematograph film is produced on at all a large scale against time, a special room is set apart, fitted with hot water pipes and supplied with a strong forced draught of warm, dry air. In this way unhardened kinematograph film may be dried in from 30 to 45 minutes without its temperature being at any moment raised to a point where there would be the fear of the gelatine melting. For particulars see next chapter. A further note on intensification will be found in the appendix to this part.

FIG. 74. FRANCE'S LEADING TRAGEDIENNE—SARAH BERNHARDT—AS "QUEEN BESS," AN EXCLUSIVE OF THE GAUMONT FILM HIRE SERVICE.

CHAPTER XI.

———

DRYING.

Drying is the final operation in the routine part of film production.

In its simplest and best form, the drying of kinematograph film, whether negative or positive, is accomplished by winding it upon a wooden skeleton drum, and leaving it to do the rest for itself. Where only small quantities of film are in question, it will be found sufficient for our purpose to make use of a correspondingly small drying drum, such as may easily be constructed by any journeyman carpenter, or even one who is not a carpenter at all. An occasional turn of such

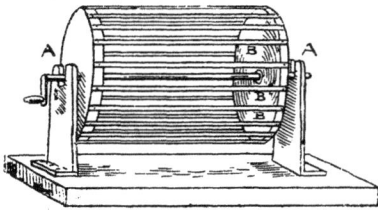

FIG. 75.

a drum, given by hand, will be all that is necessary to cause the water to dry off the film equally. Figure 75 sketches out the idea of an efficient small-sized drum, such as comes in handy for the spontaneous drying of film lengths up to 200 feet or so. The ends, composed of thick wooden circular plates three feet in diameter, are firmly threaded on to a stout metal axle, A A, composed of thick iron pipe. Between these ends of the drum thin, springy wooden slats or laths, B, B, B, etc., are nailed or screwed. The laths are the supports on which the film is wound for drying, and care must be taken that they are springy enough to allow of a considerable amount of film shrinkage during this process, which shrinkage is the counterpart of the film expansion that occurs on wetting, as already noted in the chapter on negative development. A suitable support upon which the drum may be rotated completes the whole simple arrangement. All that is necessary when using such an elementary piece of apparatus is to take care that the film is wound on to the cross laths in a regular and fairly close spiral, that it is not stretched over tight, and that the beginning and end of the wound length come sufficiently far from the drum ends to allow of the natural springiness of the slats coming into play upon every portion of the drying film. The two film ends are fastened by means of drawing pins. An occasional turn of the drum by means of the hand after winding, say once every two or three hours, will help in getting rid of collected water drops, and is all that is required to cause nature to do the rest of the drying process. Figure 76 shows a handy little attachment for use with such a small-sized drying drum, and which admits of the accommodation of longer lengths of film by allowing for contraction right to the drum ends themselves. As will be seen, the attachment consists of nothing but a short elastic loop, A,

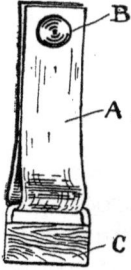

FIG. 76.

having a small wooden block C swung at one end of it, to which block the film may be pinned, while a second drawing pin, B, at the other end of the elastic loop allows of its being attached to either end of the drum, and in any desired position along its rim. Obviously, the virtue of such an arrangement is that the elastic provides the necessary compensation for whatever film contraction takes place, thus obviating any bursting of the half dry film end from its moorings, which would certainly sound the knell of part or all the film length.

DRYING LONG FILM LENGTHS.

Let us now pass to the drying drum as usually constructed on a fairly large scale. Here the only great departure from the arrangement shown in Figure 75 is in the matter of the film supporting laths. Instead of being made springy to allow of film contraction, the necessary compensation is here obtained by means more consistent with the unavoidable extra solidity of the whole construction. A way of obtaining perfect stability of the drum's structure, while still allowing for film shrinkage is by means of the system of hinged film supports as depicted in Figure 77. The small diagram A shows the actual

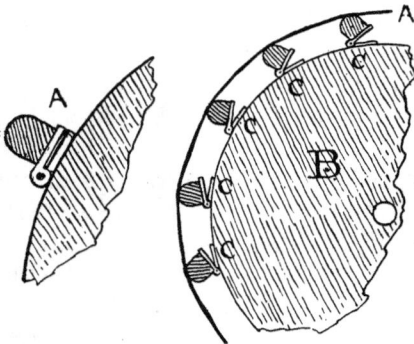

FIG. 77.

method of hingeing the slats, while the larger one B represents them in operation upon part of the surface of a drying drum. In B, A represents the film as wound upon the hinged slats C, C, C, C, and before drying has commenced. It will be seen that the hinges are partly open. As a matter of fact, provided the height and shape of the film supporting laths has been rightly adjusted, the closing of the hinged slats upon their fully open position should be automatic as the film dries. Generally, however, it is advisable to start the hinges as shown in Figure 77 B, after winding on the film to be dried. Once this is done, the contraction of the celluloid will flatten down the laths more and more up to the point where drying is complete. In practice it would not be necessary or advisable to hinge all the slats on a drying drum of this variety. One hinged one, and then two or three firmly supported ones is a better proportion. Also where film drying is being carried on upon a large scale, common sense will suggest that it is more economical in the end to pay the salary of a competent drying room attendant, who will be on hand all the while and keep constant or frequent supervision over the tension of the film upon the drum, rather than chance the spoiling of large batches of film by breakage when no one is about to set matters right.

Returning once again to the general design of the drum in Figure 75, it will be easy to see that for film drying on a large scale, constant rotation, by means of a pulley wheel attached to the spindle A, presents no element of difficulty if power is available for the purpose. Also, some experienced workers hasten drying by turning the hollow centre shaft into a species of bunsen burner, which alteration can be

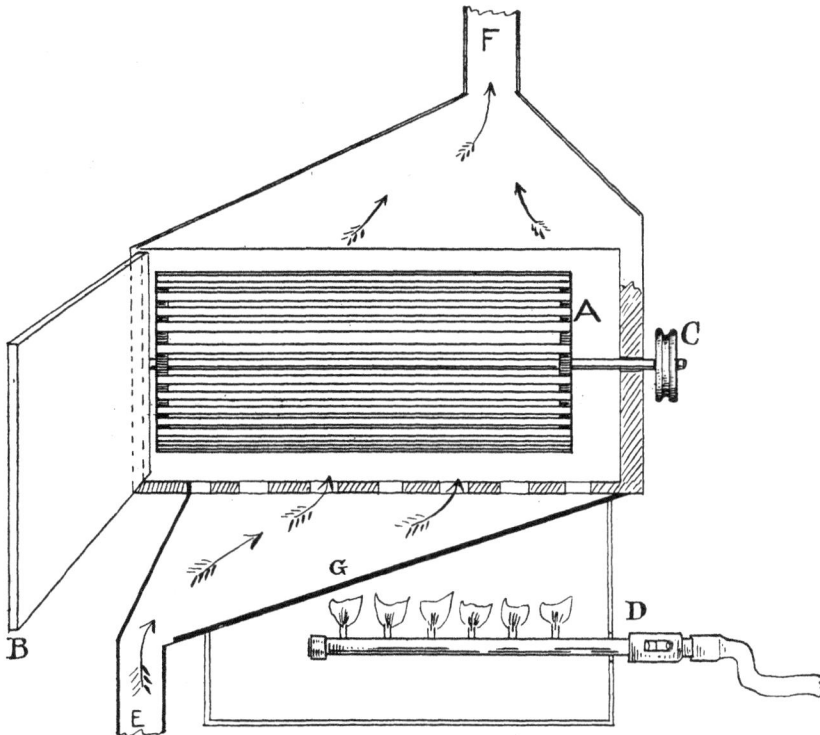

FIG. 78.

simply done if the necessary mixture of gas and air be conducted in, and holes bored in the length of the pipe within the wheel to serve as bunsen jets. The drum in this case would revolve free, while the axle would be fixed. At the same time, the process of drying film with the aid of a wheel having internal flame, though rapid, is risky. It is better to stick to a well-warmed and well-ventilated drying room with plenty of gentle heating by means of hot water pipes, and let this suffice for all ordinary purposes. For topical work only is faster drying imperative or even desirable.

For this purpose, and where large batches of film are to be dried, the water pipe-warmed drying room is fitted with a channel or channels

near the floor through which additional warm dry air is sucked in
over hot piping, the rate of air intake, and, in fact, the whole circulation of the drying currents being controlled by a powerful exhaust
fan or fans fitted in the orifices of suitable ceiling flues, whereby the
moisture that finds its way into the room from the surface of the drying film is constantly wafted upward and out to make way for a fresh
dry air supply.

Quick Drying on a Small Scale.

In the case where a worker wishes to be able to cope on occasion
with topical production on a small scale, but under the speediest
conditions of turn-out, he cannot do better than have recourse to
some form of enclosed drying wheel, such as is figured in Figure 78.
The arrangement here sketched will be found susceptible of being constructed as a small partitioned off compartment in the regular drying
room.

Moreover, there is really no limit to the heat which may thus be
fed to the film, for which reason only formalin or quinone hardened
film (see appendix for the latter) should ever be subjected to such a
forced drying system, in which ventilation depends only upon a system
of natural draught. In any case, see to it that a trustworthy thermometer is so embedded in the wall of the drying compartment
that the temperature of the inside may be seen from outside at a glance,
and do not let this temperature rise above 90 or 95 F., as no wet film,
even though hardened, could be expected to stand higher temperatures.
The above heat, combined with brisk rotation, should be enough to
accomplish the drying of film in not much more than three-quarters
of an hour. For the sake of simplicity in drawing, the arrangement
for drying by heat is represented as a cupboard. A is the drying
drum, suitably pivoted, and which may be rotated by power communicated through the belt pulley C, situated outside the drying
compartment. Following out the cupboard idea, B represents
the door shown open, but which is capable of being closed so accurately as to all intents and purposes to be air tight. D is a row
of bunsen burners, enclosed in a metal casing, and the function of which
is to heat up the under surface of the hot plate G, comprising the
under side of the air inlet E. Hot air will accordingly pass up
from here through the grating under the drying drum, and over the
surface of the wound and rotating film, till it finds its way out by the
upper air outlet F.

Such an arrangement is simply and economically installed, and
will be found quite efficient for drying topicals. Where expense is
of less object, the substitution for the hot plate of a system of hot
water pipes immediately surrounding the drying drum, and radiating
heat from water at a known temperature constitutes an undoubted
improvement, while by fitting a small electric exhaust fan in the flue
F, we have a replica on a small scale of the most approved type of
modern film producer's forced drying room.

CHAPTER XII.

DEVELOPMENT ON A LARGE SCALE.

The present chapter will seek to deal with methods of development of negatives and positives as practised and approved in works having a large output.

PREPARATION OF BATHS.

Where photographic baths for the treatment and development of positives and negatives are required in considerable quantities, it is usual to install special receptacles for their preparation and storage previous to use. Thus, hyposulphite of soda may be dissolved in large lead-lined tubs by means of super-heated steam blown into the water from a main boiler. Developing baths are also prepared by means of water warmed in a similar manner, while in order to keep their temperature up during use in cold weather, copper pipes may be coiled in the bottom and steam blown through these coils for temperature raising purposes. Where it is not considered necessary to go to this length, the ordinary bathroom geyser is a very handy piece of apparatus for quickly obtaining hot water in the kinematograph developing rooms. Receptacles of enamelled zinc are found to withstand successfully the chemicals usually employed in compounding developers, although they are useless for mixing or holding fixing solutions.

PROPORTIONING INGREDIENTS OF DEVELOPERS.

Where developing baths of constant constitution are frequently made up, there is a great saving of time, with little loss of accuracy, if the chemicals for their composition are measured out into suitably gauged measures instead of being weighed in scales.

KEEPING BATHS CLEAR.

The fixing bath will usually require to be strained immediately after making in order to rid it of small particles of insoluble foreign matter, such as paper, straw, etc., which find their way into the casks of hypo. For this purpose there is no need to use any more thorough method of filtration than the passing of the bath through one or two thicknesses of calico. Where developing baths become muddy through the deposition of lime, sulphur, etc., simple straining of this sort will not be effective. There are, then, two courses open : The bath may be warmed and subsequently allowed to stand overnight, when by morning the precipitate will have fallen to the bottom and the clear portion can be decanted into a second trough, or the bath may be filtered in the ordinary way. In either case it will be an advantage to have pumps installed in the workrooms for the raising of the solutions from the baths to the filter.

TESTING DEVELOPING AGENTS FOR PURITY.

Where chemicals for photographic development are bought in large quantities it may be necessary or advisable to resort to certain simple experiments to determine their state of purity and suitability for the purposes to which they are to be put. Below we give a summary of ways of accomplishing the above.

Sulphite of Soda.—This product is liable to be contaminated with carbonate of soda and hyposulphite of soda. To test for carbonate, adopt the following : Place the suspected chemical in a test tube and pour on it a strong solution of citric acid. This should cause no effervescence. If it does so, carbonate is probably present.

All sulphite of soda contains a certain proportion of sulphate. By keeping, and especially when exposed to the air in brown paper bags, etc., this change from sulphite to sulphate occurs naturally, and since sulphate of soda is useless and, in fact, injurious in the developing bath, it is important to find out how far the change has progressed in any given sample before it is used for development. The best way to test the proportion of sulphite is by volumetric analysis. Dissolve a known quantity in distilled water and titrate against standard normal or decinormal potassium permanganate solution contained in a burette, and dropped into the sulphite solution till a permanent coloration results, after the method so well known in laboratory practice. The percentage of pure sulphite in the sample is determined by calculation of the amount of permanganate required to oxidize it to sulphate.

Carbonate of Soda or Potash.—These can be identified for what they are very simply by pouring upon them a small quantity of dilute hydrochloric acid, when they effervesce in the manner so well known and so often seen in the case of the effervescence of seidlitz powders. To test the commercial purity of carbonate of soda or potash, it is necessary to weigh a given quantity of it in an accurate chemical balance, treat it with hydrochloric acid and then re-weigh, comparing the weight before and after effervescence by the light of the atomic weights of the elements going to form the carbonate and chloride of potassium and sodium respectively. This, again, is a matter of laboratory practice which, since it can only be satisfactorily carried out by a qualified works chemist, need not be further enlarged upon here.

Hydroquinone.—A simple way of testing this and allied organic developers for purity is by dissolving them in various solvents and noting their solubility. Thus, hydroquinone should dissolve completely in six times its weight of ether at ordinary temperature. The more accurate way of testing for purity of many organic substances of this class is, however, by means of determination of the melting point. As will be known to all those interested in such matters, the practice in determining melting point is to fill a small quantity of the substance into a thin-walled capillary glass tube, to attach this tube by means of rubber rings to the side of a chemical thermometer, and to immerse the whole in a liquid capable of being gradually warmed without ebullition to a point well above the melting point of the pure product. Hydroquinone melts at 175 degrees Centigrade, with partial decomposition. The melting point of other organic substances may be obtained by reference to published chemical tables.

Testing Metol.—Take two grammes and add thirty drops of pure hydrochloric acid. Shake for five minutes, when, if pure, the product is dissolved completely. If paramidophenol salt is present in quantity of more than one-half per cent., solution will not be complete.

TEMPERATURE OF DEVELOPMENT.

The normal temperature for the developer is from 65 to 70 degrees Fahrenheit. Whichever temperature is decided on should be rigorously kept to, both in summer and winter, as only where the temperature of development is equal can similar results be obtained upon similar lengths of negative or positive stock.

The practice adopted by some continental houses having a large output of both negative and positive film is to keep the same developing bath going for a long period, either by half emptying it and making it once again up to full quantity by the addition of fresh developer as it gets stale, or by adding a small amount of fresh developer to re-inforce the bath at short and frequent intervals. Baths so kept working will never be at the maximum strength, and will always have more or less colour, due to the presence in them of oxydation compounds as the result of their containing a proportion of used-up developing agent. Since one of the products of development of the silver bromide constituting the light-sensitive element of the emulsion is bromide of potassium, and this bromide of potassium is the well-known restrainer, it follows also that re-inforced developers will work more slowly on this account, and in the case of negative baths will not do the same justice to films which have been under-exposed as would be done by a completely new developer. Personally, we do not take upon ourselves to recommend the practice of re-inforcing old baths, but merely note it as being in extensive use abroad.

One advantage of the above system is certainly that of producing great equality in the time of development, and this of course tends considerably to simplify dark-room practice. Where entirely new baths are made up as occasion requires, it will be necessary to test the development time required with them, both at the start and as they become more and more used up. Skilled dark-room hands have little difficulty in judging this without other aid than their own experience. A method which may, however, be given is to keep in a suitably light-tight receptacle a roll of positive film printed off a negative of even density, the positive film being undeveloped. A length of this latter film should be cut off the roll and left in the developing bath for standard time, such standard time being arbitrarily determined on, but once fixed being kept to for all such tests. Comparison of the densities of such developed test lengths when treated in new, medium and old baths will show what allowance for deterioration of the developing agent must be made from hour to hour, or day to day.

Do not make up loss of fluid contents in the developing trough by addition of plain water, since a developer so treated invariably produces positives which are too soft in their gradations. For developing formulae refer back to previous chapters on negative and positive development.

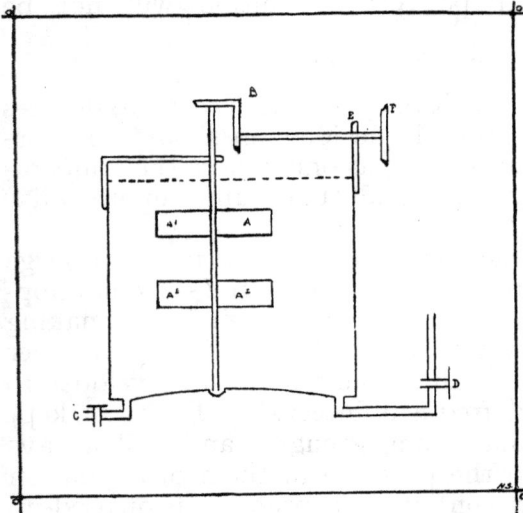

FIG. 79.

Circular Trough with rotary blades for compounding developing and fixing solutions.—B is a bevelled gear-wheel driven from a shaft E operated by the belt pulley F. The bevelled wheel B driving the vertical shaft is bushed into the centre of the mixing trough, and carries upon it the rotary blades A, A1, A2, A3. D is a pipe through which may be delivered water of the required temperature for mixing purposes, while the pipe and tap C control the outlet to storage reservoir for developing or fixing troughs, as the case may be.

DEVELOPING POSITIVES IN QUANTITY.

The method of accomplishing this in minimum time with positives printed from negatives of varying density, and with the smallest margin of error, is by means of standardisation of print exposure according to the density of negative from which the positives are printed. For this, negatives are examined both in the high lights, shades, and medium densities, and from these observations of density are sorted into groups, the printing exposure for which will be approximately equal. This sorting is skilled work, and can be undertaken only by the most experienced printing hands. The required exposure in printing may be made by means of altering the speed, or altering the light, or both. Usually it is more convenient, except in certain cases, to make the whole of the regulation by means of the speed control.

Suppose speed to be controlled by means of a rheostat possessing many points, the negatives to be printed are marked with a number or other indication to show the printer on which point the handle of the rheostat must be placed when making the positive. In some houses this information is conveyed to the printer by means of a series of holes punched in the end of the negative film similar in number to the number of points on the rheostat to be used in the printing operation. If this classification of density of the negative has been correctly made, and such indication of it correctly followed out by the printing hand, the resulting positives may be developed together promiscuously for the same time in the same trough, either singly or as a batch of frames.

TYPE OF FRAMES AND METHOD OF PROCEDURE ADOPTED BY CERTAIN CONTINENTAL PRODUCING HOUSES.

The type of frame in favour on the Continent in certain of the larger producing houses is a flat frame of a size to hold between 200 and 300 feet of film wound upon it. Such a frame is a very cumber-

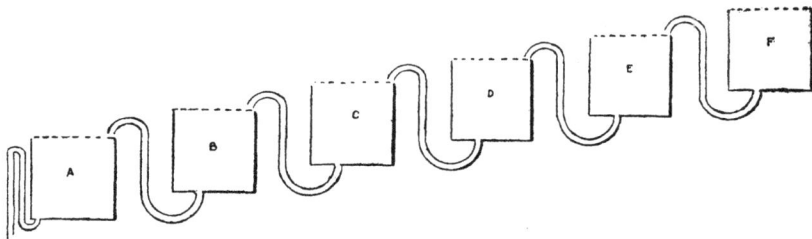

FIG. 80.

Economising Water for Washing Purposes.—Washing troughs A, B, C, D, Ξ, F are arranged in tiers as shown, so that the washing water supplied from tap G travels from the topmost trough F to the lowermost one, A, through the piping figured. In use, frames to be washed are started at trough A for their first rinse, and moved by progressive stages to trough F for the final moments of washing. This arrangement effects what is almost an economy of five-sixths in the washing water required.

some affair, but none the less is quick to wind and fairly easy to manipulate if stood upright in grooved troughs of the sort figured on a small scale in our previous chapter on negative development.

The arrangement for quick output in a factory adapted to treating say 30,000 feet of film daily would include, first a drying room for film frames, next a film winding room, where the frames would be whirled on suitable supports and the film thus rapidly wound upon them by youths, after the manner of skeining wool. Then there would follow the main developer reservoir, connected by copper piping to supply the several developing troughs. Behind each developing trough and immediately facing it must be a rinsing trough, while near by will be a fixing bath to which hypo solution is supplied from a central hypo reservoir by means of lead tubing. Large grooved washing tanks complete the necessary developing paraphernalia, such tanks being provided in sufficient quantity to keep washed at least 5,000 feet at a time. The water in the rinsing troughs must not be stagnant, but must be kept in slow yet constant motion by means of a tank supplying a fresh stream to the surface, while the lower portion of the water, which has become contaminated with developer, is got rid of by means of a syphon pierced at its upper bend as before explained to prevent the total emptying of the receptacle. The hypo solution for fixing is preferably kept acid by the addition to it of some such suitable acidifying agent as metabisulphite of potash. Acid fixing is not ideal from the scientific point of view, since it has a bleaching action on the oxydation products of development, which prevents the observer from knowing whether or not they have been completely eliminated from the film before it is put to dry, but its advantages in practice are such that for commercial purposes they entirely overshadow the disadvantage here noted.

Controlling Density by Inspection.

However carefully developing baths are standardised for print work, it is found necessary to keep a control of density by inspection. For this purpose the developing hand is provided with a well-shielded portable red electric lamp, connected to the mains by flex in such a way that he can direct the light on to the surface of the frame for a moment or two at such intervals as he shall consider necessary for judging purposes. In this way a control of density is kept throughout the progress of development from the appearance of the surface of the film. This judgment by surface density is, however, not absolute, and must be supplemented from time to time, or where difficult negatives are being printed from, by the test development of short lengths, followed by fixation, rinsing, and direct judgment of density by daylight.

Preserving the Wood of Flat Developing Frames.

Wooden flat frames, if used without waterproofing, soon become sodden through the action of the developer penetrating the pores. The following formula, culled from a Continental contemporary, is for a liquid in which wood may be soaked to render it only slightly permeable to watery solutions :—

Benzine	50 pints.
Tetrachloride of Carbon	50 pints.
Pulverised Judean Bitumen	2 lbs.
Paraffin Wax	2 lbs.

Flat frames should be soaked in the above liquid when new, and also fortnightly afterwards throughout their use. Great care should be taken that the frames have been well rinsed in plain water and subsequently thoroughly dried before treating.

DRYING ON A LARGER SCALE.

Drying can be performed by the aid of drying drums upon which the film is wound, precisely as in the former chapter appearing under this head, the only difference being that in large works the drums and drying facilities in general will be upon a correspondingly magnified scale. Personally we favour the installation of a number of drums, each capable of carrying approximately 1,000 feet of film, rather than the attempt to provide few drums of enormous diameter and which, by virtue of their weight and inertia, cannot conveniently be rotated at high speed. A 1,000 feet drum of approximately eight feet length by five feet in diameter can be rotated sufficiently fast by means of a quarter horse-power electric motor driving on to a belt-ring fastened to its side.

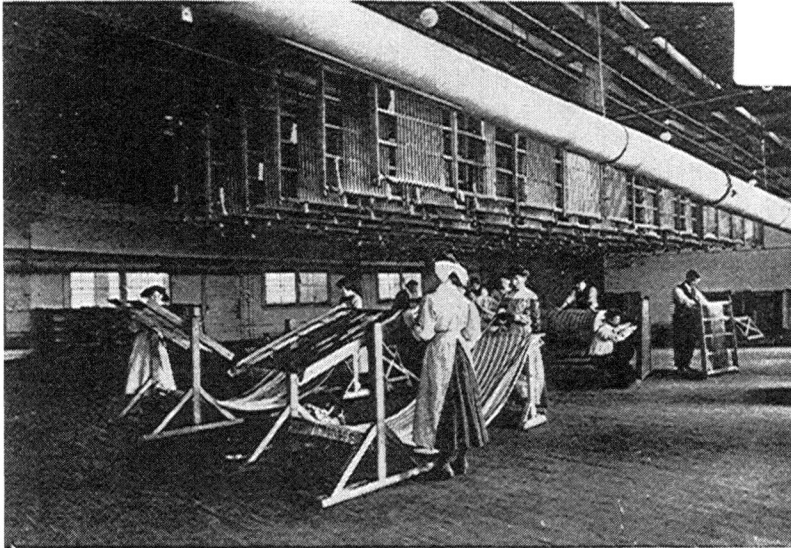

FIG. 81. DRYING FILMS ON FLAT FRAMES AT LUBIN'S WORKS.

Wet film is wound on such a drum and rotated in a drying room well ventilated and having its temperature kept at 75 degrees F. by means of electrical radiators. Thus the film will dry without coming to harm in from three-quarters of an hour to one hour. A single drum of the above capacity kept in constant operation will therefore be sufficient for an output of quite 8,000 feet of film during the working day. Four such drums would be more than sufficient for the total output of 30,000 feet a day.

Another method of drying the film is to draw it over bars suspended near the roof of a warm and well-ventilated drying room. The film thus festooned backwards and forwards across the ceiling dries quickly and evenly and without any suspicion of strain due to uneven contraction against pressure.

VENTILATION OF THE DRYING ROOM.

This is best effected by means of electrical exhaust fans placed near the ceiling. Refer back to chapter on drying.

PREVENTION OF DUST IN DRYING ROOM.

It is of extreme importance that the drying room be so constructed that every part of it can be frequently wiped over with a damp cloth and all dust completely swept up as it accumulates upon the floor. Glazed tiles are recommended for walls and ceiling, with a cement floor. In some establishments there is no corner in which dust can accumulate, all are arched with glazed tiles.

CONTINUOUS FILM DEVELOPMENT.

At least one English firm, as well as one or two Continental ones, uses for the development of negative and positive film a machine consisting of series-troughs through which the film is drawn in a continuous feed. In this way the operations of developing, rinsing, fixing, and finally washing are effected automatically one after the other, the whole process of film treatment being carried through without the necessity of hand lifting of the film from bath to bath, or rolling it upon flat or other frames. Briefly described, the perforated film is fed by means of a sprocket wheel into a long narrow trough of developer, its surface being kept under the liquid by the agency of soft fibre rollers, which effect their purpose without scratching or injuring the wet surface of the gelatine. A second take-up sprocket raises the film from the further end of the developing trough and feeds it into a rinsing trough similarly designed, from which again it is fed through fixing and finally washing baths.

Some people claim that machines of this type have already supplanted the better-known systems of development upon pin and flat frames, but such is far from the case.

SAVING SILVER FROM OLD FIXING BATHS.

In process of use the fixing bath dissolves from the photographic emulsion and retains within itself a considerable quantity of silver. It is held in the solution in the form of mono-silver-disodium-thiosulphate, but can be precipitated as black silver sulphide by the addition to the used-up fixing bath of excess of a concentrated solution of commercial sulphide of soda. (*Note.*—Sulphide of soda is quite different from the *sulphite* of soda so well known in the composition of numerous photographic baths.) To save silver residues a large tub is usually procured, into which the used fixing baths are drained. Addition of the sulphide solution to the tub causes precipitation of the silver sulphide as a black slime. On standing, the slime collects at the bottom of the tub, when the more or less clear liquid above it can be drained away, preferably by means of a syphon. Finally the black slimy matter is tilted on to large sheets of filter paper, or ordinary blotting paper laid upon muslin or calico, and allowed to drain until the whole has got to a putty-like consistency. This may be further dried off in an oven, or may be sent as it is to the silver refiners. To test if the whole of the silver has been saved, add a few drops more of soda sulphide solution to the fluid contents of the tub after first precipitation, and allowing to stand. A further black precipitate shows there is more silver to be thrown down.

FIG. 82. A MEMORABLE HISTORICAL FILM FROM THE EDISON STUDIO.
"THE CHARGE OF THE LIGHT BRIGADE."

Fig. 83.   Scene from a Beautiful Christmas Subject—"The Sleeping Beauty"—by The Hepworth Manufacturing Co.

APPENDIX TO PART I.

FUNCTIONS OF LENSES.

Lenses are in reality no more than pieces of glass which, instead of being flat, possess curved surfaces. Now it is clear that such curves may be of two kinds. They may go out, as in Fig. 84, where the lens would be said to be double convex, or they may go in as in Fig. 85, where the lens is of the double concave variety. A third class of lens extensively used in photography is the meniscus, Fig. 86, in which one of the curves goes in (concave), and the other goes

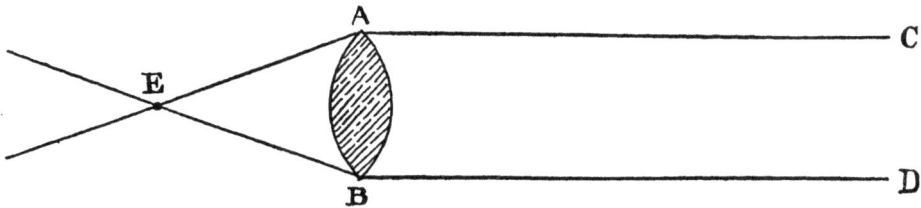

FIG. 84.

out (convex). If we refer again to Figs. 84 and 85, we shall notice that the action of the two types of lens is entirely different toward light falling upon them. In each case, CA, DB, represent parallel light rays falling on the glass. In the one case (that of the convex lens), the effect of the lens curvature upon the rays is to bend them toward a common 'focus' point at E (Fig. 84). In Fig. 85, the same rays, CA, DB, are represented as passing through the concave lens AB. But here, although a bending occurs, it has the effect of turning the light rays away from, instead of towards one another as at E, F. Since an actual or positive focus point is the only position

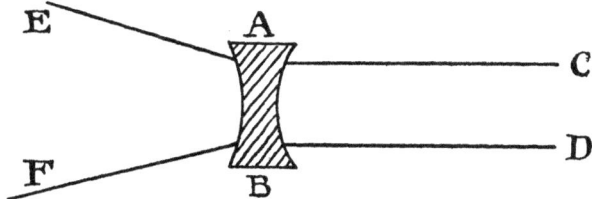

FIG. 85.

behind a lens at which a real image of natural objects is formed, and since only lenses of more or less convexity possess this, it follows that all working photographic lens combinations are of the convex variety.

The ordinary magnifying glass is of this kind, which accounts for its ability to cast behind it an image of an object placed in front. The same attribute is also shared by any lens in which the sum total of the curvature leaves a balance on the bulge-out side. Thus, in Fig. 86, the meniscus lens, although possessing distinct concavity on the right hand side (as drawn), has even more pronounced convexity on the left hand. It would therefore act on the whole as a slightly convex lens. The same rule applies to lenses made up of more than one glass or 'element.' In considering such, then, we may for present purposes include all lenses possessing a balance on the convex side as in the same category with the double convex variety figured in Figs. 84, 87 and 88.

FIG. 86.

And now to turn to Fig. 87. This seeks to make plainer the reason why the ability of a convex lens to concentrate light rays to a point confers upon it also

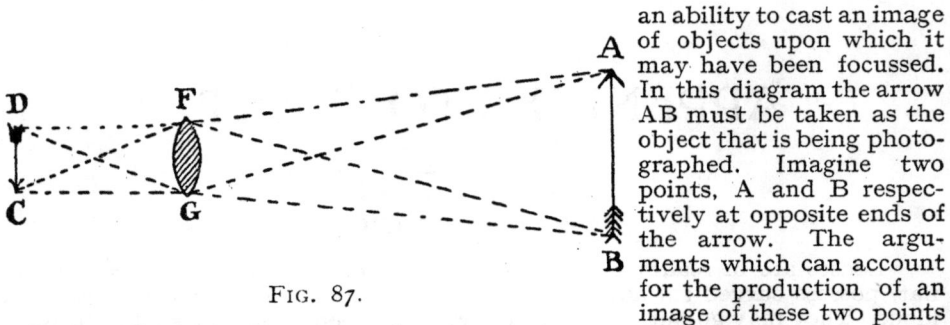

FIG. 87.

an ability to cast an image of objects upon which it may have been focussed. In this diagram the arrow AB must be taken as the object that is being photographed. Imagine two points, A and B respectively at opposite ends of the arrow. The arguments which can account for the production of an image of these two points applies equally to the formation of an image of every other point on the surface of the arrow or, in fact, of any other object photographed.

Now to reason the formation of the images of A and B. Light, as is well known, travels a straight course unless the rays are artificially turned by some substance such as the glass of the lens itself. Also, since any object can be seen from any point of view provided there is nothing between it and the observer, and provided also the intervening distance does not place too great a tax upon the observer's eyesight, it follows that light rays must be reflected from all illuminated objects in all directions. Hence, we may take it for a start, that light rays are being given off in all directions from the points A, B of the arrow AB in Fig. 87.

We interpose the lens FG anywhere within view of the points in question when pencils (portions) of light, FAG, FBG, given off from A and B, will strike upon the diameter of the interposed lens, FG. Also, these will strike the glass travelling in straight lines from A and B. Moreover, the central ray of each light pencil will follow a straight undeviated course (due to the fact that the central point of a spherical curve is theoretically a plane surface), the outer rays of such respective pencil tending more and more to meet this middle one at a point known as the focus point, which varies in position according to the remoteness of the object focussed, but we will suppose to be in the plane DC, for the object AB. We are assuming our curved glass FG to be behaving as a 'perfect' lens free from errors of spherical aberration which often arise in practice to mar the performance of the cheap commercial article. Following this out, it will happen that whereas BF, BG will come to a focus at (say) D, (a distance decided by the focal length—or extent of convexity of the lens), the rays AF, AG will come to a point at C in the same plane. Likewise, all intermediate rays will, by the like reasoning, be brought to a focus at their proper intermediate distances. Hence, an image of AB will be formed at DC. Such then is the skeleton of the reasoning underlying the formation of the optical image used for the purpose of impressing a plate with its photographic negative record.

Notice incidentally how the inversion of the image comes about as the necessary consequence of the above. With the object photographed the head of the arrow A is upward. In its image, and as the result of the crossing of the rays in the lens, the head C is pointing downward.

While we are on the subject of lens action, it may be as well to include one more diagram, Fig. 88. This has a very practical bearing upon photographic technique. It illustrates what the text books on optics speak of as the law of conjugate foci. Looked at from the utilitarian standpoint, it shows the reason why a photographic lens has to be racked inward or outward according as we are taking distant or near objects.

The diagram illustrates two point objects, A and B, which it may be wished to bring to a focus. It will presumably have been grasped by the reader that this focal point, or position where the image is concentrated (as DC, Fig. 87), is the one at which the photographer endeavours as nearly as possible to adjust his sensitive photographic surface. Reverting to Fig. 88, it will be seen that the points A and B do not focus at the same distance behind the lens, since whereas the more distant one A comes to its focus at E, the nearer point, B, does not reach a focus till F, much farther from the lens' back surface.

This is in itself a rough expression of the law of conjugate foci ; that the nearer the object to the lens, the farther behind will be the focal plane of its image. Obviously, the photographer is placed by this inflexible rule of optics

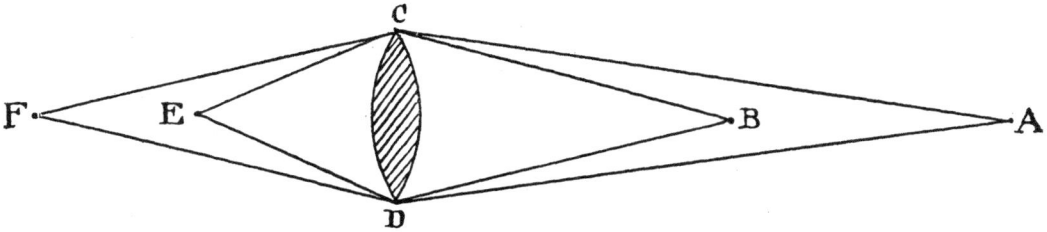

FIG. 88.

in something of an awkward predicament, for it is equally impossible for him either to insist on the objects of nature grouping themselves to order in one plane (distance) before the camera, or to make the vertically-supported plate or film receive truly focussed images of objects in different planes at one and the same time.

In practice, a compromise is effected by the process known as ' stopping down the lens.' This consists of placing a ' diaphragm ' or ' stop ' of opaque metal in front of the lens glass, the same stop having cut in it a small hole of a size only to allow a comparatively small pencil of rays to come through. While the above expedient greatly slows the action of the lens, and while at the same time it affords no help whatever in arriving at the optically impossible condition of obtaining simultaneous true focus of many planes at a time, it none the less makes the lens's departure from such a condition less noticeable to a degree depending upon the extent to which ' stopping down ' has been effected.

Stopping the lens is therefore very largely adopted in practical work both in the field and studio, and in that connection is more fully treated of in Chapter IV. For the present, it will be sufficient to append Fig. 89 by way of illustrating the theory underlying the action of a diaphragm as used for the above purpose of producing apparent ' depth of focus.'

In Fig. 89, the object A is represented as being brought by the lens BC to a focus in the plane GH, at which plane, needless to say, the sensitive surface should be placed to receive the image formed. Suppose instead, that by virtue of a greater necessity accurately to focus some still nearer object, the photo-

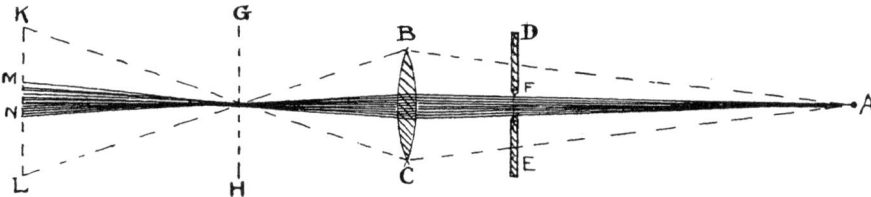

FIG. 89.

graphic plate or film has had to be moved back to the plane KL. Then, without the interposition of a stop, the image of the object A would be hopelessly blurred, each point of the original having expanded into a wide circular patch of light as KL. This is the condition of things indicated by the broken lines. The black cone sets forth the improvement introduced by the interposition before the lens of the diaphragm DE, containing in it the small aperture F, through which alone the actual utilised light cone passes. As before, we see that the true focus point remains at GH. Shifting the sensitive surface back to KL, however, now only introduces the much lesser blurring effect formed by the comparatively slight diffusion of the light rays from point formation as at MN.

The above optical notes do not pretend to do more than touch the fringe of a very wide and intricate subject, one, moreover, which is in its advanced stages right outside the scope of a work on practical kinematography. The reader who may wish to go further into the theory of photographic and other lenses is for this purpose, and as a first step, recommended to the perusal of such a well-known elementary optical handbook as Glazebrook's " Light."

NOTE ON FILM STOCK.

Needless to say, the best way of handling ribbon of all sorts in small compass is by rolling it up. It is in the form of a roll that the necessary long strips of photographically-coated celluloid, known as ' film stock,' are sent out by the manufacturers. For use, these rolls are loaded into suitable containers within the camera, from thence to be fed into the escapement as required. The usual lengths of commercial rolls of film stock are 165 feet (Continental) or 200 feet (American and English) lengths. The width of such stock is approximately one and eleven-thirty-seconds inches.

FILM MASKINGS.

The "masking" or registration of a film is a technical term expressing the relation of the perforations to the pictures. Thus a film may have its masking such that the top edge of a perforation coincides with the top edge of each film picture as in *A* fig. 90. Or the masking may be of a kind where the centre of the top-most perforation of each picture space is nearly a quarter of the picture length down from the top of the picture as in figure *B*. The masking may, moreover, be anywhere between these two extremes, according as the camera mat is adjusted.

A   *B*
Fig. 90.—Different Maskings of Film.

It is in order to compensate to some extent for variations of masking in the negatives that the printer is provided with an adjustable gate. At the same time it should be clearly understood that adjusting the printer gate will not make up for variations of masking in the cameras, wherewith two different negatives have been made in so far as the question of joining prints from these negatives together is concerned. In other words, where prints from two negatives of different masking are joined to form one positive film, the point of junction will always necessitate double adjustment of the projector gate whenever the composite film length is put through.

Consequently it is very important where film subjects are being produced to see that only cameras with similarly registered gate masks are employed upon the production of the negatives used. In this way alone can it be ensured that the one adjustment of the projector mask on starting the film will do for the whole run.

Where positives are to be made in the camera, the absence of an adjustable gate makes it imperative that all negatives printed from it shall have been taken either through the camera itself or at least by the aid of one with identical registration.

PERFORATING.

The private man, or the one starting filming on his own, should attend carefully to the following points. Have all motion picture cameras on the premises as far as possible identical of construction, having the same movement with pins or claws of one calibre, and see that all picture masks are set in the same relation to the sprocket holes. Have your perforators made to the exact gauge of the camera sprockets, with punches as nicely proportioned as possible to the claws of cameras and printers. This will materially improve the steadiness, and therefore the quality, of the film subjects you issue. Your positive stock should, however, have its perforations large enough to fit easily over the sprockets of commercial projectors.

QUINONE INTENSIFICATION OF NEGATIVES AND POSITIVES.

In December, 1910. Messrs. A. & L. Lumiere, the well-known manufacturers of kinematograph negative and positive stock, published the details of a new form of combined intensifying, toning and hardening bath, which may very possibly turn out to be of great use in the treatment of topical negatives and positives.

The formula for the bath is as follows:—

Quinone	6 ozs.
Potassium Bromide	2 lbs.
Water	60 pints.

Note.—The Quinone referred to above is otherwise known as Benzo-quinone. It is not the same as Quinol (which is another and synonymous term for Hydro-quinone.)

On placing film in the above bath it gradually changes in colour to a dark, reddish brown, also gaining in intensity. Further changes of colour and density may be produced by after treatment, according to the following table. In each case the after treatment is to take place upon the Quinone toned image.

PLACE IN TEN PER CENT. AMMONIA.

Image tones dark brown and becomes still further intensified. After drying, the colour goes back somewhat to the original Quinone tone, but the further gain in intensity remains.

TREATMENT IN CARBONATE OF SODA SOLUTION.

Tones image pure dark brown, with great intensification.

PLACING FILM IN "HYPO."

Reduces the image, making it very transparent, but still of the reddish brown colour, to which the Quinone toned it.

TREATMENT IN SODA SULPHITE SOLUTION.

Tones image greenish brown, without affecting the depth. In any case it will be found that the film, after Quinone treatment, is hardened, just as it would have been by immersion in a formalin bath. Thus the topical worker has placed in his hands a quick and simple means of simultaneously toning, hardening, and modifying the depth of image of a quickly printed and consequently faulty length of positive film which there may be no time to duplicate.

CAMERAS USING NON-PERFORATE FILM.

Although cameras using perforate film constitute the only type of present-day commercial instrument (so far, at any rate, as sales are concerned) it has always been recognised by those interested in kinematography, that were it possible to impart a steady intermittent movement to imperforate film, great advantages might accrue in the matter of motion picture taking and printing.

For one thing imperforate negative and positive film would certainly expand and contract more evenly and uniformly during development and subsequent drying than does the present perforate stock. Also whatever alteration occurred to the film, through strains in course of treatment, would not effect its perforations if these need not be made in it till after all other operations of production had been completed.

The subject is one for the earnest attention of film producers interested in the subject of steady projection.

As to attempts practically to fathom the matter of using unperforated film, the reader is referred to Hopwood's " Living Pictures," page 128, where he will see such an arrangement figured (fig. 142.)   A suggestion for projecting imperforate positive film also occurs in Hepworth's "A B C of Kinematography " (published 1900) though the practical advantage of extending the above idea to projectors might, or might not, prove so great as was there anticipated.

ANOTHER WELL-KNOWN MAKE OF CAMERA.

In our chapter on " The Choice of a Camera Kit" we omitted to mention the Urban Cameras of the Chas. Urban Trading Co., Ltd.   We have, therefore, reproduced here two cuts showing this strongly made and well-designed piece of apparatus.   This firm markets many styles of camera, from prices ranging from £15 to £50, and each has the merit of excellent workmanship and finish.

FIG. 91.   URBAN CAMERA FIXED   FIG. 92.   FIXED ON "HANDY'
      ON "MAXIM" TRIPOD.   TRIPOD.

END OF PART I.

PART II.

PART II.

PROJECTION.

CHAPTER I.

THE ELEMENTS OF PROJECTING.

The problem that confronts us in kinematograph projection is, apart from consideration of the escapement of the machine, practically no different from the one encountered in working an ordinary optical lantern. In fact, the kinematograph projector is merely the combination of the elements of an optical lantern with the escapement necessary for actuating the moving film. The intermittent motion, in so far as it applies to cameras for moving picture work, has already been gone into, and this broad principle remains little if at all altered in its application to projection instruments. We will therefore now introduce the projector firstly as an optical unit for the transmission and concentration of light rays through the kinematograph film and on to the projection screen. Discussion on projector escapements will follow.

The main spring of the projector's optical system is to be discovered in the lantern body. This is simply a roomy fireproof case, generally of asbestos lined iron, designed for the reception of the light source. Limelight or the electric arc usually provide the actual illumination within this lantern body, the light rays falling upon the 'condenser,' situate as shown B, Fig. 93, which consists of a combination of more or less crude lenses mounted in a metal cell, and so arranged as to bring the light from the light source A to a partial focus on the projector gate C.

In this gate the film moves, just as in the gate of a kinematograph camera, the light passing through it and being further collected by the objective lens D, which performs the function of forming the transmitted rays into the image on the screen.

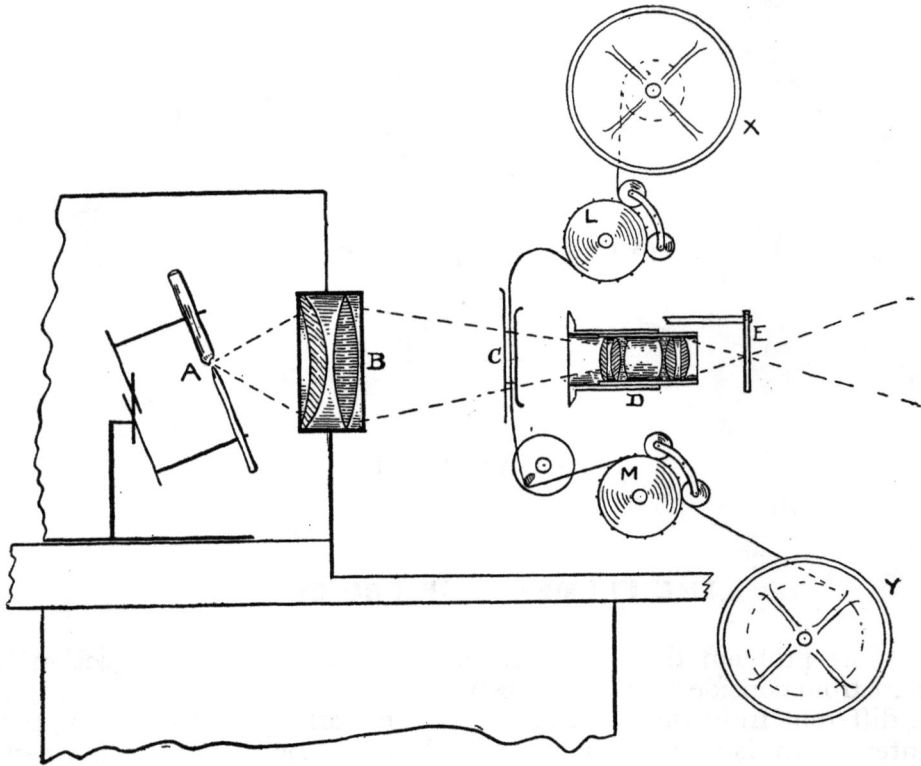

FIG. 93.—THE PROJECTOR AND ITS OPTICAL SYSTEM.

The condensing lens usually employed in projecting moving pictures has a diameter of 4 to $4\frac{1}{2}$ inches, and is either a triple condenser or one of the Herschel type, this latter being a combination of two lenses, the back one, or that nearest the light source, meniscus, and the front one nearest the gate, a double convex (Fig. 94). The objective lens is nearly always of the Petzval portrait type, consisting of a single cemented front combination and an uncemented back com-

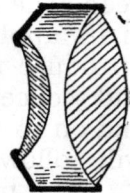

FIG. 94.

bination formed of two thin lenses separated by an air gap. When cleaning these Petzval lenses, rules to remember are to place the uncemented elements in their right order nearest to the gate of the projector, not to omit the metal ring which determines the width of the air gap in the back combination, and last, but not least, to load in all lens elements with their greatest convexity towards the projection screen. This will ensure a correct performance for pretty well all objective lenses commonly met with on a projector.

One thing will probably strike those who glance a second time at Fig. 93, and who may be accustomed to operating the ordinary still view lantern. That is the great distance of the condenser from the film in the gate. The reason for it is the comparatively small size of the kinematograph picture with the consequent necessity for concentration of light from the condenser into a small beam in order to waste as little of it as possible. Beyond this, there is really no fundamental difference between the optical arrangement of a still view and a moving picture projector.

Concerning the manner in which the condenser brings the light rays from the illuminant to a partial focus on the gate, as also the optical effect of the objective to form the image on the screen, this should be fairly plain to those who have read the remarks on elementary optics in the appendix to the first part of this book. The condenser lenses are crude and uncorrected, but they perform their function by bringing the bulk of the incident light to a partial focus on the positive film picture. From the point when this more or less parallelised light beam emerges on to the back glass of the objective the condenser's use is over. The objective proceeds to build up the image on the screen according to the laws of refraction of light. The law of conjugate foci will explain the formation in this instance of a large and distant image by means of a short focus lens. When photographing a natural object with the camera the lens is used to concentrate distant rays to a focus upon the negative film, which is then comparatively close. Large external objects, under these conditions, and following the law of conjugate foci, give a small compact image. In projection work we simply have the case in which distance and consequent comparative size of object and image are reversed. Reference to our conjugate foci diagram will make the matter easier to understand. (Appendix Part I.)

Further, as in photography, so in projection, the focus of the objective lens decides the size of image we can obtain. Thus, a two inch objective will give a clearly focussed image of twice the diameter of the one thrown by a four inch objective at the same distance. This, too, will be found absolutely analogous and explained by the diagrams and remarks on focus of lenses in our first part. But in projection it will be necessary when deciding upon the actual size of the picture to be thrown on the screen to bear in mind a law of light known as the 'law of inverse squares.' This law does not come obviously before one's notice in practical form in kinematograph photography. In projection, however, it is very important, since it is our one means of working out the comparative illumination of screens of various sizes for a given illuminant of known power.

The law of inverse squares may be stated as follows : ' The intensity of light proceeding from a small source is inversely as the square of its distance from that source.' Thus, to state the matter in practical form, the effect of doubling the diameter of the projected image thrown by a given lens with unvarying light source will be to make the illumination of any given portion of the picture, not one half, but one quarter of the former brightness.   Enlarging the projected image three times (either by shifting the screen farther away from the projector or using an objective lens of equal aperture but one third the former focal length) will cause the brilliance of the picture to diminish nine times, and so on.

Bearing this rule in mind, it will be easy for the kinematograph operator to determine at any time whether the light at his disposal will or will not allow of any given enlargement of the projected image. Later on in the book will be found precise tables tending to give more definite help along the same lines.

Having now outlined the general optical arrangement of the projector, and before passing on to deal with any particular points wherein its escapement may differ from that usually associated with the kinematograph camera, it may be as well to touch briefly upon other parts connected with the movement of the celluloid film through the machine.   Such parts will be the feed and take-up spools, the spool arms and spool boxes, feed and take-up sprockets, and the rotary light shutter.   Referring to Diagram 93, X, Y are upper and lower film boxes holding respectively the film and take-up spools ; L, M are upper and lower or feed and take-up sprockets, and E is an end-on view of the rotary light shutter which should not be confused with the sliding light cut-off fitted in practice directly in front of the condenser, and which latter being an article of practical utility rather than a fundamental item of projection will be neglected for the moment.

The film feeding and taking up mechanism consists firstly of a spool arm fixed to the top of the machine, and carrying a rotating and easily removable metallic spool or reel upon which the film to be exhibited is wound before showing.   This rotating spool is enclosed in a fireproof box, having a suitable slit in it fitted with some fire extinguishing device, usually a system of rollers, through which the easily inflammable film is led to the top or feed sprocket.   It is the rotation of this sprocket, actuated by means of gear wheels, that drags the film off the top spool and feeds it uninterruptedly into a loop on the top of the gate.   From this moment the downward motion of the film becomes intermittent, being actuated thenceforward by the escapement, till the film is picked up again uninterruptedly on the bottom sprocket of the kinematograph, from which it is fed to the second, or take-up spool on the lower spool arm of the projector.

This take-up spool, like the feed spool, is a metal reel enclosed in a fireproof box with snuffer device to prevent fire passing through the entrance slit in the event of the combustible film firing in the gate.   Unlike the upper spool, however, the take-up has to be driven forward by means of chain or worm drive from the gearing of the projector mechanism acting on a friction clutch bearing against the take-up reel.   In this manner all slack is successfully picked up by the bottom spool as soon as it is formed, while yet the ribbon film is never at any time subjected to sufficient tension to snap or damage it.

Now comes the turn of the rotary light shutter. What happens upon the screen when a 'moving' picture is exhibited is that a still picture is flashed before our eyes for something less than a twentieth part of a second. The revolving light shutter then cuts it off by rotating into the path of the light beam from the lens. The screen becomes momentarily completely darkened while the escapement moves another picture positive into the place of the first in the gate. Upon the shutter flicking once more out of. the track of the light beam this second picture flashes before our eyes in place of the first for a similar brief interval of under the twentieth of a second. These are the actual facts when moving pictures are projected.

Yet even with the first crude projectors this was not the effect communicated to the brain through the retinal nerves of the eye, while with most modern instruments there is left upon our consciousness neither the sensation of jerky movement, nor any sense of momentary transition from light to darkness. In fact, it comes to this, that while kinematograph photography is a plain sailing sort of thing, projection and the success of it depends upon an illusion of the brain brought about through some universal weakness of our visual capacity, whereby we may trick ourselves into seeming to see what is not there. We flick still pictures illustrating the successive movement phases of an object before our eyes, alternating these brief impressions with fractional moments of complete darkness, and as the result, what we seem to be watching is an evenly illuminated reproduction of the movement of nature. This illusion is brought about at will by the intervention of the celluloid positive film as actuated by the kinematograph projector. Clearly, the why and wherefore of it calls for some attempt at explanation.

Accordingly, our next chapter will be devoted not only to remarks on projector mechanisms, but also to some consideration of the nature of the particular and fundamental optical illusion of kinematography which they call into being.

FIG. 95.   AN EXCITING EPISODE IN "MONTE CRISTO."

The Selig Company have produced many successful masterpieces, including "Christopher Columbus," "Cinderella," "Kings of the Forest," "Lost in the Jungle," "Back to the Primitive," "The Still Alarm," "Captain Kate," and "Dad's Girls." The versatility of their actors is a noticeable feature in their productions.

FIG. 96.   ONE OF THE LION CUBS FROM SELIG'S ZOO.

CHAPTER II.

PERSISTENCE OF VISION.   THE ESCAPEMENT.

The essential phenomenon underlying all kinematographic projection is known in optics as persistence of vision. At the beginning of Part I. short mention was made of certain experiments of Ptolemy, the Greek philosopher, which bore on the subject. Beyond such passing notice, little has up to now been said by us of the relation of 'persistence' to kinematography, chiefly because the question assumes no practical significance during the making of negative and positive film subjects. The moment, however, we come to projecting a moving picture, persistence of vision takes its place as the main consideration controlling the performance. Accordingly, before we go further into the practical side of projector mechanisms, it will be necessary to examine this new theoretical consideration somewhat more carefully.

The phenomenon is most simply demonstrated in the well-known fire circle effect produced by a waving torch or burning brand. Everyone is aware that after a certain rate of speed has been gained, the whirling flame seems to the eye to spread out into a complete ring, or to form itself in seemingly perfect loops and spirals, according to the way such a burning torch is being brandished. In other words, the rate of motion of the flame has become so great as to bring about an optical illusion. We seem to see it lingering in a particular spot after it has really passed well away upon its swinging course. The effect of the bright image lingers in the retina of the eye after the actuality has disappeared; the verity has gone, but its echo exists in the retinal nerves for a short while only, yet long enough to befog the brain into imagining it has perceived complete fiery shapes where they have never really existed.

Precisely the same thing holds good with moving pictures. The photographer takes picture after picture on a band of celluloid. The operator throws successive brilliant images of these little pictures upon the screen, constantly shifting a new picture into the place of the last, in a series of rapid and regular jerks. And the audience watching the effect are willingly deceived by the phenomenon of 'persistence.' The dark intervals when the lens is at cover fail to impress the brain by reason of their shortness. So instead of an endless series of isolated snapshots being apparently thrown on the screen, there seems only the one persisting picture—persisting except for the minor differences of movement phase between the successive images of moving objects impressed upon the celluloid length. So much for the purely theoretical aspect of the thing. Now to consider those points in which the construction of a good projector should differ fundamentally from that of a kinematograph camera so that the phenomenon of persistence, admittedly of no account in camera work, may be given full play on the lantern screen.

Clearly we shall be helping the persistence illusion best by putting as little tax upon it as possible. There is nothing in this world that does not gain by being worked lightly and with consideration. Moreover, persistence of vision is at its height immediately after the withdrawal from the scene of the bright object causing it, in this case the projected kinematograph image. It then takes a dying-down course, occupying a total duration of from the tenth to the twentieth part of a second, by the end of which time the illusion has, practically speaking, come to an end. The moment when the rotary light shutter of the projector comes into play, after showing one kinematograph picture and before the next, persistence is at work, so that to tax the same phenomenon as little as possible the rate of picture change must be quick. In other words, the opaque portion of the rotary shutter must occupy only a small sector of a circle.

With the kinematograph camera, it will be remembered, rate of change is conveniently set at about one to one, that is to say, the cover period during movement of the film is of about the same duration as the period while it remains at rest for exposure. Even then, as often as not, it is found convenient still further to close the exposing aperture of the shutter. This may well make the effective duration of change, as compared to exposure, nearly as two to one. In designing a projector, on the other hand, three quarters exposing interval to one quarter cover period is considered a very low rate of change, while six, or even eight times the period of exposure to that of cover is reached in various projectors now on the market.

Practically speaking, it has not, so far, been found possible to make the rate of change in a modern projector greater than eight to one, for the reason that the intermittent travel of the film would become so rapid, and the grip upon it so sudden as unduly to augment the danger of breakage in the gate. Even so short a cover period as eight to one has, however, been found in practice to leave the phenomenon of the gradual dying down in intensity of persistence of vision sufficiently in evidence for a distinct flicker to be noticeable while projecting a kinematograph positive on the screen.

Several devices were invented in the early days to overcome this well-known defect. One of the first of these devices, invented and figured by Mr. Cecil M. Hepworth in his little book, "The A B C of

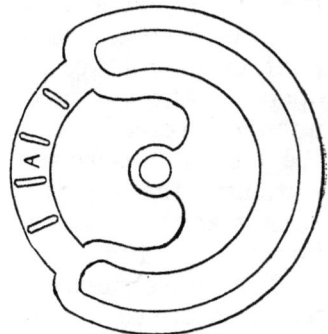

FIG. 97.

Kinematography," and here reproduced (Fig. 97), took the form of a partially perforated cover shutter. The perforated grid A, formed the cover sector of the shutter. Such a device, by lightening the screen somewhat during the dark period, certainly did relieve flicker, but it had the compensating disadvantage of bringing about 'ghost' or blurring of white outlines against dark backgrounds due to the moving film not being completely masked while being actuated by the escapement. A more recent and still very generally accepted way of minimising flicker has been, not by experimenting with the regular light intercepting shutter blade, but by balancing it with a ' non-flick ' fishtail of violet celluloid or gelatine attached to the shutter shaft so as to cross the light beam at the moment when the regular cover sector reaches the middle of its off position. Of course, such addition of a violet non-flick blade cuts down the total period of lighting of the image on the screen. But here comes in an interesting point. The second minor light flicker thus deliberately introduced has the effect of greatly lessening the apparent fierceness of alternation between light and darkness on the projection screen. A moment's thought will explain the reason of it. What we do in reality by the addition of the non-flick blade to the shutter is to call in the phenomenon of persistence a second time to help its own self out by levelling our perception of light on the screen throughout the picture projecting cycle. Fig. 98 illustrates the rotary shutter fitted with non-flick blade.

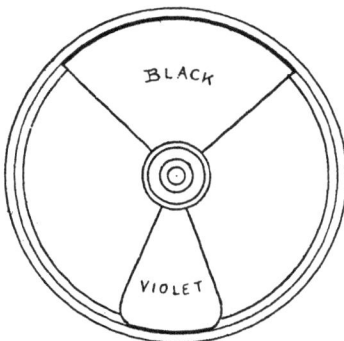

FIG. 98.

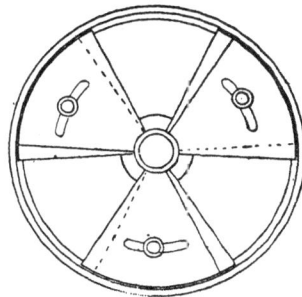

FIG. 99.

In some projectors, this same system has been carried to the length of fitting a shutter having in it three cut-away and three metallic portions. Here the light passage is deliberately interrupted twice between each necessary covering period for picture change, and in practice the resulting frequency of alternation between light and darkness proves itself so much too fast for the human eye to record that no apparent damping down effect is observable in the persistence phenomenon, and consequently flicker is very perfectly eliminated (Fig. 99). A third way of bringing about absolute freedom from flicker in kinematograph projectors is by making the covering sector of the light shutter twice as wide as usual, and revolving it at twice the ordinary speed. The loss of light is nearly the same as when working with an ordinary shutter fitted with compensating non-flick blade, but the effect on the screen is better.

Coming now to the consideration of the intermittent mechanism, we find for one thing that the kinematograph projector differs from the camera in its movement in so far as, while in cameras absolute steadiness is the first essential, and quick rate of change not a considerable item, in projection matters are just the other way about. Thus, where the projector has a movement of the pin type, the pins will be set to act with the greatest possible abruptness and celerity, even at the expense of moderate extra strain on the perforations of the film.

But in kinematograph projectors we find two other well marked types of movement in use beside the pin or claw escapement, notably the Maltese cross and the dog or beater movement. Of the two, the cross is a modified pin movement depending for its action on a system of check wheels similar to the well-known Geneva watch escapement. The Maltese cross is, in fact, practically nothing more than this Geneva escapement adapted to kinematograph purposes. Fig. 100 gives an idea of the principle.

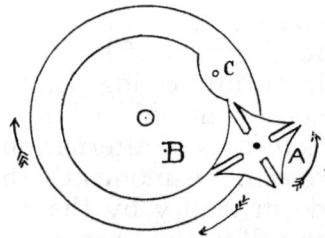

FIG. 100.

B is here a continuously revolving disc having a curved portion cut out of its periphery, while A is the cross itself fixed to the shaft of a four picture sprocket, and cut so that the in-curved faces of the cross fit tightly, yet without pressure, upon the rim of the disc B. In the position indicated in the diagram it will be seen the cross, and thus the four picture sprocket with which it is connected, is not only at rest but actually locked against the rim of the continuously revolving disc. This state of things will continue until the cut-away portion of the latter comes underneath the cross. When this happens, the lock is released, making the cross free to move a portion of a turn. At the same time, the pin C, revolving with the disc B, catches in the slot at the left hand top corner of the cross. A must now move in the direction of the arrow for a quarter turn before the pin C is released from the slot, and by the time this movement is over the disc B will have so far continued its rotation as to bring the locking portion of its rim back under the cross. It will thus be seen that, practically speaking, the cross is locked both when at rest and during the period of rotation. Consequently it follows, when the parts are accurately made and fitted, the movement is as perfect as any escapement actuating a single pair of pins can be. Formerly the Maltese cross suffered from the two great disadvantages of noisy action and want of durability. Both these drawbacks have latterly been overcome by arranging the escapement to work in an oil bath. The addition of a hardened steel roller mounted so as to revolve freely upon the pinion C still further eliminates the clatter which would otherwise result from the striking of C upon the inner sides of the radial slots of the star wheel at the moment of engagement.

A further advantage of the Maltese cross is that the four picture intermittent sprocket which the cross actuates, and whereby the downward shift of the film is made at the moment of change, may be placed very close beneath the film gate of the projector. Thus minor shrinkages in the positive stock due to strain during development, heat in the gate during projection, and such like causes do not tend to make the projected image shift up and down to the same extent as would be the case if any considerable length of film intervened between the gate and the movement device, as in the case of the dog or beater pattern projector about to be described.

At the same time, and although the dog type of movement has for long been recognised as not quite so steady as a good example of the pin or Maltese cross type, this also is in great demand, especially in the lower priced forms of projector, and where machines are intended primarily for hard and rough usage. Where a kinematograph is going to be used long and often, tended by a none too careful operator, and condemned to live its life touring abroad or in some comparatively small town where repairing and renewing of worn out parts cannot be conveniently undertaken on the spot, then the dog projector is, and will probably long remain, the one and only thoroughly reliable model.

In principle, the dog strikes out a type of movement on its own, known as continuous in contradistinction to the intermittent movement of a Maltese cross. This means that in the dog type of escapement, though the film travels in jerks its actuating mechanism does nothing of the kind. Nor is there any locking of parts at the various phases of the movement cycle, nor does any part of the mechanism come abruptly to rest and as quickly resume a high rate of speed. Naturally, therefore the dog is incomparably simpler than any other movement at any time introduced for kinematograph requirements. Fig. 101 shows it in diagram.

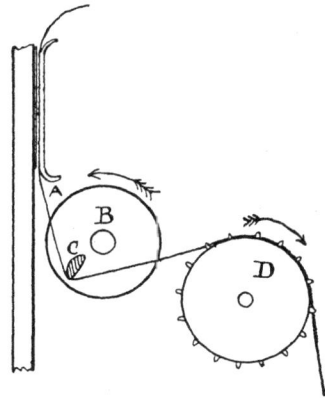

FIG. 101.

A is the film seen emerging from the film gate. D is the lower or take-up sprocket wheel revolving continuously in the direction of the arrow. Over this sprocket wheel the film passes, following a course in the track of the dog roller C, revolving in contrary direction upon the disc B. A few moments' study of this diagram will convince us as to the actual state of affairs when such a movement is in operation. The film will be constantly wound up or tightened by the take-up, this one action proceeding continuously and at an even rate. Meanwhile, the eccentric dog roller will strike the face of the film intermittently, drawing or beating down through the gate a certain length at each stroke and this at a rapid rate.   In practice, the length so beaten down is adjusted to the height of a kinematograph picture, so that each blow of the dog makes one picture shift.   Further, the rate of turning of the lower sprocket D is so adjusted that a like space of film is just wound up by the time the beater descends for its next blow.   Thus we have arrived at a state of things where our intermittent picture shifting is accomplished through the means of mechanism continuously revolving in the one direction.   Nothing could be simpler that this solution to the problem of actuating the kinematograph film in the projector gate, and nothing could be more reliable up to a certain point. But though the dog form of movement wears well, and major troubles in working seldom occur, the effect at its best is undoubtedly inferior to that of the Maltese cross also at its best.   Nor is the reason far to seek.   For one thing, the Maltese cross locks the film between each shift, but the dog movement depends entirely for its steadiness on the friction of the gate springs tending to prevent after-slip in the film, the latter arrangement being obviously the less accurate of the two.   Consequently, the residual movement of the film, which it makes by its own impetus in the dog machine in the absence of such definite locking action between picture shifts, becomes an item of uncertainty in the performance of the dog projector.   Crinkles in the celluloid will affect the steadiness of the projected picture to a far greater extent than when the Maltese cross escapement is in use. Even minor differences in thickness of various portions of the film base will be recorded as slight up and down swaying irregularities of the projected moving picture.   Rate of turning, and jerkiness due to hand turning will likewise all affect picture steadiness—in this case through the film's shift being partly dependent in its extent upon the momentum of the dog acting upon its inertia.   The necessary comparatively long interval of space between the dog and the bottom of the gate has already been pointed out as a further source of unsteadiness in projection.

All the same, speaking practically, the dog projector proves itself in use to be much better than the above considerations taken together would tend to make it seem.   Where a rough and ready knock-about machine is required it still holds its own both for economy of first cost and of running expenses.

Beside the foregoing types of escapement for actuating the intermittently moving celluloid positive film, there are several which should not go without some mention, though at present, as far as the writer is aware, they are being put to no very practical use in the moving picture world.   The intermittent grip movement, in which two wheels are set, one on either side of the film below the gate, and having parts of their circumference cut away so that their rims only come together and grip the film (thus drawing it down) through a small portion of their revolution, is a case in point.   Undoubtedly, though this particular arrangement came to no practical use, it embodies a principle which may yet show itself to good purpose in kinematography. The split screw type of movement was also undoubtedly a sound one, though unfortunately at the time it saw the light, prices of projectors ruled so low as to cause it to be abandoned, largely through the expense of construction. Still, the Lumiere pin movement, and especially the adaptation of it now to be found in the Kineto type projector, shows a certain affinity with the split screw idea.

Perhaps the worst thing that can be said of the old fashioned kinematograph projector movements is that they were not designed sufficiently with the view to easy repair, adjustment, and renewal of worn parts. Some modern makes of bioscope also show the same defects, and very glaringly, too. Thus, the best advice that can be given to the would-be buyer of a new projector is to make sure not only of its performance in the present, but also as to there being reasonable facilities incorporated in its construction for taking up and making good future wear on the escapement parts. As to the latter point, careful examination of a machine or two will soon show the buyer with a turn for mechanics what chances there may or may not be for remedying the inevitable effects of constant use. Bushings and spindles, for instance, should not only be hardened, but removable for renewal. The same applies to dog rollers, Maltese cross parts, and even to the continuously moving sprockets, especially in the case of dog machines where the steadiness of projection is quite as dependent upon the gate springs and the take-up sprocket as upon the dog itself.

In cases where the projected image thrown by a dog machine develops a sudden and unearthly kick, it is generally a sign that the gate springs or runners are at fault. Examination of them will almost certainly reveal extensive wear, together with more or less uneven spring tension. Set this right, and the kicking trouble will probably cease. Where, however, the trouble with a dog machine takes the form of an upward or downward roll of the picture on the screen, it may be looked upon as certain either that the gear wheel teeth are faulty (gear wheels have to be particularly accurately cut for use on dog projectors) or else the take-up sprocket has had a blow and thus been thrown out of truth. A loose and rattling dog roller may also prove the cause of unsteadiness.

A rhythmatic up and down motion with a cross projector means usually wrong spacing between the pins on the four picture intermittent sprocket, or of the radial slots of the cross while kicking effects are almost always the outcome of wear on the edges of the cross itself. We assume the films to be properly perforated to start with. So much for projectors, considered as a whole. The next chapter will deal more particularly with certain well-known makes at present on the English market, and it is to be hoped, therefore, that the perusal of it may prove of value, as well as merely of interest.

FIG. 102. SCENE FROM THE VITAGRAPH CO'S. "THE FRENCH SPY."

A beautifully dressed and well acted vigorous story—full of incident and varied scenery. The intense and natural acting of the Vitagraph stock companies is exemplified in this highly dramatic subject.

CHAPTER III.

PROJECTORS AND ACCESSORIES.

One of the cheapest projectors that we know designed to take full-sized kinematograph film, and is not a toy, is the Empire Home Kinematograph, model oo (fig. 103). This is a dog machine, fairly solidly

FIG. 103. BUTCHER'S EMPIRE HOME KINEMATOGRAPH.

constructed and capable of giving a very good account of itself at home or in the schoolroom.   The lantern body is of a size to accommodate a high power, limelight jet with comfort, while the projector is fitted with swing-over movement, by means of which an ordinary lantern lens in rack mount can be brought before the condenser for showing still slides, announcements, and titles.   The 'Empire Home model oo' is, in fact, a small and lightly made edition of the accepted and approved dog pattern projector, so well known and widely used for many years past.   Its price is £5 15s.

ERNEMANN HOME KINEMATOGRAPH.

Those desiring a machine of the Maltese Cross type for home use or experimental purposes, can find their wants satisfied in the Ernemann Home Kinematograph. Like the Empire machine it is, broadly speaking, a model of larger star wheel projectors. The Ernemann Home machine is, moreover, fitted with a three-bladed light shutter, by means of which flicker is practically done away with, while the escapement is particularly solid and accurate for so small a projector. Altogether, it is quite marvellous value at the price of eight guineas, which is all the makers ask for it.

FIG. 104.   THE ERNEMANN HOME KINEMATOGRAPH.

For those in search of a professional machine, however, either of the dog, cross or claw movement description, it had better be said at once there are none such (at any rate, as regards projectors with a maker's name behind them) to be had under a twenty pound note. Having stated that much, we will turn to a consideration of a few of the standard models of the present day. Generally speaking, prices for the complete projector, with take-up, spool boxes, lantern house, base and stand, range from rather under £30 to something over £40.

BEARD'S THEATRE PROJECTOR.

Illustration 105 is of Beard's Theatre Model projector. It is a professional type dog machine of first-class workmanship and construction, put out by the makers of the world-famous Beard's oxygen regulator. The Theatre Model Projector is no newcomer, but a revised and improved version of the Patent Perfect Projector which has won laurels for itself in years past. Among other important features, it has a special film masking adjustment consisting of a jockey roller between the dog and the bottom sprocket. This jockey is controlled by a lever (shown as the lowermost one in the illustration) by means

FIG. 105. BEARD'S PATENT PERFECT PROJECTOR.

of which masking can be performed quickly and accurately without in any way interfering with the centring of the illuminant in its relation to the objective. The device is picked out for special mention as typical of the many advantages of the above machine.

KINETO PROJECTOR.

With our next illustration (106) we come upon yet another different type of mechanism. In short, in the Kineto Model B Projector, we have what is practically the claw escapement of the motion picture camera adapted to throwing moving pictures on the screen. The Kineto Model B, as illustrated, is fitted with a rotary shutter of the well-known type in which a single cover blade is compensated by a violet non-flick fish tail. Yet the absence of flicker is phenomenal, the reason for such being found in the enormously high rate of change incorporated in this particular projector. By means of its quadruple claw, the film is shifted in the gate in but a comparatively small fraction of the time occupied by the complete escapement cycle, so that even without a non-flick balancing blade the period of light to darkness on the screen is very great. For this reason, the Kineto projector, divested of its non-flick addition, should possess a strong appeal to the exhibitor using limelight. The claw escapement is almost silent in operation, while as for steadiness, it is only necessary to remind the possible purchaser once again that the pin or claw is the form of escapement universally

FIG. 106.　KINETO MODEL B PROJECTOR.

chosen for present day kinematograph cameras for this very reason. The general get-up of the Kineto projector is imposing, as may readily be seen from the photograph printed above.

SIMPLEX PROJECTOR.

The latest projector to be introduced to the public by the firm of Kineto, Ltd., is, however, the " Simplex." As will be apparent from the accompanying illustration to the reader versed in the differences between English and other models, the Simplex hails from the United States of America. It is a well-made and somewhat elaborate piece of mechanism, full of novel features. For instance,

FIG. 107.—THE SIMPLEX PROJECTOR.

the cover shutter, should it be thrown out of phase through the carelessness of the operator or other cause, can be re-adjusted while the machine is running. Then, again, the works are totally enclosed, a point held to render the machine immune from the possibility of spreading danger through accidental firing of the film in the gate. The price of the Simplex is £65—next to the highest of any projector on the English market.

ERNEMANN THEATRE MODEL.

Perhaps of all silent machines, however, the palm should be given to the Ernemann (shown in illustration 108). The Ernemann also goes by the name of the 'All-Steel' projector, a title which should sufficiently indicate its durability and hard-wearing qualities. Perhaps some readers may remember that a fire occurred not so long ago at the premises of one of the Cecil Court companies ; several

FIG. 109.

FIG. 108.   THE ERNEMANN PROJECTOR.

THE SILENT EMPIRE

FIG. 110. THE MALTESE CROSS EMPIRE PROJECTOR

of the All-Steel Ernemanns came out practically scatheless from the conflagration, due to the high melting point of the materials from which they were made. Another notable point about this same projector is the large size of the Maltese Cross (shown in illustration 109). The same machine also boasts an improved three-bladed flickerless shutter, instantaneously removable condenser glasses, and, in fact, every improvement to be expected or wished for in a motion picture lantern of the highest repute. And with that we have placed ourselves in a somewhat awkward position, for the very next figure (illustration 110) shows a projector not one atom less worthy of unstinted praise. It is the

MALTESE CROSS EMPIRE NO. 12 OF MESSRS. BUTCHER.

Let us be content to say of this machine that it is all it should be, comparing favorably with others, and holding its own by virtue of general excellence.

Since the publication of the first edition of this Handbook, the Silent Empire Projector has been very greatly improved. The new 1913 Model is provided with a Patent fixed optical centre, by means of which the operator is enabled to centre his film and raise and lower the arc lamp at the same time by a single movement, operating between lenses, projector mask and lantern body.

The 1913 Model Silent Empire is also arranged in such a way that the projection arc is thrown backwards and forwards upon runners within the lantern body the correct amount to adjust itself for the showing of still or animated pictures, the movement being made automatically with the sliding of the lamp house behind the mechanism or the lantern slide objective. The principal gears of this machine are now well protected by carefully-constructed shields.

GAUMONT CHRONO PROJECTOR.

The picture which comes next among our illustrations (fig. 111) will be pretty well self-explanatory to a whole army of kinematograph enthusiasts, to say nothing of experienced operators who can scarcely have seen actice service without an introduction to the original of the photo—the Gaumont Chrono. No one wants to hear much about the Chrono's essential details now-a-days, for the simple reason that they were familiar to lovers of the best in the art of projection when other high-class present day machines were still unthought of. It was the Gaumont Chrono which first adopted the flickerless shutter (or so we believe). Certainly it was the firm responsible for the Chrono which first paved the way for the now victorious campaign of quality before cheapness in moving picture projectors. No one who purchases a Chrono expects anything but the best, and we have never heard of any such a one being disappointed.

The Gaumont Maltese Cross Chrono has, besides its wonderful reputation, many unique features to recommend it. Moreover, these exclusive features are not mere 'talking

FIG. III. GENERAL VIEW OF THE CHRONO PROJECTOR.

points,' or 'selling points,' but actual solid advantages to the buyer and user. For one thing, the cross is so fashioned that the least slackness occurring as the result of wear may be taken up with the minimum waste of time and trouble by the simple adjustment of two screws. This is, of course, in addition to the cross being bodily removable for replacement, should occasion for this eventually arise.

FIG. 112.   THE GAUMONT MALTESE CROSS CHRONO, SHOWING ARRANGEMENT OF GATE AND LIGHT SHUTTER.

Then again, the new double speed light shutter, as fitted in the Chrono, is so arranged that it travels up and down with the racking of the gate, a matter of great importance in high-class machines, where mask adjustment is effected by means of gate racking, in contra-distinction to the employment of a lever-actuated jockey roller. Other good points and special features of the Gaumont machine will be apparent from reference to the illustration block as appended. But no one wishing to hear of this projector's merits need ever trouble over worrying them out from mere printed illustrations and letter-press description. There is not a man of any standing in the kinematograph trade but knows and has handled Gaumont machines, and can tell the novice all about them.

FIG. 113. THE WRENCH PROJECTION APPARATUS.

WRENCH MODEL C MACHINE.

Messrs. Wrench have ever been modest in their claims as to the merits of their apparatus. The reason is simple, and lies in the fact that Wrench projectors have made for themselves so firm a reputation with the motion picture exhibiting public as to need no superlative epithets of the makers wherewith to label themselves before they go out on the market. We look at the illustration (fig. 113), and ask ourselves if it is not the most convincing thing possible, as setting forth the sterling worth and first-class workmanship of the Wrench Maltese

Cross Projector. Note the neat masking lever giving the whole picture adjustment, the hardened steel bearings to all important working parts, the solid steel gate runners, the excellently designed oil bath, the many other advantages plain to see, and it will be agreed the firm of Wrench can afford to go soft in singing their own praises in the assurance that the trade at large will not be slow in supplying the deficiency.

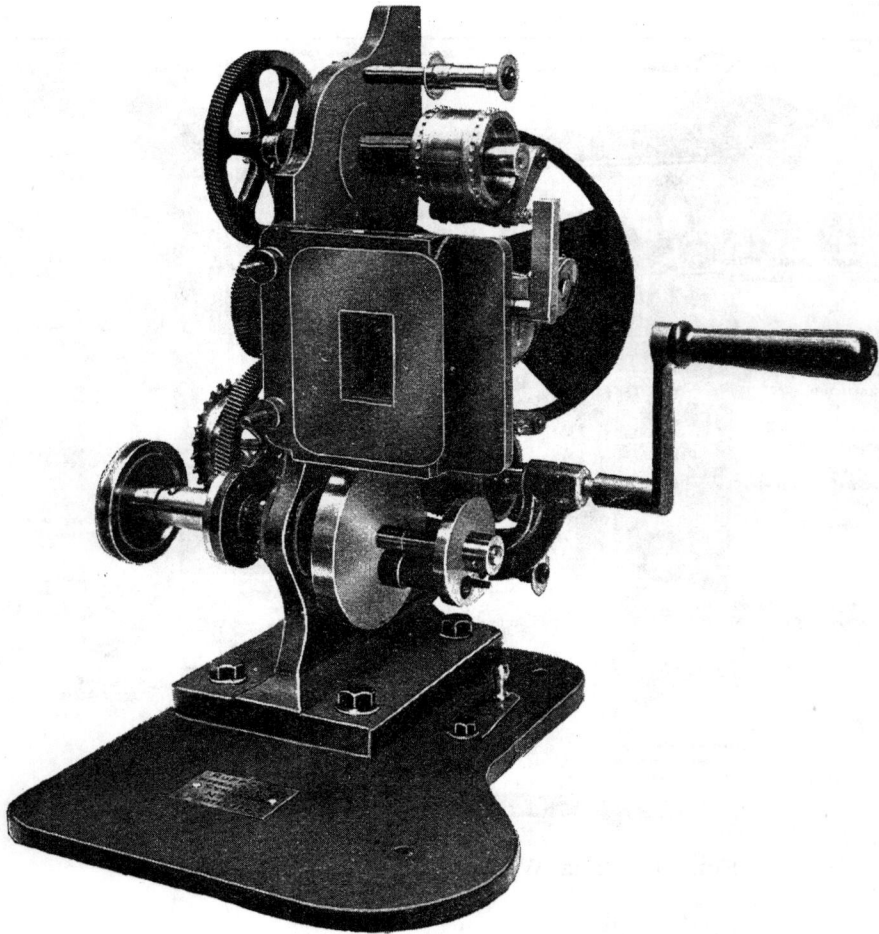

FIG. 114. RUFFELL'S SIMPLE BUT EFFICIENT PROJECTOR.

RUFFELL'S PROJECTOR.

We pass on to the consideration of yet another projector, namely, Ruffell's Bioscope. It is a machine worthy of a firm whose name has shone as a light in the kinematograph trade for many a long year—in fact, since the very early days indeed. For that matter, the author had enjoyed more than one display of Ruffell's Pictures before ever he had touched a kinematograph machine in his life. Well, then, Ruffell's Bioscope is just what one would expect under such circumstances. It is a machine of wisdom, of experience, and of a hardy and enduring value. No brilliant yet uncertain experiment awaits the purchaser of a 'Ruffell.' He puts his money on a certainty and may make up his mind to the possession of a machine with a long career of usefulness before it. What more than this need we say? Fig. 114 gives a good idea of this valuable projector.

THE BROCKLISS MOTIOGRAPH PROJECTOR.

The Brockliss Motiograph projector is the machine with the famed double cone shutter. Really this shutter needs a word or two to itself, since had the Motiograph no other striking point about it, the double cone arrangement for intercepting the light beam during picture change would alone constitute the projector as forming a class of its own. Unfortunately, the Motiograph double shutter is of a form particularly difficult to figure in print. It consists of an arrangement of two pairs of shutter blades, each pair being of 16 degrees and 32 degrees diameter, the whole bent up into a cone shape, and one cone revolving within the other very much after the style of the beaters of a mechanical egg whisk. The complete arrangement is so placed that when the metallic sectors of each cone are nearest to the projector gate, they serve to intercept the light, while when they are at their farthest point of travel, they miss the light beam entirely. Add to this that the two cones revolve in opposite directions, so imparting to the blades a kind of scissors action when opening and closing before the gate, and one has an admittedly vague idea of the absolute novelty of this system of light interception, as compared with that of all other projectors. The Motiograph has, however, beyond its double cone light shutter, a whole host of special and important features, for the mere mention of many of which we have not space at our command. For instance, there is the matter of the phosphor bronze bearings, with their fine adjustments for take up of wear in any part of the machine. Also the film is fed to the gate through a system of spring rollers which prevent side shake in the projected screen picture. Perhaps, though, we cannot do better than use what space remains to us for the purpose of impressing upon the reader the enormous saving of illumination effected by the Motiograph's shutter arrangement. From thirty to forty per cent of light, which would be lost with other machines, is conserved and used in this projector. For lime shows, therefore, the Motiograph should possess an appeal all its own, while the advantage in light saving is well worth considering by showmen employing electricity also. The Motiograph is an American-made instrument, and as such perhaps rather more delicately—that is to say, not quite so solidly—constructed as most English showmen are accustomed to. There are many points about this apparatus which must commend themselves to the skilled operator who takes pride in his projection.

FIG. 115. THE MOTIOGRAPH.

Kamm Maltese Cross Machine.

With the Kamm Maltese Cross projector (illustration 116) we come up against that very latest type of picture shutter mentioned

Fig. 116. Kamm's Maltese Cross Projector.

in the preceding chapter, namely, the double speed light shutter. We have already commented upon the marvellous effect of this high speed shutter gearing in the elimination of the last trace of flicker from the screen, so that here it will be enough to remark that the possession of such a double-speed shutter places the Kamm M.C. machine in a class by itself.   Other features of the same projector well worthy of note are the oil bath, automatic light cut-off, devised on a specially simple and reliable plan, the heavy fireproof gate, etc.

PATHE LUMIERE PROJECTOR.

Another claw system projector is that next figured (fig. 117). This time the mechanism bears the name of that great film house, Messrs. Pathe.   All the same, it is worth while noting the Pathe Lumiere projector is not offered on the market as a tyro's or handle-turner's machine.   It is intended to be used only by fully experienced operators, and only so must it be expected to develop those marvellous

FIG. 117.   PATHE LUMIERE PROJECTOR.

qualities of steadiness and precision which gained for it—and for kinematography in general—the first recognition of the theatrical and entertainment world.   For this Lumiere machine in its earliest type was the father of all publicly exhibited money-getting moving picture machines.

PATHE No. 2.

The regular Pathe projector of the present day is that next shown (fig. 118), known as the Pathe No. 2.   It is a specimen of bioscope mechanism of the French type, somewhat lighter in build than we on this side of the Channel are accustomed to.   However, the Pathe No. 2 can now be obtained in England in a form of somewhat heavier build and with its parts rather differently arranged, in which guise it takes to itself the name of the Pathe Imperial. In this and the No. 2 the essential mechanism is the same, to wit, a Maltese Cross

FIG. 118. PATHE IMPERIAL PROJECTOR.

running in enclosed oil bath. Such has been found to bring about the happy combination of great steadiness (due to the cross) combined with very good wearing qualities (the result of the constant and thorough lubrication afforded by the running of the working parts in oil). Pathe machines of this type are very silent in action.

TYLER'S INDOMITABLE PROJECTOR.

There is an increasing desire on the part of every Englishman to recognise merit in the effort to produce British productions for the benefit of the community. It is also so in the kinematograph trade ; whether it be film subjects or machines, there is an effort to obtain the all-British production. A successful achievement in this direction is Tyler's British Projector, which has recently been put on the market and has been well christened 'Indomitable.'

FIG. 119. TYLER'S INDOMITABLE PROJECTOR.

Let us say at once that it does not require a second glance to convince one that Tyler's have struck out for the best, and have attained it. In the build and in the design of the machine there is abundant evidence of the highest mechanical skill and of a determination at all costs to produce something that shall be solid and thorough in every essential. In these days, when projectors have to stand the daily strain of ten to twelve hours' work, when keen and critical audiences observe at once a badly projected and unsteady picture, and seek their recreation and amusement at halls projecting the best picture, we cannot help feeling that Tyler's will find their efforts to produce a really first-class All-British machine, will meet with a gratifying and immediate reward at the hands of the trade.

Among some of the many novel features which must appeal to users are, the heat-proof lantern body, with doors opening on both sides the full extent of the frame ; the stirrup holder for the condenser; the facility for exchanging from kinematograph to still picture lens ; the Maltese Cross movement in its oil bath ; the get-at-ableness of the gate ; the ease with which each part can be adjusted ; the solid bearings and shafts ; the automatic light cut-off ; the sheet steel fireproof boxes ; the original take-up and rewind gear ; the solidity of the projector stand ; the numerous dustproof oil caps, and the general finish and appearance of the whole outfit.

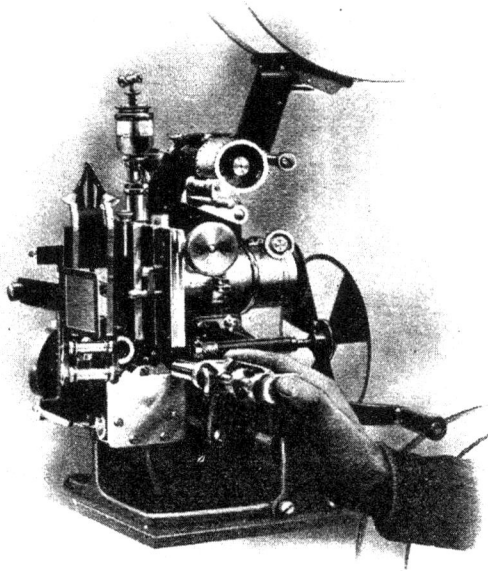

FIG. 120. THE ZAR PROJECTOR.

THE ZAR.

Needless to say, many firms are still striving to improve and beat past achievements. Whether any of these efforts will meet with success, it is not for us to hint in a machine review like the present, but the thought of all-steel projectors naturally leads us on to the Zar of Cinema-Halles, Ltd. The Zar machine combines many distinct advantages.   The makers claim for it that it combines in itself ' all the best and brightest ideas in projectors to be found both in England and on the Continent.'   What we can inform our readers with certainty is, firstly, that it is in every sense of the word a first-class instrument.   Passing on to particularise on its merits, we may just spare time to mention its adjustable and removable Maltese Cross action, adjustable gate skates, and instantly removable condensers.   It is also fitted with a patent flickerless light shutter, an excellent automatic take-up, and a whole heap of other excellent features too numerous to mention here.   The price, while not pretending to be low, is moreover very reasonable for an instrument of the sort described.   See fig. 120.

FIG. 121.   THE URBANORA SILENT KNIGHT PROJECTOR.

URBANORA SILENT KNIGHT PROJECTOR.

This is a high grade Maltese Cross projector put on the market by the Urban Trading Company.   Its main features are extreme accuracy of construction, whilst other important points are silent and steady running, freedom from flicker, a very full masking capacity (of fully one and a quarter pictures), and great moderation in price for so beautifully made and efficient a machine.   The high grade nature of the workmanship employed upon it will be at once apparent from a glance at the illustration accompanying, fig. 121.

WARWICK BIOSCOPES.

Warwick bioscopes are simply-designed machines with little complication of parts, and they possess, as may be divined from this last statement, a consequent enviable measure of durability which far exceeds that of many a projector of more complex model. Were we operating in any inaccessible part of the globe, such, for instance,

FIG. 122. THE WARWICK PROJECTOR.

as a desert or a country village, we would not hesitate to plump for such a simple machine as the Warwick, in preference to most of the highly expensive and intricate M.C. patterns which now so largely hold the field for cinema and music hall work. The Warwick bioscope is shown in fig. 122.

THE KALEE.

The New Century Kalee Projector stands out in the accompanying figure (123) like the Rock of Gibraltar. It is solid and business-like, and has with it a sort of general air of being invulnerable, which should go far of itself to reassure the intending purchasers of one of these excellent machines. We like the general design, with its firm, amply supported base and clean cut proportions, and what is more, we are sure the motion picture proprietor and operator will like it too. It will be seen, the Kalee projector is of the neat self-contained inside light shutter type, while the Maltese Cross is of generous proportions, by which means wear is minimised and steadiness maintained. Ample gate masking, diagonal cut gears, and a generally sound and scientific design and construction complete a projector which the parent firm may well be proud of.

FIG. 123. NEW CENTURY KALEE PROJECTOR.

The Projectors of Messrs. Hughes.

One of the original firms for apparatus and projectors was Messrs. Hughes and Co., of Kingsland Road, who still keep pace with the necessities and requirements of modern operating by continually improving their manufactures.

One of their cheapest and most trustworthy machines is the No. 3 Elphinstone type of Brewstergraph. This is a machine strongly built and can be hand or motor-driven. The light cut-off is of entirely new and certain movement and cannot be tampered with, and the film gate and trap is unique and simple in construction. There are not any gate springs to break or tear the film, and although the gate will never fly open, yet it can be opened when necessary to the fullest width.

FIG. 124. THE NEW BREWSTERGRAPH, SHOWING THE DOUBLE OPTICAL SYSTEM.

A better class machine, which contains a double optical system, is the Brewstergraph at forty-five guineas. Now that slides are again becoming so popular, the advantage of this extra system will be admitted by all who have small space in their operating box at their disposal. This machine can be obtained for sixty guineas manufactured entirely of steel.

Messrs. Hughes also have a projector called the Bio-Picture-scope Reverser at £73 10s. This machine has a patented movement for drawing down the film. It is a piston plunger movement, and as in the ordinary engine the piston gradually moves a wheel with an even pressure in every part, in like manner the piston movement with its aluminium roller moves the film down one picture at a time. The advantages claimed are that the strain on the film is exceedingly gentle and yet effective, and also that it is considerably quicker than the

FIG. 125.
BREWSTERGRAPH REVERSER DE LUXE.

FIG. 126.
THE PISTON PLUNGER MOVEMENT.

dog or claw movement. In Illustration 126 will be found a cut of this piston plunger, and my readers who have followed my description of the various movements will be able to understand the action of this piece of apparatus.

FIG. 127.   THE EMPIRE THEATRE LANTERN.

EMPIRE THEATRE LANTERN.

The Empire Theatre Lantern is the name given to the extremely serviceable still view lantern next figured. The lantern is especially designed for installation in the operating box to relieve the projector of its generally somewhat doubtfully performed function of projecting title and illustrated song slides. That such work should by right be relegated to a distinct lantern is a matter insisted on elsewhere in this volume, and those who will follow our advice can do no better than to instal an Empire Theatre lantern. Not only is this admirable all-metal lantern provided with its own self-contained tilting table, also telescopic three-draw front to accommodate lenses of suitable focal length for any picture hall, but it is, in addition to the above, so arranged that it can be utilised as a first-rate ' stage arc ' for throwing the well-known spot light upon variety turns, now so frequently to be seen at the better-class picture halls. A suitable miniature arc for use with the above lantern is the Klimax Parallel Arc Lamp (Illustration 128). The price of the Klimax, complete with resistance frame, is exceptionally low.

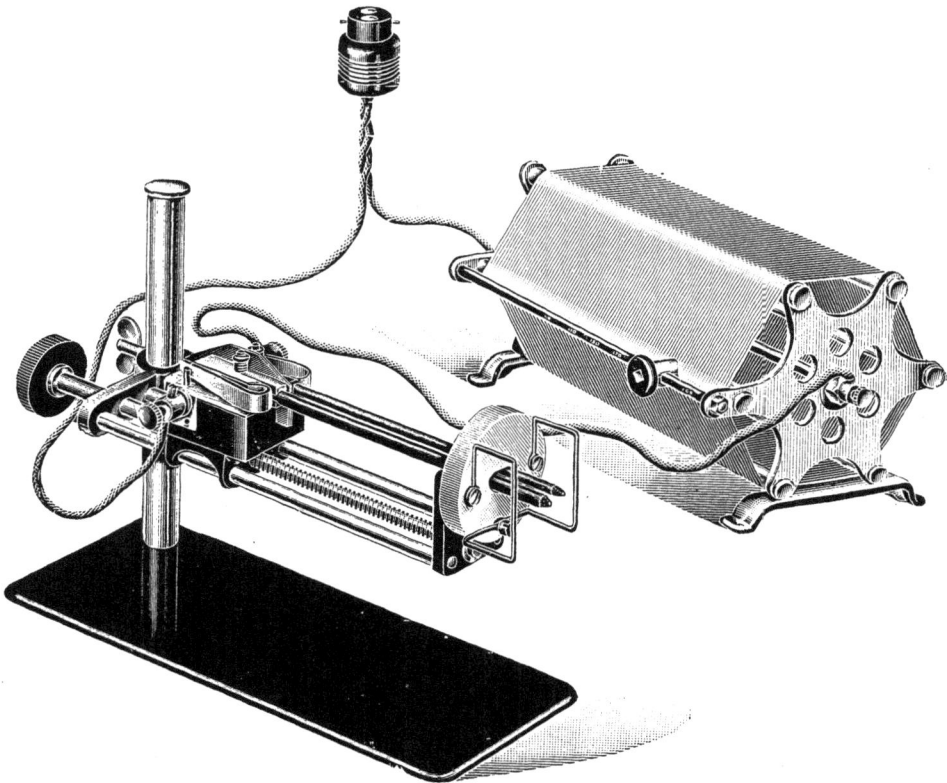

FIG. 128. KLIMAX PARALLEL ARC LAMP.

Klimax Parallel Arc Lamps.

To those whose interest in kinematography centres in its minor but sufficiently entertaining outlet for home amusement, the Klimax arc lamp (fig. 128) manufactured by Messrs. W. Butcher & Sons, Ltd., will be particularly interesting. This little lamp is of novel construction in that the carbon rods between which the arc forms itself are set parallel to one another, instead of being at right angles, or in opposition, as in more usual types of the electric arc.

The efficiency of the Klimax parallel arc lamp is very high for the current consumed, while the feeding forward of the carbons is extremely simple. The price of the whole lamp, complete with resistance, ranges from £3 to £3 10s., according to the voltage supply of the house mains. The Klimax No. 1 forms an ideal illuminant for home kinematograph machines, or where moving pictures up to not more than three or four feet in diameter are to be shown. The current, which must not exceed five amperes, is conveniently obtained from the nearest electric bracket by tapping it off with a bayonet plug.

Model No. 2 Klimax parallel arc lamp, for currents up to eighteen amperes, is a heavier made and slightly more expensive edition of the No. 1 Model. It is capable of giving a light up to 5,000 or 6,000 candle power, and would therefore be suitable for certain small kinematograph shows, such as schoolroom entertainments and affairs of the like sort. Special heavy wiring is necessary for use with the No. 2 Klimax projection arc.

And thus passing from projectors themselves to their attachments, we will yet make pause before what may at first sight look like another maker's machine, though as a matter of fact it is the already mentioned Pathe No. 2, this time fitted complete with spool boxes and—what is the present object of our attention—the Mallet patent attachment for automatically sealing the film box apertures in case of film fires. This process is accomplished by two tightly stretched strands of highly inflammable material held directly over the threaded film in its direction of travel out of the upper spool box and into the lower one. These highly inflammable strands hold open substantial sealing shutters hinged over the spool box apertures. Should the film fire in the gate and should the fire pass upward or downward toward the film boxes, the flame would be bound to ignite the safety strands, with the instantaneous result that the shutters would be released and fall.

Next (fig. 130), we have a very clearly drawn illustration of a Pathe condenser holder. A glance will serve to show how such a holder with glasses ready set in it, can be taken up in the hand by means of the top handle, and dropped into place in the front of the lamp house almost as soon as a crack in the existing condenser glass is seen. Condenser cracking is, however, to some extent at least, avoidable if due care is taken to provide for reasonable ventilation and expansion of the glasses in their cells.

THE EMPIRE COMPENSATING CONDENSER.

This is interesting both in itself and as an example of the application of brains and thought to kinematography. The novel feature of the condenser is its mount, which consists of two halves, hinged the one to the other and clasping together round the lenses of the condenser after the style of an ordinary lady's bracelet. The idea

FIG. 129. PATHE NO. 2, WITH MALLET ATTACHMENT.

FIG. 130.
PATHE CONDENSER HOLDER.

FIG. 131.
EMPIRE COMPENSATING CONDENSER.

behind this new arrangement is firstly, the avoidance of the necessity for making large air holes in the mount, which holes are considered by the designers of the Empire compensating condenser to be a frequent cause of broken glasses, due to the play of sudden currents of cold air upon their inner faces.   Secondly, the clip-over design of the mount is intended to provide a method of holding the lenses which shall be both free from shake when they are cold and capable of great elasticity when the warming of them causes sudden enlargement of the diameter.   (Fig. 131.)

The Kineto extra heavy condenser (fig. 132) is an example of another highly efficient system of mounting condenser glasses accurately and expeditiously by the employment of a suitably solid trio

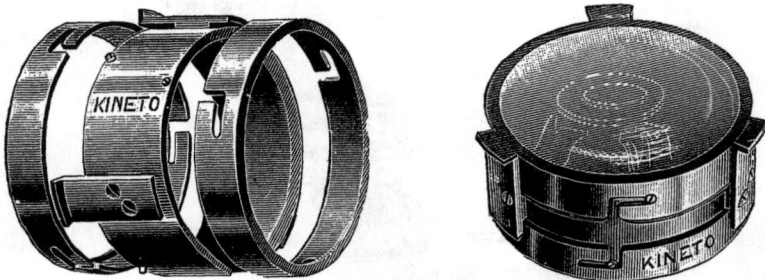

FIG. 132   KINETO EXTRA HEAVY CONDENSER.

of tubed rings, which interlock by means of quick-acting bayonet catches.   Bayonet catches also hold this extra heavy condenser in the lamp house body, thus allowing of its removal for renewal of a cracked lens in almost no time.

BUSCH PROJECTION LENSES.

These are of three types.   First come the ordinary kinematograph lenses put out by this firm.   These are listed at a uniform price of 28s. for any focus from two and an eighth to seven and a quarter inches.   They are good sound lenses, and the only marvel is that the public still go on paying a guinea or more a time for worthless nameless rubbish in the way of kinematograph lenses, when instruments by a reputable maker are to be had at this moderate figure.   Next we come to the Busch Double Illumination projection lenses.   Here a new principle is involved, in addition to the general high quality we get in the cheaper series just alluded to.   In these Double Illumination Lenses there is a large gain of effective light on the projection screen, a point which renders them well worthy the especial attention of limelight exhibitors.   Still, the price remains extremely moderate, though all the time the quality is of the highest for instruments of the class indicated.   But we pass on to the final grade in the Busch scale of excellence.   Here price becomes altogether a secondary matter, but our Busch kinematograph lens belongs to this highest plane of excellence, and is indeed a wonderful instrument. Named the Glaukar Projection Lens, it is, in fact, an instrument of a type so perfect as to be not merely fit for optical projection of the highest class, but also equally suitable for the actual taking of the pictures themselves, and everyone knows that to take a kinematograph picture nothing but the most perfect of optical combinations will serve. In the Glaukar projection lens, then, we have an instrument which may fairly claim to be absolutely and literally perfect. Other makers may equal it. Candidly, we could name at least one English firm of repute which turns out lenses equally as good. But when a thing is perfect, as is this Busch Glaukar, it cannot be surpassed, and there is no getting over it. The block hardly does justice to its importance and value.

FIG. 133.
BUSCH GLAUKAR
PROJECTION LENS.

The Walturdaw projection lens battery (fig. 131) will probably prove of service to operators travelling their own apparatus from place to place, and who are constantly being confronted with different

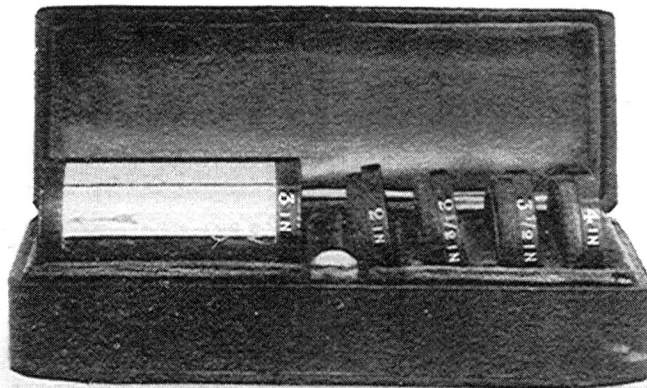

THE WALTURDAW LENS BATTERY
Nº 2 (NEW SYSTEM)

FIG. 134. A CASKET OF PROJECTION LENSES.

conditions of throw when showing pictures. Here the many foci obtainable with such a lens battery will be very welcome.

There can be no question that the man who values clear screen pictures, and who has the interest of the profession at heart, to say nothing of appreciating largely enhanced returns for small additional outlay, will insist on his projector being fitted with a lens by one of the well-known lens makers, such as Busch or Dallmeyer. The illustration (fig. 135, page 158) is of a Dallmeyer Kinematograph Pro-

FIG. 135.   DALLMEYER PROJECTION LENS.

jection Lens, which may be had in any focus desired from two inch to
six inch.   Only those who have worked with high-class projection
lenses can realise the difference they make to the clearness of the
picture, as also their effect in making possible greater economy of
current consumption for a given brilliancy of throw.

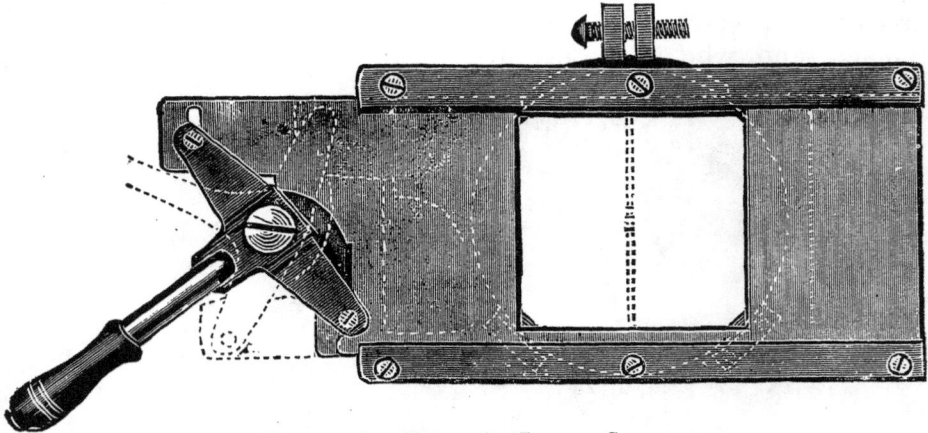

FIG. 136.   BEARD'S LIGHT CUT-OFF.

FIG. 137.   KINETO LIGHT CUT-OFF.

Figures 136 and 137 show respectively a Beard and a Kineto light
cut-off.   These cut-offs are of the hand operated type, being therefore

auxiliary to the automatic light cut-off fitted to modern projectors. Hand cut-offs are fitted on the lantern cone, or directly before the slide carrier. In this way they act as curtain cut-offs when projecting title and announcement slides. Both the makes of cut-off figured are practically identical in action.

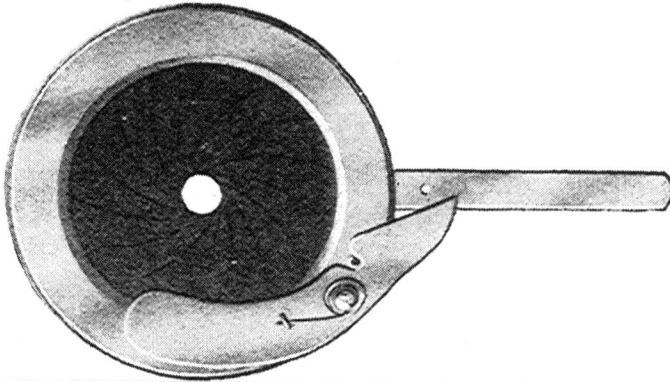

FIG. 138. THE IRIS DIAPHRAGM.

When speaking of dissolving effects with the electric bi-unial lantern in the chapter on song slides, we made mention of an iris diaphragm to be fitted before the lenses. Such a one is to be found in the 'Cat's Eye' of The Tyler Apparatus Company. We give an illustration in order to make its working clearer. (fig. 138).

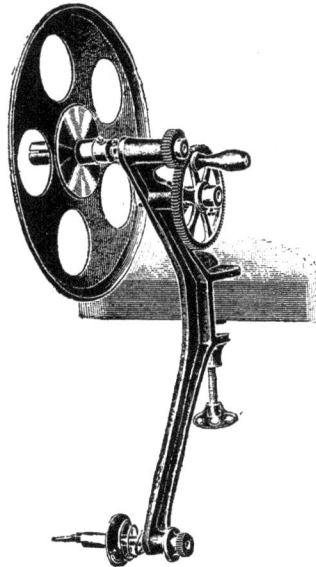

FIG. 139. THE HEPWORTH REWINDER

Among the firms who from long practical experience have developed their apparatus to the requirements of the trade, may be mentioned the Hepworth Manufacturing Company, one of the oldest firms in the trade. They issue what is called the Heptoic Bioscope, a good, substantial, steady machine, with every appliance essential to perfect projection. This firm make a feature of complete equipments at an all-round figure—a very useful fact for those who are starting in the profession. They have some unique electric appliances, including the Hepworth Patent Arc Lamp, which, although simple in construction, is effective in its working. Another very excellent adjunct to the operating box is the Hepworth Rewinder, which folds into small compass, and by adding a small sprocket wheel measurement attachment, lengths of film can be duly checked—a matter which pays the cost of the apparatus time and again.

And now we take a jump from the beginnings to, as it were, the very extreme end of projection matters. Hitherto we have been considering how to equip the operating box for the starting of a successful

FIG. 140.   SEABORNE POWER DRIVEN FILM CLEANING MACHINE.

show. But what when films have been shown time after time? It is with heartfelt regret that we have to record the deplorable state of the film selections in certain services which are neither first nor even tenth run, but where the film is literally shaggy with age, titles gone, endings abrupt, and last, but worst of all, the remainder in a deplorable state of filth and oiliness. The writer has seen film services so far gone in this respect that a run of a few thousand feet only was sufficient to clog the roller of a dog projector almost to the point of sticking. Needless to say, when such film comes into our hands, most of us will have the natural thought ' Oh, if only we could clean it before showing.' Well, as a matter of fact, this can very easily be done by means of such a film cleaning machine as the Seaborne (fig. 140). In this film cleaner, the work is swiftly and automatically performed in two definite stages. First the dirty film is well covered with a suitable cleansing fluid (be it said a very cheap one), next the wet film is dried by the train of leather brushes figured in the photo block, by which means dirt and grease are rapidly and thoroughly wiped out ; both hillocks and ruts and visible scratches are also to a great extent made to disappear. Including the cost of motor drive

FIG. 141. THE DEBRIE NAMING AND BRUSHING MACHINE.

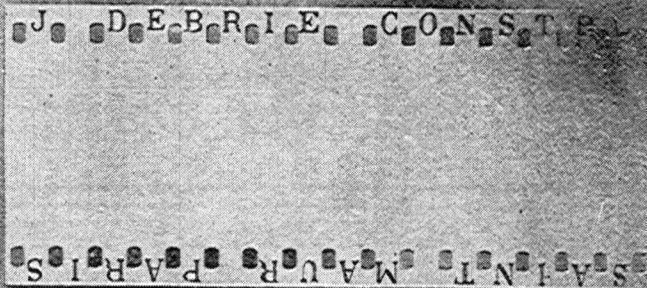

FIG. 142. FILM LETTERED BY THE NAMING MACHINE

of the Seaborne cleaning machine, the outlay on film cleaning works out at approximately 4d. per thousand feet, so that even were picture theatres to instal it as an adjunct, the present they would be making the renting houses by cleaning the worst of the film before showing would not be excessive, while for the renting houses themselves, film cleaning may now be said to have become an imperative demand. The cost of the Seaborne is not high. That of the Debrie Film Cleaner is considerably more, but then, as has already been explained, the firm of Debrie (English agents, Messrs. Brockliss) makes no bid for cheapness, considering only quality in the goods it sends upon the market. A glance will serve to show that the principle utilised for cleaning and wiping the film band in the Debrie and Seaborne machines is very similar. Another ingenious Debrie machine which we mention here for the sake of convenience is the Naming and Brushing Machine, shown (illustration 141). To the operator, the chief interest of this little contrivance will lie in the fact that it is by means of it (or some other similar arrangement) that the maker's name is put on the edge of the positive film he shows. As a matter of fact, the work is accomplished by means of an enclosed incandescent electric light shining through a rotary stencil plate, over which the as yet unexposed positive stock passes, after brushing free from dust by the little brush wheels shown in the illustration. Fig. 142 shows how such named film would develop were it placed in the developing bath without intermediate printing behind the usual kinematograph negative by means of a 'printer,' as described in the chapter on Printing (Part I).

To enumerate every projector, arc lamp, resistance, and the hundreds of other adjuncts to the modern operating box now on the market would necessitate a book three or four times the size of the present, we have therefore endeavoured to present a representative selection, and have pointed out the characteristics and leading features of each item. Makers of apparatus have seen the value of producing exhaustive and detailed catalogues and lists, fully illustrated and descriptive of their goods. To those about to purchase, therefore, who desire a further knowledge of the respective " points " of the appliances, we commend the price lists, and also the fact that makers are only too ready to give demonstrations and advice when asked for.

Finally, there is one thing we desire to agitate for, as being a necessity to all well-governed operating rooms, and that is that the iron fire shutter should be of an improved make that can readily be relied upon in all cases of emergency. Among the best we have seen on the market are those with the strong lever releasing gear, which is controlled from both the inside and the outside. Messrs. Jukes, Coulson, Stokes and Company, of Plaistow, make a big feature of these shutters, which are a real necessity for all up-to-date projection rooms.

CHAPTER IV.

THE ILLUMINANT—ELECTRICITY.

Now to the consideration of the illuminant to use in the projection of moving pictures. Practically speaking, except for amateur work —exhibiting films at home and such like—there are only two alternative forms of illuminant available :—limelight and electricity.

Even here our choice is still further limited by the recent Home Office regulations governing the conditions under which limelight may be employed. Comparing the two forms of illuminant on the grounds of economy and efficiency, there can be no doubt as to the verdict for all serious projection work lying with electricity. As to efficiency, electricity can be made to give an amount of illumination only limited by our expenditure upon current, whereas limelight, apart from every consideration of economy, can never do more than yield a light rather under than over three thousand candle power. Further, the light source with electricity is far smaller than that obtained from the glowing lime, with the result that in the former case the concentration of the pencil upon the projector gate is correspondingly more free from wasteful nebulous edge. Further, electric light for projection purposes is somewhat easier to manage than limelight (both require skilled handling) and on the score of economy may prove anywhere up to ten times as cheap in use, especially where the kinematograph show is remote from the nearest centre for gas cylinder charging, and where electric current is produced on the spot by means of a good class private generating plant.

For the foregoing reasons, electricity claims first place in our description of kinematograph illuminants. We will start upon its manner of employment in the projection arc by giving a brief sketch of its generation and measurement, also some of the most important terms of nomenclature.

Electricity, or electric current, as it may be called, can be generated in various ways. Moreover, the manifestation of it is often vastly different according to how it is called into being. For instance, lightning and the commodity which produces rotation in an electric motor are both electricity, and the only reason for the vastly different phenomena connected with the two manifestations of electrical energy is to be found in the manner of the current's generation.

The form of electricity which alone comes into evidence as the electrical supply of a picture hall is a continual 'flow' or 'current' manufactured by means of a machine called a dynamo or generator.

Such a generator consists of a soft iron drum wound about with coil upon coil of insulated copper wire and made to rotate at very high speed within the field of a powerful magnet. This rotating drum of wire is called the armature. The result of such a strange arrangement is that currents or waves of electricity are caused to form in the whirling wire coils, and this electric current is duly led to a circular arrangement of metallic conductors called a commutator, upon which press 'brushes' usually consisting of blocks of carbon. These collect the current and take it to binding screws or lugs, and from them wires known as 'main leads' further convey the electrical energy on its mission of usefulness.

Sometimes this mission is directly to supply light for the projection arc and the small incandescent lights of the picture hall. Sometimes, on the other hand, the main leads take the current to a series of glass boxes filled with weak sulphuric acid and containing lead plates covered with a paste of lead oxide. These are known as accumulators or secondary storage batteries.

When they are in use, the current in its passage through the acid and the lead plates converts the paste on the latter into a very unstable form of metallic lead. The accumulator is then said to be 'charged,' for it now has in its turn conferred upon it the property of giving out electricity from its terminals in an amount dependent upon the size of the plates and charging they have received.

Thus, we already see that besides electricity being generated as the result of purely mechanical action, it may also be given off in connection with chemical action. It is more usual, however, to take the current direct off the dynamo or generator for supplying the projection arc.

Electricity as produced for picture work has a voltage of anything from 60 to 500, the latter being very high for the work intended, and about the greatest potential to be met with in practice. This word 'voltage' will be explained a little later, together with other electrical terms. In any case, current of the voltage to be met with in picture halls only flows well through metal leads, preferably copper. Where the current is required it is accordingly led by the simple means of connecting a copper wire of suitable diameter (according to the amount of electricity wanted in any particular place) with one terminal of the electrical generator, and bringing the electrical flow back along a second copper wire to the other terminal of the generator. The current is thus supplied with a loop of wire along which it may run out from one terminal (the positive) and back again to the second terminal (the negative). Break this loop by cutting the wire at any point and the current refuses to leap the gap—unless it is a particularly short one.

That last simple fact is utilised in practice as the means of checking electrical flow when not required. The adaptation of the idea takes the form of the electrical switch.

A switch is merely a hinged metallic prong which can be made to grip firmly between conveniently situated metallic jaws, or to fly out of contact with them at will. The prong and the jaws into which it fits form part of the ' circuit ' or electrical loop of wire to and from the generator. When the prong is in contact with the jaws of the switch, current can flow along an unbroken metallic path. Pull the prong out and the track is interrupted. (Fig. 143.)

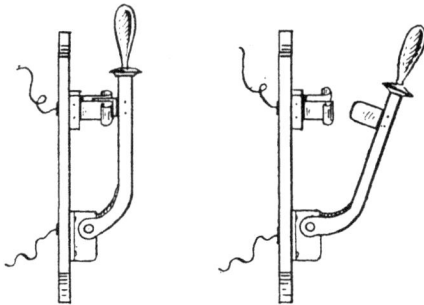

FIG. 143.

Beside providing a copper track for elecricity to run round, there is another matter which is to be attended to in order that the current, especially current of the higher potentials, may be employed in safety. This is to see that the conducting circuit is surrounded by substances through which the current has a particular objection to flowing—otherwise called non-conductors of electricity.

Non-conductors are non-metallic substances such as india-rubber, manilla, oiled cotton, silk, vulcanized rubber, paper, etc. Electric wires are insulated with such substances to make them safe to handle while ' alive,' or carrying electricity, also to prevent current from running to waste through chance metallic side tracks. Damp surfaces are also partial conductors of electricity, and where a bare wire comes against such some of the current has a habit of trickling down into the ground below our feet and disappearing. This is known as an ' earth.' Where there is a doubt that electricity bills are unduly high, ' earths ' or ' grounds ' should be tested for by the electrician using an insulation tester known as an ' ohmmeter and generator,' or ' megger.'

Below will be found diagrammatic illustration of a direct and alternating current electric generator. The most fundamental difference between them is that whereas in the direct current generator or dynamo the commutator is segmented, in the alternator the commutator is of the ' split ring ' type.

If, instead of driving a dynamo by means of mechanical power, electric current is sent through its windings in the opposite direction to which it would be given out in the usual way, the armature rotates of itself as a consequence. Thus, we may either use such an electro-

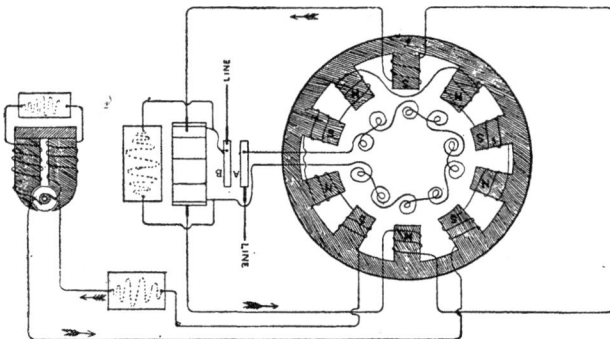

FIG. 144.   DIRECT AND ALTERNATING
GENERATOR COUPLED.

magnetic machine to make electricity (for which purpose the armature is turned mechanically by say a steam, gas, or petrol engine), or we may use it as a source of mechanical energy by turning electricity into its coils.

Electro-magnetic machines specially adapted to give power in the shape of rotation in response to feeding with electric current are termed 'motors.' Small motors of one-eighth horse power or less are now commonly used in the operating box to turn the mechanism of the projector, instead of the operator doing it by hand. These small motors consume little more current than an ordinary sixteen candle carbon filament lamp.

Now to turn to electrical nomenclature.

DIRECT AND ALTERNATING CURRENT (D.C. AND A.C.)

The electric 'current,' as it is termed (the word is not in any sense explanatory, and an attempt to give here the modern theory as to what electricity actually is would be productive of no practical good) this electric 'current' is generated of two kinds, direct and alternating. Direct current flows in a constant stream from the positive to the negative pole of the generating system, and that is all there is to say about it, but alternating current may be looked upon as a succession of electrical waves going in opposite directions. Each wave pulses through the circuit in an almost infinitely short space of time, dies down, and is succeeded in the fractional part of a second, by another one going contrariwise to the last. Thus, with the alternating kind of electricity there is really no positive and no negative pole, since both terminals of the generator become alternately positive and negative at intervals of anywhere between the twenty-fifth and the one-hundredth part of a second. The sum of alternations of direction of current flow per second is spoken of as the 'periodicity' or number of 'cycles' of the alternator producing it. Thus, a fifty cycle system would be produced by a fifty cycle alternator. All this means that with the particular description of alternating current in use, the direction of flow alters fifty times in each direction with each second of time.

Note that whereas either direct or alternating current may be produced by an electrical generator according to the system of 'commutation,' or current collection employed, storage battery systems give only direct current. Also, systems involving auxiliary storage batteries for use in case of temporary breakdown of machinery are invariably of the direct current type. In stamping the descriptive plates to be affixed on electrical machinery, and otherwise in the notation of electrical energy, a straight line stands to denote direct and a curved one, alternating current.

In kinematograph projection, employ direct current whenever possible. It is more economical than alternating when used for the projection arc. Further, the arc's crater, on which it will subsequently be found the performance of the arc depends, is formed much more satisfactorily and is much steadier when direct than when alternating current is employed. Also, where the kinematograph is to be electrically driven, this can be far more satisfactorily accomplished by means of a direct than with an alternating motor. The latter class has a very bad efficiency at starting under load, the best small power alternating motors being those of the ' repulsion ' type.

Having now tried to sketch the chief practical differences between the two great systems of electrical supply, we will go on to definite terms common to both. Instead of putting the formal definitions first, however, we will, if you please, work up to them in our own way.

VOLT.—The Volt is the electrical unit of pressure, just as the pound to the square inch is the unit of steam pressure. The word ' volt ' does not indicate quantity of electricity in the least. For instance, there might be the equivalent of a horse power of electrical energy passing through a conductor at a pressure of say ten or even five volts, while the next conductor might carry a tenth or even a hundredth the amount of current at a pressure of 10,000 volts. The term for quantity in electrical parlance is ' ampere,' commonly shortened into the familiar contraction ' amp.'

AMPERE.—An Ampere signifies a definite amount of electrical energy, the actual amount of work to which it is equivalent being decided by its pressure in volts, and the time for which such current flows. And this brings us to the consideration of our third important electrical unit, the one which corresponds to friction as met with in estimating ordinary mechanical energy. We all know that when a machine is doing work, mechanical power is absorbed by the combination of gravity and friction, which tends to stop the rotation of wheels and mechanism generally of the machine.

These electrical terms may be compared to the action of a man pushing a truck along a road. The man presses the handle of a truck (this is the voltage), he overcomes the friction (the resistance) of the wheels on the axle and against the surface of the road, etc., and the truck moves. The rate at which the truck moves is equivalent to the electric current. The more the man pushes (viz., the greater the voltage or pressure) the greater is the movement of the truck, which corresponds to the greater flow of current which would accrue from an increased voltage. If, on the other hand, he suddenly wheels his truck off wood pavement on to a rough gravel path, then the same pressure will only allow a slow speed, and to get the same speed as when on wood pavement he has to exert himself more. That is to say the greater the resistance, the greater is the pressure or voltage required to get the same current of electricity. Electricity in itself is practically useless. It is the *flow*—the electric current— which is of value.

In electricity the flow of current along even the best conductor is attended with the necessity for similar driving power to send the current on its way. It is this driving of the current that calls for the pressure—otherwise voltage—in an electrical circuit. The voltage expends itself against the circuit's resistance—the equivalent of mechanical friction—only that amount of ' amperes ' of current travelling through the circuit which the voltage is sufficient to drive. Thus the third electrical measurement to be taken into consideration is the internal resistance of the circuit. This resistance is measured in ' ohms.'

The OHM is the unit of electrical resistance. It is that resistance to the current which is exercised by a column of mercury one square millimetre in section and 106.3 centimetres in height. That gives us our first *tangible* electrical measurement, and from it the volt and ampere become also tangible electrical units, for :—

ONE VOLT is that electrical pressure which is required to cause ONE AMPERE to flow through the resistance of ONE OHM.

The actual pressure corresponding to one volt has been originally decided by calibration with a standard type of electrical primary cell. It is also possible to state the actual equivalent in horse power of an amount of electrical energy, and this is done in terms of ' wattage.' Thus :—

ONE WATT is the energy represented by one ampere at a pressure of one volt. Seven hundred and forty-six watts is the equivalent of one electrical horse power, so that it becomes comparatively easy to work out the equivalent in horse power of any dynamo — which we shall remember is the name given to the machine used to produce electrical energy. For instance, take the case of a five kilowatt dynamo. This will give an electrical output of five thousand watts, one kilowatt equalling a thousand watts. Divide 5,000 by 746 and we shall find the electrical output of the dynamo to be the equivalent of 6 7-10 horse power (approx:)

We cannot pass on to other considerations without setting forth Ohm's Law :

OHM'S LAW :—Current equals pressure divided by resistance. Let C stand for current, E for pressure (electromotive force), and R for resistance, then setting down Ohm's law as a simple algebraic equation—

$$C = \frac{E}{R}$$

The above simple formula is of endless use to the electrician. By the aid of it, he can ascertain for himself either the current, voltage, or resistance of any given circuit where the other two electrical quantities are known. Thus by simple means of algebra we see that if

(1) $C = \dfrac{E}{R}$ it must also follow that

(2) $R = \dfrac{E}{C}$ as also that

(3) $E = C \times R.$

As an example of the use of the above formulae derived from Ohm's law, suppose the voltage of a given circuit is not known, but the amperage and resistance are, then, from formula (3), multiplying the two latter together will give the required potential.

Perhaps the simplest of all forms of stating Ohm's Law is by means of the 'rule of thumb.' Here it is :

$$\frac{V}{O \quad A}$$

V here means, of course, voltage, A amperage, and O resistance. The rule is when wishing to find out the third unknown quantity where two are given, cover up the letter representing the unknown and proceed to divide or multiply the amounts represented by the two remaining letters according as to whether they show themselves on the same side or on opposite sides of the line. The result is precisely the same as when Ohm's Law is worked intelligently and takes the same amount of trouble, only the rule of thumb seems on the surface to call for less intellectual effort, and will doubtless therefore be appreciated.

ELECTRICAL UNITS OF THE ELECTRICITY SUPPLY CORPORATIONS.

The electrical unit used when computing the charge for electrical service is the watt-hour, or rather, the amount of electrical work represented by 1,000 watt-hours. The watt-hour is just the thing it calls itself : the service of one watt of electrical energy for the space of one hour, or of a correspondingly larger or smaller amount of energy for an equivalent shorter or longer time. Two watts running for half an hour would thus be one watt-hour. Also, the twentieth part of a watt running for twenty hours would be one watt-hour. The reason for making the practical commercial unit one thousand times the watt hour is purely a matter of convenience. This thousand watt-hour electrical quantity is known as the Board of Trade unit— familiarly the 'unit' or 'B.T.U.' A unit of electricity may cost anything from one penny to eightpence when bought off the public supply. When generated by means of a suitable private plant, a unit may cost the producer scarcely more than a halfpenny, according to how generated. The unit will be seen to be the equivalent of about one and a quarter electrical horse-power for the space of one hour. Also, taking the voltage of the projection arc at 70, one unit of electricity would provide about 14 amperes for one hour. In other words, a 40 amp. projection arc will consume about three units of electricity per hour. We are here well up against the important item of running costs of projection. Accordingly, it may not be out of place to note that supposing the arc is on for three hours and the electricity rate fourpence per unit, the cost of current (exclusive of upkeep of carbons, etc.,) would be 3s. This gives a fair idea as to what electricity charges would be where town electric supply is in use. Later on, it is hoped to indicate methods of obtaining one's own electrical energy in more economical fashion. This talk of quantities and cost of current brings us to the consideration of electrical measuring instruments.

The instruments necessary on every well-equipped switchboard are an ammeter and a voltmeter.

An AMPERE METER, often abbreviated to 'Ammeter,' depends for its action on the fact that a coil of wire carrying current is magnetic and will attract an iron core, the amount of attraction being proportional to the number of amperes applied. Current to be measured by this instrument is made to flow through the windings, and the movement of the core is then indicated on a dial by a pointer attached to it.

A VOLTMETER is an instrument for measuring the voltage or electric pressure between any two points of an electric system or circuit. The usual form of voltmeter for practical work is a core or coil arrangement similar to that of an ordinary ampere meter, in which the movement of the core depends on the magnetic pull of the coil. The amount of this pull, in its turn, is governed by the number of turns of wire in the coil, and the strength of current running through same. By reference to Ohm's Law it will be seen that the voltage of an electric current is dependent on the resistance of the circuit, and the number

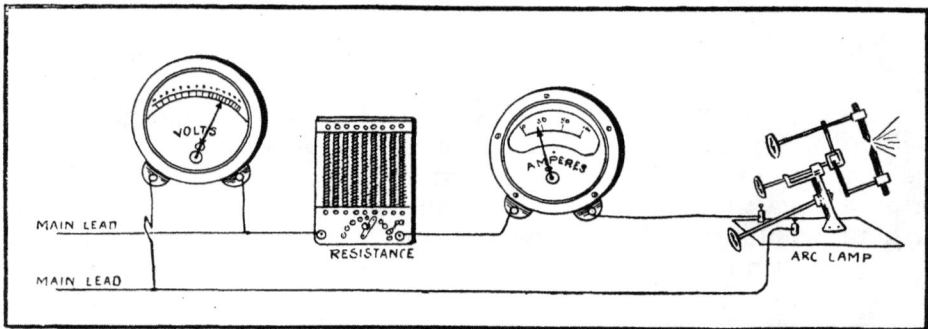

FIG. 145.   VOLTMETER AND AMMETER CONNECTED UP.

of amperes flowing. Accordingly, where the resistance is kept constant the current will depend on the voltage applied. The movement of a voltmeter's core depends therefore on the amount of current in the instrument, and the deflection so produced will record the voltage of the circuit. The resistance of a voltmeter is usually very high in order that the current absorbed may be negligible, and therefore very many turns of fine wire are necessary. For this reason it is very easy to burn out a voltmeter by over-running. Fig. 145 shows the method of connecting voltmeter and ammeter with the necessary wires. Technically, the ammeter would be said to be connected in series, and the voltmeter in parallel.

THE PROJECTION ARC.

The projection arc lamp on which the bioscope depends for its source of illumination is a heavily made instrument of the hand-feed type. The electric arc lamp consists essentially of two carbon points or rods, one of them being connected with the positive and one with the negative cable of the electrical circuit. If current of more than 40 volts potential be turned on and the carbons momentarily 'struck,' or brought together and then as quickly parted again, the electricity

FIG. 146. DIRECT CURRENT ARC SHOWING ANGULAR TILT TO BRACKET.

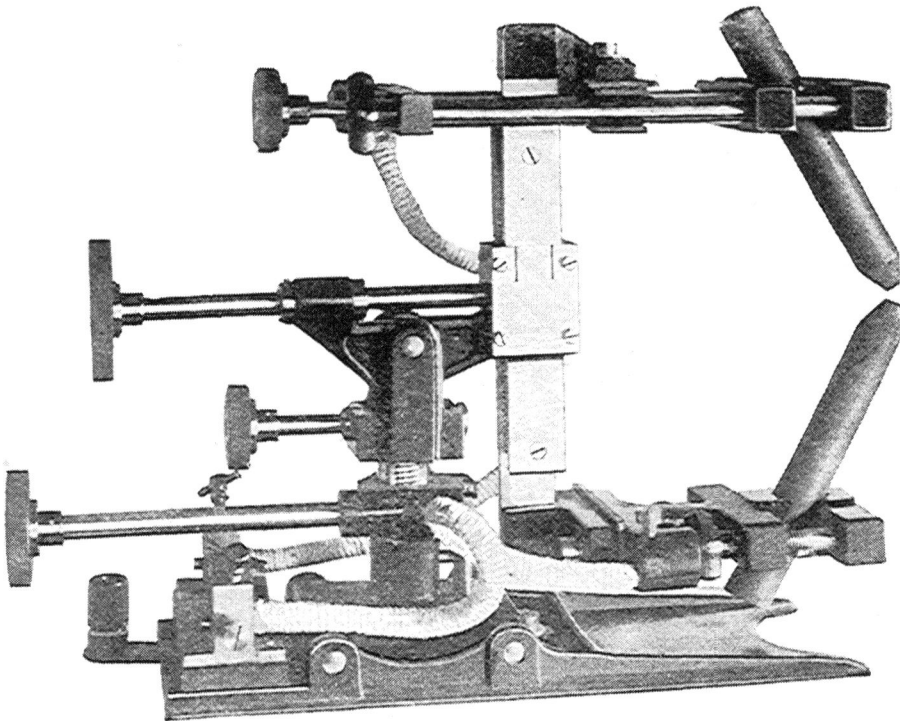

FIG. 147. ALTERNATING CURRENT ARC SHOWING VERTICAL BRACKET.

will be caused to jump from one carbon to another over a short air gap. Incidentally, the positive carbon will become incandescent, the amount of light given off by it depending upon its size and the quantity of current flowing.   While the light continues the carbon is burning away from both rods, though chiefly from the positive one. The positive being made of larger diameter, burns short at the same rate as the negative and so keeps the arc at a constant position when the carbons are fed together. All the same, the air gap gradually widens till it becomes so great as to put the arc out.   To cause the arc to remain burning therefore, some device is necessary whereby the carbon rods can be 'fed' together as they are consumed.   Further, to ensure keeping the position of the arc's 'crater' upon the positive pole (from which the major portion of the light emanates) exactly at the focus of the condenser, a second movement is necessary to the arc feed whereby the two carbons may be raised and lowered together as a whole. We must bear in mind when dealing with D.C. arcs that the crater when properly formed occupies a slope of about 45 degrees upon the end of the positive carbon, while the light from it is thrown, not straight ahead, but partially downwards. Therefore, to get it through the condenser lens, the entire bracket holding the carbons has to be tilted backward about 25 degrees.

THE WALTURDAW
ACME ARC LAMP

Fig. 148.

The Walturdaw Acme Arc is a lamp of the latest and most approved pattern, being fitted with every possible movement. See the six insulated milled heads. (Fig. 148.)

A recent and very excellent arc lamp, possessing novel features of its own, is the new model Kamm projection arc. In this lamp every possible adjustment is supplied, each movement being controlled

FIG. 149. THE KAMM PROJECTION ARC LAMP.

by insulated milled heads. The Kamm projection arc is as yet a new arrival, but none the less it has already become very popular. (Fig. 149.)

The subjoined illustrations of practical hand-feed arc lamps show the various movements referred to and how they are accomplished by means of insulated milled (handles) heads. It is significant that while from time to time automatic feed projection arcs have been placed on the market, they have made no headway. In truth, the crater adjustments necessary for maintaining a steady light of high efficiency on the gate of the projector are of so delicate a description as to defy mere mechanical means of regulation.

With alternating current arcs other conditions are met. Here, since both carbons are as much positive as negative they both burn away at the same rate, also, there is a crater on each. The light given off travels straight out at right angles to the carbon set. Fig. 150 gives the older arrangement for setting carbons when using alternating current. It is known as the 'scissors' arrangement. While giving a good light efficiency this set has of later years been more or less supplanted by the one shown in fig. 151, the latter set being, in fact, practically identical with the D.C. method, except that the backward tilt of the bracket carrying the carbon feed arms is absent. The latter set, while not giving so great a light efficiency as the scissors, has the advantage that the crater, when formed, keeps its shape far better. It will be noticed that with the direct current set either as used for actual direct or for alternating supply, an essential point is that the lower carbon shall be somewhat advanced in relation to the upper one. This forward position of the lower carbon determines the form of crater obtained,

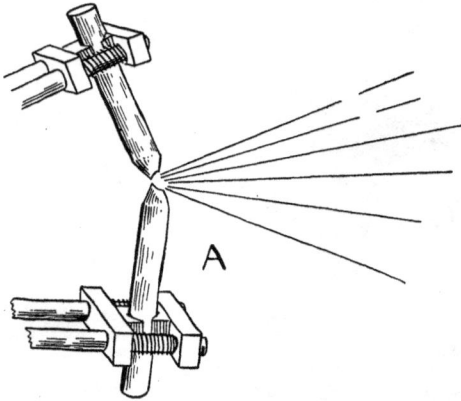

FIG. 150. " SCISSORS " SETTING OF CARBONS.

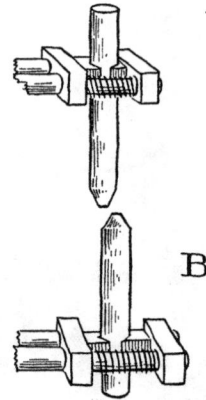

FIG. 151.   ANOTHER SETTING OF CARBONS.

and the skill of the operator in managing the projector illuminant is very largely shown by his ability to keep the crater right through the medium of such adjustment. Where the current is alternating, the carbons used in the lamp are both of one size (figs. 150 and 151), and both 'cored,' that is to say having a core or stuffing of soft carbon pressed through a central hole, like the lead in the centre of a lead pencil. Flame arc carbons have a chemical core. With direct current, however, it is only the upper or positive carbon which is cored. This positive carbon must be of considerably larger diameter than the negative one, as has already been noted. For a 35 amp. D.C. arc, the minimum size of carbons should be, upper 16 millimetre diameter cored, lower 12 millimetre solid. Where 50 amps. are being taken, the top carbon should be at least an ' 18 ' cored, and the lower a ' 14 ' solid, to use the customary abbreviated way of speaking of them. Many operators use larger sizes for the same current consumption. Size of carbons will also be found to be in a measure dependent upon the voltage of the electrical supply.

For instance, considerably larger carbons can be used at a given amperage where the voltage is say 100 or 110, than where the voltage is only 60 or 65. With low voltages, moreover, the air gap between the carbons has to be kept so short as to cause the lower tip to interfere more or less with the light from the crater. Also low voltage arcs have a very bad habit of collecting conglomerations of incompletely volatilised matter from the core of the positive carbon upon the tip of the negative one. The projection light is thereby ruined until the collected matter has been knocked away by a sudden blow of the operating box screw-driver or other equally handy and unsuitable tool. On the other hand, high voltages have their own drawbacks, such as wastefulness of current. An arc consuming 30 amps. at 110 volts will give a light practically no different from one consuming the same current at 60 volts, yet the running cost of the former will be almost twice that of the latter. Moreover, where the voltage across the arc is comparatively high, the light will burn long without attention but with an ever-diminishing efficiency —very much longer than where the voltage is low. Consequently, the temptation to a careless operator to feed his lamp but seldom becomes greater the higher the potential across the arc.

The best voltage for projection is 70 to 75. This is very economical. At the same time it is just high enough to ensure a good clean burning negative carbon, with unobscured crater upon the positive pole.

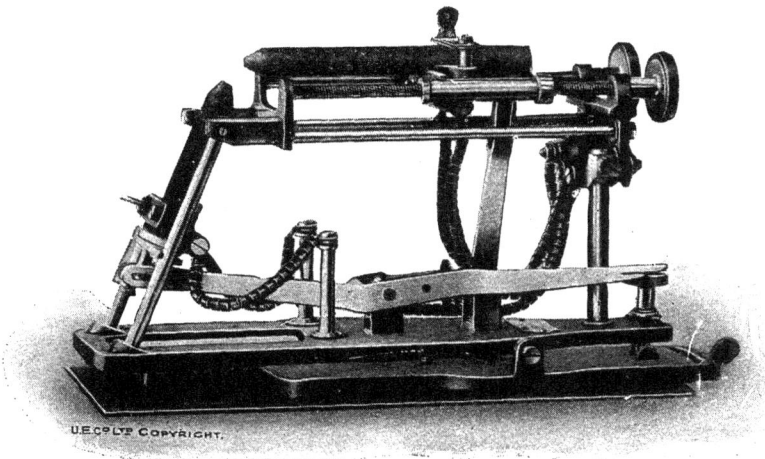

FIG. 152. HAND-FEED KINO LAMP.

RIGHT ANGLE PROJECTION ARCS.

As has been foreseen by the writer for some time past, the right angle or obtuse angled projection arc is slowly, but surely, beginning to come into its own. The model is one capable of giving a very high efficiency, particularly with direct current, and now that the popular prejudice against this type of arc is dying down, a serious attempt is being made to give to the question of its design some of that earnest attention that has been so long grudged it.   The Union Electric Co., Ltd., of Park Street, Southwark, in particular, are doing good work in this direction, though up to the present this firm, like many another, appears to regard the limit of current for a right angle arc as being in the neighbourhood of thirty amperes.   The model figured is that of a hand-feed obtuse angle lamp (fig. 152).   This type is supplied for direct or alternating current, as may be specified upon ordering.   For the obtuse angled lamp a slightly better crater formation is claimed than in the case of the actual right angled type.

As we go to press word comes to hand of a fifty ampere lamp of similar pattern, put on the market by the Union Electric Co., Ltd. We are particularly glad to note this, since for years past we have been sure there was a great future for the medium to high amperage horizontal projection lamp on account of its naturally high light efficiency.

The Resistance.

A resistance is employed to limit and control the amount of current which will flow in a circuit.   A resistance is absolutely essential in every arc circuit.   It is sometimes asked why kinematograph dynamos are not made to give the exact voltage required for the arc and so avoid wasteful resistances.   The reason for this is as follows : The arc itself has practically no resistance, the voltage which is measured across the arc being the result of a back pressure, which is generated by the arc, and which acts in opposition to the main supply.   The back E.M.F. of an arc is about 35 volts.   If the pressure in the mains were no higher than this each would neutralise the other, and so no current would flow, making an arc impossible.   The amount of current which will flow through an arc is therefore exactly dependent on the number of volts over and above this first 35, and which superfluous voltage acts on the line resistance.

This number is obtained by deducting the 35 arc volts from the supply volts.   The number of ohms required for the arc resistance is then arrived at by dividing the resulting figure by the required amperes.   (See Ohm's Law, page 16 .)

The usual type of kinematograph resistance is one which can be adjusted to give various strengths of current, and generally consists of a metal frame carrying suitable insulating panels, between which spirals of resistance wire are fixed   These spirals are so connected that current passes through each in turn.   Connections are also made from a number of these coils to contacts on the lower panel, and by means of a regulating switch on these contacts the amount of resistance in the circuit, and hence the current, can be varied.   The resistance figured (fig. 153) is so planned that as the switch is rotated from right to left, the current is increased accordingly, as the resistance coils are cut out of circuit.

The diagram will make clear the arrangement of connections.

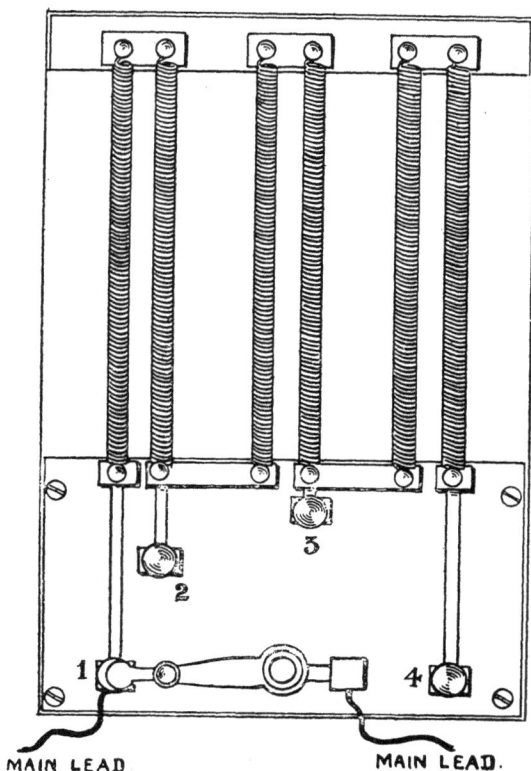

MAIN LEAD

Fig. 153. Simple Regulating Resistance
with Three Points and 'Full on.'

Of course, in addition to the resistance frame mentioned above, a certain amount of ohmic opposition to the flow of current is always to be found in the circuit. There are the carbons, for example, and bad connections, etc. In the case of the carbons, the resistance is a varying quantity, for it decreases as the carbon burns away. For this reason, it will be noticed that on a low voltage supply, say 70 volts or so, a small variation in the resistance of the circuit, due to the carbon burning away, will make a considerable difference to the amount of current flowing, but on a high voltage supply this same variation will be relatively small, and therefore will not alter the current value so much. The importance of careful feeding and good quality carbons will now be seen, especially for the lower voltages

Resistances should be capable of reducing the arc current to relatively small proportions, so that at starting up, the lenses and the apparatus generally may be warmed up gradually, to avoid sudden expansions, which would cause breakage, to say nothing of burning out the windings of motor generators through overload.

There is often much misunderstanding as to the correct gauge of resistance wire required for certain currents. In this connection, ventilation is a more important factor than the mere gauge of wire, and calls for consideration first. Efficient ventilation is essential. This means the coils must not be arranged too close together. Air must circulate freely between the spirals if it is to carry away the generated heat. Where resistance frames are designed with proper regard to their ventilation, the following table of gauges may be taken as fairly reliable. It should, however, always be borne in mind that smaller gauges of wire can be safely employed where there is plenty of ventilation, but in enclosed situations it may be desirable to use much heavier gauges. It is here also important to note that where the current is large, considerable saving will accrue from using a number of thin wires in parallel in preference to one thick one singly.

SAFE GAUGES OF RESISTANCE WIRES FOR VARIOUS CURRENTS.

For resistance wires having a specific resistance of 50 microhms per c.c. Such alloys are known by the names of Eureka, Constantan, Manganin, Platinoid, German Silver (30 per cent.), etc.

6 amps	10g
7 ,,	18g
9 ,,	17g
12 ,,	16g
15 ,,	15g
17 ,,	14g
20 ,,	13g
25 ,,	12g
30 ,,	11g
35 ,,	10g
40 ,,	9g
50 ,,	8g

FIG. 154. A PRACTICAL REGULATING RESISTANCE.

FUSES.

These are of the greatest importance. Of the few fires which start from electrical causes the majority probably owe their origin to carelessness in regard to some fuse or other.

A fuse is a short length of metallic conducting wire suitably enclosed and connected in series with the circuit through which current runs. This wire is purposely chosen of such a current-carrying capacity that should the circuit become overloaded, the fuse will get hot enough to melt, thus breaking the circuit and cutting off the current. Fuses are of several different kinds. Some are made of lead, some of tin, such being employed where the current in the circuit or sub-circuit is only of small quantity, say up to twenty amps, or thereabout. For larger loads, tinned copper fuses are admittedly the best, and for use in the projection arc circuit they are the only kind which may be relied upon, since they are far more tolerant of the sudden overload unavoidable at the moment of striking the arc than are fuses of the softer metals. The usual tin and lead fuse capacities are five, ten. and twenty amps. Reels of such wire are sold at all electrical stores, and should never be far from the operator's hand when in the box, or by the switchboard. For the fuse controlling a forty or fifty amp projecting arc, a single strand of No. 20 tinned copper wire is the thing. It is purchased wound ready for use on pound or half-pound reels.

The best form of fuse at the present time consists of tinned copper wire made up inside an insulating cartridge. Cartridge fuses are fitted with copper lugs at either end, which grip by means of spring pressure upon terminals on the inside of a covered terminal box. With these fuses there is absolute protection from the splashing of molten metal. Also, the cartridges being enclosed, it is not easy for an incompetent electrician to introduce fuse wires into the circuit of such over-large capacity as to be no real protection against overload of the regular cable. Lastly, cartridge fuses are renewable in a minimum of time, an item of consequence when one blows in the middle of an exhibition.

TABLE OF FUSE WIRES.

Approximate Fusing Current in Amps.	APPROXIMATE STANDARD WIRE GAUGE.		
	Tin.	Lead.	Copper.
5	25	23	38
10	21	20	33
15	19	18	30
20	17	17	28
25	16	15	26
30	15	14	25
35	14	13	24
40	14	13	23
45	13	12	22
50	13	12	21
60	12		21
70			20
80	Strip fuses above	Strip fuses above	19
90	this gauge	this gauge	18
100			18
120			17

NOTE.—The full normal load on a fuse should be two-thirds of its fusing load. For projector arcs however, it is wise to allow a margin of 50 per cent., or double the current between full and fusing load. Always use copper wire for arc fuses.

SIZE OF CARBONS FOR PROJECTOR ARCS.

CONTINUOUS CURRENT.			ALTERNATING CURRENT.	
Current in Amps.	Lower Solid Carbon.	Top Carbon Cored.	Current in Amps.	Top and Bottom Carbons, both cored.
10-15	10 m/m.	13 m/m.	15-25	10 m/m.
15-25	12 ,,	16 ,,	20 35	13 ,,
25-40	13 ,,	18 ,,	30-40	16 ,,
35-50	14 ,,	20 ,,	35-50	18 ,,
40-60	16 ,,	22 ,,	45-65	20 ,,
60-100	18 ,,	25 ,,	60-80	22 ,,
			75-100	25 ,,

CARRYING CAPACITY OF WIRES AND CABLES.

It will be noted that the standard adopted is that in which a conductor with a cross section of one square inch is considered as able to carry a current of 1,000 amperes. This standard is sufficiently exact for all ordinary purposes, but it may be pointed out that the carrying capacity of conductors has been the subject of much investigation, and that the Institution of Electrical Engineers has revised the figures somewhat. The difference between the two standards is not great, and for the sake of reference, both figures are given in the table; it may be said, however, that the kinematograph operator will be erring on the safe side if he adopts the 1,000 amperes to the square inch standard for ordinary use.

Standard Wire Gauge.	Amperes at 1000 to 1 square inch.	Amperes at I.E.E. Standard	Standard Wire Gauge	Amperes at 1000 to 1 square inch	Amperes at I.E.E. Standard
22	.61	1.7	7.21	5.53	10.63
21	.80	2.2	7.20½	5.86	11.19
20	1.01	2.6	7.20	7.00	12.90
19	1.25	3.2	7.19	8.64	15.34
18	1.80	4.2	7.18	12.46	20.68
17	2.46	5.4	7.17	16.95	26.62
16	3.21	6.8	7.16	22.14	33.12
15	4.07	8.2	7.15	28.03	40.22
14	5.02	9.8	7.14	34.59	47.80
13	6.64	12.4	19.20	18.99	29.23
12	8.49	15.0	19.19	23.43	34.74
3.25	.92	2.45	19.18	33.75	46.85
3.23	1.33	3.30	19.17	45.93	60.33
3.22	1.81	4.25	19.16	60.00	75.06
3.20	2.99	6.44	19.15	75.86	91.12
3.18	5.32	10.31	19.14	93.72	108.30
7.25	2.16	4.92	19.13	123.85	136.2
7.23	3.11	6.63	19.12	158.26	166.4
7.22	4.23	8.54	37.16	116.80	129.6
7.21½	4.86	9.56	37.15	147.8	157.3

Single stranded conductors, from 22 to 12, have been included in the table. This has been done for the sake of reference, but it must be pointed out that modern practice does not favour the use of single wires. Of the sizes given, only the 18 S.W.G. is used to any extent at the present time, and many engineers prefer to use instead the 3.22 size, which is a stranded conductor made up of three wires of 22 S.W.G. The objection to single wires is that they are less flexible than stranded wires of the same total carrying capacity, they are more liable to injury when the insulation is bared, and cases have been known where they have fractured when bent at a short radius. For interior wiring, the sizes with which the kinematograph operator will be called upon to deal are 3.22, 7.22, 7.20 and 7.18. For the lantern, however, such heavier sizes as 19.16 or 19.15, according to the amperes required, will have to be used.

DISTANCES FOR LANTERN LENSES.

Distance between Lantern and Screen.	FOCUS OF LENS. DIAMETER OF PICTURE (obtained with 3 in. mask).					
	4 in.	6 in.	8 in.	10 in.	12 in.	14 in.
	ft. in.	ft. in.	ft. in.	ft. in.	ft. in.	ft. in.
10 feet	7 6	5 0	3 9	3 0	2 6	2 2
12 ,,	9 0	6 0	4 6	3 7	3 0	2 7
15 ,,	11 3	7 6	5 8	4 6	3 9	3 3
20 ,,	15 0	10 0	7 6	6 0	5 0	4 3
25 ,,	18 9	12 6	9 4	7 6	6 3	5 4
30 ,,	22 6	15 0	11 3	9 0	7 6	6 5
35 ,,	26 3	17 6	13 1	10 6	8 9	7 6
40 ,,	30 0	20 0	15 0	12 0	10 0	8 6
45 ,,	33 9	22 6	16 10	13 6	11 3	9 8
50 ,,	37 6	25 0	18 0	15 0	12 6	10 9
60 ,,	45 0	30 0	22 6	18 0	15 0	12 11
70 ,,	52 6	35 0	26 3	21 0	17 6	15 1
80 ,,	60 0	40 0	30 0	21 0	20 0	17 3
90 ,,	67 6	45 0	33 9	27 0	22 6	19 5
100 ,,	75 0	50 0	37 6	30 0	25 0	21 7

DISTANCES FOR KINEMATOGRAPH LENSES.

Distance between Lantern and Screen.	FOCUS OF LENS. DIAMETER OF PICTURE (obtained with 1 in. mask).					
	2 in.	2½ in.	3 in.	3½ in.	4 in.	5 in.
	ft. in.	ft. in.	ft. in.	ft. in.	ft. in.	ft. in.
10 feet	5 0	4 0	3 4	3 0	2 6	2 0
12 ,,	6 0	4 9	4 0	3 6	3 0	2 6
15 ,,	7 6	6 0	5 0	4 6	3 9	3 0
20 ,,	10 0	8 0	6 8	5 8	5 0	4 6
25 ,,	12 6	10 0	8 4	7 2	6 3	5 6
30 ,,	15 0	12 0	10 0	8 6	7 6	5 10
35 ,,	17 6	14 0	11 8	10 0	8 9	6 2
40 ,,	20 0	16 0	13 4	11 6	10 7	7 8
45 ,,	22 6	18 0	15 0	13 0	11 3	9 2
50 ,,	25 0	20 0	16 9	14 3	12 6	10 0
60 ,,	30 0	24 0	20 0	17 0	15 0	12 0
75 ,,	37 0	30 0	25 0	21 6	18 9	15 0
100 ,,	40 6	40 0	33 5	29 0	23 0	20 0

INSULATED CABLE AND ITS CURRENT CARRYING CAPACITY.

Needless to say, no system of fuses can be of avail unless the cabling of the electrical circuit is properly insulated, and the joints well and carefully made. Of all substances which act as insulators or checks to the flow of electricity, india rubber, paper, tarred braid, and bitumen are among the best. Transversely cut electric cable of good quality will therefore invariably show several distinct yet closely superposed layers of these current resisting substances. Only specimens of electrical wiring where such covering is stout and well put on should ever be included in the electrical installation of a kinematograph show. When ordering such insulated cable, one should specify distinctly ' association cable.' This stipulation assures that the insulation will be up to a definite standard of reliability. Also, one must be very careful to see that electrical wire is never overloaded whether it be of small or great current carrying capacity. Appended is a table giving the current-carrying capacities of wires of various gauges.

ELECTRICAL JOINTS are to be avoided whenever possible. When, however, they are essential they should *always* be " sweated " ; that is to say, ends of wire intended to form part of an electrical circuit should be so affixed to each other that the cable is electrically continuous. A badly made joint may get hot, and may thus cause a fire. Large cables should never be joined by an inexperienced hand as the consequences of bad workmanship would be serious. Before cable ends can be sweated together with solder they must be thoroughly cleaned of all rubber or grease and then carefully twisted together in such a manner that good electrical contact is made. A small quantity of ' flux ' is then applied to the joint. This prevents oxidation of the wire and allows the solder to run freely when the joint is heated. Success with soldering depends on using a very hot clean iron, on thoroughly cleaning the joint, and on using a good flux; Acid fluxes must not be used for electrical work. The joint, when made, is neatly taped up with rubber and special black tape.

Leads of large capacity are usually sweated into lugs of copper or brass. These lugs may then be conveniently bolted up with main switches, ammeters, etc.

LAMP INSULATION.—The current-carrying parts of a projection arc lamp are insulated with mica, this insulator being perhaps the most suitable, as it is capable of withstanding the great heat. Should the insulation fail for any reason, then the current will pass through the metal parts of the lamp, avoiding the carbons and so not forming an arc. This would be called a short circuit, or, more simply, a ' short.' It is always desirable to keep a small quantity of mica at hand for temporary repairs.

WHEN CONNECTING THE D.C. ARC with the leads for the first time it may give some difficulty to the novice to determine whether he has really made his top carbon the positive, and the bottom one the negative pole. The simplest way to test is by striking the arc and letting it burn for a minute or two.   If now the current is turned off and the two carbons examined after the lapse of 15 seconds, whichever shows the hottest tip will be the positive one.   Should the ruddy cherry glow indicative of the positive pole be on the upper carbon, we shall know all is as it should be.   If, on the other hand, the best part of this after glow is given off by the underneath carbon it is a case of reversing the wiring connections to the lamp terminals.

Other indications that the poles of the projection arc are wrong are the casting upward instead of downward of the light, refusal of a proper crater to form on the upper carbon, and an unsteady puffy flicker of the flaming gases in the air gap.

CURRENT CONVERTING AND TRANSFORMING.

We have already pointed out in this chapter that the best voltage of electric supply for kinematograph projection purposes is 70 to 75. Incidentally, this same voltage is by no means over low for the incandescent electric lighting of a single building, especially where metallic filament lamps are in use.   It may therefore be taken that when—as where a picture hall owns its private generating plant—the whole installation is at 70 or 75 volts, there will be a great gain on the running of the arc and little or no loss elsewhere.   When, on the other hand, the hall takes its electrical supply off the public mains, it is likely the voltage will be a higher one.   Suppose it is 220 or more, then the only practice consistent with economy will be to 'transform' or 'convert' down to the required pressure.

The voltage of alternating current is easily altered to almost any value, either high or low, by means of a static transformer.   This apparatus consists of two coils of wire arranged around an iron core, the number of turns of wire on these coils being proportional to the ratio of voltage transformation required.   One coil—the primary— is connected to the mains, and the effect of the flowing current is to create a magnetic field in the iron core.   This magnetic field threading through the other or secondary winding causes a new current to be generated in it, which has a voltage dependent on the number of its turns. A static transformer only alters the potential or pressure of the current. It does not alter the quality of the current.   Current transformed in this way is still alternating, and is of the same frequency on the secondary as on the primary side of the transformer.   The actual value of the current itself is transformed in inverse ratio to the voltage.

Thus, a transformer that is used to reduce the supply voltage say 3 to 1 will incidentally increase the amperage in the proportion of 1 to 3 with an efficiency loss of about 5 per cent. or 6 per cent.   For illustration of a static transformer see fig. 155.

When dealing with direct circuit the matter is quite different. Here, since the electricity flows steadily in one direction instead of pulsating in cycles, no method of converting by means of simple induction could be of avail.   Accordingly, resort is made to a transformer of the rotary type. Such transformers are in reality nothing more than small high potential electric motors driving low potential dynamos direct coupled on the one shaft. The waste of current in transforming by this method is much greater than that where high potential alternating current is to be converted to low, since now we have an actual transformation of our original electricity supply into mechanical energy on the one end of the shafting, the same mechanical energy being re-converted back to electrical force on the other end. The actual amount of current lost in process of conversion depends on the make of the machine, but is anywhere from 30 per cent. to 15 per cent.

FIG 155.—STATIC TRANSFORMER.
Alters voltage of alternating current but does not convert it to direct current.

FIG. 156.—THE ROTARY TRANSFORMER OF THE VICTORIA DYNAMO AND MOTOR CO.

Machines of the rotary converter type which give high efficiency differ from simple combinations of a separate dynamo and motor on the one shaft in that with them both fields are excited direct from the same main high voltage supply. The method of arranging them in this way for the least loss in the transformation of high potential into low potential electrical energy is by exciting the field of each machine on the high voltage side, as before stated, and putting the armatures in series and winding each for the correct voltage, *i.e.*, the generator for the arc voltage and the motor for the difference between the arc voltage and the line voltage. The generator armature is made with a special winding in order to give the large current necessary for the arc.

Sets made on this plan and of extremely compact design and equally precise workmanship are marketed by the Electrical Company, of 122-124 Charing Cross Road, London, W.C., one such being figured on the next page (fig. 157).

FIG. 157.   CONVERTER SETS.

With each set sent out a carefully drawn diagram of the wiring connections is given, a facsimile of one of which we are courteously permitted to reproduce here (fig. 158).

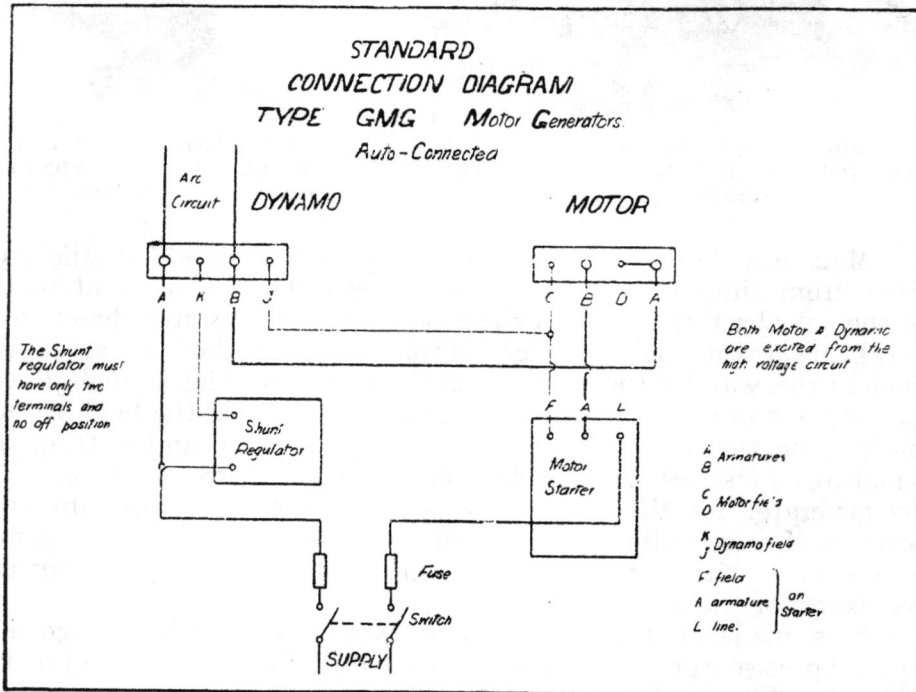

FIG. 158.

FIG. 159. MOTOR GENERATOR SETS (Two Machines on a Combined Bedplate).

FIG. 160. DYNAMO DESIGNED FOR KINEMATOGRAPH WORK.

PRIVATE GENERATING INSTALLATIONS.

Where a public electric supply is not available, and unless lime-light is decided upon as the illuminant for the projector, there is no alternative to making one's own current on the premises by means of suitable plant. The generator here will invariably be of the direct current type, and should be specified 'compound' wound.

As previously explained, current is got from a dynamo by revolving a wound armature between the poles of a magnet. This magnet is itself electrically excited from current generated in the dynamo armature. Upon the amount of current allowed to flow through these magnet windings depends the strength of the magnetic field, and hence the voltage generated by the dynamo. In order to regulate this voltage, it is usual to put a variable resistance in the magnet winding to control the amount of current flowing. This latter is known as a 'field' or 'shunt' regulator.

So much for the dynamo itself. We already know that the voltage to stipulate is 70 to 75, at least, the latter is the writer's personal preference, though some current economists profess to find no great trouble in use and some further current saving by installing a 60 volt supply. For a medium sized hall the arc will probably take 50 amps, so that allowing 25 amps more for interior and frontage lighting and a small margin on top of that, we shall find an 85 amp set to be about what is required.

Now to consider how the dynamo is to be driven. The following are alternative possibilities. We may drive by means of :—

> Steam power,
> Town gas (ordinary gas engine),
> Suction gas,
> Petroleum gas,
> Petrol,
> Water power.

The last of all would, of course, be the cheapest in those country districts where it could be installed. Occasionally in small country towns or their outskirts one comes across a water wheel converted so as to drive a dynamo to good purpose. This experience, however, is by no means a common one in England, and with that we will pass on to the other more likely forms of driving power.

STEAM is in many ways ideal for large electric installations. The running of high speed steam engines is particularly smooth and free from jar. The same applies in even greater degree to steam turbines, which are, of all forms of driving power, quite the best for running dynamos. Steam is not, all the same, by any means the most economical form of power, besides requiring more attention than will usually be convenient to expend upon it when utilised for kinematograph purposes. Also steam engines with their attendant boilers are both costly and bulky. Small steam engines are even less economical than larger ones. Practically, therefore, good as is this form of motive force, it has to give way before others in the driving of small private electric supply installations.

Exception to this last statement must, however, be made in the case of touring and portable kinematograph shows which travel their own fit-up by road. Here the ideal lighting system is to use electricity generated by means of a high class compound steam road (traction) engine fitted with dynamo carried on the front plate. Such a road engine is employed both for lighting and also for haulage purposes, whereby the expenses of travel are cut down to a minimum. In fact, the system of lighting and haulage here touched upon has been in constant use for years by proprietors of roundabouts and large movable bioscope shows.

Town Gas.—We now come to the most popular source of energy for our purpose. The gas engine is known to everyone as a cleanly and simple means of obtaining mechanical energy for all manner of diverse purposes. It nearly always works on the Otto cycle. That is to say, power is communicated to the fly-wheel as the result of an explosion of mixed gas and air occurring inside the cylinder once in every two revolutions. Thus :—

Revolution One.—Mixed gas and air are drawn into the cylinder through suitable inlet valves as the result of suction brought about by the outward thrust of the piston. The energy for this is derived from previous momentum of the fly wheel. As the crank turns into position to send the piston back again, the inlet valves automatically close. Consequently, this backward strike compresses the gas and air mixture into small compass in what is termed the 'explosion chamber' at the far end of the cylinder. At the end of this backward stroke and when compression has reached its height means are found of igniting the compressed and explosive mixture in the cylinder end, and

Revolution Two.—The gases expand enormously as the result of explosion, the pressure of the burnt product in the cylinder tending strongly to force the piston out again. This outward thrust causes the crank and fly wheels to take on further and increased momentum. On the second backward stroke of the piston, the exhaust valve of the cylinder opens, blowing out the burnt-up gases and leaving the cylinder clean and ready to take in further charges of gas and air wherewith to repeat the above 'Otto' cycle.

Well-known and trustworthy examples of the gas engine are to be found amongst such models as the National, Crossley, and many others. These gas engines work very evenly, give little trouble, and only require a comparatively small amount of cleaning to do their work well. Usually they are connected with the dynamo for driving by means of an endless belt. Latterly, however, several direct-coupled sets have made their appearance. These possess the advantage over belt-driven sets of a saving of something like 15 per cent. of power otherwise lost in belt transmission.

When belting is used for driving purposes, allow at least one-half inch width for every horse power to be transmitted to the dynamo. This presupposes the belt to run at normal speed, about 2,000 feet per minute. Driving should always be forward, that is to say, with the slack of the belt on top. In apportioning power of engine to dynamo for belt-driven sets it is useless to have the dynamo of much more than two-third power as compared to the driving power. Thus, a nine horse gas engine will not comfortably do more than drive a four and a half kilowatt dynamo on the belt system, though with direct drive, it might conceivably produce nearly an extra kilowatt of electrical energy.

SUCTION GAS.—The gas here made use of is not town gas at all, but a special brand produced by burning anthracite coal or coke in a 'producer.' The disadvantages of a suction gas plant lie in comparatively heavy first cost, coupled with a certain lurking suspicion of possible explosions if the producer is not looked after intelligently. The advantage lies in extreme economy of running cost of the installation. There is no doubt that where properly understood and reasonably carefully controlled, suction gas is next to water power the cheapest of all sources of mechanical—and hence of electrical —energy.

PETROLEUM.—Where town gas is not available for our dynamo driving, and it is not wished to go to the somewhat heavy first cost of a suction gas plant, we may substitute oil in the shape of ordinary petroleum. Oil engines are manufactured by several reputable makers such as National, Blackstone, Tangye, etc., and are of solid construction, and in appearance very much like gas engines. Also, their performance is equally satisfactory for short runs. Their disadvantages are smell (which is usually cruel), and the necessity for constant cleaning, involving taking the whole engine to pieces pretty well every week. If cleaning is neglected ever so little power begins to be lost, and running costs in oil consumption to go up enormously. Even at their best, petroleum engines work out more expensive in running—perhaps half as much again—as town gas engines.

Both town gas, suction gas, and petroleum engines are now made in models expressly intended for electric lighting. Such are provided with extra heavy and specially balanced fly wheels, and are capable of driving a dynamo so as to give an output steady to one volt on the meter. This performance is very good indeed, as need hardly be pointed out.

Whatever type of engine is used, great care must be exercised over lubrication, or bearings will seize and soften. Once this happens they will give trouble ever afterwards. Never start an engine until it has been ascertained that all ring bearings and oil cups are properly fed with lubricating oil.

PETROL SETS.—Petrol sets are the order of the day. They possess many attractive points, notably small and compact configuration, lightness, portability, simplicity in starting (provided adjustments are correctly made) and such like interesting features. Petrol comes

FIG. 161. THE TYLER-ASTER GENERATING SET.

FIG. 162. A COMPACT PETROL GENERATING SET.

out in working somewhat dearer than petroleum, but these portable petrol sets being of the direct drive type are thereby more economical than if a belt drive were employed.

Like all oil engines they have to be kept clean if satisfactory results are to be expected. Mostly they are fitted with high tension magneto ignition which is in itself very reliable, as is shown by the fact that it is coming in more and more for gas and petrol engines of every description.

For touring kinematograph shows of the kind which hire and fit up in provincial halls these petrol sets may and should prove very useful. Needless to say, where long runs in one place are to be coped with, the advantage would seem to lie with a more solidly constructed town or suction gas plant.

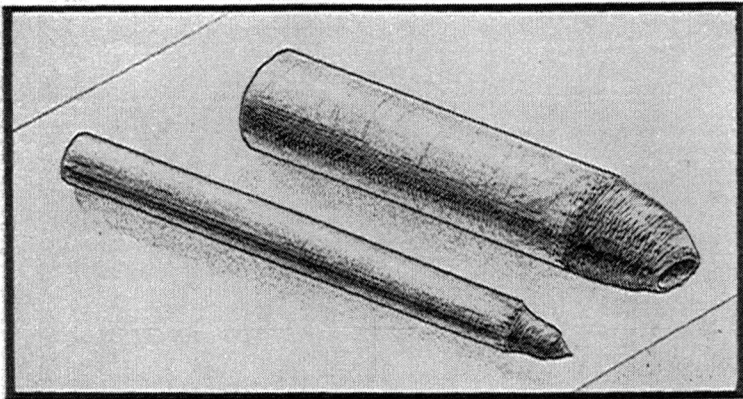

FIG. 163. A WELL BURNED PAIR OF CARBONS.

CHAPTER V.

––––

LIMELIGHT AND MINOR ILLUMINANTS.

Where the kinematograph is only to be exhibited occasionally and in neighbourhoods distant from a town electric supply, then the one real alternative light to electricity is limelight as produced by the impinging of a burning jet of mixed oxygen and hydrogen (or coal gas) upon a cylinder of hard lime.

Under these conditions, a very good light may be obtained emanating from a comparatively small source, and approximating in intensity anywhere up to 2,500 candle power, according to the skill and lavishness of the operator in using his gases. With a wide aperture projection lens such a light will prove adequate for a well illuminated moving picture up to eight feet diameter. The writer has read wondrous stories of fourteen feet pictures illuminated brilliantly by means of the oxy-hydrogen jet, but he would not personally care to attempt the projection on this scale and with this illuminant of any but specially picked, lightly printed film subjects.

Years ago, when kinematograph projection was in its infancy, the bulk of shows were given with limelight, and it was then the rule to keep the positive pictures very thin so as to make the illuminant go as far as possible. Nowadays electricity has come in almost to the exclusion of the other, and consequently, modern kinematograph films are made correspondingly dense in the shadows. Hence the fact of it is, the limelight operator has to curtail the dimensions of his picture more, and attempt a far less ostentatious show now than formerly. He may help himself to some extent by employing as the objective of his projector one of the newer extra wide diameter makes. Even here, however, there are pitfalls in his way, since, unless this same wide aperture lens be the somewhat expensive product of a reputable firm such as Busch or Dallmeyer, he will find the clearness of projection, especially at the corners of the screen, diminish in proportion as added brightness is gained.

Thus, if a rule be laid down at the start for the guidance of lime-light operators in deciding upon throw and dimensions of the picture, it had better be the following admittedly conservative one. Keep to projector lenses of good quality and wide aperture, also limit the throw from lens to screen as much as possible, and do not attempt to show a large picture where the throw is great any more than where it is small. Where limelight is in use a wise limit of throw (distance between projector lens and projection screen) will be thirty-five feet or thereabouts in the case of small exhibitions.

Within these limits, however, really brilliant limelight pictures may be projected.

The actual apparatus for the work consists of the jet, connecting tube, limes, oxygen and hydrogen (or coal gas) in cylinders, cylinder regulators, gauges, cylinder key, lime tongs and borer, lime tray for the jet, and wire for wiring on the tubing.

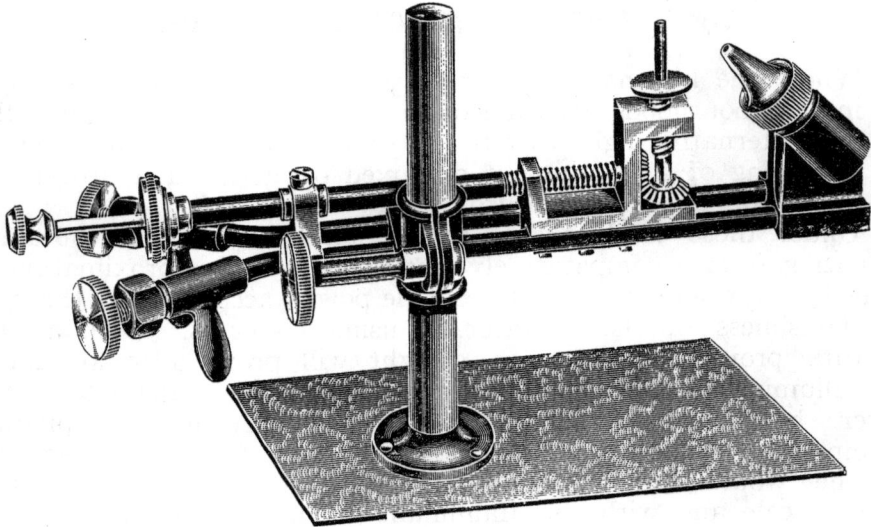

FIG. 164.   THE 'PRIMUS' HIGH POWER MIXED JET.

The jet to use is technically known as a 'high power mixed.' It consists of a strong metallic chamber filled with sheets of perforated metal or metal gauze through which streams of the two gases are forced by the pressure behind them. While penetrating the gauze the gases mix prior to issuing from the nozzle of the lime jet. To start a mixed jet a tube is connected with one of the taps and its other end wired to the regulator upon the oxygen cylinder. A second similar connection is made up with the hydrogen cylinder. With limelight of this class it does not usually matter which tap on the jet is connected with which cylinder. See that the jet taps are closed in starting. The main valves of the cylinders are now opened wide by means of the cylinder key. If the regulators are working correctly nothing will happen beyond the accumulation of a certain amount of compressed gas in the respective lengths of tubing. Now turn on the tap admitting hydrogen or coal gas to the mixing chamber. There should be placed upon the lime pins a cylinder of lime previously made hot. Apply a match to the hydrogen issuing from the nozzle and it will burn in the ordinary way. We now adjust the distance of this jet nozzle to about one eighth of an inch, or slightly more from the surface of the lime. This is done by means of the screw adjustment provided for shifting the lime gallery backward and forward. Finally, turn on the oxygen tap gradually. The first effect will be to make the hydrogen flame appear to get smaller. If it gets too small turn on more hydrogen and also more oxygen and shortly one of two possible things will happen. The jet will begin to hiss loudly, or the light at which we are aiming will show itself. If the former, turn off the hydrogen gradually till the hissing stops, and then turn on more oxygen, and so on till the light comes.

The sought-for illumination will show itself as a spot of incandescence arising and growing in brightness upon the lime cylinder. Careful

FIG. 165.
GWYER SPECIAL KINEMATOGRAPH LIME-LIGHT JETS.

adjustment of the gas taps will cause this incandescence to increase till the whole front face of the lime is white hot and glowing fiercely. Hard limes for kinematograph purposes are usually one inch high by one or one and a quarter inch in diameter, so that high power limelight does not give nearly so concentrated an illuminant source as electricity. This difference will duly show itself as a woolly yellow margin to the light pencil around the projector gate, necessitating a larger circle of illumination with consequent loss of effective light on the mask aperture. Moreover, the impinging of the extremely hot mixed gases upon the face of the lime cylinder has the effect of burning it away, more or less, such burning or volatilisation taking the form of pits which necessitate turning the lime round from time to time. For this reason, every limelight jet is fitted with a lime turning adjustment in addition to the backward and forward motion of the lime gallery from the nipple. The lime turning actuates corkscrew fashion, so that theoretically it should be possible to pit the lime over the whole of its face before it would be burned out. Practically, no lime will withstand the temperature of the mixed burning gases for so long without cracking. It is the business of the operator to turn the lime slightly every couple of minutes, otherwise, in addition to loss of light, there is great danger of the hollow cup-shaped pit formed in the incandescent material causing the flame to strike back at an angle and hit the condenser, with the inevitable result of a smashed glass.

ECONOMY IN THE USE OF MIXED GASES.

It is possible to burn a mixture of gases widely differing from the theoretical correct proportion of each constituent and still get a very passable light. Such mixtures will, notwithstanding, be inefficient and wasteful. The way to ensure that the mixture of oxygen and hydrogen passing through the mixing chamber and to the jet nipple is rich enough without being too rich is as follows :—

Having got the lime to glow by means of the rough gas adjustment already described proceed to turn down the hydrogen or coal gas (not the oxygen) till the quality of the light suffers. Now once more turn up the hydrogen slowly till the point is just reached at which full light is maintained for the existing oxygen consumption. This will now be the perfect mixture of gases for the work. Should it be desired to increase the light, turn on more oxygen slowly and follow by admitting correspondingly more hydrogen (or coal gas) till the advance in brightness of the glowing lime ceases. To lessen light with economy of gases, turn down the oxygen first, then proceed to turn off hydrogen till the diminution in the lime's brightness which took place on lessening the oxygen supply partially recovers itself —that is to say, till it recovers itself so far as is possible with the reduced amount of mixture.

Centring the illuminant will be dealt with in the next chapter, the remarks to be written concerning it applying equally well both to lime and electricity.

Turning to the gases themselves, we have already stated broadly that these are stored in cylinders. Such cylinders are supplied of mild weldless wrought steel of great strength and comparative lightness. A twenty-foot gas cylinder, for instance, will weigh somewhere about twenty-five pounds. For kinematograph work small sized cylinders are not so useful or so economical as larger ones. Sixty-foot sized cylinders come under the cheaper charging rates of the companies supplying compressed gas, while they are also sufficiently portable to be moved single handed by a muscular man. Gas cylinders of 100 foot capacity are made where even larger supplies are necessary. All these are thoroughly tested before leaving the compressing houses, and only such as have stood on test an internal strain approximately three times as great as the normal charging strain are allowed to go on the market. The security of the public in handling them is thus seen to be very great.

Oxygen cylinders are painted black, and have the ordinary right handed threads cut upon their valves. Hydrogen cylinders are painted red, and the screw threads are left handed, this affording a further safeguard against the possibility of wrong charging at the works. Oxygen for storing into the oxygen cylinders is obtained from the air we breathe by means of the patent 'Brins Process,' in which the substance Barium Peroxide is made alternately to discharge oxygen and re-absorb it from the air under the influence of varying pressures. Pure hydrogen gas (where this is stipulated by the consumer) is made from zinc and sulphuric acid after the manner adopted by the old gas bag operators. More usually, however, coal gas is used with the oxygen to form the gas mixture. Coal gas does not give quite so high a temperature on burning, but it is both cheaper to buy in its compressed state and also much more economical in use. Ten feet of oxygen require twelve feet of coal gas, or in the alternative, twenty feet of pure hydrogen to form the burning mixture, and the difference of light obtained is only slightly in favour of the latter much more expensive material.

A high power lime jet burning its best will take at least the last mentioned amounts of gas per hour. Thus a sixty foot oxygen and eighty foot coal gas cylinder will be sufficient for about six hours limelight with the kinematograph.

The gases, as stored in cylinders, are under so great pressure that adjustment of them by means of the jet taps would be a sheer impossibility were it not for the employment of special regulators affixed to the cylinders themselves.

THE WALTURDAW
GOVERNOR FITTED WITH
BABY GAUGE

FIG. 166.

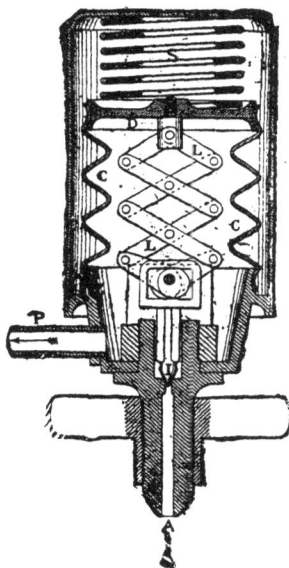

FIG. 167. SECTIONAL VIEW OF IN-
TERIOR OF GAS PRESSURE
REGULATOR.

Gas regulators work upon a simple principle. A lazy tongs is enveloped in a strong airtight leather bag or 'bellows,' having a metallic cover to the inside of which one end of the tongs is pivoted. Turning gas from the cylinder into the regulator fills this bag, thereby causing it to stretch upwards towards a counter spring placed outside its stiff metal cover. This upward movement is transmitted to the lazy tongs as a downward thrust of the end of its arms nearest the gas orifice, and the downward thrust acting on a finely adjusted metallic plug stops the gas flow as soon as the pressure in the leather bag is sufficient to press back the external counter spring to a pre-determined amount. Seeing that the internal pressure of a full cylinder is 120 atmospheres, or 1,800lbs. per square inch, it goes without saying the work the regulator is called on to perform in bringing this enormous pressure down to the equivalent of two or three inches of mercury is by no means light. It is therefore necessary to keep a sharp eye upon this part of our apparatus, and be ready at once to detect minor leaks or signs of wearing in the bellows or bag.

Leaks are best detected by putting one's ear to the side of the regulator while the gas is turned on at the cylinder tap, but not at the jet taps. An internal hissing will mean leaking either of the regulator bellows or of the tubing between it and the jet. Which of the two is really at fault is a matter that ought not to take any operator long to discover for himself. Another way of testing a regulator is to remove the tube from its delivery pipe, close it tightly with the thumb, and then turn on the cylinder cock by means of the cylinder key. Any continuous hissing heard must now result from leakage of the bellows or around the screw threads and their connections, to find which, plug the regulator delivery pipe, turn on the gas again, and immerse the whole upper end of the cylinder, with regulator, in water. Bubbles coming from the hole in regulator top then denote worn-out bellows, while bubbles from elsewhere tell their own tale as to indifferently made connections or battered screw threads, resulting from knocks in course of railway transit.

One of the latest ideas in regulators is to have the counter spring upon which pressure of gas delivery depends made so that it can be tightened up at will. Both Beard and Brin have a regulator fashioned on these lines, though in Brin's pattern the leather bellows gives place to a metallic diaphragm. Such variable gas pressure regulators are chiefly of use in controlling the oxygen supply where limelight is produced by means of the injector jet.

CYLINDER GAUGES.

The cylinder gauge is—like the motor drive of a projector—a matter which may prove a blessing or a curse according to how it is used. The careful operator will be able to save pounds in a very short time by the intelligent checking of his cylinder contents by means of gas pressure gauges. On the other hand, these same gauges are very delicate pieces of mechanism, and rough usage of them has to be strenuously avoided or they will turn out more trouble than they are worth

Undoubtedly the best way to run a gauge is to have it permanently fixed upon a branch connection of the regulator fitting. Thus mounted it is always available for consultation, just like the gauge of a steam engine. Also, it is for ever at the mercy of the rough-handed should they take it into their heads to push the heavy cylinder about in a careless manner. It will then only take a comparatively slight bump to smash the gauge glass and bend the branch tube sufficiently to make the whole fitting leak badly.

A sort of half-way house in the use of gauges is to have them fitted so as to be interchangeable with the regulators. In this case they will only be available between, and not during, shows. Moreover, the constant screwing and unscrewing of threads is none too good, and minor leakage may well also result from it.

Oxygen and hydrogen gauges work upon the well-known principle used in the case of testing steam pressure, and also adapted in modified form when testing atmospheric pressure by means of the ordinary aneroid barometer.

Under this principle compressed hydrogen or oxygen from the cylinder passes without entering the regulator into a thin-walled curved metal tube contained within the gauge cover. The tube has a tendency to straighten itself in increasing extent according to the difference between its internal and the external atmospheric pressure. As the tube straightens, the movement of its free end causes rotation in a series of toothed wheels actuating the pointer on the gauge dial. Barring accidents due to carelessness in handling the only thing about a gauge which is liable to go wrong is the breakage of the thin internal pressure tube itself. Should this burst one soon knows it by the rush of escaping gas, coupled with an unearthly buzzing sound due to the vibration of the broken end. There is no way of plugging up a broken gauge tube and going on with the show, so the light will just have to be shut off while the whole fitting is removed, and a new regulator union without gauge branch substituted.

In reading a gauge, whether oxygen or hydrogen, the great thing to remember is that thirty atmospheres indicates quarter full, sixty atmospheres indicates that the cylinder is half full, ninety indicates three-quarters full, while at the figure 120 will be found a red mark showing that this is where the pointer should come to rest when the cylinder is returned quite full after charging. From the above figures it will not be difficult to calculate how many feet of gas there are actually in any cylinder at any time. For instance, say our cylinder is a forty-foot one and it reads thirty on the gauge. It is then quarter full, which means that there is in it ten cubic feet of gas. Supposing it to be an oxygen cylinder we shall know ourselves to have just enough gas left for one bare hour's show.

In addition to the foregoing, some gauges are now also figured to show the number of feet there would be in a ten-foot cylinder. With such a gauge, supposing the case of a sixty-foot cylinder and the pointer standing at five (meaning five feet in a ten-foot cylinder), multiply the figure by six, since our cylinder is of six times the capacity of the one for which the gauge was calibrated, and we get as our result the figure thirty. There are thus thirty feet of gas in our sixty-foot cylinder—the cylinder is half full.

In making connection between cylinder and regulator always see that the separate wing nut upon the regulator union is screwed down all the way into the cylinder thread before commencing to tighten up the regulator itself. In this manner very strong and airtight joints may usually be made. Occasionally the writer has found even this to fail to make absolutely gas-proof joints. In such a case a very little hard grease run into the screw threads works wonders. Such practice cannot, however, be conscientiously recommended, since in the case of oxygen fittings the procedure is not entirely free from danger (at any rate, in theory) should any of the grease later find its way into the body of the cylinder. The writer does it all the same with the best results, only, it needs a lot of care.

It is possible to work the gases successfully for mixed lime-light without either gauge or regulator. The omission of the former means that there will be a great danger of running short of gas unexpectedly, the only alternative being that the operator should keep well on the safe side of his cylinder capacities, entailing sending back cylinders before all the gas is used out of them. The absence of regulators is attended with many difficulties, one of these being the need to give constant attention to the main gas taps of the cylinders. When working without regulators the cylinder threads must have screwed into them what are known as fine adjustment taps. These, then, serve to control the gas flow in its entirety, both jet cocks being left full open at all times, otherwise the connecting tubing will be blown off and ripped by the internal gas pressure. Fine adjustment taps are merely strong screw valves controlled by means of milled heads. The reason of the fine adjustment taps needing constant attention, say every ten minutes or so during the show, is to compensate for lowering of cylinder gas pressure, which is now unbalanced by the bellows action of a regulator.

Injector Lime Jets.

These differ from ordinary lime jets in that while they obtain their feed of compressed oxygen from a cylinder, the coal gas they consume with it comes from the ordinary house supply, from which it is conveniently obtained by affixing a rubber tubing connection to any handy gas bracket. The system of the injector jet is the same as that of the steam injector of an engine boiler. A fine spray of steam blowing into a funnel-shaped passage way creates a draught, which gives rise to strong back suction tending to draw air or other gases in its track.

With the oxy-hydrogen light used on the injector principle the mixing chamber of the jet is modified into more or less of a cone through which a high pressure oxygen stream is driven, thus sucking into its track and driving through the jet nozzle coal gas, which fills the rest of the chamber. Needless to say, the mixture of gases in an injector jet is not so intimate as with the regular mixed gas variety. Consequently, the candle power realised on this system is not so good. 1,000 to 1,500 c.p. is the most to be expected from any injector jet. This power will be found fairly suitable for kinematograph projection up to say six feet diameter with two and a half and three inch focus objectives. Further, since no licensing authority would countenance this system of lighting in regular kinematograph shows, the power available will probably prove amply sufficient for those conditions where the light is practicable, such as small charity shows, private house exhibitions, and the like. Remarks referring to the mixed gas display apply for the most part also to injector work, except that here it is necessary to have the cylinder regulator adjusted to deliver oxygen at not less than seven to ten pounds per square inch pressure. This entails the use of specially reinforced and extra thick 'injector' flexible tubing for making connections between regulator and

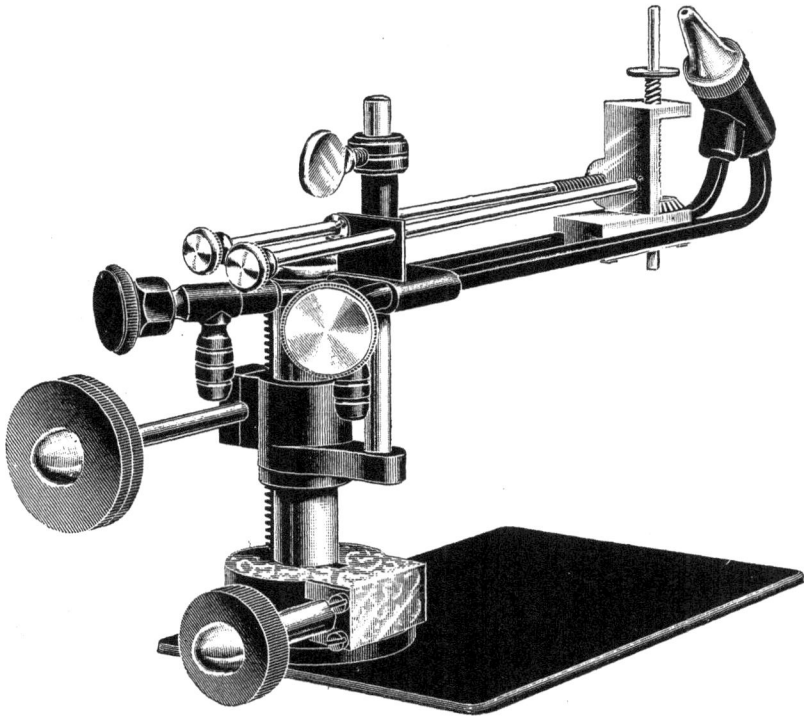

FIG. 168. THE PRIMUS INJECTOR JET.

jet tap. With the injector jet it is, moreover, essential that the oxygen is led into the oxygen feed of the jet, for which purpose this tap will be found to have the letter O engraved upon it. Wastefulness of the injector system is due to the high pressure oxygen stream inevitably drawing after it rather less than the theoretical amount of coal gas which would be necessary to bring about its complete consumption. For all that, relief from the necessity to run the second compressed gas in a cylinder will be found to make injector work very much cheaper in practice than the employment of the mixed jet.

Injector jets are always more or less noisy in burning.

The following systems of illumination in optical projection as applied to the kinematograph are only of service for very small pictures and for those projected at home or in the schoolroom and experimental laboratory.

THE BLOW-THROUGH LIMELIGHT JET.

With this jet, as with the injector type, coal gas is taken from the house supply, but here no internal mixture of any sort is attempted.

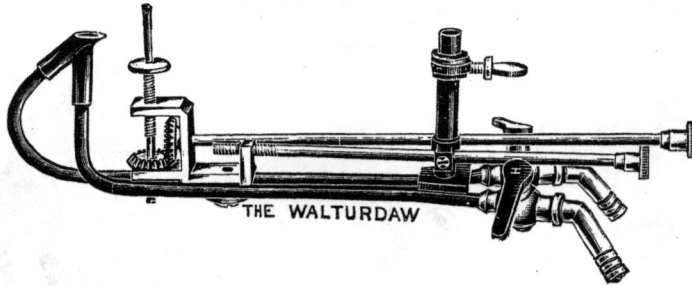

FIG. 169.   THE WALTURDAW BLOW-THROUGH JET.

Indeed, the coal gas is first made to burn in a wide based ragged flame against the side of a soft lime cylinder.   When light is required oxygen is blown through a narrow orifice into the middle of this coal gas flame. In the result, a portion of the coal gas becomes so raised in temperature as to transmit to the lime heat enough to bring about incandescence. Needless to say, this system is very wasteful of both gases, a consump-

FIG. 170.   COMBINED ETHER SATURATOR AND JET,

tion of six feet of oxygen per hour giving a light not much over 400 candle power, or 500 at the most.   The light is comparatively silent when skilfully managed.   Any attempt to force it, however, at once gives rise to that peculiarly irritating hiss familiar to all of us who have attended parochial ' limelight lectures.' Blow-through limelight will serve for pictures up to three or four feet in diameter with the average modern kinematograph films.

Oxy-Ether. Oxy-Petrol.

This form of limelight would be most useful in kinematograph work were it not for a lurking suspicion as to its safety which cannot be dismissed from the mind of the conscientious operator, also for a tendency on the part of ether or petrol fumes, as the case may be, to pervade the air at such times as the light is burning. The form of jet utilised with oxy-ether and oxy-petrol may be the same as that used for high power mixed gas work. One cylinder of gas only is required instead of two, this gas being, of course, oxygen. Instead of employing the house gas supply, however, a branch off the oxygen supply tube is connected with a tank containing sponge or tow saturated with methylated ether, or in the alternative, ordinary motor spirit.

As the oxygen forces its way through the ether or petrol it takes up a surfeit of the vapour of it. This ' saturated ' oxygen vapour mixture is then led to the hydrogen side of the jet. When the saturator is working well the charging of the original oxygen with vapour may be so thorough that the explosive point of the mixture is over-passed. Thus a quietly burning hydro-carbon vapour finds its way to the jet nipple on the hydrogen side. We then have what practically amounts to a lime jet burning gasified ether or petrol in place of coal gas, this being capable of being enriched with oxygen turned in from the oxygen lead for the purpose of raising the lime to incandescence, just as with the ordinary mixed jet. Moreover, the oxy-ether and oxy-petrol light is almost as brilliant as mixed gas at its best. Well over 2,000 candle power is available from such a source when the ether tank is full and working well—which it does when slightly warm.

But there is with all such systems the lurking fear that the ether or petrol supply may give out unexpectedly, and that the combustion of the impoverished mixture may proceed down the length of the jet and through the connecting tubing to the tank itself. An internal explosion would then be inevitable, and though a strong walled metal saturator might come out of it scatheless a weaker one may burst and do great damage. In any event, and even where the saturator withstood the explosion, there would be the sudden pop of the back-firing jet, the rip of bursting tube, and the nauseous escaping ether fumes permeating a darkened projection chamber, and with kinematograph audiences all on edge, as they are, for danger scares and causes of panic the prospect is not a nice one to contemplate. Latterly, the Home Secretary has ruled out as illegal systems employing saturators in kinematography. This can only be called a very wise precaution, though for laboratory purposes where a cheap and powerful illuminant is required in connection with kinematograph experiments the oxy-petrol light is well worthy of remembrance as an alternative to electricity. Many patterns of saturators now on the market seem as safe as houses, judging from their construction, but then——

Oxy-Spirit.

About a year ago, a French firm put on the market a projection lamp wherein boiling methylated spirit supplied the vapour necessary to the hydrogen side of a mixed gas limelight system. The writer has come across an example of this form of jet, and has heard well of it from the owner. It is said to give a light of quite 2,000 candle power. Moreover, it is economical in use, requiring only a comparatively small oxygen feed, but is very hot in working, owing to the spirit boiler with its attendant auxiliary flame which has to be kept going during exhibition. Altogether the light seems good enough and simple enough to merit careful consideration by those private individuals interested in projection work who may live away from a town gas supply and yet require some more powerful illuminant than acetylene. This spirit oxygen lamp is reported to be good for a six-foot projection with a throw of twenty-four feet.

Acetylene.

With acetylene we come to a class of illuminant which is barely on the brink of utility for the amateur projection of moving pictures, but it may be used where a two or three foot picture will satisfy requirements. Acetylene, as everyone who owns or has owned—or has a friend or relation who owns or has owned—a bicycle, will know, is made by dropping water upon calcium carbide. When water falls upon carbide there arises a—an aroma. This is the aroma of acetylene, celebrated as at once the most highly illuminating and one of the most noisome gases known to science. Incidentally, its mixtures with the air are very explosive in very wide proportions, so that acetylene generators should be carefully looked after, especially when their containers are large and pretty full.

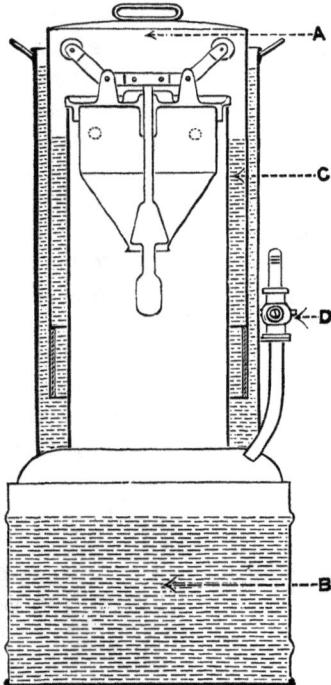

FIG. 171. A 'CARBIDE TO WATER' ACETYLENE GENERATOR.

A Gas Container.
C Carbide Container fitted with automatically operated outlet for carbide at bottom.
D Acetylene delivery tap.

Acetylene generators are broadly divided into two classes, those in which the gas is produced by water flooding trays whereon is spread calcium carbide, and those in which the calcium carbide is automatically discharged little by little into water as circumstances may require. The first class of generator is a good knock-about form, but has the disadvantage that once the flow of gas starts it is difficult or impossible to stop it completely till the whole of the carbide charge is used up. Gas production may be stopped off partially, but there will always be more or less leakage going on—with attendant smell—due to the carbide remaining in an atmosphere full of water vapour.

The alternative or carbide discharge system is under the drawback that the mechanism here is more complicated and requires to be more carefully looked after. Further, the carbide used in charging the ' carbide to water ' generator has to be crushed to a definite calibre and screened, all of which makes it more expensive to buy than that which suffices for the ' water to carbide ' generator. But where the system involves carbide discharging into water, the gas supply may be turned off or on with much greater freedom.

For kinematograph purposes, the acetylene jet may consist of three or four Beta Bray burners arranged with suitable attachment to the lantern tray. Preferably, each burner should have its own controlling tap, and the better class acetylene jets are

FIG. 172. FOUR-BURNER ACETYLENE GAS JET

thus provided. A reflector completes the arrangement, and unless the light is skilfully managed, this same reflector may, and probably will, give a lot of trouble in the way of unequal illumination effects upon the screen.

Acetylene projection in kinematography generally takes about one pound or a little more than one pound of carbide per hour for a four-burner jet. Taking the retail price of a pound of best carbide as sold in tins at the cycle shops at 6d., we shall see that acetylene, while giving a vastly inferior light to oxy-hydrogen, is also very much cheaper—roughly six times. This is not reckoning light for light, but merely putting the actual cost of an hour's run of the one form of illuminant against an hour's run of the other. Small wonder then if the hard-up amateur decides to content himself with a diminutive two-foot acetylene show in lieu of the more pretentious one possible with limelight. Acetylene gives a light of about 300 candle power, 350 candle power is the outside limit.

ELECTRIC NERNST LIGHT.

Where high voltage house mains are available, a very handy as well as inexpensive illuminant for home kinematograph exhibitions is to be found in the Nernst light as adapted to optical projection. The Radax Company, of 38 Great St. James Street, W.C. put on the market a five-filament Nernst lamp for which is claimed a candle power of 1,600 when running on a 200 volt circuit. The same lamp as adapted for 100 volt circuits only gives half the above amount of light, while on account of the length of the filaments used in this form of illuminant, only about one half of the nominal illumination would be capable of being usefully condensed upon the picture gate. This form of light further suffers from the drawback that in order to start it up, the extremely delicate filaments have to be heated in the flame

FIG. 173. THE RADAX CO.'S NERNST LAMP.

of a methylated spirit torch till they reach a temperature at which they can conduct the electric current sufficiently well to be kept in a state of incandescence by its passage. Against this must be placed the fact that the projection Nernst is exceedingly light and handy for the comparatively high candle power obtainable from it, while the first cost of the lamp being only two or three pounds should further endear it to the amateur to whom high voltage mains are available. In running cost this form of projection light compares with acetylene.

INCANDESCENT SPIRIT LAMPS.

Most of the cheap spirit burners which have come to our notice are quite unsuited to serious consideration in connection with even the home exhibition of moving pictures, since even at best they give a light of very little over 150 candle power. There is an exception to the rule, however, in the case of Hughes' Luna Spirit Lamp, an illustration of which is given (fig. 174).

FIG. 174. HUGHES' LUNA LAMP.

As will be seen from the illustration, the Luna lamp consists of a reservoir in which the spirit vapour is generated under pressure, the same being then led to the burner proper, where it goes to supply a spirit bunsen. The flame of this bunsen, which is exceptionally hot, causes the mantle to give off a light of well up to 300 candle power, which illumination may be regarded as just enough to produce small but reasonably well-lit moving pictures for the benefit of the home circle. At the same time, we strongly advise the amateur exhibitor while he is about it, to invest an extra guinea upon the price of the Luna and purchase Hughes' Universal lamp, which not only does all the Luna lamp can do, but is also capable of

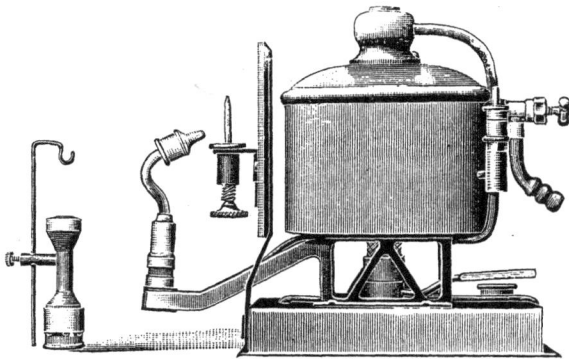

FIG. 175. HUGHES' UNIVERSAL LAMP.

being converted as required into an oxy-spirit jet on those occasions where the special importance of the exhibition warrants going to the expense of hiring a cylinder of compressed oxygen. This Universal lamp when reinforced with the oxygen supply can be relied upon to give upon a lime cylinder a light of well over 1,000 candle power, or enough to do justice to a picture up to six feet in diameter, while for more modest occasions it is simply converted into a plain spirit burner, giving about 300 candle power, the same as the Luna.

Among other firms supplying compressed spirit vapour lamps of more than the usual efficiency may be mentioned Messrs. Wrench, who have a very nice if somewhat high-priced lamp of this type.

Hughes' Chromatic Film Tinter.

We take the present opportunity as being the best that offers (at any rate, so far as the present edition of the HANDBOOK is concerned) of referring to the above very useful accessory. By its use the kinematograph showman, not only amateur but professional also, can flood his picture with any one of five appropriate tints the better to set off the artistic qualities of the subject being shown. Thus, snow scenes may be given a general prevailing tint of rose pink to their considerable enhancement; night scenes (where not already tinted in the film length) can be turned blue. In fact, the Chromatic Film Tinter has many and varied uses, which will speedily reveal themselves to the man who decides to give so clever a little accessory a trial. We figure the Chromatic Film Tinter above (fig. 176).

FIG. 176.
HUGHES' CHROMATIC FILM TINTER.

Incandescent Gas. Oil.

Incandescent gas, as adapted to projection, even at its best rarely touches 100 candle power, while the best oil lamps, such as may give an effective 100 to 150 candle power in the case of still view work are not feasible even for amateur kinematography on account of the abnormally large light source involved, with the attendant difficulty of concentrating anything like the whole of the emerging rays upon the gate.

Those who wish to find out more concerning these totally inadequate lighting systems, may therefore be referred to works on still view projection and on photographic enlargement making, for which purposes alone they are fitted.

CHAPTER VI.

———

IN THE OPERATING BOX.

The operating box of a modern picture theatre should be a substantially built brick chamber provided with fireproof—preferably concrete—floor. It must allow sufficient elbow room for the operator and his assistant to get about freely between the projector or projectors and winding and film storage benches situate around the sides of the chamber. The winding bench will, as its name implies, have screwed to it or otherwise made firm upon it, a film winder, the best kind of winders being those in which two separate uprights carry respectively the full and empty spools, thus allowing of a good expanse of film between the two for purposes of examination while in passage from the one spool to the other. The same table will also be of sufficient size for the convenient accommodation of the pile of empty spools necessary to the conduct of the exhibition, while the full ones will be kept in one of the specially constructed metal cases, well away from where hot carbons—or limes, in the case of lime-light—may chance to be dropped or thrown.

One half of the second table or bench in the operating room forms a handy place for the reception of boxes containing song slides, announcement slides, title slides, etc., while the opposite half of it, divided off by a ridge, serves for such indispensable tools as electrical pliers, box containing bioscope spares and renewals, and also for fuse wire reels. The winding table accommodates the film mender and mending appliances including scissors, sharp knife, film cement, brush and duster. Beyond the items already enumerated, place also has to be found among the tools and spares for lubricating oil and oilers, cleaning brushes and dusters, and such like necessary odds and ends of the operating box. But when all these necessaries have been accounted for, there comes in a further and no less important point from the view of efficient operating. This is to see that no litter of unnecessary trifles, beyond those enumerated, or rubbish is allowed to accumulate on the operating box floor and under the benches. Numerous shelves are likewise out of place in the operating box, though it is a very neat plan to have hooks or nails for the accommodation of such tools as can be readily hung up, instead of allowing them to lie about when not in use.

A box or tray for the reception of new and used carbons, both for the kinematograph and announcement lantern is necessary in the case of electric shows. This should be fireproof or lined with fireproof material, and should also be compartmented so as to allow of the

SOME OPERATING BOX REQUISITES.

FIG. 177.   METAL FILM SPOOL STORAGE CASE

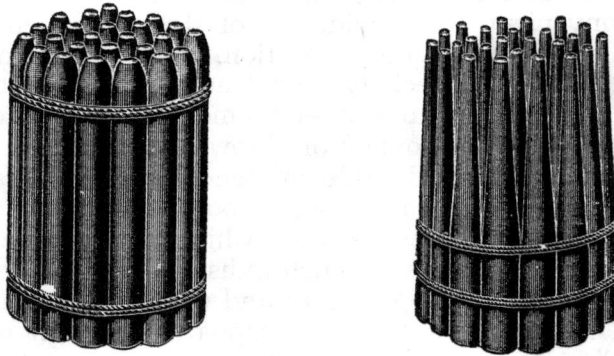

FIG. 178.   CARBONS.

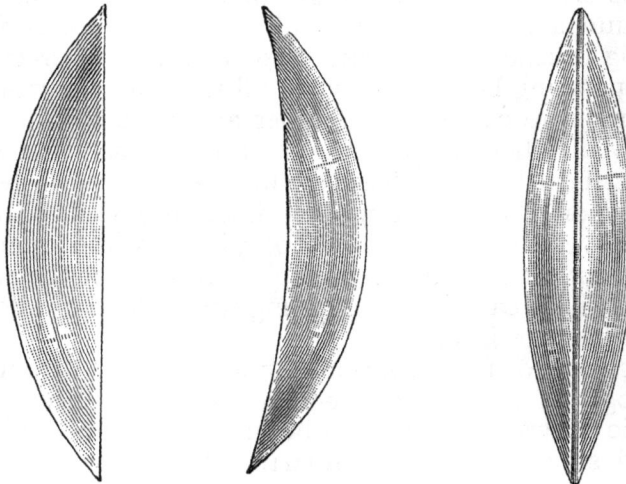

FIG. 179.   SPARE CONDENSER LENSES.

various sizes and descriptions of carbons being got at at a moment's notice. Red hot stumps will be thrown into the waste compartment. In the case of limelight shows, an old tin into which to throw the used and cracked limes will answer all practical purposes. All benches inside the operating box should be composed of, or covered with, fireproof material. Latterly the trend of licensing authorities is to eliminate as far as possible every speck of wood and such like combustible matter from the box equipment, so that where new boxes are being put up it will probably not only be best, but also cheaper in the end to be done with makeshifts.

In the case of a lime show, a good place for the cylinders is to have them tied on to the iron projector stand—either that, or they may be accommodated in proper cylinder stands fixed permanently near to the lamp house of the projector. With electric shows, the metal conduit leading the mains into the box goes first to the enclosed double pole main switch controlling the entire operating box circuit. From here, the current, after flowing through enclosed main fuses, placed on either pole, passes on to the variable resistance and the sub-circuits for incandescent lighting, the latter being branched off on the live side of the resistance frame. All sub-circuits must be provided with their own individual switches and double pole fuses. The conduit leading from the variable resistance (which latter must be well protected and right out of the way of the celluloid film used in projection) mounts up the side to the top of the box, where the leads issue from it, and falls directly to the terminals of the arc. Asbestos braiding is here a necessity. A similar arrangement of the smaller leads supplying the announcement lantern completes our projection current supply.

As to the sub-circuits mentioned above, there may be several, of which one may control stage lights, footlights and battens, should these be installed in the electric theatre in connection with incidental turns, song slide work, lecturing, etc. A further sub-circuit will control the lights in the auditorium, which go up and down between the showing of pictures. But here it is necessary to insist that where the latter arrangement is made, a second hall lighting circuit be also provided, controlled from the pay box or vestibule. Sometimes the theatre will be arranged so that the bright lights in the auditorium are on the operating box circuit, while a dull red glow from obscured secondary electric bulbs, which are never extinguished, even during showing, comes straight off the mains independent of any control, save that in the pay box. The reason for such an arrangement, as also for similar independent illumination of the exit signs, is to prevent the possibility of the audience being plunged in complete darkness, which might otherwise happen through an accident in the box causing the operator to pull his main in a hurry.

Having now roughly sketched the electric system of a picture theatre from the operator's point of view, we will pass on to consider matters connected with the art of showing.

SOME OPERATING BOX REQUISITES.

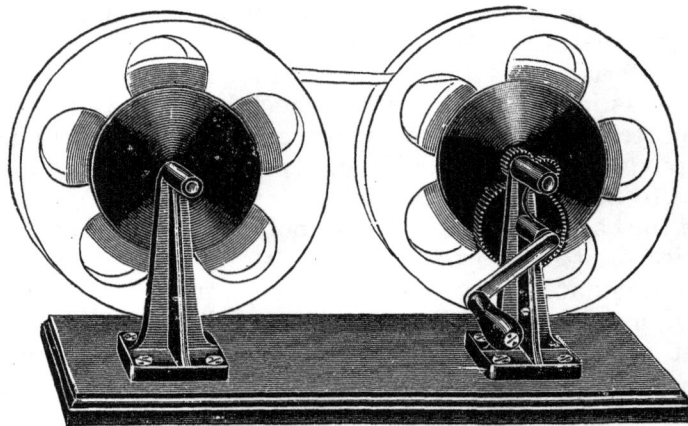

FIG. 180.   FILM WINDER (APPROVED PATTERN).

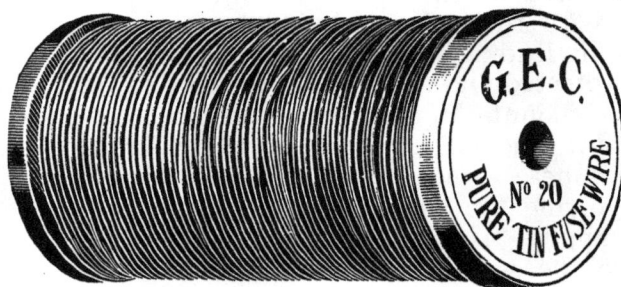

FIG. 181.   FUSE WIRE.

FIG. 182.   FILM MENDER.

Firstly, when film consignments arrive from the renting houses, it should be insisted that the operator unpacks them outside the operating chamber. The films are too often done up with more or less of a litter of odds and ends of paper. Even promiscuous shavings from short lengths of old and worn out spacing are by no means always absent. A little of this sort of stuff getting about where a red-hot carbon stump might conceivably fall might well be the cause of incalculable damage. Make a rule, therefore, that packing and unpacking of films are not to be done in the operating chamber.

There is another class of work which should also have a place assigned to it as far as possible away from the box. This is the class of job connected with repairing of the projector fittings and of the arc. Some minor repairs and most adjustments, as also the cleaning of the projector, are inseparable from the operating chamber. Here the best thing that can be done is to try and see that the one engaged upon the job uses clean dusters, brushes, etc., and that he shakes them out each time after use, and well away from the operating room. But when it comes to the use of the file and such like more daring repairs executed in the box, the risk to working parts of the mechanism, to say nothing of risk to the travelling film, through grit getting in the gate, becomes too serious to be tolerated. A repairing bench should accordingly be provided for the operator whenever possible right away from the projection chamber. If this bench is fitted with a few decent tools, such as tap and dies, small hand drill, small turning lathe, even of the most meagre description, together with an assortment of files, pliers, and screwdrivers of reasonably varied sizes and characteristics there can be no question a good mechanic will do wonders in the way of keeping the projector running sweetly and of prolonging its working life. On the other hand a bad worker will never be able to resist experimenting with that concerning which he knows nothing. If, therefore, your operator or operators are not absolutely up to snuff, discourage all attempts by them at repairing on the grander scale. It will pay you better to buy a spare projector right away, so that you can send the old one off to be refurbished by the makers on the first signs of approaching senility and decrepitude.

Cleaning the Projector.

Next to the glasses of the optical system, the parts of a projector which require most frequent and most careful cleaning are the gate mask and gate runners. In the case of a dog machine, the sprockets of the lower or take-up sprocket wheel are also of the utmost importance. However, the gate is best left till last when cleaning a projector throughout, so we will get to work systematically on the machine as a whole.

The first thing to be seen to will be the lamp house. Remove the arc or lime jet, and take it with its attendant mess of carbon and silicate dust, or lime ash, right out of the operating box. Proce d to dust the lamp house carefully, and without stirring more than necessary the debris into the air. Remove the cell holding the condenser lenses and place on the winding table for cleaning before returning the illuminant source to its place.

Having now got the lamp house clean we go on to the mechanism. If this is in a passable state it will be sufficient to first thoroughly brush the cogs of the gear wheels so as to remove collected dust and oil blobs. Next oil the wheels with clock oil and turn the mechanism. Of course, it will be understood that during these cleaning operations there is no film threaded in the gate. Also it will be wise at the start to remove the objective lens from its jacket and place it with the condenser out of harm's way.

If, on turning the mechanism, it runs smoothly with no shake, and no jar or 'grind' in the wheels, then we may leave it at that as far as the cogs are concerned. If, however, shake or grind manifest themselves, the thing to do is to wipe off as much as possible of the sur- plus clock oil and anoint the cogs with vaseline, alternately applying it and turning the projector handle till it works its way well into them. This is a wonderful treatment for grind. Careful wiping of the spindles with liberal oiling of the oil holes in the bushings and subsequent cleaning up of all surplus which may exude, completes the treatment of well kept gear wheels. Sprocket wheels are polished up like door knockers, collected cakes of oil and dust around the sprockets being first rubbed away by means of the cleaning brush, or by gentle removal with a paper knife.

Where the gear wheels and pinions show signs of being clogged with collected muddy-looking cakey matter—which condition of things is pretty constant where the film service is cheap and consequently the films run old and dirty—there will be nothing for it but to take out the screws binding gear wheels and pinions together and remove both for thorough burnishing and internal oiling.

Take a clean oily rag and thread it through the holes from which shaftings have been removed for cleaning purposes. Pull the rag backwards and forwards till the bushing is thoroughly bright and lubricated. The polished pinion shaft may now be returned to place, when it should work easily and give no more trouble.

When a machine gets into the condition known as 'running hard,' and which condition is baffling to many operators, it is really a sign the time has come for such thorough internal cleaning and burnishing of bearings.

To clean the gate runners, also the gate and lens tube, usually entails no more than their removal, dusting and burnishing with a chamois leather. The rim of the gate mask must be gone over very carefully to take away all trace of the furred edge which from time to time gets to show on the projected picture. Gate runners and springs are of several different models. In some of the older fashioned and cheaper ones, the two are combined, the runners being in them- selves f'attened spring surfaces. Such are usually referred to as 'bow springs.' Gates fitted with these usually give trouble sooner or later. A spare back plate with bow springs attached must always be kept handy with such gates, for when in use the thin steel bows rapidly wear down and snap. The broken ends are then in condition to rip off the film perforations till further orders, in other words till the evil attracts attention, and the new plate and bow springs can be slipped in place of the old and worn-out set.

Modern forms of gate are fitted with comparatively heavy rigid polished runners, which serve to keep the film close against the film mask, these runners or 'skates' being backed by separate adjustable tension springs bearing against their outer surfaces. Gate tension may here be adjusted to suit the requirements of any individual film, whether it be new or one worn and thin in the perforations. This system is far better than the old one of bow springs with their unalterable tension. Gate runners, however, require careful cleaning, both in themselves and as to the grooves in which they lie. Otherwise they may get stiff and fail to transmit to the film the spring tension behind them.

When cleaning the gate, start by polishing with a duster. Should any old gelatine from the films have caked upon the film track and be difficult to remove, it may be scraped off by means of a metal scraper having a straight semi-sharp edge, and being of not quite the width of the gate track. A penny will also serve the same purpose in most cases, its edge, though round, having just about the required amount of bite upon the gate. Personally, the writer uses neither. He discovered for himself some time ago the advantages of a piece of ordinary typing eraser. This, besides most thoroughly cleaning the gate and runners of all suspicion of accumulated film coating, serves at the same time to burnish the metal, thus making one job of what would otherwise be two separate operations.

After cleaning the gate, wipe it over with a very slightly oiled rag More than a mere suspicion of oil is not permissible.

The dog roller of a dog machine is also very liable to collect about it waste matter from much used film subjects. This waste material prevents its rotating freely, and later on it will work into the dog spindle and spoil the snugness of the bearing, and consequently much of the steadiness of the machine. With Maltese cross machines, the intermittent sprocket must be kept equally clean. The oil bath must also be kept filled, while now and then the old oil should be completely run off and a new supply substituted.

Occasionally—as for instance, when the shaft spindles of projectors have been removed from their bearings and replaced after cleaning—it will be found that the synchronisation of the cover position of the rotary light shutter with the picture change has been interfered with. Here it will be necessary to re-adjust the covering shutter, except in those rare cases where this part is non-adjustable. Then the still more arduous operation of fitting the picture change to the light shutter becomes inevitable. The former adjustment, however, is by no means difficult

Thread a piece of positive film in the projector gate, as for showing Now place yourself with the eye looking straight into the projector lens at the threaded positive film.   Turn the projector handle very slowly until a shift of the film in the gate warns of the escapement coming into operation, then proceed to set the light-cut-off so that at the moment this movement of the film starts the cover sector just completely covers the lens.   Continue turning till the covering sector of the shutter clears the lens again, and if adjustment has been correctly made the eye will just miss seeing the last trace of the picture shift in the same way that it grazed the beginning of the movement.   There are besides this simple method, several mathematical ways of measuring the middle point of the picture shift and setting the cover shutter accordingly, but in practice the one given above is at least as simple and also far more certain. One point must be borne in mind. When adjusting the light cut-off upon a projector fitted with rackwork masking to the gate, see first of all that the gate rack is in its central position. Where the masking of the film is effected by means of a jockey roller riding upon the film between the gate and escapement, as in some types of projectors, no precaution as to the mask setting is necessary

The machine being now well cleaned in all its metal parts, there only remains to polish the glasses of objective and condenser before fitting them back in their places.   Instructions for cleaning and replacing the objective elements have already been given earlier in this part.   The condenser lenses are easy enough to replace, since in the case of triple and Herschel condensers the fittings usually only allow of the right glass being dropped into the right position, always remembering that the concave side of the meniscus (smaller) lens must be toward the illuminant.

Plano convex condensers consist of two identical plano convex lenses, placed in a cell with their flat sides outward.   Such condensers are not much used in kinematography, but where met with the replacement of the glasses after cleaning is easier still, since both being identical one cannot well go wrong.   Selvyt cloth kept scrupulously clean and for the one purpose only will be found excellent for wiping over the optical glasses of the projector.

We now come to centring and adjusting the projection light ready for showing.   To do this, first turn on the current into the arc and strike carbons, or light up the mixed gases and adjust lime, in the case of limelight. The light source is now to be considered as back once again in the projector's lamp house. Leave the gate unthreaded. The sliding light cut off, as well as the rotary light shutter, must, further, be out of the way, so that as soon as correct illumination has been obtained, it will be seen in the form of an evenly illuminated picture disc upon the projection screen.   Notice at first whether the light beam streaming through the condenser strikes any part of the gate, or if not, where it does go ; up, down, or one sided, or both.   The object will be to get the light shining in a neat even pencil just sufficiently large to cover to the corners of the aperture of the mask, and illuminate the projection disc equally all over. If now the light beam strikes too high, lower it by raising the illuminant source ; if the light strikes too low, bring it up by reversing the above process. Similarly, a left hand turn to the source of illumination will switch the light beam to the right, and *vice versa*. Sooner or later we cannot help getting the light, such as it is, to strike into the gate aperture. But this is not to say the effect will be right. Perhaps, instead of a compact bundle of rays about the diameter of a five shilling piece or less, there will be a large and correspondingly dimly illuminated area widely overlapping the gate. This will mean that the light source is too near the condenser. Pull the arc or lime jet bodily backwards as though sliding it out of the lamp house, and the light pencil will come together till it is as it should be. On the other hand, the light, on first centring, may show a curious bluish cruciform effect upon the centre of the gate. Where this manifests itself, it means the light source is already too far from the condenser. The remedy is to shift it nearer up by pushing the lamp bodily forwards further into the lamp house.

Even now, unless the front of the condenser is the right distance from the gate, the light on the screen will not be even, but will exhibit a more or less circular or zonal gradation of colour and brilliance. Where such effect shows itself, the lamp house itself must be shifted further back upon its runners, so as to increase the distance between condenser front and gate mask. From four to six inches is the usual separation required between the two with a four and a half inch condenser, though the individual characteristics of the condenser can alone determine the matter.

Making up Programs.

Before a picture program can be exhibited properly and without long and totally unnecessary gaps between the showing of the various photo-plays, it is necessary to subject the films to the process known as ' making up.' Making up consists in collecting together the films comprising the program, into groups of a length such as can be conveniently accommodated upon the several spools. Not only must the films be selected into aggregations totalling, say, 1,200 feet in each, so as to wind on the minimum number of spools, and consequently show with the minimum number of change intervals, but subjects must be arranged in such sequence that each one will, by contrast, help the next as much as possible.

Thus, suppose our film consignment has in it two Wild West films, each of 600 feet, it would still be very bad making up to join them together, although by doing so we should get our exact 1,200 feet spool length, for in this case it would mean that two similar subjects totally devoid of contrast would appear one after the other. A man who is good at make up understands the value of light and shade in the picture program. But this is a matter on which more may be said subsequently.

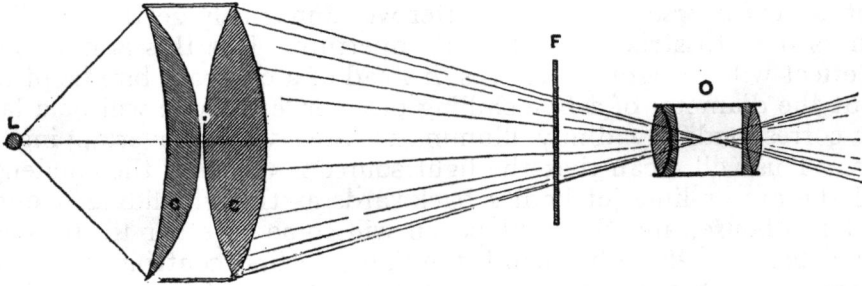

FIG. 183.   A CORRECTLY CENTRED LIGHT BEAM.

L, light source. CC, the glasses of a Herschel condenser. F, projector gate, in which is cut a hole of suitable size for the picture mask. O, objective lens of the projector.

Note how the light beam is here adjusted, and try to centre it the same in your projector.

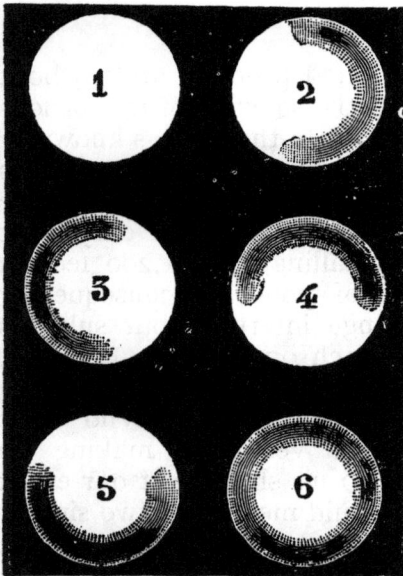

FIG. 184.

HOW WANT OF CENTRING OF THE LIGHT SHOWS ON THE SCREEN.

1.—Light correctly centred.

2.—Light source too much to left.

3.—Light source too much to right.

4.—Light source too low.

5.—Light source too high.

6.—Light source too far from condenser.

To make up a spool, the film which is to show last upon it is wound up backwards, and to its latter end is attached about a foot of blank spacing, either the white, black, or the blue variety. The film is then rewound right way on to the empty spool. Its title will come outermost after such winding. Affix to this title a foot of white blank spacing, and to the other end of it attach the latter end of the second film, and so on. When the last film the spool will accommodate has been wound upon it, a further ' threading up ' length of blank spacing is attached, and the reel is ready for exhibition.

White blank spacing is obtainable from all film renting houses at a cheap rate. When splitting up the spool, or 'cleaning' the films off it for sending back to the renting house, the spacing is removed and retained for further use in making up the next film program

To join film for the purpose of mending it or when attaching spacing, adopt the following routine. Cut an edge to be joined level with the top of a picture. Cut off the edge to be attached to it about one quarter of an inch or rather less below the bottom of the picture on the end of its length. Lick the portion of the picture last cut into so as to moisten the gelatine coating. Then lay film down, gelatine uppermost, and proceed to scrape away the coating from the licked flap, till clear celluloid only is left.

Dip a camel hair brush into a bottle of film cement and apply rather freely to the scraped flap, then press this flap down upon the celluloid side of the length to which it is to be joined. If rightly done both emulsion sides of film will look the same way. Shift the cemented flap rapidly into place so that the lowermost sprocket hole of the one length coincides with the uppermost on the other, and hold the two thicknesses of celluloid together for a couple of minutes. They will then be sufficiently stuck to adhere, and ten minutes more will make a tight joint of them.

A reliable formula for ordinary film cement consists of commercial Acetone and Amyl Acetate in equal parts. In this mixture allow to dissolve suffcient clean celluloid chips (old cleaned off film will do) to impart a slight degree of viscosity.

FORMULA FOR CEMENT FOR NON-FLAM FILM. Dissolve non-flam film base in chloroform till a viscous liquid results. Use in the same manner as ordinary cement, but bearing in mind that it evaporates quicker, so leaving less time for effecting registration of the sprocket holes.

Where the operator's skill in film joining is not too great, he may press in the services of a film mender. This inexpensive little accessory accomplishes the task of correctly superposing the sprocket holes upon the two lengths to be joined, and holding all in position till dry. It is a neat device but not necessary, and certainly not time saving, in comparison with the hand mending of a good operator.

Film breakages are doctored by cutting out the portion of celluloid which has been damaged and connecting together the nearest perfect pictures, in the foregoing way.

PUTTING THROUGH.

This is the actual thing—the projection of the kinematograph picture itself. It is set about in the following way.

To load the upper spool box, open the door and place the ready made-up spool in position upon the central bobbin. Pass the film end through the slit between the spool box feed rollers. If projecting upon an opaque screen, which is now the almost universal practice, the emulsion side of the film must unwind towards the condenser. If it does not, it means that the spool has to be taken out and reversed, the inner side becoming outermost, and *vice versa*.

Pull down about three feet of film, which corresponds with the thread-up length, and close the spool box door after making sure that everything is running normally inside. Snap down the jockey roller from the upper feed sprocket, pass film between jockey and sprocket then snap jockey up into place again. The film between film box and upper sprocket wheel should be left fairly tight, that is to say, without any slack lopping over the lens and light shutter. Now open the gate and pass the film end into it, leaving about a six inch. free loop between the gate top and upper sprocket feed. Pull the film well into its place in the gate track so that it lies both flat and even, and proceed to snap the runner plate into place. Try the film by pulling slightly on the film loop at top of gate. It should slip evenly, but with a gentle friction as the result of the pressure of the runners upon its edges.

Feed the film, which now lies free below the gate, over the jockey roller of the masking adjustment, if the machine is one of this kind, and round the dog of a dog machine or over the sprockets of the intermittent sprocket wheel in the case of a Maltese cross projector. The film next passes over the take-up or bottom sprocket in the same way as it was led over the top one, and from thence goes to the take-up spool (empty) within the bottom spool box. This take-up spool will have affixed to its hub a spring arrangement for gripping the film end. Wind the mechanism of the projector sufficiently to cause the take-up to pick up one complete turn of film. This ensures that nothing will fail to act, and with it threading is accomplished.

Adjustment of the light is presumed to have been made as described earlier in this chapter. There is still the adjustment of the gate mask, which has to be made before showing each picture. Make it thus:

FOR RACKWORK GATE.

The shutter of the sliding light cut-off should have a very small pin hole pierced centrally in it. This will pass an equally small light pencil, almost devoid of heat and therefore harmless to the film. With this arrangement it will be possible to look through the lens and see for oneself if the masking is right, the sliding light shutter meanwhile remaining closed. Adjust the mask and everything will be ready for throwing the light cut-off out of the way and starting projection.

Another way of going to work is this : Paint the inside of the operating box safety shutter white, when it will be found that the pictures to be projected on the screen may be seen fairly distinctly upon this whitened dropped shutter flap as the result of the narrow pencil of light streaming through the pinhole of the closed light cut-off in front of the condenser. Such light would, however, not be sufficient to cause any visible image upon the comparatively distant projection screen. The image on the shutter is used to adjust the mask and also for centring the light, after which the shutter may be drawn up, the light cut-off opened, and projection proceed.

Fixed Gate with Jockey Roller Adjustment for Masking.

The difficulty of masking is here much greater, since with this system no adjustment is possible until the projector mechanism is actually at work. The best way is to start the projector slowly with sliding perforated light cut-off closed, and with the operating box shutter down. As an alternative to using the box shutter, the assistant operator may hold a white card well in front of the l ns. While the projector is thus running dead slow, the jockey roller masking device may be brought into operation until adjustment is seen to be effected. The light cut-off is then opened, the card or shutter withdrawn from the track of the light beam, and projection proceeds as usual. It will be seen that masking in this way with short titles, there is the danger of their being lost. This may be overcome by joining to the front of such titles, other scrap film bearing an image or imprint of some sort and having the same masking. Adjustment is made upon the latter, and afterwards the cut-off is drawn out, and projection proceeds upon the title proper.

Dangers to be Guarded against in Operating.

Breakage of film, either through burst perforations, fault in the celluloid base, wear, or bad film joining, is bound to occur more or less often. Where such breakages take place in the gate, the film may stop dead in the track of the light beam. If the operator is not on the look-out to close the light cut-off instantly, the celluloid will certainly, under such circumstances, fire. Such firing should not spread if the gate is well designed. Still, the very fact of possible combustion of any part of the highly inflammable film is enough to warn the operator before-hand to be on the constant look-out all the while the film is going through.

After a break, and when the light has been cut off, the thing to do is to open the gate quickly, wind down enough film to carry it over the escapement, and proceed to pin the free end to the broken one for the purposes of taking up. Projection may then go on as before. Do not use large pins for the purpose, and try not to do more injury than necessary to the broken film ends. Every picture that can be saved on the edges of a break is so much more film length, with its representation of incident preserved. An experienced operator can dispense with the pinning operation altogether by simply winding down the film sufficiently and then making a hand wind of a turn and a half upon the already partially filled take-up spool. After this the film will hold on of itself again.

Occasionally, portions of film perforations will split and stick in the gate in the middle of projecting. If such splinters do not spoil the effect of the picture on the screen one need not stop till the end of the picture, since the moving celluloid between them and the light source acts as an effective cut-off to the heat rays. It is well, however, to increase the speed of projection considerably the moment any splinters make their appearance, and to keep it up till the subject is over, when, of course, the light cut-off is at once thrown in, and the gate opened and cleaned.

SPOOLING SINGLE FILMS FOR PROJECTION.

Single films are sometimes required to be exhibited in a hurry and without winding previously on a regular film spool. In such cases it is usual to spool the film on a split spool, but when wound tightly in the first place, the hole in the centre of the wound film may not be sufficiently large to admit of the hub of the split spool going

 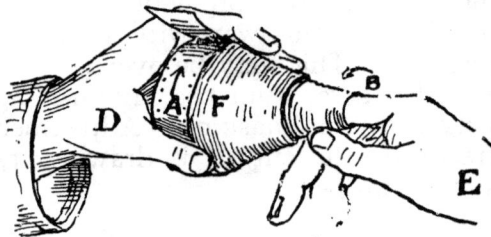 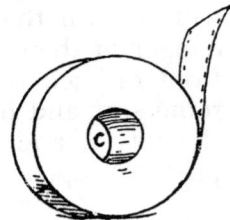

FIG. 185.   FIG. 186.   FIG. 187.

through. In such a case, which is figured in fig. 185 C, the opening can be enlarged in the following manner. Take hold of the roll with the left hand as shown at D, fig. 186, and then place the forefinger of the right hand in the centre of the roll, as shown. The roll may then be drawn out horizontally, forming a cone-shaped mass, as indicated at F. Now grip with both hands, turning the left hand in the direction indicated by the arrow at A, and the right hand in the direction indicated by the arrow at B. If the larger end of the roll at A is allowed to slip through the fingers whilst the right hand forces the film from right to left, as shown by the arrow B, then it will be found that the roll is gradually increasing in size, and that the opening in the centre becomes enlarged, as shown in fig. 187.

JOINING FILMS.

Film ends are joined together by first cleaning the extremities as shown in fig. 188, and then cementing the one on the other with film cement. The accompanying detailed and illustrated description may be of service to the novice.

Cut one end at the junction of the pictures, and the end of the film to be joined thereto three-sixteenths of an inch from the junction of the first picture. Take a rule as at C, fig. 189, and place it over the film last mentioned, with the edge of the rule in such a position that a penknife E may be taken, and the gelatine scraped away in a straight line across the film in the direction of the arrow. There will now be a clear space of celluloid surface at A, Fig. 190. Now wet the fore-

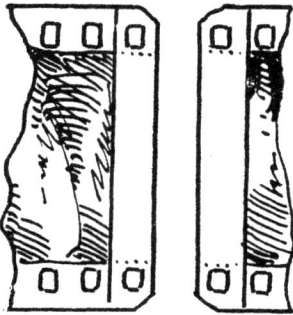

FIG. 188.

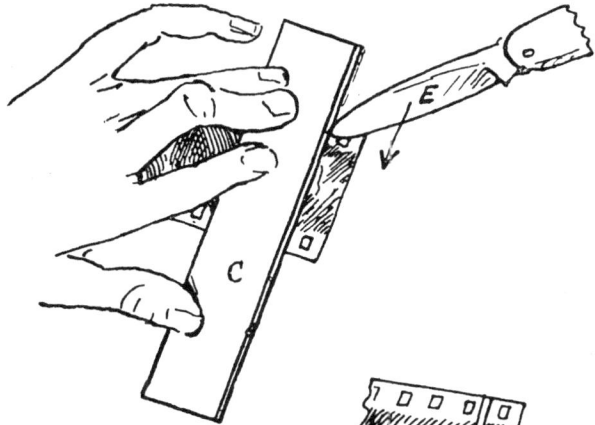

FIG. 189.

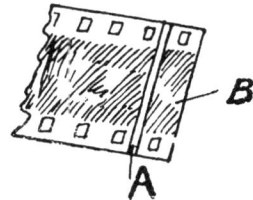

FIG. 190.

finger and moisten the remaining gelatine B. After a few seconds, this strip may be pulled from the celluloid support, so that there will be a piece of clear and clean celluloid at the end of the film measuring about three-sixteenths of an inch. Having cleaned and prepared the film, as shown in Fig. 191, cement is applied to the cleaned surface, the second film laid upon it with the sprocket holes in register, and the whole pressed together or put under pressure in a film mender till a strong join is effected, Fig. 192. It should be noticed that the film

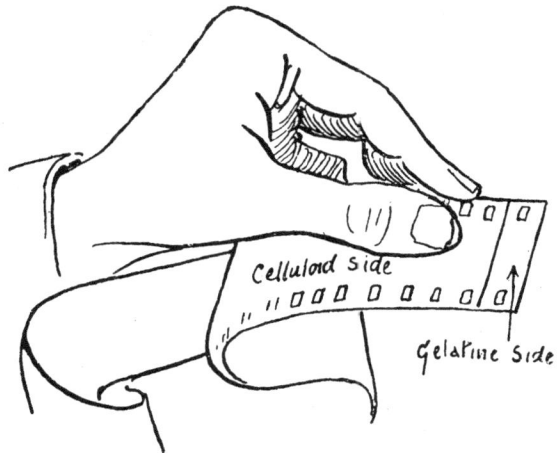

FIG. 191.

cut at the junction of the last picture is laid celluloid uppermost upon the film with the clear space extending, and the gelatine side upwards, as indicated in the cut. The gelatine, however, has been removed from this part, as already described.

FIG. 192.   THE FILM IN THE MENDER.

Failing of the take-up is a very real danger to be faced when operating. This danger is, moreover, greatly increased by the necessity of using a lower as well as an upper spool box in compliance with Home Office regulations. If the film begins to pay out on the floor there is always a risk of its becoming ignited by a stray spark or red hot particle from the light source. An assistant in the box to rectify such a condition of things as sticking of the take-up spool by if necessary completing the winding by hand, is a very wise precautionary measure. If there is no second person handy when the take-up fails, then the operator must manage to hand wind and attend to the other parts of projection at the same time, and as best he can. It is at such moments as this that masking is liable to go wrong, and indeed such a reason should be about the only valid excuse for it doing so and remaining out of adjustment for any length of time. After the show, a faulty take-up is adjusted by tightening or renewing the spring clutch.

ORDERLY SHOWING.

The moment a film subject is concluded, the lights in the auditorium should be switched up, so that the audience may consult the program as to the synopsis of the next motion picture story. Meanwhile, the masking of the forthcoming title is adjusted and the illuminant looked to. When all this is satisfactorily managed, the auditorium lights once more go down, the light cut-off of the projector is opened, and projection proceeds again.

As the spool of film becomes nearly exhausted, the attendant's business is to fetch a new one ready for instant threading and to open the film box doors. The moment the last subject on the spool comes to its end and the cut-off is thrown in, the auditorium lights go up and the operator quickly whisks the empty top spool from its place, and replaces it with the new full one, proceeding to thread up without delay. Meanwhile, the assistant removes the loaded take-up and transfers it to the dead arm of the rewinder, returning immediately to place the empty reel from the top box in position in the lower spool box, where it will now act as the new take-up spool.

While the operator completes threading, the assistant may commence rewinding the former spool on the rewinder, or he may stand by the projector holding the adjustment card in front of the lens, etc., until the signal is given for the auditorium lights once more to go down, and projection of the second spool commences.

It is possible for an operator to do all the above single-handed, but in such cases the light and masking of the projected image usually suffer while his back is turned attending to the rewinding of films for the next show. The latter remark refers only to motor-driven shows, which only lend themselves to one man control.

MOTOR DRIVEN PROJECTORS.

Many projectors are now motor instead of hand driven. Motors for such a purpose are almost invariably of the direct current type, developing a horse power of from the one sixteenth to the one sixth, and are generally shunt wound, the speed being controlled by a

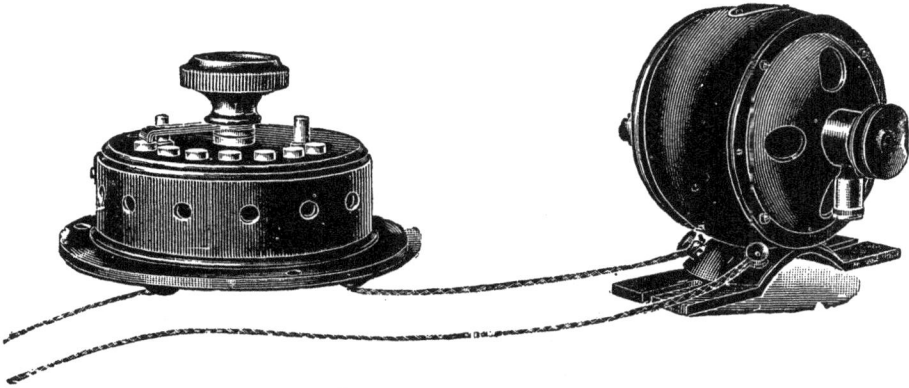

FIG. 193. BUTCHER'S MOTOR FOR DRIVING PROJECTOR.

multiple point rheostat, or shunt regulator. Fig. 193 gives the method of connecting such a motor with the electric supply taken as a sub-circuit off the dead end of the main operating box switch To start up motor, put in switch and turn rheostat handle till the required speed is attained. The rheostat is conveniently bolted to the side or end of the projector stand, so as to be controlled by means of the left hand while masking and other adjustments are made with the right.

FIG. 194.   UP TO DATE KINEMATOGRAPH THEATRE IN NEW ZEALAND

FIG. 195.   AN AUSTRALIAN TOURING COMPANY.

PART III

PART III.

CHAPTER I.

TRICK KINEMATOGRAPHY.

Hitherto we have confined ourselves to the consideration of ways of photographing actually proceeding actions. With trick kinematography, however, an entirely new element is introduced into the work of the picture maker, for by its means it is not only possible but often easy to turn out film subjects representing actions and situations which never could have arisen in real life.

Let us try to enumerate some of the various devices made use of in obtaining trick effects.

MIRACULOUS APPEARANCES AND DISAPPEARANCES.

These are amongst the easiest of trick effects to produce. Indeed they are supposed to have had their inception through a pure accident which came about in the following way :—

A well-known kinematographer (quite in the early days of the industry) had taken a film exhibiting the departure of a train from a railway station. One of the last people to enter it before it steamed off was a certain young man known to the photographer. This passenger hurried up, newspaper in hand, and made a run for a near by compartment just as the whistle of the engine was going.

Now it so happened that some months later the maker of the film happened to see an old copy put on in a touring kinematograph show. Naturally he looked out for his friend to come on the film and make the wild dash for the carriage during which he had been photographed, and in due time the young fellow with the newspaper appeared, ran half way to the compartment door at which he should have entered, and————of a sudden he was no more. He had vanished. Of course, the reason was easy to divine. The positive film had got worn and had broken at the point where the incident should have culminated, the result being that a foot or more of it had been cut away by a none too careful film mender. But the sudden disappearance of the traveller was destined to be the starting point of many another deliberately produced effect of the same kind.

The motion picture producer hurried home and set himself straight off upon the production of a ghost film, in which the whole effect was obtained by cutting out portions representing the moment of appearance and disappearance of each white-clad sepulchral figure, the result being that these ghosts came and vanished on the screen in the same sudden and unaccountable manner.   Such, at any rate, is the story of the manner of the inception of appearance and disappearance effects as told to the writer by one whose word he has no cause whatever to doubt.

According to modern methods, where it is desired to bring about a miraculous disappearance, one goes to work much in the same way. There is, however, no need to waste film in cutting when photographing such trick effects, since the same result is better obtained by the simple device of stopping the camera handle during the ghostly entrances and exits.

Let us take a case in point and examine how such a magical appearance or disappearance can be made use of, and how its accomplishment is set about in practice.   Take the once well-known Pathe

FIG. 196.—A SIMPLE TRICK EFFECT.   The gentleman clinging to the lamp-post is acting as though intoxicated.   Still further to heighten this effect, the camera man, while taking the motion picture, rocks the tripod top by means of a suitable screw action, with which it is provided.   The result is to give a picture which sways on the screen as projected.   This effect can be obtained with an ordinary 'maxim' tripod head by screwing on the camera at right angles to its usual position.

film, " The Enchanted Glasses."   This now almost forgotten film was famous in its day as one of the finest hand-coloured trick subjects ever issued.

A part of it represents a young woman flourishing a piece of cloth in front of a dark curtain.   Suddenly, as she twirls the cloth about, another girl appears behind it as though from nowhere.

To photograph such an effect, the camera handle is stopped abruptly when the cloth is in the act of being waved about in front of nothingness.   Now while the camera is out of action, the girl who is to "appear" steps into position for her "appearance."   The waving of the cloth is recommenced, the camera handle is once more smartly started, and the resulting film negative will show two adjacent pictures, in the first of which the magically-produced young lady is not visible, while in the next she is.   On putting through the projector the positive printed from such a negative, the effect will show the seeming production of a girl from nowhere. For a marvellous disappearance, the above course of events is merely reversed.

In all work of the above description, a great deal of the effectiveness depends upon the final making-up of the negative, choosing for the pictures which stand at the point where the camera has been stopped and restarted such images as show as little as possible of movement variation, except in the matter of the object produced or vanished. Thus, in making up the negative for the disappearance effect described above, much care would have been bestowed upon ensuring that the position of the waving cloth in mid air in the picture immediately after the production of the girl was approximately the same

Fig. 197.—THE DANCING MIDGET. This effect depends simply upon an observer's comparative inability to perceive distance except by relation to intermediate objects. The camera D is set to photograph the table A, which stands before the partition G. In this partition is cut an aperture C, behind which and at a suitably great distance, is the living model E. The background F is of the same tint as G, so that the want of continuity is not easily apparent. When carefully planned out, the effect may be as though a figure much smaller than life-size was situate at B. The lens of the camera must be greatly stopped down.

as in the one next before. This is adjusted finally by careful cutting and rejoining of the negative film prior to printing from it, omitting in the process whatever pictures may be superfluous or prejudicial to the general apparent continuity of action depicted.

MAGICAL METAMORPHOSES.

As an instance of this sort of trick work may be cited a film in which a beautiful young lady is in the act of being married to a very fine young fellow, when the latter changes in a flash to a giant-sized dutch doll. The effect is really the combination of one of the already described "disappearance" effects with an "appearance." The young fellow taking the part of the bridegroom steps out of the picture, and the monster dutch doll is placed in position during the one interval in which the camera turning has been stopped.

A particularly effective and surprising instance of the use of the metamorphosis comes to mind in a film issued by the Gaumont Company some years since.   The sensational quality of the whole was here greatly heightened by the fact that the film did not ostensibly figure as a trick subject at all, but as a drama pure and simple.   It shows a woman who has planned to run away from her husband.   She is taking a last snatch of rest before meeting her lover when she falls into a troubled sleep, and dreams a dream which is thrown on to the projection screen, and wherein the trick effects take place.   We see the woman in her vision actually hurrying off with the other man, but time after time the various incidental characters she encounters turn for a brief flash into the semblance of her deceived husband, always looking at her in the same reproachful way, one hand raised in denunciation of her conduct.   Yet so cleverly are the substitutions managed that the movement of the various dream characters even throughout the course of the transition and back again seems to be continuous.   Thus, a cabman after receiving his fare, raises his hand to his hat in a respectful salute.   He has half lowered it again when he changes for a brief half-second to the accusing husband.   Then, almost before the audience has realised fully what it has seen, the cabman is back in his place, and his hand continues its descent to his side as if nothing had taken place.   The technique of the film, both as to the acting, timing and final make-up of the doctored film lengths was truly wonderful in its way, while the whole wound up in a suitably dramatic curtain showing the wife newly awakened from her nightmare rushing to the telephone to inform her lover she has changed her mind and will not leave her husband after all.   In this connection it may be pointed out that most trick effects are doubled in intensity as well as in mystery by being wrapped up, more or less, in some reasonably plausible story, and not served up raw like the conjuring tricks in the windows of a " magical " toy shop.

FATAL AND COMIC ACCIDENTS.

Although neither of these usually figure before the public as trick effects, they would both be out of the question save for the technique of the magical metamorphosis given above.   The fatal accident occurs more and more often in modern dramatic films.   Perhaps it is a distracted young girl who determines to throw herself out of a top floor window, and does so.   At least, the audience sees her climb to the window ledge, give a last convulsive shudder, and pitch forward and down past storey after storey, until the body flashes out of view at the bottom edge of the picture mask.   Or, again, it may be a comic accident, such as the submerging of a couple of tramps by a cartload of shingle, which submersion would hardly have been good for the actors taking the parts in question had they really remained to bear the brunt of the accident. Sometimes even a steam roller is requisitioned to go right over a man in a comedy film, in which case he invariably gets up again and resumes normal activity in a surprisingly short time. Small wonder if the audience marvel how it's done. The above instances and all of a similar sort are worked on the principle already alluded to, a metamorphosis being effected in each case between the living subject and a more or less life-like dummy.

Thus the suicide girl is only a flesh and blood creation up to the moment when she gives her last convulsive shudder on the window ledge. From that instant she retires from the stage (the camera handle being conveniently stilled to allow of her doing so). When it restarts its record-making revolutions it is a dummy which goes pitching down to its death somewhere beneath the picture mask.

The comedy man who lies down in the track of the steam roller takes good care not to remain there so long as he seems to do. It is a dummy which is gone over and duly flattened, while a second convenient pause in taking, allows of the effigy being hastily removed for the real man to resume his place in the track of the steam roller as it once more passes on its way.

GHOST EFFECTS. MATERIALISATIONS.

Here is another class of effect which, though usually realised by the audience as of the trick variety, has, none the less, its place in many an otherwise " straight " dramatic film. Although ghost films of a sort may be produced by no more elaborate a method than that of the trick appearance and disappearance, explained at the commencement of the chapter, yet the modern mode of going to work is very different and much more complex. For instance, we may see the signalman sitting in his cabin contemplating the result of a mistake he knows himself to have made in the setting of the points. In the semi-darkness and silence there flash upon his mind thoughts of the train wreck and consequent loss of life he believes to be inevitable. Suddenly, as he sits horror-bound, the thoughts take tangible form before the audience. Thin white hands appear from the darkest corner of the signal cabin and growing momentarily in substance, seem to reach out and demand vengeance for the wretched man's fatal mistake. Little by little the ghosts of the killed passengers take shape, till they come clamouring one after another, nearer and yet nearer to the object of their hatred. And all the while the signalman sits glaring wildly at the phantoms in a frenzy of dread. How is it done ? There are no tame ghosts, even in the most up-to-date film producing studios.

The secret of it lies in two things. One of them is a special dead black floor covering and heavy black velvet background, which are always kept handy wherever ghost production is a feature. The other secret lies in the correct use of the feet film indicator, to be found affixed at the side of every good-class kinematograph camera of recent design. Background and indicator are worked together in the following way. Firstly, the subject who has to be ghost-haunted goes through his part before an ordinary background and is duly photographed, the only odd thing about it being that though when the critical moment arrives he makes every indication of having seen whatever spooks are to be in evidence, he really sees none whatever, because they are not there to see. No matter. When he has to be scared, he makes sure his hair curls and his face gets contorted with horror enough for the occasion. Meanwhile, an assistant standing by the camera man is diligently reading the camera feet indicator. His business is to register accurately the number of feet exposed both just before and just after the supposed spook invasion. When this " straight " part of the scene is concluded, the exposed film is

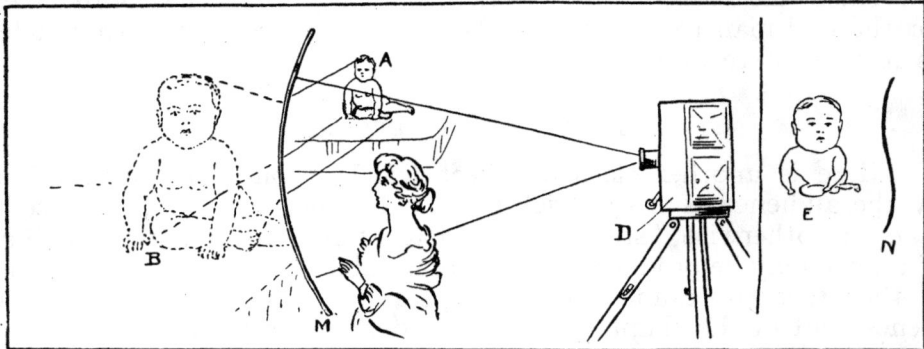

FIG. 198.—MAKING A GIANT BABY FROM THE REFLECTION OF A REAL ONE. The original subject A is reflected in the concave mirror M, and it is this reflection which is photographed. The presence of the mirror need not be apparent in the result. N shows an undulating mirror by means of which a still further distorted rendering of the baby would be given ; this time with big head and tiny legs, as depicted in E.

wound back again from the take-up to the top film box by means of a special device fitted to cameras used for this work, and indeed to all instruments of the " reversing " order. Now for the black background and the spirit manifestations. Once again we wind forward our film, without exposure, up to the point where the feet indicator tells us the ghost-seer is about to be tormented by supernatural manifestations. This time, however, we have the manifestations ready in the shape of suitable actors, draped in white, and posed before the special velvet curtain, with full instructions as to their actions, etc.

Now to turn the camera handle once more, while the assistant gradually opens the lens iris from its smallest to a suitable working aperture. The result will be to impress upon the already once exposed roll of film a second record of the white-draped figures, which record grows in intensity as the stop aperture gets larger in the camera lens. When the film indicator indicates the point at which the ghosts must disappear, the diaphragm is first turned down to its smallest and the camera handle then stopped. Result : filmy white spooks, which grow in body, fade once more, and disappear. As such, at any rate, will the audience see them when the print from the negative comes to be put on the screen.

In working effects of this kind one should see to it that the part of the " straight " background against which the spirit manifestations have to be made is suitably dark in tone. Also such effects to be worth seeing must be very carefully rehearsed and arranged. For timing them, the film indicator checked off by a smart assistant is the one and only reliable guide.

Sometimes the kinematograph film will show a figure which

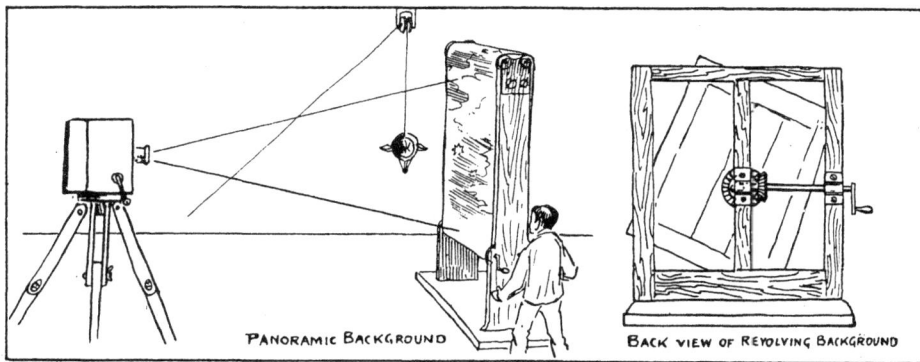

FIG. 199.—This illustration gives the method of obtaining airship effects by means of trick kinema-tography, as explained in the text. The toy airship is suspended by fine thread from a suitable overhead travelling trolley, while the background, representing sky, can be wound up or down by the assistant, as depicted. The other background support (shown in back view) is fitted with a rocking device for use when photographing earthquakes, rough seas, and such like effects in trick work.

appearing gradually (as a faint mist which builds and builds itself up in body and intensity, as in the case of the ghost effect above de-scribed) finally turns into the semblance of a real flesh and blood person. Thus, for instance, might be depicted Cinderella's fairy godmother, or the good fairy in any other children's play. In this case the method of going to work is not quite identical with that al-ready given. It is done in the following way.

First the " straight " figures are grouped in what is considered by the producer to be a suitable manner for the production of the super-natural being. This grouping having been made, it is essential that the actors keep perfectly still and rigid from now on till such time as the materialisation of the fairy has been fully recorded on the film. For the actual recording of it, let the lens iris be slowly closed down until completely shut, the operator meanwhile keeping the camera running as usual, while the exact amount of film so passed from the commencement of closing the iris till the moment of full closing is read off on the film feet indicator. The camera is then stopped. Now proceed to wind this film length as read off back into the feed film box, place the figure to be materialised in position, the other actors meanwhile still rigidly maintaining their former attitudes, and once more start the camera, the assistant this time opening the lens iris slowly at precisely the same rate as he formerly closed it. At the moment the iris is fully expanded to working aperture, he pronounces the word " open " in a loud voice for actors and producer to hear, and from this moment the action of the play proceeds as usual. Needless to say, in materialisations carried out on the above plan, much depends upon so arranging the poses of the actors prior to the double photographing that they shall appear on the projection screen to have paused naturally, remaining still for the time being simply through surprise at the strangeness of the sight they are witnessing in the gradual production from nothing of their supernatural visitors.

NOTE.—Lenses of cameras intended for the above sort of trick work should be fitted with diaphragms capable of closing completely so as to shut out all light when turned to their uttermost extent. A type of diaphragm particularly suitable for the above, with which the writer has had recent acquaintance, is a square or diamond-shaped aperture formed by the drawing to or away from one another of opposing thin metallic leaves. These may be controlled by the operation of a screw-head which rotates a double-threaded pinion, upon the threads of which the leaves are caused to work.

REVERSING EFFECTS.

Although the more blatant reversing effects are now to a great extent out of date, trick work of this kind is still sometimes seen.

In essence the reversed effect is the result of turning the camera upside down at the time of taking. When this is done it will be found the positive subjects may still be threaded through the projector so as to give an image right way up as usual. Only now the action of the subject on projection will proceed in the contrary direction to that ordained by Nature. For instance, suppose in the subject photographed with reversed camera a tea-tray, full of china, has been allowed to fall, and the china smashed. The projected incident will show the start of the film with the broken tea service lying upon the ground. Suddenly the pieces will be seen to spring together, the whole will be met by the tea-tray, which will trundle up from whatever may have been its final resting place, the ware will set itself magically upon the tray, and the latter, now fully loaded, will spring up into the outstretched hands of the one who was destined to be carrying it at the time of the accident. The end of the film would, in fact, depict the beginning of the scene.

In practice, this extraordinary reversed movement has been applied to a host of weird situations. One of Pathe's earlier films

"Quick, I'm on fire!" was almost wholly dependent upon reversal for its drawing quality. It was a film of the "chase" variety, illustrating a man who had been set on fire in the seat of his trousers, running madly on and on in the effort to put the fire out. Every now and then he would spring up to a house-top or slide up a sloping board at the speed of an express train, or roll hard up hill, always followed by the usual yelling crowd which imitated his strange gymnastics. In the end he is seen to emerge from a river by a reversed high dive, coming out of course still alight.

Recent cameras, intended more especially for trick work, are fitted, in addition to the ordinary take-up, with re-wind or take-up to the top spool box, which can be put in or out of operation as required, and alternately to the ordinary one. Such cameras have also a special driving shaft, which turns the intermittent motion the reverse way without having to reverse the turning direction of the handle. With such a system no inversion of the taking camera is necessary. The above, together with the addition of a film indicator, renders the instrument useful as well for ghost effects and many other purposes away from the usual run of everyday work. Part of the "Enchanted Glasses" film, already alluded to, where the wine pours upwards from the glasses and back into the decanter, is a good instance of effective, yet not obvious reversal.

AERIAL EFFECTS.   AIRSHIPS, BALLOONS.

The above class of trick effects seem to be worked rather extensively at present. Probably the aviation craze is at the root of it, though the same system which reveals to the watcher of the kinematograph sheet the "heights of the air," may also serve equally well to set forth a more or less garbled version of the supposed depths of the ocean. To be specific, let us confine our remarks here to the type of effect where the picture projected before us shows a glimpse of a balloon or airship moving upwards through the clouds, till suddenly it explodes and falls headlong earthward. As we watch, we see the rolling vapour before and behind the balloon basket. Probably the cloud effect will not be entirely convincing, yet the very ability to depict a balloon soaring up and up through any sort of clouds strikes wonder into our hearts, until we know how the photographer set about it.

As a matter of fact, the above class of thing is done with the help of models, combined with the more or less skilful use of what is known as an ascending and descending background. For the latter, two round rollers are arranged on a suitable frame, and canvas stretched between them so that it can be wound from one to the other after the manner of a child's myriorama. Suppose one of the rollers situate at such a height as to be well above the picture, while the lower roller is equally below the bottom of the picture. Our whole picture then depicts "sky." If we paint clouds upon the canvas we have only to wind slowly upon the lower roller to give the idea of ascending to anything in the way of a model aeroplane hung before the "sky," while a sharp turn of the higher roller will impart to the model the idea of dropping, since the clouds will appear suddenly to run upwards.

As to the model balloon itself, it is a tiny affair cut out of suitably painted paper, or if it is to appear on a larger scale it may be an ordinary toy one. When photographing the balloon ascent, all we need to do is to get one assistant to introduce the model before the camera lens on the end of a bit of fine silk, as though it were travelling along in space, while other assistants make the clouds descend slowly and regularly. Mist effects are imparted by the usual thickness or thicknesses of gauze allowed to drop down between the model and the camera. An aerial explosion is easily worked with the help of a suitably contrived smoke puff, following which the cloud rollers are reversed, while a dilapidated balloon "double" is rapidly lowered down through the picture and out of sight.

A great number of such kinds of subjects are worked by means of models and panorama backgrounds of this sort, while in other cases larger panoramic backgrounds, either ascending, descending, or moving from side to side, are employed with living subjects to impart to the latter the illusion of unnaturally quick or eccentric movement.

Tom Thumb in his seven-league boots is an instance in which a laterally moving background was effectively combined by two separate printings (see later) with the subject of a boy performing the action of running seemingly in mid-air. The well-known, not to say classic film, "A Trip to the Moon," also made use of the descending background, though here still another principle was involved, which latter should be dealt with by itself.

The Downward Pointing Camera.

For a diagrammatic arrangement of such a camera, reference should be made to the chapter on Title Production. The principle there set forth of pointing the camera vertically downward is one which can be easily applied to trick work on a large scale. Where necessary the camera can be placed up in the roof of a lofty studio so that people can be taken full size while lying down, etc. Obviously, with such an arrangement, the camera lens will have the same relative position to the prostrate model as would the lens of a normally-supported picture camera to an upright model. It will therefore be possible to obtain many seemingly baffling travesties of the action of gravity by means of the downward pointing motion picture camera arrangement.

As has already been hinted, "A Trip to the Moon" remains probably the most classic of all films which go to exemplify how the vertically pointed lens may be used in trick work.

In this film an elderly gentleman was depicted as climbing up into the night sky, past the stars, and right on to the moon's disc itself. The moon then opened its mouth (if memory serves) and swallowed the traveller.

It was all contrived by means of a descending background worked in this case flat on the studio floor, while the taking camera was perched up above, looking downward. The man who had to make the journey to the moon, in reality crawled slowly along the star-painted canvas as the latter was wound from roller to roller. Finally the moon's disc was wound into position to occupy the centre of the kinemato-graph picture in process of being taken. Thereupon the gentleman taking the "trip" crawled through the slit of the moon's mouth, which had been made practicable for the purpose.

A far different and yet equally amazing effect of the downward pointing camera is the self-forming title, which used to be so much in evidence a few years ago. In reality it was formed by the gradual displacement of the letters of the title during the time they were being photographed by means of the downward pointing motion pic-ture camera. For the purpose threads are attached to opposite ends of suitable block letters before lay-ing them out to spell the word or words desired. Fig. 200. The motion picture titling camera is then started when the letters are moved out of the field with a slow zig-zag motion, imparted by as-

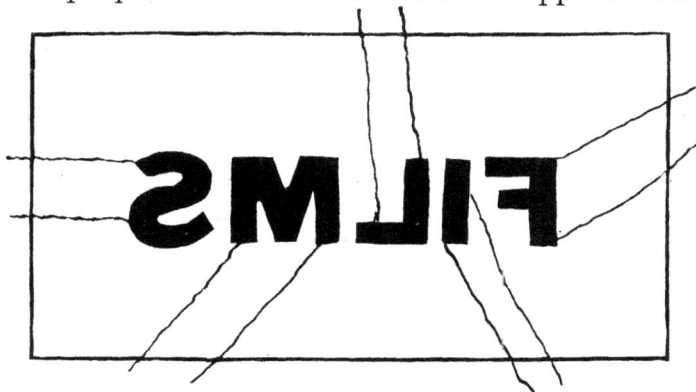

FIG. 200.

sistants actuating these invisible cords. The letters may be moved in various ways, all at once or one at a time, just as the taste of the one arranging the trick title may incline. Two points, however, are noteworthy in this description. The first is that in the accompanying diagram showing suitable positions for attaching threads to moveable letters, these threads are shown as black upon a white ground for the sake of clearness to the reader. In reality, of course, they would be the same colour as the ground, black for white letter titling, or white for black letter work.

The further point to be noted, since it is an essential part of the process, is that when working on the foregoing system, the actual title must be photographed with reverse movement, the *modus operandi* of which has already been explained in this chapter. Clearly this is necessary, since the effect we want on the screen is that of a title miraculously built up, and not one in the act of being torn apart, as is the case in actuality.

The particularly puzzling and odd step by step effect exhibited by films of the " Affair of Hearts " order, in which purely mechanical arrangement and re-arrangement of geometrical areas of black and white follow up each other in a sort of kaleidoscopic sequence, are also produced by means of the vertical camera, combined with infinite pains on the part of the artist operator. By the same means also, automatic writing, drawing, etc., of all sorts is produced, the camera being stopped after each picture or two for a few more short strokes to be added or taken away.

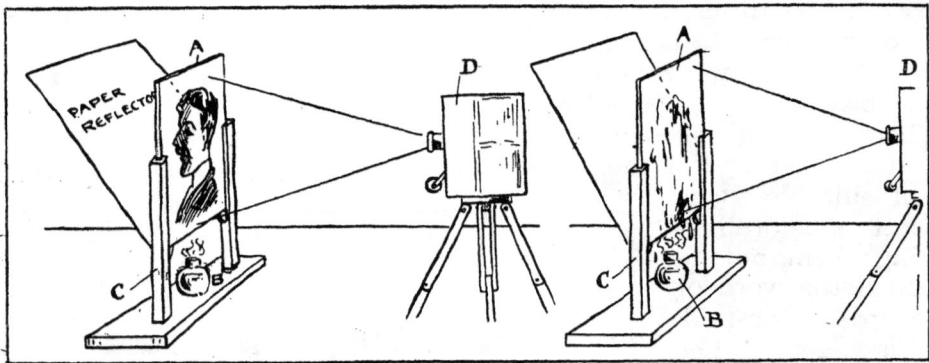

Fig. 201.—A CURIOUS REVERSING EFFECT. A wet photographic transparency plate A on which is a picture, title, or portrait, is stood in a special support C, and photographed with reversed action by means of the kinematograph camera D. Meanwhile the spirit lamp B causes the wet gelatine of the photographic emulsion to melt, so ruining the plate. (See second diagram to note this effect.) The effect on the screen when showing the kinematograph film so taken will be that of a picture, portrait, etc., which gradually forms itself out of nothingness.

" ONE TURN ONE PICTURE."

The more elaborate present-day motion picture cameras have all got what is known as a " one turn one picture " movement. This takes the form of a driving shaft for the camera handle (or driving pulley in the case of an electrically driven kinematograph studio camera) in addition to the regular full speed and reversing driving shafts. The third shaft drives at such a rate that each turn of it accounts for the exposure of only one negative picture—hence the name. The one turn one picture movement, in conjunction with the downward-pointing camera, is made extensive use of in the production of films of the more mechanical order of trick subject last alluded to. Many very surprising effects, such, for instance, as that shown in the Urbanora film, " The Wooden Athletes," are also contrived by the use of the one turn one picture movement in conjunction with suitable flat or other models—in the above case none other than a row of ordinary wooden Dutch dolls photographed against a dark background. In its more elastic connection, the matter of speeding down in kinematograph photography is mentioned in a succeeding paragraph.

SMOKE PUFFS.

The use of these and similar methods of distracting the attention of the audience at the moment of introducing a trick effect into a film takes much the same place in kinematography as " blacking out " does on the stage. As we all know, in " blacking out," the stage lights are turned suddenly down, while a line of brilliant red blinders is flashed in the eyes of the audience in order to distract its

FIG. 202.—A VERY PRETTY TRICK EFFECT. Mamma gives the children a magic box. On opening it a little figure is found to be alive inside. The secret lies in the bottom of the box, which is either a plane or slightly convex mirror. The fairy in the box in reality is an ordinary person so placed in regard to the reflecting mirror and camera lens as to satisfy the well known optical law that the angle of incidence shall equal the angle of reflection of the mirrored image. The illustration makes this plain.

attention from some hasty scene re-arrangement in progress behind, and which is not considered to occupy enough time to justify a regular interval being made for it.

Just so with the kinematograph film. Something is to be done, and done mysteriously. So instead of merely stopping the camera and re-starting when the re-arrangement has been made, the transition may be rendered even more mysterious by a suitable smoke puff thrown out before the lens at the critical moment.

Smoke puffs are of many origins, from the regular smoke rocket to the steam jet or spilt bag of flour. Either will serve for its special use, and which of them is most suitable to any particular subject is a matter best left to the experimental genius of the stage manager.

That smoke and dust thrown into the atmosphere at suitable times and places are true friends to the picture man cannot be denied. With comic work in particular they are in constant use, generally in order to perform the same kind of function as in real trick work—the throwing over a faked incident of the glamour and mystery of detail, which makes it go down as genuine.

GEARING DOWN THE CAMERA.

Previously we have given advice in the case of all ordinary kinematograph photography to take the pictures at the one constant rate of sixteen per second. There is, however, an exception to this in certain trick subjects. Then it may become advisable or necessary to stop down the lens suitably and photograph at a much slower speed than the normal. The film " Something Wrong with the Time " shows a clock, the hands of which suddenly begin to race round madly while those people within its influence have their movements enormously augmented in rapidity. Undoubtedly much of this film was photographed very slowly, while the ordinary rate of action was maintained by the models taken.

Occasionally one sees a " chase " photographed in this same geared-down way. The camera, instead of going full tilt, is worked only at a fraction of its usual pace, with the result that chasers appear literally to gallop this way and that over the picture. An ordinary street scene photographed at half speed will show everything going along at double its usual pace, while should the camera handle be turned much too fast, the relative pace of natural objects will be correspondingly slowed.

NOTE.—Wherever a camera is to be used for trick work it is important to ascertain the exact point nearest the lowermost phase of each handle turn at which the shutter is at cover position over the lens, since only when turning is stopped exactly at a " cover " point does one avoid the last picture of a series being hopelessly overexposed. Find the " cover point " nearest the lowest position of the handle, mark this position boldly on the camera body, and see to it thereafter that when pausing in trick effect production the handle is brought smartly to the marked point and there stopped dead. Doing this properly will take a little getting into, but the acquirement is well worth the trouble. When turning is resumed, this should also be done as smartly as the camera mechanism will stand without undue jar.

DOUBLE PRINTING.

This is the only other phase of trick photography which will be touched upon here. Nor will much be said concerning it, not because it is not a very important branch of trick work, but because it is in itself so complicated as to be more easily approached by the man of experience than by the one newly interested in film production. Still, it is possible to sketch out the general method adopted in double printing, and this will now be done so far as may be.

A double printed film is one in which two separate and distinct negatives are used over the production of a single final positive. Each negative illustrates a different subject, and each subject is so arranged that it may be printed over the image formed by the other, without effecting an unsuitably jumbled-up result. Double printing is being used more and more in modern trick work, but a single instance of its application should serve to show both the principle and broad method of employing it.

Let us take for our case in point the production of a "vision" film, in which someone is depicted in a trance or sleep, while the thoughts in his or her brain are shown enacted as varying scenes on, say, a wall of the room behind. A method of producing the above effect by double printing is illustrated with reference to Diagram 203. Here (A) shows the "straight" part of the subject, consisting of A, a bed on which lies the sleeper, B, a fairly light dado running around the lower half of the wall behind, and C, a black, or very dark tone on the upper portion of the wall. Such is the subject as

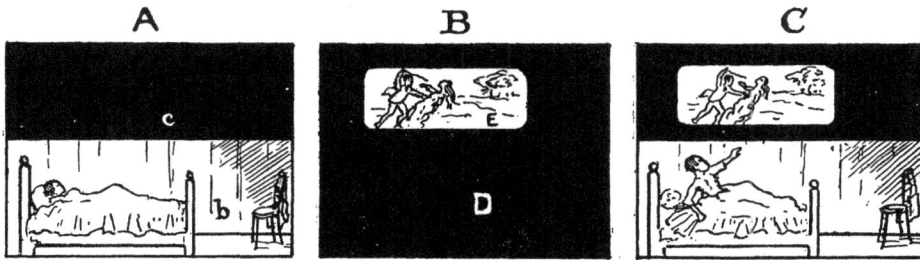

FIG. 203.

it is arranged for photographing, and the "straight" negative produced from it will illustrate just that and no more. Now turn to (B). Here we have a very different state of things. In the first place, before going on to photograph the "vision" negative which (B) illustrates, the ordinary camera mask is replaced by one having in it only a small aperture E, so cut as to photograph a scene lying on a portion of the film which would correspond with C in picture (A). Having provided such a mask for the camera, we now proceed to stage our vision scene and photograph it with the small mask in place, so that the resultant negative will give the whole of the picture area D as blank, with only the "vision" picture of the part E where the mask has been cut away. The printing of the "straight" negative and the "vision" or trick negative together superposed over the positive film will now give us a positive picture in which a sleeper is seen in bed, while various dream pictures flash across the wall above, as may be determined by the different subjects acted when making the trick or second printing film. Whenever a "vision" scene is required to fade, the trick or second negative is replaced by a length of

transparent perforated celluloid (cleaned film base). Then when
another " vision " has to flash on to the wall the celluloid is joined
up with another trick length of (B) negative.

Working on the foregoing system it will be seen that instead
of a single negative, two thicknesses of negative film have to be carried
forward by the claw of the printer along with the positive stock in
course of printing, the " straight " negative being always threaded
nearest to the positive stock.   There is another way in which double
printing may be effected.   It has the merit of giving sharper outlines
to the " vision " portion of the print, though certain complications
also follow upon working by this alternative method.   Such an alternative way of going to work is to dispense with the small cut camera
mask in making (B), and substitute for it a wide white frontage to the
stage E, on which is enacted the dream "scene" to be photographed. The
resulting (B) negative will now have an opaque, instead of transparent
D portion.   Such a negative will be used to print in upon the positive
stock at a different printing from that which prints (A).   In other
words, the negative (A) will be printed as usual for single printing. The
once-printed positive will then be wound back and reprinted with
(B) negative in place in front of it.   Where the impression of the
" vision " has to disappear, it will be necessary to use lengths of plain
opaque blank spacing between the (B) subjects, instead of cleaned celluloid as in the former instance.   This second system is only of use
where the C portion of the " straight " scene is white, or very light.

The number of effects possible by means of double printing is
so great that a list of them would occupy much space, as well as being
hardly sufficiently explanatory to be of service.   Careful examination
of those more modern trick subjects which cannot be duly explained
by the simpler methods, will, however, generally give the key to the
form of double printing involved in their production.

MASKS.   RETOUCHING.

Though hardly connected of necessity with trick work, this is
thought to be the place to say a word or two about the above.

As has just been explained, picture masks for special purposes
may be cut for the camera of different aperture to the usual one,
Sometimes even with " straight " negatives and single printing, an
enhanced effect may be got by varying the mask aperture more or
less from the usual and admittedly monotonous horizontal cushioned
oblong.   For instance, a scene may portray what is being viewed
through a round window.   In such a case a circular-cut camera mask
will photograph the subject with a round dark border on the print,
which will often be extremely effective.   A lady looking in a looking-
glass may see her reflection portrayed as a picture cut the exact shape
of the hand-mirror.   Other similar ways of utilising this possibility
of varying the shape of the camera mask should easily come to the
mind of the reader.   Many modern cameras are fitted with simple

means of taking out and replacing the ordinary mask with ones cut to openings of special proportions.

Retouching kinematograph film is not a matter calling for anything like the amount of remark which is properly lavished upon similar treatment in the case of still view negatives. Practically speaking, the multiplicity of tiny negatives to be dealt with in modern motion picture work renders anything like careful individual work upon each out of the question. One thing can, however, be done to a kinematograph negative before printing. What is more, it should be done and done carefully. The film length should be gone over, and any large transparent spots, technically known as " pin holes," filled in with a touch of paint applied with an ordinary small paint brush. Light red is a good coloured pigment to use for the purpose, or a special photographic preparation sold under the name of " Photofake " is excellent.

Needless to say, only such pin holes as occur in dense portions of the negatives should be thus touched out. Those occurring in places where the silver deposit is thin would only be rendered more conspicuous by filling in, and had consequently best be left alone.

Fig. 204. M. Proszinski and his Automatic Camera.

CHAPTER II.

REHEARSED EFFECTS.   STORY PICTURES.

Story pictures form the preponderating class of present-day kinematograph releases. They may be roughly classified as follows :

COMEDY.	SERIO-COMEDY.	ADVENTURE.
TRAGEDY.	DRAMA.	DETECTIVE.
FARCE.	HUMAN INTEREST.	

Of all plots, the human interest and farcical kinds are probably most sure of a good reception by any audience, while farce is almost certainly the easiest of all to put together and produce in something approaching a satisfactory manner.

THE SCREAMING FARCE.

The typical farcical kinematograph plot is, in fact, nothing more than a glorification and amplification of the well-known music hall knock-about turn. Both rely for their drawing power on that subtle appeal to the primitive emotion of the masses, known as " biff humour." In other words, they make their bid for success through the exhibition of unlimited horse play. But, strange as it may seem, even horse play has its psychological side, which must be attended to or it will fall flat.

Thus, it is well known and accepted by all psychologists that the humour of a ridiculous situation lies chiefly in its mockery of the accepted and respectable. For instance, suppose we are to depict that oft-filmed man staggering along with a ladder over his shoulder, knocking into various people as he goes, it would not be half so funny for him to knock into a labourer trudging to work as if he drove the ladder into the stomach of a well-dressed city man, thereby causing the latter to fall into a pile of road refuse or other suitable and handy means of causing his respectable clothing to be held up to mockery.

So much for the motive power underlying screaming comedy. Summed up in a few words, it is mockery and horse play judiciously combined. See to it that someone is always getting into bad trouble from start to finish of the film, and let it be trouble of a sort to render dignity undignified and set the laugh against human frailty, either mental or moral, so long as the joke is not of the kind to come home to roost with the audience who are to witness the film.

USE OF VEILED TRICK EFFECTS.

Films of this class are often heightened in intensity and rendered correspondingly more effective by judicious trick effects of a sort which, not being obvious, will not appear as unreal to the observer. Thus, a man may be running from his mother-in-law when he slips and falls down a precipice. We see his body actually come hurtling down to what would in the ordinary way be certain death. But no! In some manner he manages to cheat destiny, and get up after the fall with nothing worse than a bruised face and bad limp. Of course, the fall is contrived by a trick already fully explained along with

FIG. 205.   FILMING A COMEDY SCENE IN THE LUBIN STUDIO.
Note the overhead lighting and reflectors.

numerous others in the chapter dealing with Trick Kinematography. At the same time, such unsuspected trick effects undoubtedly add to the breathless interest of the " chase " variety of farce film.

ADVENTURE AND DETECTIVE DRAMA.

Next to the farce in order of easiness of portrayal probably comes the adventure and detective classes of motion picture story film. The reason of their simplicity is to be looked for in the highly coloured incidents portrayed. Moreover, the bulk of modern motion picture detective films are of the " Nick Carter " and " Sexton Blake " variety. Nor should we forget, when setting this forth, that both the above heroes belong to the realms of gutter literature, and not to those of high-class legitimate fiction at all. Small wonder, then, if there is but little subtlety called for in the interpretation of plots stamped with the hall-mark of Messrs. Blake and Carter. Still, even here it is essential to success that the conscientious portrayal of the smaller details should not be lost sight of. The thrills of either detective or adventure stories lose nothing of their power for being reasonably plausibly worked up.

Of course, there is a reason for the comparative shallowness of even the best adventure and detective films, and to the student of picture plot writing or moving picture production it is a reason well worth enquiring into. In the case of both classes of film it arises as the necessary consequence of the construction being usually undertaken the wrong way round. To make this plainer, when planning out and producing a drama or a human interest film, the point uppermost in the mind and always to be strived at is the presentation of a natural series of events leading up to the final and supremely important *denouement*.

In the adventure film, on the other hand, the culminating point is of secondary importance to the lurid depiction of an exaggerated series of over-thrilling adventures leading up to it, while in the detective play the humanity of the characters is usually sacrificed in the necessity for keeping up a sense of baffling mystery and general apprehension throughout. Detective and adventure films are therefore, as a rule, essentially artificial in their conception, and this applies to all of them, the bad and the good alike. The outlet for real genius on the part of the actors taking part in these is accordingly curtailed. It behoves the producer to recognise the fact, and make up for it as best he may by the introduction of elaborate spectacular effects, mysterious trick illusions, or what not, whereby the interest of the audience may be so far kept up that the essential shallowness of the thing shall not strike in upon its consciousness. In other words, with the production of picture plays of the artificial type, far more is placed upon the producer and far less upon the artistes than where a genuine human interest of some sort (however banal or hackneyed such interest may be) is to be depicted.

Where Higher Talent is Necessary.

Let us pass from the consideration of the above class to say a few words about certain kinds of kinematograph story which call for an exhibition of higher talents in those concerned with their production. Such types of kinematograph plot are the light humorous, the more serious dramatic, and human interest varieties. Of them the easiest one to manoeuvre to a measure of success is probably the human interest tale, only it must be really well acted, with no slips and no unrehearsed ridiculous situations to spoil it. Human interest being entirely savage—like the appeal of " biff humour "—we must not attempt to look for it outside of the emotions. But whereas humour may be regarded as the making of a brutal exhibition of some person or estate with which we have no sympathy, human interest is the ringing of the changes upon emotions and situations in real life near to the audience itself. Nor in the " strong " human story need we hesitate to lift the veil from the most private and sacred of human hopes, griefs and attachments. It may be somewhat of a grisly business, this digging up of mouldering bones wherewith to decorate the projection screen. Still, it pays.

Love constitutes a great human interest, of course. Money has an appeal as strong, or sometimes even stronger. Then there is death, horrid enough, one might think, yet capable like the rest of being turned for the occasion into an unwilling pay-box attendant. The ill-treatment of the old by the young whom they have raised up, or the cruelty of a hard-hearted landlord to his tenant, to say nothing of themes involving cruelty to pet animals, all go to swell the human side of a motion picture film. In fact, to the man with his eyes open

FIG. 206. TWO WELL ARRANGED MELEES.

there is no common cause of distress which cannot be successfully played upon for the purposes of the more lachrymose type of kine-matograph film.

SYMPATHETIC AND UNSYMPATHETIC PARTS.

In the construction of picture plays of the dramatic or human interest variety it is before all things essential that the sympathetic and unsympathetic characters shall be well and correctly understood and interpreted both by plot writer, producer and actors themselves, otherwise the audience will certainly be dissatisfied with the result as shown on the screen. Sympathetic characters are those whose parts are intended to arouse the sympathies of the audience, while the unsympathetic characters are those concerning whom the opposite applies. But here again are pitfalls for the unwary, inasmuch as a character which is highly sympathetic to one person may be equally unsympathetic to the next. To take the most obvious instance—a political one—it will be clear that a picture play representing the defeat of the Orange-men and formal inauguration of the first Home Rule Parliament at Dublin might meet with a rousing reception in many Irish picture theatres because to the audiences it would be sympathetic. But take the same film to Belfast, and which picture theatre proprietor would care to screen it ?

That case is, as already admitted, an extreme one. None the less, it points the finger of warning at what is probably the most insidious of all the pitfalls besetting plot writer, producer and showman alike. For instance, in a certain film one of the unsympathetic characters represents a hard-hearted Jew. Such a character would excite no adverse comment in many parts of Great Britain, but here and there—say in the Whitechapel Road—it might be most unwise to screen it. The showman in that part of the world who carelessly exhibited the film as part of a hastily made-up program might wonder why the attendance of the public suddenly fell off.

FIG. 207. WELL-ARRANGED ROMANTIC DRAMA.

Nor would he possibly ever wake up to the real reason for his decreased receipts.

The thing to do, then, as regards the decision as to which characters in a film shall be sympathetic, which unsympathetic, and which merely neutral, is first to think well over the probable geographical distribution of the film and the class of people who will witness its exhibition, and proceed to adjust the characters so that, as far as can be foreseen, no possible offence will be given to any well-marked section of its public. This is best arranged by making all doubtful characters mere neutrals—that is to say, having no particularly emphasised moral peculiarities, either good or bad—while the unsympathetic characters are painted so villainously black that no right-minded person of any shade of thought can be sorry when they get the worst of it in the final *denouement*. This last course is obviously not the most artistic one, but it is certainly the safest. It is the course invariably adopted in producing music-hall sketches, where the whole chance of success lies in capturing the approval of stalls and gallery alike, but especially the gallery—the place where the dreaded "bird" comes from.

Sometimes a film subject will rise far above the usual dead level which we have tried to depict above. When this is the case, careful investigation will usually show the idea to have been taken from a more or less well-known work of classical fiction. But classical or not, film plots have to be pretty well handled if they are to stand out from their fellows as worth seeing by the critical man. And here it might be well to say a few general words about sundry conditions which should be looked to in the photographing of rehearsed effects.

THE ACTORS AND STOCK COMPANIES.

First as to the artistes themselves. Needless to say, in order to produce a picture play one must be able to call upon the services of a company of actors and actresses, precisely as one would do for the presentation of any other type of staged production. Picture play companies then take their place as a fundamental consideration to be faced and grappled with in this connection. There is, however, more than one way of going to work when constituting them. If one is constantly producing it may be well to run a stock company. This is one in which a sufficiency of useful artistes are kept permanently on the pay-roll to be able to tackle any ordinary type of picture plot. Stock companies are necessarily costly, and are only justified where a firm is engaged in the production of a continuous stream of this type of kinematograph film. They may consist of anything from a dozen or less to fifty or more members, but in any case will include first and second lady, first and second male heavy, at least one good comedian, a really versatile juvenile, preferably female, and a backing of three or four sound character impersonators for the lighter, but still important parts.

Naturally, such a company is going to run into money, as does everything even remotely connected with stage production. The exact figure cannot, of course, be laid down, but it may be said as a rough guide that a fairly good first male lead would be worth at least £5 a week on contract, while the corresponding leading lady, once she hit on with the public, would probably soon be worth considerably more, in which case she would be the first person to spot the fact and keep the management duly reminded of it long before it came to renewing her engagement. The salary above quoted would not be nearly large enough in the case of artistes having a ready-made reputation with the general picture public.

Second leads might be picked up for anything over £3 a week, while there are plenty of fairly sound artistes for the lighter parts to be had for even less. On the other hand, it should never be lost sight of that if talent is worth paying well for in moving picture production, the other thing is dear at a gift. It would be easy to ruin the best of plays by giving the minor parts to premium-paying amateurs of the stage-struck order or even by entrusting such parts to the tender mercies of down-at-heel professional wasters, who soon come to beset the doors of the kinematograph studio like a flock of faded harpies, luring the producer ever on to the rocks of cheap and talentless " talent."

Supposing a stock company to have been successfully got together, either as the result of judicious advertisement in the recognised stage journals or otherwise, it is not to be thought one's troubles in this matter are at an end. Far from this, it will very soon be discovered that—especially as regards the female side of the company— the more talented it is and the better suited to its work, the more independent and generally unreliable will its behaviour become with the passing days. Let but the first lady discover that the producer finds her invaluable and his reign as organiser and director of the

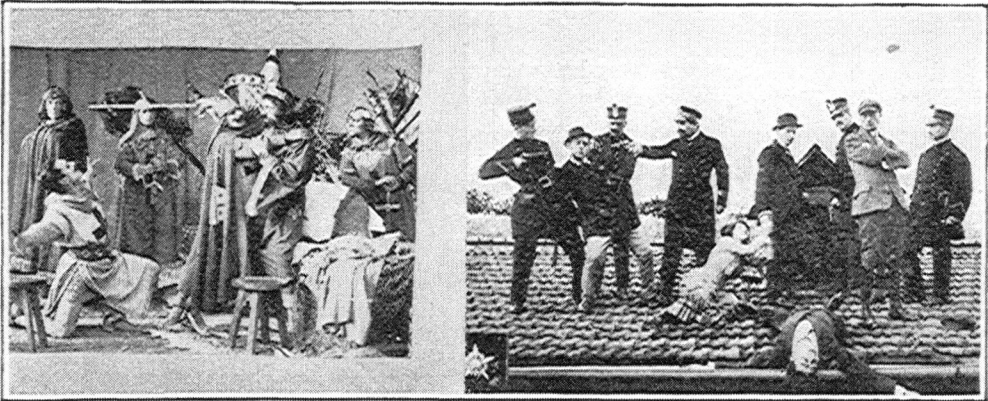

FIG. 208. THE HISTORICAL AND THE SENSATIONAL.

company is over. He may post his calls for rehearsals for what hour he likes. The actual rehearsal will commence when Miss —— turns up, a very different thing. Nor should existing producing houses remain blind to the fact that the present day idea of cultivating the admiration of the public for Miss This and Mr. That by the sale of picture portrait postcards and the distribution of portrait posters is going in the near future to recoil on their heads just as it already done in the case of the mpresarios of the legitimate and musical comedy stage.

WORKING WITHOUT A STOCK COMPANY.

A way of somewhat avoiding the state of things hinted at above, and at the same time limiting expenditure where the number of picture plays produced does not warrant the permanent upkeep of a stock company, is to work with a nucleus company of five or six good, sound, all-round character artistes, and augment it by the addition of temporarily engaged actors, both as regards the light parts, and even where a specially good and expensive first lead is deemed to be justified by the nature of the picture play in hand. In such cases, a record of available male and female leading and other artistes is compiled, and these can then be drawn upon as required. This gives the producer the benefit of fresh faces, while, the engagements not being of a permanent order, there is far less tendency on the part of the actors and actresses to forget their position and assume airs which are not helpful to the general conduct of stage management.

Where picture production is only occasional, artistes can be engaged on short contract either through the medium of stage adver-

FIG. 209.   SIX SCENES BEING SIMULTANEOUSLY FILMED IN THE LUBIN STUDIO.

tisements, or by arrangement with the management of local theatres (of not quite the first grade order) whereby a notice is posted on the call board from time to time inviting the members of the visiting company to make a little additional pocket money for themselves by picture play acting during blank days. In the latter case, ten shillings a day is usually gratefully accepted as payment by the artistes in question. Once they are employed it is of the highest importance that the producer shall immediately assume full command in the fatherly, yet completely autocratic way loved of and recognised by the real "old pro." In this manner a good day's work may be got for the money expended. Otherwise, all that is likely to result is a lot of wasted time on the part of the producer, eked out with advice tendered to him on how to manage his own business, which advice he could well do without.

REHEARSING THE CHARACTERS.

To rehearse a company well is the key to successful picture production. This must be proceeded with smartly. Have an assistant stage manager by your side to time each act from the word " go " to the " stop " which signalises the cessation of acting. Also decide beforehand on just how long each scene is to take, and see that such time and no more is occupied by its presentation. Do not attempt to get picture artistes to learn up long written parts. If they know their business and have been given a brief explanation of the intention of the scene, they should be able to supply impromptu the words or sentences necessary to carry the whole through. And in this matter it might be well to counsel actors not to keep repeating their pet sentences over and over. Quite a number of the audience at any picture show are more or less proficient in lip reading, and it is ridiculous in the extreme to see the frantic mother, whose child has just fallen down the well, rush in and exclaim, " My child has fallen—has fallen down the well—the well.—The well, she has fallen down—fallen down—my child. My child—oh, my child—my child has fallen down the well— the well—well—"

As to whether the producer of a picture play shall also act as camera man, this is a point variously decided by various firms. The rule is usually to have the two offices separate, the producer acting as head stage manager, with the help of the assistant manager as timer, the camera operator being also under his control. Sometimes conditions are reversed. The writer could mention at least one firm where the camera man is paramount, the stage manager being little more than an adjunct in the picture production, while in many small producing houses a separate stage manager, not to say assistant stage manager, is dispensed with altogether, the offices of camera operator and the rest of it being combined, often with quite satisfactory results. And here we will leave the more intimate side of the management of a picture play company and pass on to some considerations as to the arrangement of the films themselves. We might, however, mention by the way that in the matter of facial make-up of the actors and actresses in moving picture production, the usual flesh-tinted grease paints give place to either white and black make-up or to the still simpler and almost equally effective treatment of powdering the face with white face powder. In female subjects especially, the latter treatment is excellently adapted to showing up facial expression in the resulting kinematograph film.

AS TO INCIDENT LENGTHS.

The aim in all story film production is to make the pictures explain as much as possible without the necessity for sub-titles (or explanatory sentences interspersed between the picture subjects).

A film helped out by a great number of sub-titles thereby shows itself, amongst other things, as capable of improvement either in plot or stage management.   This is not to say that a sub-title may never be admitted.   That would be going too far altogether towards the other extreme.   Where titles or sub-titles are photographed they should be of a length of not less than six feet if a few words are only included.   If many words or sentences are necessary upon a sub-title, as, for instance, in the portrayal of a hand-written letter, or in giving a sketch of the story leading up to some historical presentation, the film length may well be from ten to twelve feet, or just so long as it would take an ordinary reader to go through the whole of the written matter twice slowly.

The pictured incidents themselves should never be of a length less than ten feet, or they will flash off and on the screen in an abominably jumpy way.   Needless to say, this remark does not apply to tableau effects.   Twenty feet is a fair length for a good story incident, though this may be increased to forty or even sixty feet if circumstances seem to warrant.   With long films, individual incidents may even be spun out more than this, but then there is always a danger of sameness spoiling the snap and go of the production.   Such an exceptional picture incident as the telling of a ghost story might, however, go on just so long as the narrator's pantomimic genius enabled him to hold the audience.   As to rate of turning, it should always be the same—sixteen pictures a second for every subject, whether grave or gay.   So many modern projectors are motor-driven that an even taking rate becomes daily more and more a necessity.

Thus Far and no Farther.

Perhaps it may be the lot of the reader who makes his first attempt at story film production to have to work with actors and actresses not accustomed to playing their parts in the focus of a kinematograph camera.   In such a case there is likely to be some difficulty arising through the fact of the artistes' inability to gauge accurately the limits of the stage as seen by the camera lens.   With a set studio gauge the complication may not be a serious one, but when acting outdoor episodes where the action is confined to a small and important space in the foreground, one cannot be too careful in ensuring that no important bit of business takes place " off," when it should have been " on."   The way to accomplish what is necessary is by means of small flags or tapes, planted or laid in V shape, from camera lens outward, as illustrated in Chapter on Rehearsed Effects.   The tape lines must be just invisible on either edge of the picture mask.   Chalk marks may also be used for a like purpose.   All the actors and actresses have then to do is to be sure that they make their entrances from outside to inside the chalked or taped area, that their action is gone through strictly within the same area, and that no exit shall be deemed complete till after the outer side of the tape lines has been crossed.   This will ensure acting strictly within the limits of the picture.

Probably where anything of the nature of a regular set kinematograph stage is attempted for the first time, this will take the form of an outdoor one. In such a case the scenery is best painted on supported canvas, exactly after the manner of mounting and painting ordinary stage " flats," except that for motion picture photography we work out the original in black and white instead of colour. Flatted oil colour is the thing to use ; also the " fit up " must be so made as to be easily removable from place to place and aspect to aspect, according to time of day, weather and general circumstances, not excluding the possibility of sudden squalls of rain and wind.

THE INDOOR STUDIO.

Covered-in studios, provided with expansive glass roofs for daylight work, to say nothing of arc or mercury vapour light installations for

FIG. 210. A ROOMY STUDIO.

photography in dull weather and at night, are hardly among the first flights of commercial kinematograph enterprise, for which it is hoped this part of the book may do something to fit the prospective motion picture photographer, so it will hardly be necessary to say much concerning this indoor work. Since here neither wind nor rain has to be guarded against, flatted oil scene painting may be, with advantage, superseded by distemper work, the latter then having everything to be said for it on the score both of speed of production, low cost, and quick-drying qualities.

A roomy indoor studio would be one from thirty to forty feet broad by sixty or seventy feet long. For daylight work it would be glazed for two-thirds its length and to within three feet of the floor level, the best glass for the purpose being colourless glass of sufficient stoutness to withstand gales of wind or driving hail-stones, and with an uneven surface the better to break up and diffuse the sun's rays when these strike upon it. The aspect of the studio would be such that it gets the benefit of the full sun at about mid-day. Special directions of lighting are contrived by the producer by arranging the setting of the scenery more or less obliquely with regard to the studio walls, or by stretching between the top of the scene and the glass roof an awning or awnings so disposed as to direct the lighting as may be required for the particular effect aimed at. The position for the camera is in the solidly built end, where the lens is projected from the direct glare off the glass.

Such a studio will naturally be erected on a site chosen with great care so as to command free and uninterrupted daylight all round. Where the position is at all enclosed it will be necessary to elevate the whole structure sufficiently for it to command the light required, and a good way of effecting this is to make it the upper storey of a two storey building, the ground floor of which may conveniently be used as green rooms, stores, scene painting and carpenters' shops, and the rest of it.

Needless to say, a studio of the dimensions above indicated, and proportionately solidly constructed, though by no means so very imposing as studios go, is none the less a pretty expensive affair. For this reason, few would think of going to the expense of building one such unless the finished article were to be of use for more than the limited number of days in the year when we happy Englishmen are favoured with a good bright sample of daylight. Accordingly it will be almost a *sine qua non* that as well as its glazed roof our studio shall be equipped with a good effective artificial lighting system for use during dull weather, or in the dark winter afternoons and evenings.

The actual arrangement of the indoor kinematograph stage is practically similar to the outdoor one as regards facilities for erection of scenery, this being also according to the lines usually adopted upon the regular stage, indoor scenes being usually of the boxed-in chamber variety, with or without practicable doors or windows, or both, giving scenic vistas produced by back sheets, etc. The boxed-in chamber is in itself composed of flats and is self-supporting when fully erected, but this is the province of the stage carpenter, who will certainly (like the scene painter) be a permanency on the staff of the producing house owning its own indoor studio.

How the Scenes are Lighted.

A further word or two may, however, be said as to lighting methods in vogue where daylight is dispensed with in the filming of motion pictures, since this lighting is completely different to any other stage system. The most usual way is either by means of a row or rows of mercury vapour lamps suspended above and also at the side of the stage, or else by similarly placed rows of enclosed " photographic " arc lamps, which latter may be furnished with slightly obscured or merely ground glass outer globes to obliterate the harsh shadow outlines otherwise thrown by them.

The advantages of mercury vapour lamps over arcs are to be found in their far greater actinic efficiency, with consequent economy of current, their large light source, their portability, steadiness and comparative lightness in weight. A disadvantage is their great liability to break and give out when least expected.

If enclosed arc lamps are used they will possess the counter advantage of great physical strength to resist the knocks and bumps that come of careless scene-shifting operations. Also, if photographic arcs are installed, the efficiency will be fair. A photographic, or " long " enclosed arc, it may be mentioned, is one constructed to pass the highest possible voltage across the carbons consistent with the E.M.F. of supply mains. This long arc, produced by the high potential across the poles, is proportionately blue and rich in actinic rays. An up-to-date indoor artificial light studio might be fitted with two to three rows of these long arcs overhead, each row consisting of, say, ten 10 amp lamps, the outermost row being somewhat nearer the camera than the front of the stage, the second row about level with stage front, and the third row, where such is used, being placed as the producer may direct to obtain any special lighting required. All direct light from the arc craters must be shielded from the camera lens by means of suitably placed reflectors. Sometimes the lamps are wired up into combinations of three or four in parallel, the aim being to group each four lamps thus wired together so as to produce a different, but in itself satisfactory lighting effect upon the stage. For actual photographic work, a sufficient number of groups of lamps would be turned on to get the particular lighting effect aimed at, the lens diaphragm being adjusted accordingly. The foregoing is only a brief sketch of one of the many satisfactory ways of achieving successful artificial lighting of the kinematograph stage. It should, however, serve the purpose of the experimenter in the above direction, and for the rest, the matter is essentially one for the display of individual fancy and original artistic talent in the production of chiaroscuro. No two existing artificially lit kinematograph studios have their lamps arranged quite alike.

STAGE LIMITATIONS. A WARNING.

It is felt the time has come to utter a word of warning as to superabundant and unnecessary recourse to the scene painter's art in the filming of staged productions. In order to compare in any way with the real thing, artificially-produced scenery has to be of the very highest order, and since such a condition is never easy to fulfil in practice it must accordingly follow that, where Nature can by any reasonable means be made to serve, scene painting should be rigorously avoided.

For instance, we may be called upon to depict a love passage between the hero and heroine. If possible, such a passage should be represented as enacted out of doors in the garden of the girl's father's country mansion, not in the drawing-room, which would then necessitate studio and painted scenery. Of course, it is not possible to do without such studio work entirely. Still, one should try as far as one can to get away from it, and indeed, we only have to study carefully the latest and best film productions to realise more and more the trend among high-class houses to keep away from the " boxed-in chamber with scenic ornaments " of olden time.

FIG. 211. MAKING STAGE PROPERTIES.

Don't let the leads " take the footlights " for every effect or incident on which the film's strength is going to depend. Why ever the motion picture stage manager doesn't put his foot down on the present prevailing and wholly pernicious practice it would be hard to surmise. Lurching into the exact centre of the picture at three-quarter length point for every telling situation is not really the way to make that situation more telling. In fact, it is the reverse. The centre of a picture is admitted by art critics to be its weakest, and not its strongest portion. It is half-way between the middle and the extreme side that the real strength of composition lies. But there is another reason why " taking the footlights " is not going to be of any use to the picture actress. It shows up her face too fiercely in the resulting print, with the consequence that, if she really be pretty, half her attraction for the audience will be lost through her features being too completely seen and taken stock of early in the film picture, while if she be not quite so pretty——.

How to Photograph Beauty Becomingly.

We have just touched on a very common way in which its effect can be and is lessened in many moving pictures. The best method of doing justice, or maybe a trifle more than justice to a pretty and capable female model is to photograph when feasible with the sun out and high in front of the camera. That way the features will be thrown into a very delightful silhouette, while if the sun is a trifle more on one side, Rembrandt effect is the equally satisfying result. Only in trying the above beauty formula see to it that the lens is well shaded and the camera shutter and gate are thoroughly dead black or there will be trouble from fog and internal reflections.

A Final Word.

A final word about the taking of rehearsed effects. Insist that these be gone over time and again and made absolutely perfect before there is any attempt whatsoever at photographing them. Even then, Heaven knows, enough things can go wrong and ruin films at the critical moment. The snorting charger may jib when it should be racing the Scotch Express. The murder in the lonely wood may be ruined by the casual appearance on the scene at the crucial moment of a mildly interested tramp. The writer has even witnessed a terrible accident—the rolling of a young girl down a precipice—which was rendered so ludicrous through unforeseen circumstances that it could only have done as a roaring comic of the continental type. That represents a negligible part of the tricks Nature may play you, so don't add to them by allowing any on the part of the artistes.

Fig. 212.—Military Manœuvres.

FIG. 213.   SCENE FROM VITAGRAPH CO.'S BEAUTIFUL CLASSICAL
SUBJECT, "THE LADY OF THE LAKE."

CHAPTER III.

————

ON ACTING BEFORE THE KINEMATOGRAPH.

BY

MR. HENRY MORRELL, OF HIS MAJESTY'S THEATRE, HAYMARKET.
(*Sir Herbert Beerbohm Tree's Company.*)

————

The more I have thought—the more I have tried to give you something intelligible on the subject of acting before the kinematograph—the more conscious have I become of the difficulty of my task.

I could not write a chapter on how to act! A book would not teach a man that. I may be able to write a few remarks on how to adapt stage acting to the requirements of the camera, though much of what I say on this head seems after all only what would occur to an actor of experience as readily as the way to remove ink-stains would suggest itself to an experienced chemist. But how to give help to the promising novice, that is the real difficulty I am now to try and face.

So many books have been published on " How to become an actor," " How to comport oneself like a gentleman on the stage " (id.), etc., etc., that I feel rather guilty lest anything written by me may seem like an attempt to add to the number. Let it be hoped that in what follows I shall come rather nearer than that in my effort to be of use to the would-be dumb show artist. And with this I will pass on to the subject in hand.

It has always been a matter of regret amongst men and women engaged upon such evanescent acts as singing, playing upon the piano, or the violin, and acting on the stage, that the results of years of patient and close application should be destined to perish at the very moment of their birth.

True, an impression may live in the memory, but in being handed down it becomes considerably changed, for better or worse, until at length a very hazy and imperfect idea remains of what originally was. And this is not to the artist, at all events, a very satisfactory state of affairs. The image which we conjure up of the past is the product of a number of psychic factors. It results in part from the impressions we receive from those to whom we have listened, or whose writings we have read.

But these impressions, we must remember, bear a stamp of the individuality of the person through whom they have come. They represent only his personal view ; so that, however good the writer, he offers an incomplete picture of his subject, limited by the standpoint from which he has seen it. Limited, that is, by the bias of his own taste and judgment. One has but to compare a criticism of a play with one's own impressions upon seeing it, to realise how great this difference can sometimes be. So, I am sure, it is with our idea of the great actors of the past.

FUTURE POSSIBILITIES TO THE ACTOR.

If it were possible to see Edmund Kean or David Garrick, we should probably find them vastly different from what we had imagined.

FIG. 214. A PRODUCER DEMONSTRATING JUST HOW A PLAYER SHOULD STAND.

Not that I think we should be disappointed. I firmly believe those elements in their work of perennial human interest, the depth and sincerity of their passion, the truth of their emotion, would be as moving as ever.

But we might find some difficulty in dissociating them from the style in which they would be presented. Unhappily, that IF is an infinitely large one. To our eyes, the panorama of the past is hidden. We shall never see it. But posterity is destined to be more fortunate. The kinematograph will bring the past before it, and it will be able to look back, across centuries, maybe, to the distant present.

It will be able to judge with its own eyes of the past . . . of the great actors of to-day . . . . . though still somewhat imperfectly perhaps, for that elusive element in a man's success—his personality —makes no appeal from the photographic screen.

But that may come.

One could assign no limit to human ingenuity in face of the progress of science during the past sixty years.

Well, here is comfort for the neglected genius whom the world to-day refuses to recognise. He can appeal to the wider jury of time—if he is lucky enough, that is.

This is our aspect of kinematography, of interest to the actor. But I am not sure it is of so much interest to the film makers.

The latter, whilst appreciating the actor's desire to be alive a hundred years hence, might well wonder in what way the returns then are going to benefit him to-day. And there is still this difficulty

FIG. 215. A CORNER OF THE WARDROBE ROOM, WHERE THOUSANDS OF GARMENTS ARE STORED.

for those who desire to go down to posterity : They must be sufficiently popular to pay for their taking.

But there is another side : The art of acting applied to the kinematograph. Here is a field in which actor and film maker are interested equally.

The kinematograph as a form of entertainment has come to stay. It offers so many possibilities at once amusing and instructive that its future is, without doubt, in every way assured. And perhaps its most popular appeal is with the kinematograph play. So great is the demand for this now, one might safely say there is not an hour of the day or night, but that somewhere dozens of comedies or dramas, farces, melodramas and plays are being exhibited upon the screen.

With its growing popularity, more and more attention will be concentrated upon its various factors, and one in particular, the question of adapting stage acting to the requirements of the camera, must come in for especial consideration.

Now, in order to gain a clear notion of kinematograph acting, it will be best, perhaps, to make an analysis of the methods of stage acting, and observe in what respect thay need adapting to the requirements of the camera.

We have on the stage three modes of expression, viz.:—

    1. Voice,
    2. Gesture,
    3. Facial expression.

Action, which is a combination of these, is the medium with which the actor works. Of these modes of expression, by far the most important is the voice. Indeed, this organ is capable of infinite expression, for not only does it convey in words a definite train of ideas to the minds of the audience and so, by a psychic process on their part, make its appeal, but by proper modulation it can be made to express every emotion that we are capable of feeling. And this to a degree which depends upon the actor's genius.

A line which to all appearances might be quite commonplace, suddenly becomes electrified by the personality of the man or woman whose whole being vibrates in the expression given to the words. Since, then, in kinematograph acting, we are deprived of the use of the voice, every other available means of expression must be used in an enhanced degree to make up for the loss. We must convey through gesture and facial expression the whole movement of the play. This is by no means an easy business. Indeed, it is a high tribute to an actor to have succeeded in holding an audience for any length of time by the sole use of pantomime.

GESTURES.

In the old days, both in England and on the Continent, gesture was recognised as an exceedingly important factor of expression, and it received accordingly a good deal of attention. Those were the days of Drama, Melodrama, and Farce. Many so-called authorities however, approached their subject from anything but a scientific point of view, with the result that much that was accepted as good gesture was in reality clumsy and artificial.

It was left to M. del Santo to found the school which to-day enjoys universal acceptance.

This man was a pioneer in the science of psychology, and his methods are founded upon accurate observations and extensive experiment. They can be used in every type of play—it is merely a question of adjusting breadth to circumstance.

In modern plays the gesture is obviously somewhat curtailed in England, at all events, because it is not in the nature of Englishmen to use much gesture. In the classic play, on the other hand, gesture plays a more important part, and finally, in the kinematograph play, it has the chief part.

The kinematograph actor will need, therefore, to be above all things, an accomplished pantomimist. He will also need to have a very expressive face. There will then remain only the circumstance of adapting his skill to the requirements of the picture screen.

The Requirements of the Kinematograph.

Now in acting before the kinematograph, there are one or two important points to be borne in mind. In the first place, it must be remembered that although the photographic plate is, under certain conditions, a perfect rendering medium, the swiftness of movement and general defects attendant upon the reproduction of living pictures render the latter more or less insensitive to minute detail.

For this reason it would be a mistake to strive for subtlety of effect. Even on the stage, and especially in large theatres, much of the actor's finest work is lost to the audience. So much that can be conveyed in a look or compressed into a whisper is lost immediately these are exaggerated to carry to distant parts of the house. Now, in acting before the kinematograph, all this applies very much more. It is therefore necessary to adopt a style which shall be impressionistic rather than otherwise; a style wherein effects are obtained by methods at once broad, deliberate and incisive. One should, besides, act a little more slowly than on the stage; this gives the film a better chance of taking the impression. On being reproduced, it can be quickened again to whatever speed is required.

Besides the actor, the playright is called upon to adapt his act, for the dramatic possibilities of the kinematograph plot are limited by the resources of the camera. A play that is built up of intuitions requiring a lot of words to interpret them is out of its element on the picture screen.

Each situation should carry no more words than are necessary to suggest the pantomime that will convey the dramatic movement of the scene.

The subject should be preferably of the strong and gripping order. This will stir up the audience to a high degree of interest that will carry them over any moments that might not be quite clear to them in meaning.

The chief point to remember, then, is to write for pantomime, and in producing to point out to the actors the spirit to be conveyed; to pick out, as it were, the essential idea, and interpret it in pantomime, all other language being merely incidental and of no vital interest to the story.

This is the ideal form of kinematograph play. Often, of course, a certain interest prompts a film maker to photograph a stage play, when the scenes most full of movement are usually chosen, but this is not by any means a satisfactory kind of entertainment on the kinematograph.   The play was intended for stage representation, and its general movement to be interpreted with the aid of the voice, what gestures there would be being accidental or accessory, rather than playing the vital part in the general interpretation of the dramatist's work.

Nor is it easy, nor satisfactory, except in those cases where the subject lends itself especially well, to adapt this style of play to the kinematograph.   Rather does it require a special play—the pantomime play—written for the kinematograph stage.

Of late an attempt has been made to use the gramophone in conjunction with living pictures, but without results that are quite satisfactory.   In time, however, there is no doubt this question will be solved.   Then matters will be a good deal simplified, but at present, the kinematograph actor must be a master pantomimist, and the writer of kinematograph plays must write for pantomime.

FIG. 216.   CURIOUS ACTORS FOR THE KINEMATOGRAPH.

CHAPTER IV.

PICTURE PLOT WRITING.

Since the appearance of the first edition of this HANDBOOK, a great number of letters of enquiry have reached the author from journalists and amateurs alike anxious to try their hand at picture plot writing, or wishful to know if a field is offered for their activities in such a direction. It is on their account, and also in the hope of being of service to others who may care to take up picture play writing on their own, that the present chapter is penned.

First of all, and by way of answering one of the most constant questions, let us start by saying it is undoubtedly true that picture plots are purchased from outsiders by important producing houses, both in England, on the Continent and in America. All film producing firms do not demand a like quality in the plot they select, nor do they all pay for those selected on the same scale, but the last is another matter, to be dealt with in its proper place. For the present, let us be content to know the bare fact that a good plot written by the man in the street will find its buyer. We will take this fact then as our starting point in a short enquiry into the sort of plot to write, and how to set about writing it.

THE KINDS OF PLOT.

As to the kind of plot which sells, there can be no better rule given to the tyro than to decide in his mind upon the firm he intends sending the picture play to, and then to endeavour as far as possible to let the writing up of his idea—no matter how original be that idea in itself—fall somewhat into the pattern the firm in question is seen to favour for its film subjects. This advice may possibly seem to the amateur to be anything but of the best. None the less, so well is it understood in general journalism that no writer for the popular weekly or monthly magazines would think of embarking on a story without glancing over a sufficient number of back copies to make sure he had caught the note favoured by the particular editorial staff to which his own work would have in its turn to be submitted for consideration. Nor can it be argued against this that in the case of picture plots no such a course is possible. As a matter of fact, it is so. Week by week *resumes* of the plots of current films appear in the pages of the journals devoted to the kinematograph trade, of which the *Kinematograph Weekly* is, of course, the leading one as regards Great Britain. Moreover, nearly all the best film producers send out at frequent intervals sheets or leaflets containing similar condensed plots or synopses of their forthcoming productions. Then there is the *Monthly Film Record* to be consulted, while as a last resort in the same direction, there is hardly a picture show, even in the depths of the country, which does not give or sell to its patrons a programme containing short descriptions of the plots of its leading feature films.

SPECIALISING IN THEMES AND CHARACTERS.

Let us examine any one of the above sources of inspiration and we shall very soon see there is much of valuable import to the budding plot writer which may be gained by a little reading both on and between the lines. For one thing, we thus begin to perceive which are the firms that turn out this or the other series of comics, which put forth serio-comic films, which specialize in " life portrayals," which are in the habit of spending fabulous sums of money over " feature films," involving the most gorgeous and elaborate of scenery and costumes, and so on. Armed with such knowledge, we shall soon get into the way of asking ourselves the question as each new idea for a picture play occurs to our mind, " Which film-producing house would it be best suited for ? " and so we take a first but still a very important step towards turning our new mental activities into a direction where solid profit may sometimes be looked for.

Often enough it will happen that our query as to the best firm to send this or that plot to will seem hard, or even baffling, to answer. Here, again, there is a more or less cut and dried way out of the difficulty. It lies in the adaptation of the central character or characters of a picture plot to fall in with those figuring in a series of favorite feature films of one or other of the well-known firms. Thus we may have a good comic idea, but for the moment it seems difficult or impossible to decide as to the house to whose consideration it shall first be submitted. Then, if we have followed the various film plots published in the several ways already alluded to, we shall remember for instance Cricks and Martin's laughable series of the adventures of Constable Smith. Yes, but our central comic character is not a constable at all. Never mind, you proceed to ask yourself the question " Can he be made one ? " and can the comedy be linked on to him in this guise ? If it can, well and good. The producers of the " Constable Smith " exploits are ever on the look-out for new laughable ideas in which that comic hero may play the central part, and for this very reason your plot in its new form will stand an additional chance of favorable consideration by the firm in question. Needless to say, in the event of its rejection, the thing would be to re-write or re-type it in its older and less distinctive form before submitting the picture plot to another producing house.

Perhaps the reader has a rattling idea for an adventurous and dramatic picture play dealing with life in the mercantile marine. Well, can it be turned into a drama of the Royal Navy instead? If so, it may be waiting to add yet another laurel to the wreath of fame of Lieutenant Rose, R.N., to the mutual satisfaction of the Clarendon Company and the happy plot writer. And here let us digress for a moment to clear up a small matter which has obtruded itself, sideways, as it were, in the course of our preceding remarks.

MANUSCRIPT OR TYPESCRIPT?

Hardly a minute or so since the talk turned on the subject of re-writing or re-typing our MS. (abbreviation for manuscript, also used to denote typescript). This raises the obvious question as to whether plots written out in handwriting stand the same chance of acceptance as if they were typed. Frankly, they do not, and that for two simple reasons. One is the score of legibility. There is no getting away from it, the clearest handwriting—and no one would be so foolish as to send in for consideration a picture plot that was not written plainly—is still somewhat more difficult to read than is the case where printing characters are employed. But the second reason for counselling typewritten plots wherever possible is the perhaps even more cogent one, that from a literary standpoint, an author's work, otherwise " copy " or " stuff," invariably carries more weight, or at least seems more prepossessing to the professional reader after it has got into typescript. This curious property of the typewriter of casting a halo over literary work of all sorts is appreciated by no one more than by those who are making their living out of letters. To the journalistic hack, the typewriter is as the French polish to the cabinet maker, while even editors when in doubt as to whether a particular story or article is " up to " their standard of publication have a practice of sending the doubtful effort to the compositor to be "set up." This is equivalent to giving it a last chance. If it " reads well " when in type, it may scrape through its editorial examination. Needless to say, it follows from this that if copy looks better in typescript than it does in manuscript, it looks better still in real type than in either. The idea of having picture plots printed before sending them round for consideration is, none the less, far too outlandish to be thought of. Typing out is, on the contrary, comparatively inexpensive, and certainly more usual than not. Notwithstanding all the above, it is not to be taken as the writer's intention to make out that hand-written copy does not stand a very fair chance of careful consideration at the hands of any reputable picture plot reader. Quite on the contrary, many manuscript plots have been sold for good prices, and many more will be so sold in the future.

CONSTRUCTING THE PLOT.

We have now got a fair insight into the way of preparing oneself for the ordeal of kinematograph play writing. We will proceed to go into the actual construction of the plot itself.

Probably in almost every case where a bright inspiration occurs which seems to the reader to be worthy of sale for purposes of pictorial portrayal, such idea will at first be of a more or less disconnected sort. For instance, we are passing a cook shop when a small child happens to drop a beef steak pie as it emerges from the doorway. By a freak of thought, for which we are unable to account, we hit upon the fancy that if an old gentleman was to happen to step in the greasy mess, he would probably fall down, and it might go to make an amusing kinematograph film. And so it might, but only one incident out of a whole heap which will have to be thought out to complete that film. True, this first idea is of the nature of a gift to us from the gods, but after that all the rest must be thought out by long and perhaps even painful effort before the plot is in a shape where it may hope to become saleable. Thus, it is apparent, that if we are to save ourselves worry when we have an idea, it should be noted down at once in a note book and stored up until a sufficient number of other happy thoughts of a similar nature have been collected, to turn the whole into the skeleton of a really good picture plot.

Should Dialogue be Introduced ¿

Supposing we have got our plot, not merely a single good idea without either a bright beginning or a satisfactory end to back it up, but a whole plot in our minds—or note books—how then are we to write it up in its final form? Shall we merely copy out our rough notes in a sufficiently connected style to make them intelligible, and leave it at that? Or shall we attempt to add more or less conversation, otherwise dialogue of the characters? Or shall we write the thing up in the form of a short story, as though it were to be submitted to *Home Chat* or say, the *Strand Magazine*, instead of to the reader employed by a film producing company; or shall we do what would seem on the first glance to be the most sensible thing of all, and write up the picture play after the manner of a legitimate dramatic or real stage production?

The answer is not altogether easy to give, since different producing houses use their plots in a rather different final form. The final technical alterations are, however, usually supplied by the producer, with or without consultation with the principal artistes in the company. One thing, however, is quite certain, and that is that in no case can the plot writer do more than he is capable of in the direction of brushing up his work. Where, then, there is grave doubt as to a budding picture play writer's literary capabilities, it will always be best for him to be content with the simplest or " once upon a time " style of writing. Even so, his ideas will sell if they are really good, for the ideas are far more to the buyer of plots than their literary excellence of presentation.

Here is an example of a picture plot for a " Western " drama told in this simple way, a way which anyone should be well able to emulate without previous practice. We will put the title first of all, nor will we ever fail to give our plots titles of some sort, if only for convenience in the event of correspondence arising in regard to them :

BRONCHO BILL STRIKES LUCKY.

Broncho Bill, a poor miner, becomes attached to the daughter of a wealthy ranch owner dwelling in the neighbourhood. He asks the girl's hand in marriage, but the father, who is noted for his money-grubbing nature, will not hear of so poor a union. Broncho Bill is not to be beaten. Soon after he is seen by his mates to be acting in a queer and excited way. For days at a time he disappears and when he returns he always carries a little bag, which he guards jealously and refuses to let his mates look into. He has given up his own work, but is seen at dead of night carrying mining implements into the hills. The whole settlement gets filled with suspicion, and soon the rumour gets round that Broncho Bill has discovered a gold vein and will not tell anyone. His mates tackle him. He only smiles darkly, but in the midst of the whispering and general wonderment, word goes round that the thing is an actual fact, and that the next day Broncho Bill purposes riding into the neighbouring township to register his claim with the sheriff. Broncho Bill's sweetheart tells her father, who has already heard much of this, how, by refusing to let her marry the man she loved he has driven away vast wealth from the house. Aroused at last to a sense of the mistake he has made, the wealthy ranch owner decides to race after Broncho Bill, who is already on his way to the township, and get him to agree to marry his daughter. The race takes place, Broncho Bill is caught up just outside the sheriff's office and made to sign a paper before a crowd of miners by which he agrees to marry the girl he is in love with and share his new fortune with the father. As soon as the paper is signed he discloses to the father in confidence that he has struck no gold, but has only been playing a trick on him with the help of the daughter in question. In order to avoid being the laughing stock of the place the father of the girl agrees to allow the marriage to take place.

The above is a specimen of perfectly plain, straightforward writing without any attempt at turning the work into either a story or a play in the ordinary sense of the term, yet the thing, as it stands, would be quite sufficiently intelligible for a film producer to be able to grasp not only the main idea, but also the general run of the incidents and their natural sequence, and it would therefore have a chance of favorable consideration. Also, the plot being thus condensed, does not take half so long to wade through as it would do if set forth more elaborately, and this is all on the side of the reader having more patience with it, and so giving it a better consideration than if the verbiage spread over say half a dozen closely written foolscap sheets. At the same time, and admitting that the skeleton plot is all in the above and that what remains to be done before production might quite well be undertaken by the producer and his staff, it should still be borne in mind by the plot writer that the work up to this point, though it may quite possibly sell without further exertion on his part, is still very unfinished. The plot as above written out should be prefaced with a "cast," or list of the characters included in it.

Suppose we wish to submit a more finished picture play, what is the first obvious improvement or addition to make to the bare bones of the plot or "skeleton scenario," as we have it above? Undoubtedly, the answer is to divide the whole up into scenes. This is best done on a separate sheet of paper in something after the following style, and the latter pinned to the scenario proper. In order for the writer of this chapter to make clear the sort of thing he means it will only be necessary for him here to show the first few scenes so sketched out:

EXTENDED SCENARIO FOR "BRONCHO BILL STRIKES LUCKY."

SCENE 1. *Exterior of the "Sunrise" Mine.*

Action of the film starts with the arrival on the scene of the heroine and her father. The wealthy ranch owner has business in the managers' office, which brings about an exit on his part and leaves the opportunity for Broncho Bill and the girl to have an affectionate meeting. In the midst of their chat enter the father again, and he then proceeds to send Broncho Bill angrily about his business.

SCENE 2. *Behind the Manager's office.*

Broncho Bill is walking off in a huff when the girl runs after him and they are seen to be talking earnestly. " The plot is hatched."

SCENE 3. *Interior of a saloon.*

Miners drinking and joking with one another. In the midst of it all Broncho Bill slouches in excitedly, calls for drink, then seats himself at a far table and makes as though to examine the contents of a small bag without being observed, though it is made apparent to the audience that he is really gloating over the excitement his mysterious bag creates.

Etc., etc., etc.

Even though the writer of a picture plot should take the trouble to set out a complete scenario of the sort indicated above, it must be distinctly understood the producing house which might buy it would not in any way bind itself to keep to the scenes suggested. As already stated, such intimate arrangements are always at the final determination of the producer and stage manager. Nevertheless, it may well happen that such a division of scenes will often be of service to the producer, and for this reason may make the plot as a whole more easily understood, and correspondingly more valuable.

We do not counsel any attempt on the writer's part at giving full dialogue, as though the play were to be produced on the legitimate stage, though sometimes where there is a rather nice point to be brought out, it may be set down in dialogue style for the sole benefit of the reader entrusted with the task of judging as to the plot's merits.

Later on, it will fall to the lot of the film producer to determine how best to translate this same dialogue into a series of actions or episodes such as shall be equally, or almost equally, intelligible. As to the idea held by some would-be plot writers that a picture play should be written up in novelette form, this is utterly wide of the mark. In point of fact, the aim and object is here precisely the opposite of that governing the art of novelette writing, since in the latter case the usual rule is that the plot is made to serve to last over just as many words as the author thinks he can get payment for, whereas in putting on paper the scenario of a picture play, the system to go by is to use the least number of words which will serve to convey the author's idea to the reader, and convey it with sufficient force and a sufficiency of grip to give the plot reader a good opinion of one's handiwork.

Where to send the Plots.

When the plot is written, and provided the suggestions contained in the early part of the present chapter have been carried out, it will in many cases be simply a matter of posting it off to the firm for whose consideration it is intended, enclosing a stamped addressed envelope for its return in case of unsuitability. On the other hand, there may still be cases in which a picture plot has been written out without there being in the head of the author at the time of its inception any very clear idea as to what firm of film producers it is most likely to be suitable for. In the latter event, the only thing to do is to run over the names of the better-known producing houses and try and pick out some well-known one that appears to deal in plots as nearly as possible of the kind in question. Sometimes even the writer has been appealed to as to what firms are film producers although such a query as this may seem to be sounding somewhat deeply into the depths of human ignorance. It must not be forgotten that the names and addresses of every film maker in the world, and their various agents, can be found in the *Kinematograph Monthly Film Record*.

What is the Value of a Film Plot?

The price to expect for a given picture plot is a question almost invariably asked by beginners in this branch of the kinematograph industry, but unfortunately, and chiefly owing to the comparative newness of the market, prices have not as yet settled down to a sufficiently fixed scale for it to be possible to render all the help one would like on the point. With things as they are, the matter is really a very difficult one for a third party to speak about. For instance, the seller of a picture plot may be in a position where he can afford to make the resolution to sell at what he judges to be a fair price, or not at all. Undoubtedly, in this case his position, as far as it goes, is a strong one. On the other hand, unless he is careful in the estimate he forms of his own capacity, he may permanently keep himself from success, simply through the exorbitance of his demands on producing houses, which might otherwise be favorably impressed with his efforts. Then again the converse equally holds good. It is possible to submit a really good plot with a humbly worded note asking whether in the event of its being of use, 7s. 6d. would be too much for it. In such a case as this—and the kinematograph trade being what it is—no one should have cause for surprise if the ensuing post brought with it a remittance for 5s. (or perhaps even less) by way of making a hasty completion of a profitable transaction.

Thus the matter is difficult enough to advise upon, nor is it made any the easier by the practice (which we do not favour) of many film producing houses of notifying an outside contributor of the " provisional " acceptance of his plot, and asking him to write back naming the price he wants for it. The underlying idea is obviously that in the case of one unversed in the mysteries of plot selling there will be a tendency to take almost anything that can be got in the way of cash rather than scotch—or run the risk of scotching—the deal at the last moment. Candidly, this is not cricket on the part of the producers, and it may be laid down for their spiritual benefit here and now that the best journalistic talent will never be at their disposal in the matter of outside contributions until they alter their tactics and adopt the obviously fairer practice of making their own bid for the work submitted. It may be argued that no man is called upon to be buyer and seller too, but the argument, like many another evergreen one, is as hollow as a spool box. Further it can be added for their edification, that all the best literary magazines have recognised this last fact, and either buy their outside contributions on a set scale of payment, or else make use of a form somewhat like the following, which film houses might do far worse than copy, to the ultimate benefit of all concerned :

" The Editor of the...............................will buy your contribution entitled...................................at the price of ....for full rights. Please reply on the attached slip as to whether you are willing to dispose of it at this figure."

There is a perforation line, and following it :

" I will (not) accept the offer of...............................made for my contribution entitled....................."

(*Signed*).....................................

Meanwhile, and until Utopia is heralded in by some such general rule as indicated above, it can only be given as a necessarily vague guide that plots may be worth anything from say 7s. 6d. for a short comic to several pounds in the case of a theme capable of being worked up into a long and powerful dramatic picture play. American houses will cheerfully give as much as £5 to £10 or more for a plot of precisely the sort they know to be useful to them, but the very fact that prices rule high across the water means that the level of merit necessary for acceptance of a plot is accordingly raised. On the whole, the British plot writer will probably be doing wisely if he decides to start, at any rate, by sending his work to the British houses for consideration. For one thing, postage in the British Isles is so much less than it is abroad. In other words, you can send a plot to a home producing firm, enclosing stamped addressed envelope for its return in the event of unsuitability, and the total postage is twopence. On the other hand, you would be lucky if in trying your luck with the American market you got off with fivepence.

One last word. If you are going to start plot writing, don't begin by being swelled-headed about what you can do without practice. It is a notorious fact that everyone who knows nothing of writing for money imagines there is little or nothing to be learned. It is only when the re-reading of your old work makes you thoroughly disgusted with yourself that you are beginning to suspect your limitations. Be humble then, by all means, but on the other hand, don't be easily daunted. There is a journalistic aphorism that " a man's twenty-first literary effort is always accepted," which is only another way of saying that in every branch of literary work it is the rule, and not the exception, for success to come late.

FIG. 217. AN AUSTRALIAN OPEN-AIR SHOW.

CHAPTER V.

PLAYING TO PICTURES AND EFFECTS.

There is a certain part of the kinematograph entertainment which the average member of the audience takes no very particular notice of, and yet if it were absent he would notice it fast enough. This is the music which sometimes of better, sometimes of less quality, invariably accompanies the progress of the picture on the screen.

Now, music can be of many sorts. It may be orchestral, it may be vocal, it may be piano, or for the matter of that, it may be artificial music. Artificial music is generally considered highly inartistic, and for this reason it would not do for anyone calling himself a picture pianist to admit it as having any good points about it whatever. None the less, to be perfectly fair, the so-called electric piano is not always utterly bad, and is often quite passably good by comparison with some of the picture pianists one hears from time to time.

There is an electric piano put on the market by Messrs. Keith, Prowse and Co. which is capable of rendering many a homely melody, such, for instance, as " Alexander's Rag-time Band," with the greatest of verve and precision, while almost any electric piano, provided it is properly attended to and kept in good condition, will be voted pleasing by at least 80 per cent. of picture patrons.

Perhaps it would not be fair to dismiss the subject of automatic pianos without mention of the Harper Electric Piano, and the Harper Piano Player. The first is intended for installation in halls where the electric current is available and where the major portion of the program is intended to be automatically produced. The Player model, which is somewhat cheaper in first cost and does not call for the use of electricity, is for halls where a regular pianist is engaged, the use of the automatic playing attachment being reserved for odd times and emergencies.

Passing from artificial music, of which, after all, it is not so easy to write, since the A and Z of it is contained within the folds of the music roll, we come to picture pianists Here, as may be expected, the division of first class, second class, and other classes is pretty much one of salary. A manager who wants a good pianist must be prepared to pay at least a reasonable price for his services. The pianist who receives, say, £1 a week or less, is giving quite good value for his money if he can play a dozen or so different pieces of music fairly accurately, and bring them in with the pictures in a way that is not absolutely absurd. Provided, however, a reasonable salary is paid, the showman should expect a program of music carefully chosen by the pianist and in every way suitable to the pictures the individual pieces are intended to follow, since there is no doubt audiences are becoming daily more discriminating in such matters.   And this leads us to the question how far should picture music take the form of actual tunes, and how far should it be considered as a mere following of the pictures and nothing more?   Personally the writer has no love for a succession of more or less meaningless triplets, even though it may be accepted in some quarters as the last word in the picture pianist's art.   To his mind it is both far cleverer and far more effective to make use of good published music, chosen with care, and when necessary, varied just sufficiently to fall in with the incidents and motions of the scene portrayed on the projection screen.   There is no need for this music to be either particularly new or particularly heavy, both extremes being better avoided.

We should recommend that the basis of the stock repertory be culled from the minor and more melodious classics.

A word as to a habit which is much in vogue with picture pianists of the present day when accompanying films.   It consists in stringing together the refrains of a number of more or less well-known popular songs, which songs happen to bear titles somewhat applicable to the scenes of the moving pictures being shown.   This practice is evidently considered, in some quarters, as being both the height of smartness and of art in picture music technique.   As a matter of fact, two thoughts on the matter will show it to be the height of silliness, since unless the songs played are so hackneyed as to be a bore and a nuisance to the more cultured members of the audience, their titles will not be recognised, and thus this musical pun (for to such class the system appears to belong) will go unrecognised and entirely flat.   If, on the other hand, the song titles happen to strike home, they will worry the better portion of the audience immensely by forcing them to think of the pianist when they wish to be following the incidents of the picture.   What is even worse, the chances are that the cheap seats will take up the refrains and bawl them deafeningly to the lasting discredit of any picture palace with a reputation to lose.   The popular refrain, if admitted at all to the musical repertory of a good class picture show, should be in evidence but seldom, and then only to follow the incident of a screaming farce film.

There is a tendency in accompanying moving pictures on the piano to make the music much too jumbled and theatrical by exaggerating expression to a point where tune is lost and the melody becomes nothing but a succession of infantile fireworks.   It is strongly advised that picture pianists bear in mind that their function is to follow, and not lead, the pictorial side of the entertainment.   Their work will take all the more credit to itself if subdued sufficiently to leave the picture its prominence in the mind of the spectator.

It is advisable to sink the piano in a well close to the picture. Have the player sit where the screen is clearly visible, but if a piano light has to be used, be sure if does not shine into the eyes of those in the front rows. If your house is semi-lighted, the piano light will not be needed.

Do not expect your pianist, however clever he may be, to make good music with a poor piano. A second-hand instrument in good condition from a reputable maker is greatly to be preferred to the gaudy new fraud that is made up solely to sell. A baby grand takes up a lot of room compared with an upright, but it yields a splendid return. An organ can be used with good effect, either in combination or by itself.

Pictures can, of course, be played to by an orchestra, but to do so properly, it is necessary to have the very best talent. It is an impossibility to gain results by engaging inferior talent. As a rule, the majority of managers take the responsibility on their shoulders of engaging musicians and the chances are that not one in fifty has the least conception of what is required.

Where an orchestra is to be employed, always leave the choice of musicians to the leader. If he is capable of leading an orchestra, most assuredly he is capable of selecting his musicians. The whole responsibility is on his shoulders of having the music rendered in the proper manner. If he has an inferior class of performer who only murders the music, he is the one who is ridiculed.

FIG. 218. THE CINECHORDEON.

The Cinechordeon, for which the agents are Messrs. Jury's Kine Supplies, Ltd., is not an automatic but a hand operated musical instrument, including within itself a combination of piano, organ, zither, etc.

Next to the installation in the picture show of a full orchestra the Cinechordeon is the most complete thing in the way of musical equipment we have seen. Piano, organ, or both can be played at the same time or separately at will by the single musician who controls the instrument. The Cinechordeon provides really high class music of a most refreshingly varied description in the hands of any reasonably capable player.

But no matter what form of music you employ, you will find that motion pictures cannot be played without a proper repertoire of incidental music. This class of music is an absolute necessity, and can be used for any situation. It is selected as before explained, and should include pieces suitable as hurry music, that can be used for fights, Indian attacks, duels, sword fights, etc., sentimental music for death scenes, despair, sadness, meditation, and special music for military, comic, love, exotic, racing, and a hundred other scenes too numerous to mention.

And what sounds more encouraging to a manager than to hear his patrons complimenting him on the fine orchestra or the capable pianist he maintains, and the excellent manner the pictures are played. When the public begins to talk in this way, you may rest assured that you are giving satisfaction, and satisfaction is what brings your profits each week.

In many places it is found wise to introduce one or two vocal or instrumental solos, but the practice should only be adopted by the manager who is able to afford really good talent. Fifth or sixth rate variety turns do more harm than good, but real concert artistes lend tone to a picture theatre, as has been proved over and over again at the shows run by Mr. T. J. West, Mr. Dove Paterson and other leading showmen.

As to the question whether stage effects other than those produced by musical instruments are really artistic and helpful in kinematograph exhibitions, it is undoubtedly a vexed one, and as such should be answered by each showman to his own satisfaction. For those who favour them, a few of the many effects, with methods of production, are appended.

HORSES' HOOFS ON HARD AND SOFT ROAD SURFACES.—Procure two half cocoanut shells and a square of slate. Hold the cocoanut shells one in either hand, and knock rhythmically upon the slate to simulate the clattering of horses' hoofs upon hard ground. Alter the beats for cantering, galloping, walking, etc. The effect of riding on soft ground is produced by tapping the shells lightly on wood.

WAVES ON THE SEASHORE.—Procure a long wooden case and place in it a quantity of split peas. The rolling of the peas from one end of the case to the other simulates the sound of waves beating upon the shore. The faster the peas travel, the stronger and more furious the sound of the waves.

THUNDER.—Rivet together two or three sheets of thin sheet iron and suspend from the ceiling in a convenient position. Thunder is produced by shaking the iron sheets to make them rattle.

WIND.—This is produced by a wind drum fashioned somewhat like a film drying drum ; that is to say, a hollow wooden cage rotating on a central axis. Against this cage is stretched a length of silk on which the slats of the drum rub, producing a whistling sound. The wind drum is turned by means of a handle attached to it.

SMASHING CROCKERY, SMASHING GLASS, ETC.—A quantity of broken china or glass is placed in a box, and this box is dropped to simulate the sound of smashing crockery.

RIFLE SHOTS.—These can be simulated by striking a cushion sharply with a cane. The hardness of the cushion and amount of spring in the cane will determine whether the sound simulates a revolver, rifle, field gun, etc.

For those who require more ambitious effects than the above, it will be best to instal one of the machines sold for the purpose of producing various effects in great quantity. These effect machines are known by such trade names as the " Pathe Box-of-Tricks," " Andrews' Allefex," etc.

The scope of the present Handbook is so great that it would be impossible in it to deal at length with the various matters pertaining to picture music and effects without robbing of their just place many references to other highly technical aspects of kinematography. Accordingly the present *resume* of the subject must not be taken for a serious attempt at grappling with it in detail. Fortunately for the man to whom picture music is a vital or at least an important consideration, there is a book ready to hand, easily obtainable by him, and full of just the very information he requires. In fact, it is a capital book. Its name is " Playing to Pictures," and its author Mr. W. Tyacke George. It is produced by the publishers of the present volume at a price within the reach of all. Here will be found sections on the Musician, Music Arrangements, Classifying the Picture, Music to Prevent Panics, The Art of Improvising, How to Produce Effects, Music Licenses and How to Obtain Them, Musicians' Salaries, How to Choose a Piano, Small Bands, Making up Programs, Musical Copyright, List of Music Publishers, List of Specially Written Music, A Suggested List of Appropriate Music, List of Popular Songs, etc., etc.

FIG. 219. A WELL PACKED AUDITORIUM.

PART IV

PART IV.

CHAPTER I.

SCIENTIFIC AND TECHNICAL KINEMATOGRAPHY.

Scientific kinematography is a branch of the motion picture art the details of which must be worked out by each investigator in conformity with his particular line of research. At the same time, there are certain broad hints which may be given, and which may help towards making a start in a particularly fascinating and almost unexplored branch of moving picture work.

MICRO-KINEMATOGRAPHY.

This is a combination of the microscope with the motion picture camera, just in the same way as the microscope and still picture camera have for many years been combined for micro-photography. Broadly speaking, the same fundamental considerations as to technique apply in both cases. Such main considerations may be summarised as the obtaining of 'critical' illumination, absolute rigidity, and sharp focus with what is known in microscopy as good 'resolution,' or differentiation of minor microscopic details by the objective lens of the optical system. In motion picture micrography we shall in addition to the above require that the light be sufficiently powerful to permit of such turning rate as may be necessary for any given piece of work.

Turning rate, let it be noted, does not in scientific kinematography mean of necessity the regular sixteen pictures a second of ordinary studio and field work. Quite recently, a form of high speed micro-kinematograph camera has been invented in France with which as many as two to three hundred pictures a second are obtained. This particular camera is not fitted with intermittent movement. It relies on the light from a stream of sparks given off by a static electrical machine as the source of illumination of the successive pictures. The duration of each spark being almost infinitesimal it has been found that quite clear-cut images may, by such illumination, be obtained upon the fast rotating kinematograph film as it whirls round upon the rim of a drum in the plane of focus of the objective lens.

As an example of a contrary class of scientific motion picture may be cited the 'Bud to Blossom' series in connection with 'Kinemacolor' two-colour kinematography. Apart from the question of colour, the interest of the films here depends upon great speeding down of the camera mechanism during taking of the subjects. The films so produced depict the opening of various flowers before one's eyes.

To obtain such a speeded-down series all that is necessary is a system of gear wheels driven by a small electric or other motor, whereby the motion picture camera escapement may be driven at a constant rate, such rate to be far below the normal. Thus, suppose it is found by experiment that a certain flower bud placed in water takes from two to three days to open, and such opening of the bud is to be recorded so as to show in the space of one minute, we may arrive at the exact speeding down required as follows :—

Three days equals 72 hours, or 4,320 minutes. One minute's exhibition of kinematograph film at normal rate equals 60 feet, or 960 pictures. Therefore our 960 pictures must be divided into taking intervals spread equally over 4,320 minutes. That is to say, the interval between the exposure of each successive picture in the speeded-down camera is to be $4\frac{1}{2}$ minutes.

We accordingly arrange that our speeding-down gear shall operate the picture movement once every $4\frac{1}{2}$ minutes for three days. What portion of this time shall be actually occupied in exposure may be determined within certain limits by the adjustment of the camera shutter opening. Suppose each exposure is to give one minute of actual light impression on the film, then it is obvious our light source need be much less than that obtainable from daylight. Also, since daylight will wax and wane three times in three days, it must be equally obvious such in any case would not be available by us. Accordingly suitable artificial illumination has to be provided in the speeding down laboratory.

For such comparatively large-sized objects as flower buds, where no microscope attachment is needed, a couple of small and suitably shaded metallic filament electric lamps, placed one on either side of the object to be illuminated, would be in most cases quite sufficient. With microscope attachments, however, the light source will have to be much stronger. Also, a great deal depends on how the original light beam is collected and parallelised prior to striking the microscope's optical system. We append a sketch showing the microscope with its illumination as arranged for micro-kinematography.

A (fig. 220) is the light source, shown here as an electric arc lamp, such being the most powerful, and generally speaking, most suitable light for the work. From the lamp A the light beam passes outward to the lens B, known as a stand condenser. Stand condensers for micrography are (unlike those used in moving picture projection) highly corrected instruments. The stand condenser should throw a clear achromatic or colourless light beam through the cell X, which contains glycerine or water, with, perhaps, the addition of some colouring matter, according to the work in hand. The functions of the cell X are to cut off as much as possible of the heat rays from the microscope stage. Also, where colouring matter is added, the resolution of the microscope objective may be improved thereby.

Other reasons for the use of a colour trough in special cases may deal with the production of contrast in the film image, and similar points not necessary to go into at length here.

Leaving the glycerine cell, the light pencil falls upon the substage condenser C, in a very brilliant and concentrated patch, which in its

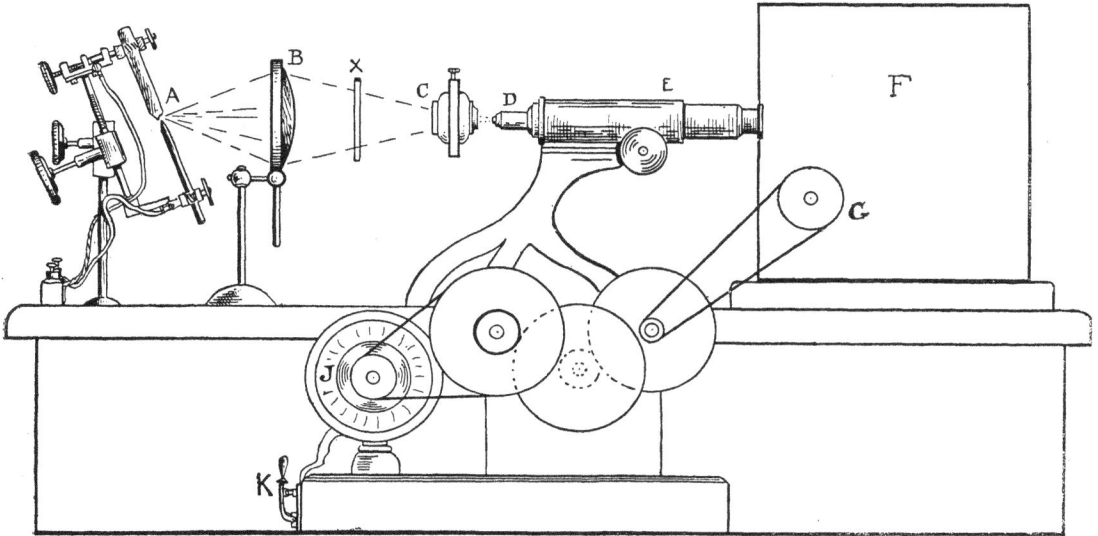

FIG. 220.

turn becomes further concentrated by this second condenser emerging upon the object on the microscope stage as almost a pin point. It is in this way that the object to be photographed is illuminated. Afterwards, the light beam passes on through the objective lens D, and the eye piece E of the microscope, till the image is brought to a focus upon the film in the gate of the motion picture camera attachment shown at F.

FIG. 221.
WESTMINSTER RIGHT ANGLE SEMI-AUTOMATIC ENCLOSED ARC LAMP.

The camera lens will, of course, have been removed before the adaptation of the instrument to its use in micro-kinematography. G shows the driving pulley actuating the picture changing movement and connecting by means of a belt through the gearing down wheels H with the electric motor J, the latter being controlled by a switch or rheostat K.

Fig. 220 shows the micro-kinematographic system arranged in horizontal position, in which case the microscope stage will be vertical. When photographing such subjects as animalculae moving in liquid and such like, it will be necessary to tip up the whole arrangement on end so as to make the stage of the microscope horizontal. When starting first experiments in this line of research, it will be advisable to use only microscope objective lenses of low power, say from two inches to half an inch focus. With very low magnifications the eye piece E may well be dispensed with altogether. For higher magnifications, one of the 'compensating' type eye pieces, or better still, a 'projection eye piece' will be used.

Where the electric arc is not available for experimentation in micro-kinematography limelight may be substituted. Also, water motors or hot-air motors can be made to take the place of electric ones for such light work as the turning of the geared-down escapement where such is used. In high magnification work, where great resolution is required, and consequently wide apertures of objective and substage condenser become a necessity, it may be found necessary to have the optical system of the microscope of the apochromatic variety.

The Ernemann Micro-Kinematograph Camera.

Since the publication of the first edition of this Handbook, a beautifully made and highly efficient micro-kinematograph camera has been placed upon the market by the well-known firm of Ernemann, of Dresden. Messrs. Ernemann also have a depot at 9 Great Newport Street, and the English agents are Messrs. Jury's Pictures, Ltd., which firm has opened a special showroom for the purpose of housing and demonstrating this micro-camera, as well as the Ernemann all-steel Imperator projector.

The micro-apparatus consists firstly of a heavy iron pillar-supported base, which acts as a rigid stand for (*a*) the kinematograph camera body, carrying within it film boxes and escapement, and (*b*) the microscope attachment, which takes the place of the camera lens.

So far, the whole merely follows out the invariable principle already laid down for work of the class to which we are referring. Several convenient arrangements, however, tend greatly to ease and accuracy of the results obtained. For instance, the camera mechanism is controlled by a small electric motor placed upon the ground under the supporting table. A special form of foot-operated switch controls this motor, so that pressure of the sole of the foot is all that is necessary instantly to start or stop record-making. Both hands and arms are thus left free the while for the delicate manipulations connected with focussing, light centring, arrangement of objects in the field of view, and such like.

The illumination used when working with the Ernemann micro-camera is usually supplied from a small hand-fed arc. The light beam from it is concentrated upon the microscope stage through a system of condensing lenses supplied with the outfit, a liquid cell

FIG. 222. THE ERNEMANN MICRO-KINEMATOGRAPH CAMERA.

being provided for obtaining approximately monochromatic light. The focussing of the image is done by means of the microscope coarse and fine adjustment in the usual way, but an extremely simple, accurate and reliable reflecting system enables the worker to view the actual focussed image upon the film in the camera gate right up to the moment of exposure. The value of this last attachment cannot be over-estimated when dealing with such problems as the recording of moving bacteria, living protozoa, and the like. These flit across the field of view so swiftly and at such irregular intervals that the making of moving pictures of them by means of apparatus not equally well provided in respect of focussing and viewing of the image previous to exposure would be almost impossible, and in any case attended with an enormous wastage of film.

Considering what it is capable of doing, the Ernemann micro outfit is extremely moderate in price, and can be conscientiously recommended to those in need of a really fine piece of apparatus for this particular class of scientific kinematography.

As we have already pointed out, for high power micro-work it becomes a practical necessity to use only apochromatic objectives, with a compensating, or even better, a projection eye-piece, and preferably also an apochromatic oil immersion sub-stage condenser.

TELE-KINEMATOGRAPHY.

There would seem to be a considerable field for the application of the motion picture camera to the telescope, especially to the astronomical telescope. At the present moment, photographic charts of the heavenly bodies are made through the telescope with ordinary still camera attachment, working on just such a general system as the one in common use for photo-micrography of still objects, except that in tele-photography the distant objects provide their own natural illumination. Now, as made by tele-photography star maps either show one fixed position only of the heavenly bodies, or else they give the general direction of these in the form of lines due to the movement of the earth during exposure.

The motion picture combined with the astronomical telescope affords a ready means, not only of recording the direction of apparent travel of the heavenly bodies, but actually of recording the motion itself. For this purpose, undoubtedly, some system of gearing down the rate of taking to compensate for want of light in the bodies themselves, as also for reasons of economy of film length exposed, would, however, be necessary.

In terrestrial tele-kinematography also there is a wide field and a very interesting one for the exploitation of the motion picture man with ideas of his own. Who, for instance, has not from the sea-shore looked through a high power glass at shipping passing over the horizon? Such effects of distant ships passing, to say nothing of many another odd and interesting subject, would most certainly be in range of the owner of a good terrestrial tele-kinematographic outfit.

At the time of the appearance of the first edition of this Handbook the remarks appearing above, which were to be found in it, were written in a purely prophetic spirit. They indicated no already commercialised field in the art of motion picture making, nor at the time did it seem as though makers of kinematograph machinery had any definite intention of interesting themselves in the present aspect of the subject. However, so swiftly do matters move with us that already there comes an intimation from that enterprising and go-ahead firm of Dallmeyer that they have got seriously to grips with the problem of tele-photography as applied to moving picture work. This is no wonder, seeing that they were the first to perfect and commercialise telescopic photography in connection with still view work, yet it does not make less interesting the announcement of their latest Kinematograph Telephoto lens, having a working aperture of F 4.5 and capable of giving a picture of any given object three times as large as that obtained from the same position by means of an ordinary lens with the same back focus. When using the Dallmeyer tele-kinematograph lens, the operator may be three times as far away from his subject as when using an ordinary lens, and yet the object he wishes to record will be of full size in his picture.

The adoption of the telephoto construction has also enabled Messrs. Dallmeyer to make the lens far smaller and lighter than would otherwise be possible. As a result the design of the lens allows of it fitting into quite a small flange, so that it is easily adaptable to any ordinary kinematograph camera, at once turning it into a low or medium power telescopic motion picture apparatus.

The above is a striking instance of the quickness with which the voicing of a need by the responsible moving picture press is followed on the part of go-ahead business firms by its almost instant gratification.

Natural History Kinematography.

While micro-kinematography and tele-kinematography largely depend upon the skilled use of extra attachments to the kinematograph camera, there is a field of the art of motion picture making equally scientific, yet in the main calling for little extra apparatus beyond the ordinary kinematograph outfit, for a successful incursion into it. What it does call for, however, is an abundance of patience and care, a natural power of contrivance, and an untiring perseverance in the study of the habits of the smaller living creatures that surround us. This natural history kinematography has produced a whole number of films combining in themselves not merely technical excellence, but also amusement and instruction combined. Needless to say, the man who intends to carry out work of this description must have his own equipment for it, which equipment is to be found in the careful and painstaking reading up of books such as will provide him

with an adequate working knowledge of the habits of the creatures
he intends to photograph.   Thus, in making a film of a particular
insect, it would first of all be necessary to know the part of the world
where it was to be found and the time of year to be seized upon for
the illustration for each phase of its life.   Next, the form and size
of the creature would come up for consideration, and would decide
the focus of lens to be employed for the work, and the nature of the
surroundings which might best be provided for it during photographic
operations.   Habits must be studied up beforehand and watched for
at the right time or times and in the right places, until it is possible
to obtain the coveted record of them.   Further in order to make the
whole interesting and instructive at the same time, the film must have
a considerable measure of technical excellence, combined with evidence
of knowledge behind the mere record making, so that in the end the
life history of the creature, or those points about it most interesting
to the naturalist, will be sufficiently brought out in the complete
record.

Sometimes it may be desired to show off a peculiar point of elementary intelligence or instinct in an animal of a low order of development, and as a last resort it may be considered necessary to have
recourse to artifice to demonstrate the existence of such, where it is
found practically impossible to obtain an entirely genuine film showing
it.   We do not know what to say of such proceedings.

Perhaps if they are embarked upon as the result of a full and
accurate knowledge of the point it is desired to convey to the audience,
they may be somewhat justified.

A type of film which is, perhaps, hardly scientific in character
and yet may be dealt with in the present chapter as being at least
pseudo-scientific, is one in which animals, birds, insects, or such like
are shown performing various tricks, such, for instance, as the film
depicting a fly twirling a straw dumb-bell, a mouse taking tea with a
tortoise, and a host of others of the same type.   Here we think it is
certainly quite permissible to resort to artifices, for the result aimed
at is such as cannot often be conveniently obtained by perfectly straight
means, and since even though the film be, strictly speaking, turned
thereby to one of the trick variety, there is little or no fear of impressing the audience with false knowledge through its projection
upon the moving picture screen.

Thus the writer has in mind a film wherein a mouse was shown
as nibbling through a paper bag in order to liberate a captive snake.
The snake then proceeded to circle round and round it in gratitude.
As a matter of fact, it must be fairly evident the snake would not
really be liable to do any such thing.   What was done to obtain the
film was this.   The snake was placed in the bag along with some
lettuce leaves, and a tame field mouse placed near by.   The smell
of the leaves inside the bag caused the little animal to nibble through
the paper to get at them, and as it did so a surreptitious poke by means
of a concealed rod disturbed the snake and caused it to emerge from

the hole. Mr. Snake soon began to walk out of the picture, but before it had quite disappeared, the camera was stopped, its direction of crawling was changed, and the camera once more re-started, this proceeding being continued laboriously until a sufficient number of short lengths were obtained, showing the reptile in more or less suitable positions for the final operation of negative make-up. 'Make-up' took the form of cutting out the stops, or portions of over-exposed film between the short length records, and also removing such pictures as appeared superfluous for the purpose of giving the effect aimed at. In the end, a print from this heavily edited negative gave a result sufficiently like the scene it set out to depict.

A great future for natural history kinematography undoubtedly exists in connection with natural colour work. Already there have been secured in Kinemacolor a wonderful series of moving pictures depicting the life of fish under water, also showing fish in the act of taking the fly of an angler, played on the end of a line, and landed in true sporting fashion.

The now famous Kinemacolor subject, 'The Birth of Flowers,' taken by means of a geared-down colour camera, is an instance of natural history trick photography, having the additional advantage of being executed in a process giving approximately natural colour rendering.

FIG. 223. EXTERIOR AND INTERIOR OF A MODERN PROVINCIAL MOTION PICTURE THEATRE.

Fig. 224.   "The Earth Divided, the World United."   A wonderful Kinemacolor Series showing the construction of the Panama Canal.   Among other triumphs of Kinemacolor may be mentioned The Durbar, Unveiling the Statue of Queen Victoria, The Coronation, and many topical subjects of historical value.

CHAPTER II.

KINEMATOGRAPHY IN COLOURS.

While it would be rash to prophesy that kinematography in black and white has seen the best of its days, or even that it has yet reached the height of its popularity, there can now be no shadow of doubt in the minds of those intimately connected with the industry, that the immediate future is going to witness an early and highly important development of the production of moving pictures in natural colours. Perhaps a year, perhaps two years, possibly only six months will witness something of a popular revolution in this direction, and the only thing which remains in doubt in the minds of those who can see most clearly ahead, is as to who will reap the richest reward out of this new phase of the picture art.

But a word of preliminary explanation. Kinematography in colours, as the term is at present understood, goes to include two distinct classes of moving pictures. These are produced in entirely different ways. The first is one which we shall only touch upon here, for it does not properly belong to the present chapter at all. It concerns itself with the effect produced upon the projection screen by painting or colouring a black and white positive by means of dyes or transparent pigment applied to the surface of the film by handwork, or by the use of a stencilling machine. To this class of coloured subject belongs that extensive range of highly pleasing views to be met with week by week in the modern picture theatre under such trade names as " Pathecolor," " Gaumont Color Cinematography," and the like. In both the above, as in the case of all other commercial film subjects where the colour is apparent on the celluloid positive film upon hand inspection, the system employed does not involve the making of any real sun record of the actual colours of nature. Consequently, whatever tints are shown are entirely empirical in their origin ; that is to say, they result from the will of the particular gentleman or gentlemen who decide on the colours to be used for tinting, and do not depend really upon the colour of the original subject at all. Thus, a certain lady may have been photographed in a bright blue dress, but if it occurs to the film tinter that the dress would look better pink, then pink it is made, and pink it appears on the projection screen. This pink dress may look very pretty, but still, it is not the original blue one, nor would anyone be able to suspect that a blue gown had ever been within a hundred miles of it for all the audience sees of the original's natural colour. This simple explanation may do something to explain just how much—or how little—guarantee of fidelity to Nature is carried by the colours seen upon hand or stencil-tinted subjects.

Let us pass on to the matter in hand and try to get an insight into a means whereby the actual colours of Nature can be in some wise recorded upon the negative so that they and they alone, or at least a latent record of them, are in their turn communicated to the positive.

To start our explanation, we will first give a brief description of the principle on which all colour photography and colour kinematography is based. This principle takes the form of a theory of colour vision originally propounded by the investigators Young and Helmholtz, at the beginning of the Nineteenth century. It was years before the theory was adapted to a commercial use in connection with photography, and it was very many more years again before anyone thought of re-adapting the whole to the production of natural-hued kinematograph films. The Young-Helmholtz theory, put briefly and somewhat crudely, is as follows :

The perception of colour by the eye comes about through the medium of three colour nerves, or colour sensitive elements in it, each one sensitive to waves of a definite length. One colour element of the eye has its maximum sensitiveness to red light. The second is particularly sensitive to green light, while the third colour nerve is chiefly sensitive to blue, in the region between indigo and violet. Now, since these principles involve the possession by the eye of only three distinct colour sensitive nerves, sensitive to three colours of light as stated, the question immediately arises, how is it the eye sees also intermediate colours such as yellow, pink, brown and the rest of them ? Young and Helmholtz decided that these colours made their impression on the brain by virtue of the fact that they had the power of exciting more than one of the colour elements in the eye at the same time. Thus, yellow light would be the result of the simultaneous excitation of the red and the green colour nerves ; pink light the result of the simultaneous excitation of the red and the blue ; while, for instance, such a dimly perceptible colour as greyish-brown could be transmitted to the brain by a gentle and simultaneous excitation of all three colour sensitive elements, the impulse of the red and green sensitive nerves being slightly in excess of that transmitted by the blue. How did Young and Helmholtz suggest that we saw white light ? In their view we saw it as the result of a strong equal and simultaneous excitation of all three colour elements in the eye. Pause and consider what this means upon the application to it of a simple deductive reasoning. It means, if the theory be sound, that since white light is to our brain no more than the simultaneous record of three definite colours, then the mechanical mixture of these same three colours should, under proper conditions, give to the eye the same effect as though it were viewing a pure white light. We should, in fact, be able thus to make a sham (or, as it is now called, ' synthetic') white. This we can actually do. Young and Helmholtz did it, thus demonstrating that as far as their optical theory went, it was correct enough for all practical purposes, and later on, in 1861, James Clark Maxwell, one of the fathers of photography, and THE father of colour photography, adapted this same principle to what we now know as 'three colour.' At a demonstration given before the Royal Institution, he projected in super-position upon the lantern screen three photographic transparencies, one illuminated by red light, the second by green light, and the third by blue light, and the result was not merely that where these lights mingled in equal amounts it formed synthetic white upon the screen, but he also showed the first actual colour photographs ; that is to say, photographic projections, however imperfect, which gave something of the original colour of the objects back to the audience. How did he manage this last ? It is clear that in order to do it, if he worked upon the Young-Helmholtz theory, it would be necessary to do more than use three transparencies taken in the ordinary way in a black and white camera. As a matter of fact, he took a special set, using before the lens during the exposure of each one a screen of coloured glass of the same colour as that of the light which was destined to be used for the projection of the transparency. Here, then, we arrive at the beginning of practical color photography. The wide principle, even in modern practice, is practically the same as above, whether we are working in still or moving pictures, whether we continue to use all three colour records to obtain our results, or whether we decide to forsake somewhat theoretical accuracy and get the best effect we can with two only of the colours, namely, the two brightest—red and green. And now to try to make matters clear as to how this photographing through coloured glasses plays its part in natural colour photography.

We will take the simple case of the actual photographing of an original, and follow it from start to finish. Thus, suppose three negatives to be taken from a coloured original—one through a red, one through a green, and one through a blue glass. It is obvious that the opaque silver deposit on these negatives will represent partially the light and shade of the object or objects photographed, but also this density of deposit will vary with the colour possessed by the original objects, since the glass transmits its own colour and absorbs other colours. Suppose positive transparencies to be made from the three negatives, and that these three positive transparencies are backed by glasses of the same colour through which their respective negatives were taken. We have then a set such as was used by Clark Maxwell in his experiments, and we may reasonably expect to obtain upon super-position of the three images by means of a triunal lantern, a reconstruction of the colours of the original. Thus:—

Suppose the object photographed to consist of a red flower with green leaves. Arguing the matter out as simply as possible, we see that the red record negative would show the flower as a heavy deposit, while the leaves being green—that is to say, of a colour which is not transmitted by red glass—will have little or no effect as regards recording upon the negative. In other words, they will give us practically no deposit on the negative at all. With the green negative matters will be just the other way about. In it the leaves will have made a heavy record or deposit of silver, while the position of the flower will be left as practically a blank, without silver deposit. Positives made from these negatives will show the relation of the deposit to the original colour as exactly reversed, for the reason that a positive always has its density of silver deposit directly the opposite to that upon the negative. Thus the positive from the red negative will now show the flower as transparent, while the leaves will be opaque ; while the positive from the green record negative will have matters exactly the other way about.

We now back each positive with a glass similar in colour to the one with which its negative was taken, and project the two images in super-position on the screen. The result will be a red flower projected through one lantern, and green leaves projected through the other ; that is to say, the red flower with its green leaves is reproduced before the eyes of the audience. It will be noted that for the sake of simplicity in the above description, we have neglected the blue-violet record altogether, since neither red nor green being transmitted by a true blue-violet glass, the blue-violet record may be looked upon as a blank one, in other words, one showing no colour recording deposit on any part of it. The transparency made from such a negative would be nothing but an opaque black glass, so that the blue-violet unit would contribute on projection no light whatever. Had there been blue or violet in the original, it would have added itself on where required, exactly as with the red and the green in the above example. This omission of the comparatively dim blue-violet record is, actually, not solely confined to the present description in the HANDBOOK OF KINEMATOGRAPHY, but is sometimes successfully made use of in practice.

The best known commercial process of colour kinematography at the moment of writing neglects the blue record, and trusts to the fact that deep pure blues and violets are comparatively rare in Nature for the omission not to be too keenly noticed by the audience.

But to return. Red, green and blue-violet light have come to be known as the three primary colours, and are often referred to by the simple term of 'primaries.' When two of these are mixed together, the resulting colour, which may be either yellow, blue-green or pink, is known as a secondary colour or may be referred to as 'minus' that colour which, when mixed with the secondary would go to form synthetic white. Thus the secondary colour, pink, resulting from the mixture of red and blue light, but not of green, is referred to as 'minus green'   yellow, being a mixture of red and green, but not blue, is referred to as 'minus blue,' while blue-green, being a mixture of green and blue, but not red, may be referred to equally as 'minus red.'

There are two points still left for us to go into briefly, after which we will pass on to see how much has, up to the present, been done towards adapting the mechanical, or rather optical and photographic record of colour to the uses of the moving picture.

The first point we shall try to make plain will be one over which the uninitiated usually blunder. It is the difference between the addition to and subtraction from each other of colour and colour.

The second point deals with the rendering colour sensitive of photographic emulsions, especially with colour-sensitising to red rays, since the obvious weak point in that part of our description which has gone before is the fact well known to every camera man, that while other colours are not safe as illuminants of the dark-room, yet there is no ordinary negative stock but can be handled in perfect safety in a reasonably subdued red light. Now to our first point.

The simplest case of the addition of one colour to another, as imagined by the ordinary reader who has not studied the subject, would be the case of the mixture of coloured paints.

If we were to turn the contents of a red paint pot into that of a green one, we might claim to have mixed colour and colour, the resulting mixture being of a dull and dirty brown hue. As a matter of fact, in the scientific sense, we have not mixed two colours at all. We have merely subtracted the one from the other, and the reason of this is that colour, in its strict sense, is not a substance, but a form of light. We call red paint red because it has the property of reflecting red light, but the colour we see is not that of the paint at all, but of the light which strikes upon it. A red-painted wall will not appear red in a totally darkened room. It will then be just as black as everything else in the room, whereas a room cannot be made so dark but that a beam of red light passing into it will throw its own coloured illumination.

Now to review our simple, if not particularly sensible proceeding of mixing a red and green paint together. All we have really done is to make a subtraction of the colours of the two paints from each other. Thus, roughly speaking, red paint reflects only red light ; green paint reflects—for practical purposes—only green light. We mix the two together and the mixture reflects scarcely any light at all, each paint killing the other in this direction. It is on the same system that a water-colour artist mixes his paints before applying to the paper. By him, green is regarded mainly as a mixture of blue and yellow. He is right in the case of his water colours, and for the following reason. These two colours mixed will give a green, because while yellow has the power of reflecting both green and red light, blue has the power of reflecting green and blue light, so that when the two paints have mutually killed by subtraction those colour-reflecting properties in each other which are antagonistic, they still both possess in common the property of reflecting the green rays. Green alone is therefore given back to the eye from the mixture. Thus, to the artist blue and yellow make a green. But to the scientific mind the process of paint mixing is not an additive one, but a subtractive proposition altogether ; thus the product of the mutual interference of the light rays by a blue and a yellow pigment leaves a residue of green light to be transmitted to the eye.

Let us pass on to enquire as to what constitutes a real colour mixture, as against a mixture of substances possessing a mutual absorbtion of certain colour waves. In colour photography it is the former we must deal with. We must consider the colours themselves, that is to say, beams of colour in the form of light, as it is only with coloured light rays that mixtures or additions, as in contra-distinction to subtractions, become possible.

Let us imagine ourselves seated in a totally darkened room when a beam of pure red light is thrown upon the projection screen in front of us. Let us also imagine that a second and distinct beam of pure green light, coming from another quarter of the room, is allowed to strike upon the same part of the screen as the previous red beam, so that both lights fall upon the same part of the screen and intermix. We shall now obtain not a dirty brown, but a pure yellow as the result of the mixture, and this for the simple reason that in the present instance the experiment is one of genuine addition of light to light. Imagine a third blue-violet light beam coming to play upon the other two. Provided its proportion as regards quantity was correctly adjusted, we should get the effect of white upon our screen, this being in fact not a spectrum white, as is real daylight, but the synthetic white to which we referred in an earlier part of this chapter. Roughly speaking, the correct proportions of red, green and blue-violet light which go to form synthetic white are 39 parts red, 60 parts green, and one part blue-violet, the last being, it will be noted, in far the least proportion.

In the case of two-colour processes, advantage is taken of the very small proportion of blue-violet present in synthetic white to so arrange the green record that blue also is passed by it in amount partially to supply the want of this third colour.

Colour Sensitive Emulsions for Colour Work.

We have mentioned that the ordinary photographic emulsion is not sensitive to the red rays of the spectrum. It was this want of sensitiveness which greatly curtailed the early experiments made in three-colour, with the result that it is only within the last few years that practical processes of colour photography, and later of colour kinematography, have come before the public, although the scientific bases on which these processes rest was fairly well-known and understood to investigators nearly half a century ago. Clark Maxwell had to make his red records by exposing ordinary, or non-colour-sensitive emulsion to red light for 10,000 or more times the normal period, while his green records were only a trifle more easily secured. Yet even in those early days the hope was expressed that a substance or substances might be eventually discovered which would render photographic plates capable of very much quicker colour recording. The first practical results in this direction were secured some fifteen years after Clark Maxwell's original experiments, by Professor Vogel. He found that by bathing plates in ammoniacal erythrosine solution, very greatly increased yellow and green sensitiveness with slightly increased orange sensitiveness was obtained. That started the ball rolling. From then onwards it was recognised that the problem of colour sensitising plates had ceased to be an insoluble one, a conviction which was deepened by the discovery some years later again of the red sensitising properties of cyanine, and other dyes belonging to this group. Photographic emulsions bathed in cyanine solution acquired a degree of red sensitiveness which, though but slight to our modern way of thinking, rendered them sufficiently suitable for the making of the red record of an experimental tri-colour set. In fact it was at about this point, and well before the introduction of the isocyanine derivatives which have so completely revolutionised colour work, that the earliest patents for apparatus for colour kinematography were filed. Thus, a patent of 1898 in the name of W. Friese-Green which purports to produce moving pictures in colour, clearly shows that the minds of investigators were already beginning to turn, however haltingly, to the proposition of making and projecting such kinematograph pictures ; while the following year, 1899, is historic in this connection in that the month of March saw the filing by Lee and Turner of the first patent describing a practical and workable adaptation of the system of three-colour to the making of moving picture records. Unfortunately, this particular patent, or at least the process which it described, was marred to the point of impracticability by the fact that the means proposed by the inventors for the projection of their colour records when obtained, consisted of an apparatus so faultily conceived and clumsily designed as to mask and for practical purposes nullify the value of the recording system that went with it.

It was in the era between the unsuccessful attempt at working out the Lee-Turner patent in a practical form, and the filing of George Albert Smith's Kinemacolor patent which supplanted it, that the isocyanine colour sensitisers made their bow to the public from the works of Meister-Lucius and Bruenig, Hoechst-on-Main. The first of these to come to us was ethyl-red, but almost before it got known it was supplanted by the substance orthochrome T. With the advent of the latter dye, the colour sensitiser's troubles began rapidly to fade, and even had no isocyanine derivatives been worked out, it is probable that a good deal of successful colour work might, under favorable conditions, have been undertaken with its agency. None the less, orthochrome was speedily followed by pinachrome, and panchrome by pinacyanol, to say nothing of such other less used sensitisers as pinaverdol, dicyanine and the rest. It is with dyes belonging to the above class that the present-day seeker after highly colour-sensitive emulsions prosecutes his investigations. Without them, Kinemacolor would not to-day be the successful commercial colour process it is, nor would there be the very good reason we have for feeling sure that the era of general natural colour kinematography is about to dawn to an extent which will stupefy the less go-ahead members of the black and white side of the business.

To leave film sensitising and go back to the year 1904, that is to say, a couple of years before the Kinemacolor patent was filed, we find that at this time there took place in Paris and also in Brighton exhibitions of a system of two-colour motion projection invented by Dr. Jumeaux and Captain Lascelles-Davidson, which exhibitions have an interest of their own as marking early and partially successful attempts at obtaining *actual* colour on the projection screen by a system of optical super-imposition, as against the later if more successfully exploited colour effects obtained by persistence of vision. In the system in question a red and a blue record of the original were made side by side on the colour sensitised film stock, which had been treated to render it orthochromatic. On projection, the light going through the positives printed from the colour record negatives was filtered through respectively red and blue glasses, and the two beams were then combined in front of the lens by a system of prisms, or, in a modi-fication of the patent, by means of suitably disposed mirrors. The writer has been given his description of the Brighton exhibition by one who actually witnessed it, and from all accounts, although from the commercial point of view the result could not have been described as successful, yet from the scientific aspect, enough was accomplished to show that the principle of optical super-imposition of coloured images held within it a distinct promise of better things to be evolved some day.

In the above system the two images were recorded by means of prisms set in front of the lens.

It will be noted that these early attempts of Dr. Jumeaux and Captain Davidson were made on the two-colour and not the three-colour principle. Though no two-colour process can ever give natural colour results (any more than any photographic lens can ever realise true depth of focus, both suppositions being in the realm of sheer theoretical impossibility), the above experiments served to reveal to investigators several important things. One of these was that the two-colour system, while not being true to Nature might be expected with careful handling and under favorable circumstances to yield quite pleasing results. Also it was noticed that prismatic splitting up and reblending of the images as then accomplished tended greatly to want of sharpness in the result obtained. So the practical investigation of what might and might not well be attempted in colour projection is found by now to have proceeded somewhat.

It was at this point that word came of Kinemacolor. Here we have a system which adopted the eminently sensible course of follow-ing the line of least resistance as it then appeared to the inventor to have been mapped out by prior investigation in colour kinematography.

In Kinemacolor, panchromatic film (that is to say, film rendered sensitive to all colours by means of suitable sensitising dyes) is exposed in a special kinematograph camera. This instrument is in many ways similar to an ordinary black and white motion picture camera, but between the rotary light shutter and the gate is a second rotating filter frame, carrying in its opposite halves the two colour filters respectively employed for making the red and green record, for Mr. Albert Smith, the inventor, decided very wisely to substitute in his process a green record for the blue one of Dr. Jumeaux and Captain Davidson.

Kinemacolor being, as we have before stated, a two-colour and not a three-colour process, makes use of filters of these two colours only for taking and projection. Usually in the case of taking filters, one is a reddish orange, while the other is a pure or very slightly bluish green. The projection filters are respectively scarlet and blue-green in colour. In many Kinemacolor film results, the variation from theoretical perfection in the projected pictures is surprisingly small. The process is, moreover, deserving of all honour as the first commercial adaptation of colour photography in any form to motion picture work.

When operating a Kinemacolor camera, the turning of the handle causes the rotating filter frame which carries the red and green colour filters to turn round once for every two pictures taken, so that the records made upon the film are the result of the action upon it of red and green light, picture by picture alternately. Needless to say, special care is necessary in developing panchromatic films, since the operations have to be gone through in practical or even total darkness ; but once safely developed and fixed, the film is printed from as if it were ordinary black and white negative.

In projecting a print, a projector is used fitted with a rotating colour filter frame carrying coloured projection filters in the same way as the camera. The positive film is threaded into the gate so that the picture produced in the camera by the action of the light passing through the red filter will once more show on projection through the red projecting screen, while the green record in its turn receives green light through the green filter of the projector. Thus, every alternate picture will flash on the screen illuminated by red and green light respectively.

It is found that when these light impulses succeed each other at a rate of approximately thirty-two a second, they blend together in the retina of the eye to form seemingly natural colour through the well-known and already explained principle of persistence of vision, which same principle is the basis of the whole illusion of kinematography. Thus, in the case of Kinemacolor, the willing member of the audience is treated to not one, but two separate and complete illusions, for whereas the black and white exhibitor merely makes you believe you see movement which is not there, the Kinemacolor operator does the same for the perception of colour also.

At the moment of writing there is on the market no commercial process of colour kinematography which has for its basis the principle of actual optical super-position of two or three separate images illuminated by corresponding coloured lights for the purpose of giving an actual and non-illusory coloured picture on the screen, after the manner first attempted by Jumeaux and Davidson.

The writer has some patents directed towards the accomplishment of this end, and founded on his original patent No. 1,642 of 1911. Moreover, from present experiments, his process appears promising, but we will not waste time by saying more. Several other inventors are working out their own particular patents. The Cine-colorgraph Co., of New York, send word of a system whereby it is proposed to put on the market positive film base of light lemon-yellow colour, having on one side a chemically prepared image printed from a suitable record negative in pink while the other side of this same base bears upon itself a second colour record positive in blue-green. The whole is designed to make an actual coloured picture which can be seen in the hand or projected on the screen. When this film comes upon the market it will falsify the statement at the beginning of the chapter that films in which the colour can be seen on hand inspection are not true colour photographs.

Mr. Thornton is, we understand, turning his attention to the adaptation of Pinatype, or a process somewhat allied to it, for the projection of similar coloured kinematograph positives. In his case he aims at a true three-colour result, and is not content with making the third or lemon-yellow a solid colour. Let us hope the future will deal kindly with his ingenious invention. Tompson and Campbell have latterly evinced a disposition to file many patents in connection with colour kinematography, and, in fact, for the last year or so the patent agents have been becoming quite brisk in such matters, so that short of a small glossary to contain the names and numbers of inventions it is hard to know how to set about naming them all.

Suffice it to say that what with the energies that are known and with those that are suspected in the realm of moving picture colour work, what with the numerous attempts which are certainly being made, and the undercurrent of dark rumours as to even more miraculous feats accomplished, we have come to a point in this fascinating branch of the motion picture art where ' anything may happen.' The one thing that seems to stand out from all the rest as practically certain is that the public are not for much longer to be denied a full share of genuine colour pictures, quickly recorded and as quickly presented for their delectation at the bulk of the picture shows.

SAFE LIGHTS.

While ruby and yellow glass may prove fairly suitable in combination as a filter for the light utilised in dark room illumination during the loading and development of ordinary non-colour-sensitive kinematograph film, such will be useless when handling the panchromatic film necessary in colour work. Further, even when dealing with non-colour-sensitive stock, the amount of light which may be passed by commercial ruby glass without injury to the film is very small in comparison with that which might safely be allowed to issue through a proper ' safe light.' A suitable safe light is a necessity when handling undeveloped colour stock, and a great luxury at other times. Directions are therefore appended for the making of safe lights such as will be found of use in the dark room lamp or lamps when handling any sort of film from slow positive to fastest colour-sensitive negative stock. Needless to say, the same coloured safe lights will not do for all purposes. A series of three graduated ones will therefore be given, with directions such as will enable the experimental photographer to make each for himself.

CANARY YELLOW SAFE LIGHT.

This safe light allows of a brilliant yellow illumination, which is yet quite safe for use when handling positive stock. The light is at least four times as bright as that passed by commercial yellow glass, which latter, however, would not be safe for use at all. The safe light is made thus:

Fix out two undeveloped photographic plates of a size to fit the dark room lantern to be glazed. Wash the fixed plates, and they will now have left on them only a coating of clear gelatine. Proceed to dye one plate in a strong (5 per cent.) solution of filter yellow K, Hoechst. Dye the other in strong Metanile yellow, Grubler. Rinse both plates after dyeing and stand them up on end to dry. When dry, bind them together face to face, having placed a sheet of tracing paper between the two to diffuse the light from the light source. Engineer's tape is suitable for binding the glasses together, and is applied round the edges after the manner of lantern slide binding strips.

SAFE LIGHT FOR HANDLING ORDINARY NEGATIVE FILM.

Treat one plate with filter yellow solution as above, but dye the second a deep rose in Rose Bengal solution. Bind the two up when dry, having interposed between their faces a sheet of tracing paper soaked in strong Metanile yellow solution so as to make it almost orange in colour, and subsequently dried. This will give a deep ruby coloured filter, passing considerably more light than ordinary ruby glass, and at the same time far more safe for use in dark room illumination.

SAFE LIGHT FOR USE WITH COLOUR SENSITIVE FILM.

Dye one of the fixed out plates deep violet in Methyl Violet solution. Dye the second plate orange yellow in a solution of strong mixed Filter Yellow and Metanile Yellow. The translucent paper bound between the two plates must be stained green in Naphthol

Green dye solution. This filter when made up will be very dark, and will pass only a small quantity of light in the pure green to bluish-green part of the spectrum (technically known as little b). Though the light is very faint, it will be found to penetrate the darkness comparatively well, so that after a little while, the eye will be able to distinguish objects in the dark room more or less. Thus, this faint green glow becomes a considerable help in the admittedly difficult operations of winding and developing colour sensitive film. A brighter safe light can be made by substituting Filter Blue Green, Hoechst, for the Methyl violet wherewith to dye the one plate, but in this case the filter will have to be used with much caution, or fogging of the panchromatic film will result.

NOTE.—Even the deepest *red* filters are useless when handling panchromatic film.

SCREEN RULED COLOUR FILM FOR KINEMATOGRAPHY.

Mention has already been made of the possibility of a future type of colour kinematography utilising some such system as that now employed in the celebrated Autochrome plate for direct still colour photography. This, which is known as the 'screen plate' system, depends upon covering the base upon which the photographic emulsion is afterwards coated with a patchwork of minute areas dyed in the three primary colours. Exposure is made through the back of the film or plate, and the resulting patchwork colour record 'reversed' in a chemical reversing bath instead of being fixed in the ordinary way. The Lumiere autochrome process utilises dyed starch grains for the purpose, but other kindred screen plate systems rule minute microscopical or crossed lines of clear primary colour on the glass or celluloid emulsion base.

The present difficulties in the way of adapting screen plate systems to the motion picture record are several in number. For one thing, there is the trouble of obtaining sufficiently rapid exposures even in the brightest light. Then the amount of light absorbed by the coloured film base on projection is very great. Also, where magnification is high, a spotty effect may be produced on the projection screen.

Still for all its present drawbacks, both in manufacture troubles, expense, and difficulty of working, there is at least a sporting chance for the future of the screen-ruled motion picture film.

CHAPTER III.

THE KINEMATOGRAPH CAMERA ABROAD.

So great a part of kinematography now deals with the production of films of foreign scenes and customs that no text book on moving pictures could be looked upon as complete without mention being made of this branch of the art. It is to be hoped the following hints on the exposing of film abroad will be of use to at least some of our readers.

First and foremost, when touring in foreign lands with the moving picture camera, one must know just what kit is necessary for the work and just how it may be carried from place to place with the minimum amount of trouble, expense, and anxiety. Needless to say, the camera, tripod and spool boxes are always necessities, as is also an adequate stock of perforated negative film to last through the trip, or so much of it as may elapse before the opportunity arises of replenishing the supply. But with regard to the carriage of developing kit there are two courses open to the photographer. Either he may re-box his exposed film and send it home for development, or he may carry portable developing kit with him and do the work himself while on tour.

The first of the two expedients is not only by far the most simple, but will obviously be the one to commend itself in every way where possible. Where exposed film is sent home undeveloped one simply has to save the original tin and wrappings of the film stock and repack after the day's work, using for the purpose of obtaining the necessary red light a small portable dark room lamp, such as are sold by the hundred at all photographic supply shops.

Loading and unloading film stock in and out of spool boxes in hotels or other houses where there is no regular darkroom available is done at night. When it is dark draw down the window blind closely as a further precaution. If the room is then so free from stray light beams such as moonlight, the reflection from street lamps, etc., that one cannot see one's hand before one's face, the portable ruby lamp may be lit and the work of loading, unloading and repacking of films for shipment home proceeded with. Often, however, no mere drawing of a window blind in a hotel bedroom will give the necessary pitchiness to the apartment's interior. It then becomes essential to drape the bedclothes, carpet, or whatever material may be handy, over the curtain rods, or tack it up against the window apertures until a real ' dark room ' has been manufactured.

Having got the exposed film safely reboxed in its tin cases, and the edge of the tins sealed round by means of the usual adhesive tape, the repacking is completed by affixing to the top of each tin a label bearing the following data :

> Title of subject taken.
> Length.
> Stop used.
> State of Light.
> Suggestions for development.
> Special remarks.

The package in which tins of exposed film stock are put up for sending home should have attached to its exterior a label printed in the language of the country and plainly declaring the nature of the contents ' Exposed kinematograph films (undeveloped). Sensitive to light.' It is well to add the following : ' To customs officers. Examine only by ruby light, or the contents of this package will be spoiled.'

If such labels are duly placed on the packages, all that is possible will have been done to save the films from ruin through over-assiduity of foreign customs officials.

Many kinematographers who adopt the system of sending home exposed film stock for development take with them besides the ruby lamp a small supply of photographic developing and fixing solution and an ordinary quarter-plate developing dish. With these simple additions to the travelling kit one can develop test slips off the ends of exposed stock before sending home. Thus, one can satisfy oneself from time to time that all is well with camera, film, etc. In short, one knows pretty well from such test developments how the bulk of the film may be expected to turn out at home.

This, then, is the simple way of getting over the development difficulty where such a way is applicable. Unfortunately, there are numerous occasions which confront the kinematographer in foreign lands where the method cannot be resorted to. For instance, many of the most interesting travel films are secured under such climatic conditions as to render it impossible to retain the undeveloped film in good condition sufficiently long for despatch home. Sometimes one may contrive matters by hermetically sealing the tins in which exposed stock is returned. M. Andre Barlatier, the well-known kinematographer for Messrs. Raleigh and Roberts, also the Eclipse Company, says in this connection that it is an impossibility to return exposed and undeveloped film stock from India in good condition, unless such is absolutely hermetically sealed in tins as soon as used. Needless to add, the tins in which the unexposed film is taken out must also be closed with an airtight seal. Film kept in India in unsealed tins is generally useless in about fifteen days, says this authority.

Another operator having great experience of work in India, Mr. McKenzie, of Kineto and the Natural Colour Kinematograph Company, makes no attempt to preserve exposed film stock in its undeveloped state. Here, then, we come to the second alternative in actual operation. Mr. McKenzie on his last Indian tour took with him a self-contained developing plant, including hundred foot folding pin frames for development, developing, washing, and fixing tanks, made of waterproofed wood and nested for convenience in carrying, and last but not least, a folding drying drum. The latter instrument was, by all accounts, particularly cleverly constructed. The light wooden lathes of which it was made took apart and folded up in a bundle for purposes of transit. Of course, with complete portable developing kit one is confronted with the necessity of carrying a correspondingly weighty and bulky amount of chemicals. At the same time, the writer is informed the system of nesting the chemical troughs and providing a collapsible drying drum, as above referred to, allowed of the whole developing kit being loaded on to the shoulders of a couple of Indian coolies and by them carried in comparative comfort.

Where film is thus developed abroad, especially where the water supply is not good, it will often be found impracticable to give it more than a very superficial washing after fixation. In fact, in very hot climates thorough washing would be impossible without recourse to ice cooling of the washing water or the intermediary use of a hardening bath. Otherwise the gelatine would melt and leave its celluloid base entirely. Practically therefore, the way generally adopted is to give the fixed film a good ten minutes' rinse in three or four troughs full of clean cooled water, then to dry it at once on the wheel and despatch home for further thorough washing prior to printing.

Developing, washing and fixing baths should be iced down to 70 F. or thereabout before the film is immersed in them. Otherwise, the subjects run a big risk of being spoiled.

Where, in the tropics, it is decided to harden film prior to fixation, the formalin bath, as given in Part I., should be used. It must not, however, be employed till after development and subsequent washing of the film, or fog will result. A better way would be to employ a fixing bath containing alum or chrome alum and plunge the developed film straight into it. Such an alum fixing bath would harden the film at the same time, and so tend to prevent solution of the gelatine due to subsequent too warm a temperature of the washing water.

M. Barlatier has found that working in Southern India, where it is not uncommon for the temperature to go up as high as 120 F. in the shade, a reaction will sometimes set in between the emulsion and base of the dry unexposed film stock. This causes the emulsion to become brittle and shale off in flakes from the celluloid as it passes through the gate of the kinematograph camera. For such a state of things as this there would seem to be no possible remedy.

Mr. George Albert Smith, the inventor of Kinemacolor, informs the writer of a very ingenious dodge of his for preserving exposed and unexposed Kinemacolor stock in good condition during its voyage on shipboard to and from a foreign country. The same dodge would undoubtedly be applicable to any other film stock. It is simply to tip the head steward on board the ship to store the tins containing the stock in the ship's ice safe, or refrigerating room if there is one. Under such circumstances film keeps in prime condition. On account of its extreme simplicity the tip is well worth remembering by those going abroad on kinematographing expeditions.

FIG. 225. ENCHANTING THE NIGGERS.

CHAPTER IV.

THE STILL SLIDE.

Although the bulk of projection in the modern cinema theatre consists in showing moving pictures, yet there is a certain amount of still projection which gives relief to the eyes and variety to the program.

Still slides shown in the electric theatre consist of titles photographic and non-photographic, illustrated song slides, and topical slides illustrating local events.

TITLE SLIDES (NON-PHOTOGRAPHIC).

The usual hurriedly prepared title or announcement showing on the projection screen in thin, somewhat ragged lines upon a black, or reddish ground, is made thus :

A photographic lantern plate of the 'slow' or 'gaslight' variety is withdrawn from its box without any precautions against light fogging, since it is not going to be employed in its photographic capacity. A needle is stuck through a cork so that only about quarter of an inch of its point projects. With this needle held almost vertical the necessary wording is scratched upon the emulsion side of the lantern plate.

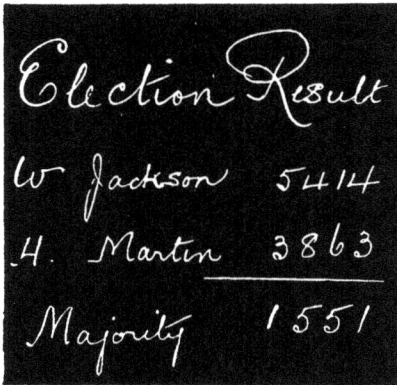

FIG. 226. A TYPICAL 'SCRATCHED IN' ANNOUNCEMENT SLIDE.

The above procedure, though producing slides of a distinctly home-made appearance, has the merit of being within the reach of operators possessing neither photographic nor artistic skill. At the same time, where the producer is more or less of a draughtsman, the following way of making announcement slides will be found far preferable.

METHOD 2.—In this case, start with a plain piece of glass of the regulation size ($3\frac{1}{4}$ by $3\frac{1}{4}$ inches). The materials required for putting on to it the announcement consist of a good medium sized camel hair or sable brush and a bottle of 'photographic stopping out medium.' The Vanguard Company's 'Photopake' is a very good medium for such work.

Apply it by means of the brush and it will be easy thus to produce the necessary wording upon the glass in dead black opaque characters. When the announcement is painted and dry back it with a piece of tinted glass—red, green, or blue—such as is obtainable at any glazier's, and bind the two together around the edge by means of binding strips, after the manner of an ordinary lantern slide.

PHOTOGRAPHIC TITLES.

The title slide used for projection purposes is in this case a photograph from an original, which original may take the form of a title card neatly printed in black on white at the nearest printer's. If the projected title or announcement is also to show black on a white or tinted ground, then the procedure is to photograph it in the ordinary way and proceed to print a positive lantern plate off the resulting negative, also by means of photography. If, on the other hand, the title or announcement is to have white letters on a black background start from the ordinary black or white printed original just the same, but use the negative itself for projection. Often such a negative as photographed direct from a printed title card will show inordinate weakness of contrast between what should be the white and the black parts. In that case, it should be intensified by means of the copper-silver intensifier after fixing and washing.

TOPICAL SLIDES OF LOCAL EVENTS.

The making of these is by no means difficult, nor does it call for any great skill in photography. Also, the first attempts on the part of the operator to master the rudiments of the art can be made best and cheapest upon the production of topical lantern slides. If successful, these same attempts may then prove the thin end of the wedge towards mastering the much more difficult management of the motion picture camera.

The apparatus required to start snap-shotting consists, first of all, of a small quarter-plate hand camera. Such may be bought for anything from about 5s. upwards. Besides this, we shall require the following sundries: Packet of quarter plates, (ordinary brand), packet lantern plates, developing dish, printing frame, dark room light, photographic measure, jug of water for washing, one bottle (or packet) developer, one pound 'hypo' for fixing. The whole of the above will cost about another 5s. Thus, 10s. is the amount which must be speculated if we are to try our hands at topical still view work.

TAKING THE NEGATIVE.—Having loaded the camera with negative plates, which loading must be done only by the light of the dark room lamp, it is taken out into the open, the lens pointed at the object to be photographed, and the knob controlling the shutter pressed. Provided the light is good at the time (sunlight), and that the camera is held steady, a photographic record should be made on the foremost plate in the camera's magazine. This plate will, however, require to be developed to make the record visible. Take the camera back to the darkroom, remove the exposed plate, place it in the developing dish and flow on the developer. After a short while the invisible 'latent' image will come out. Fixing and washing complete the photographic operations.

MAKING THE LANTERN SLIDE.

After the negative has dried by itself (which will take about eight to twelve hours), place it in the printing frame in the dark room and put behind it one of the lantern plates out of its box. Expose the two in contact to light according to directions supplied with the lantern plates, and develop the latter in the same way as the negative was developed. When the lantern plate is dry it has a mask placed over the edges and parts which are not required to show on projection. This mask takes the form of a piece of black paper, with a hole either circular, oblong, or lozenge-shaped in it. The slide is spotted upon this mask, and finally a plain piece of glass, known as a cover glass and of the same size as the lantern plate, is bound over the emulsion side in the well-known manner by means of gummed paper strips stuck round the edge. More detailed instructions in the making of lantern slides by photography may be found in any beginner's handbook of the still picture camera. Those capable of using their own judgment and of adapting methods to their needs, will also find all they want—only given in its relation to motion picture making—in the first part of this volume.

SPOTTING LANTERN SLIDES.

This matter, although very trifling from the point of view of trouble involved in carrying it out, is of absolute importance to the exhibition of all still view slides, whether announcements, title, or otherwise. The word 'spotting' means in this case the actual provision of a white paper spot or patch which must be stuck inside the cover glass or on the mask before binding the slide up. This spot must be so placed as to be visible on one side of the slide only, and in such a position that when the slide is in its carrier with the white spot in the bottom left hand corner on the side away from the screen, projection will be right way round and right way up.

Where the spotting of a lantern slide is omitted, there is always even with the best operators an element of uncertainty as to the projection being correct as regards way up and way round.

FORMULA OF THE COPPER BROMIDE (Copper-silver) INTENSIFYING BATH.—This bath was mentioned earlier in the chapter as the one for increasing contrast in black and white titles. Its formula is here appended.

SOLUTION I.		
Copper sulphate ...	100 grains
Potassium bromide	100 grains.
Hot water	2 oz.

Dissolve the chemicals separately each in half the water, mix, and allow to cool.   Then bathe the negative in the mixture till it is bleached white.   Wash quickly and transfer to

SOLUTION 2.   Silver nitrate   ...   45 grains.
                     Distilled water   ...   1 oz.

In this second solution, the original black parts of the negative should darken again and become very dense, while where the veil over the clearer parts was not pronounced, it will lift completely away
    Wash well and dry.

ILLUSTRATED SONG SLIDES.

Most of these are supplied ready made and coloured by the various firms dealing in picture and variety show music.   At the same time, there may be occasions where a local effect introduced here and there will add greatly to the point of a song.   A certain song now being issued, with slides for the picture theatre has a refrain introducing the catch words ' Beautiful Devonshire.'   Obviously, when singing this in another county the name of that county would have to be substituted.   But if also a slide of some local scene were introduced upon the screen from time to time, interspersed with the regular illustrated slides, the local colour would undoubtedly become far more convincing.   For such local scenic lantern slides the nearest professional photographer may be found a satisfactory source of supply, or where the operator is handy at snap-shotting he can turn out the necessary for himself.   In the case of utilising posed figures to heighten the effect of the song the matter becomes considerably more intricate. Not only shall we have to find suitable models for the work, but also we must evolve pleasing poses wherein to arrange them.   This is by no means an easy matter, though where the best is to be made of a fair to medium model one can often gain a considerable advantage from what is known as front lighting.   By this is meant not that the light is arranged to strike towards the front of the model from behind the camera, but that the light source is itself in front of the lens.   In such a case the faces of those posing before the camera will be more or less in complete shadow, while in the case of female models very pretty effects of light playing through the hair may be obtained, and these often go a long way towards success in the general impression left upon the audience.

Song slides are usually coloured, this being invariably done by hand.   For colouring them solutions of the aniline dyes are used, and these are applied by means of ordinary paint brushes.   Where the surface of the gelatine of the finished lantern slide shows a tendency to repel the dye or to absorb it unevenly a drop or two of prepared ox gall, obtainable from the artists' colourman, will put things right.

Keep the first washes of dye well on the light side, also select good large areas for their application.   Sea, sky, banks of foliage and such like should first be coloured lightly.   After this, more concentrated colour is applied to the smaller objects in order of their brightness. Where very brilliant flowers, jewels, or other small and gaudily tinted things come into the view they may be touched up with transparent oil colour, obtainable from the larger dealers in artists' materials, and selected especially for the purpose in hand. Needless to say, no oil colour should be applied to the gelatine till after it has got bone dry again following the application of any watery dye previously used for tinting.

DISSOLVING VIEWS.

Song slides undoubtedly gain much from being shown as dissolving views. Dissolving view work necessitates the installation in the operating box of a special ' biunal optical lantern.' This is quite distinct from the moving picture projector. In fact, with such a biunal lantern installed in the box the usual shift-over lantern slide showing attachment of the projector is not needed.

A biunal lantern consists of two still view projection lanterns mounted one over the other with their lenses so tilted on their axes that the projection discs cast by each superpose on the lantern screen. The light sources (two in number, one for each optical system of the biunal) are so arranged that turning on illumination in one lantern simultaneously (or nearly simultaneously) turns it off from the other. In the case of limelight biunals this effect is gained by the turning of oxygen into one mixed jet and off from the other, while with electric biunals it is best to leave both the actual light sources on all the while and operate the dissolving effect through the interposition of iris diaphragms fitted on either objective, and so connected that the opening of one iris closes the other.

To dissolve one view into the next by means of the biunal lantern place the two slides in position in front of the two condensers in their respective carriers. Show the first one. Then at the moment for change turn off the light beam from the one showing, and turn on the other. Such is the operation of working the dissolving view lantern in its simplest form. As an outcome of this same system, and by means of careful centring of the projected discs of light, coupled with equally careful centring of the slides in special wooden holders, it is moreover possible to conjure into effect the many startling optical metamorphoses common in the old-fashioned still view displays of the better sort. For instance, a certain cathedral is shown on the screen. While the audience watches the windows become lighted up from within, etc. Triple lanterns consisting of a combination of the biunal with yet a third optical system have, in the past, also had their vogue, the advantage with them being the possibility of still more daring optical metamorphoses than those of the sort before mentioned.

A very good way of showing song slides in the single lantern with partial dissolving (or rather curtain) effect, is by means of what is known as the Davenport carrier. With this carrier a curtain rolling up and down covers the face of each slide at the moment when it is being changed for another, the whole idea being very like the covering of the kinematograph film picture during picture change. The only drawback—if it can be called such—to the use of the Davenport carrier is that, in common with the exhibition of dissolving views, it necessitates a separate (in this latter case, single) announcement lantern being installed, apart from the projector. As a matter of fact, however, the push-over movement of the projector for lantern slide showing is only at best a makeshift. It is far preferable, whether forced to or not, to run announcements and song slides in a lantern of their own.

FIG. 227.—A QUICK VISIT TO THE SCENE OF A UNIQUE TOPICAL.

CHAPTER V.

THE MANAGEMENT OF A PICTURE THEATRE.

Although somewhat outside the province of a Handbook on Kine matography, it is necessary, as this book will be used and referred to by every section of the trade, and by those desiring to enter it, that a brief chapter should be devoted to this important part of the profession.

The keen competition among the numerous halls in every part of the country makes it incumbent for the management to be entrusted to a man who possesses not only a thorough knowledge of the technical side of picture theatre management, but one who can realise and tactfully judge the desires and requirements of the inhabitants of his neighbourhood. He must be a capable organiser, a strict disciplinarian, able and willing to make himself popular with every section of his patrons, and above all, must judiciously economise so that the proprietor of the show, or its shareholders, can reap return for their invested capital.

FIG. 228. A HANDSOME ENTRANCE HALL.

It is the intention of the writer of this chapter, therefore, to deal particularly with the qualities necessary of the successful showman, and the way for him to go about his most important duties. The successful picture theatre manager will be *showman* in many senses, not only for showing the advantages of his picture programs, but in emphasising the comfort, cleanliness and beauty of his hall. He will further be *showman* of his own personality and ability; *showman* in catering for the continual education and amusement of regular and chance patrons; and *showman* in judicious advertising and skill in inducing people to visit the establishment under his charge.

And now for the particular functions of which he should have complete control

The Building.

We take it he comes on the scene when the actual hall is erected and furnished suitably for the class of public who inhabit that particular district.

The opening, with the usual " send off," has to be arranged. It is wise to obtain the assistance of a popular individual—the mayor or local member of parliament—to perform the opening ceremony, assisted by subordinate magnates and big-wigs. This not only gives the local papers a chance of making much of the event in their columns, but binds the hall up with other social affairs, and proves one of the best advertising wheezes that can be adopted. It is up to the manager to " pull the strings " and induce the right man to take on the job. He seldom pleads in vain if he argues that a strong feature will be a clean and healthy entertainment, good class films, and—wise man—that the proceeds of the day will be entirely devoted to a local charity in which the opener is particularly interested. Having obtained his opener, he sends a well-printed and high-class looking invitation card " requesting the honour of the company of Lord and Lady——(or other notabilities) to support ' T. B. Windbag, Esq., M.P.,' on the occasion of the opening of the Grand Electric Empire, etc., etc.," not forgetting the " R.S.V.P.," so that he can invite others if there is a deficiency in the number of replies. Having been successful in this direction, the next step is to have everything complete and ready for the momentous event. Now this is where the manager must shine. He must hustle the various workmen and yet see that no portion of their work is stinted or badly finished, but in this hustling he must look well ahead, clearing everything at least a day before the opening, for he will find many little details needing attention at the last moment.

We take it that the building is all he desires ; it complies with the necessities of the local council, the Cinematograph Act and the police requirements. It possesses an excellent lobby and waiting rooms, the rake of the floor has been judiciously arranged at the approved slope of one in ten, and the walls are ready for the final decoration.

It is here that artistic taste is necessary so that there is a general appropriateness in the embellishment right through the building. The first consideration is the lobby, which has to be depended upon to create the best impression in the minds of patrons. A dingy lobby betokens in the thoughts of many a dingy entertainment. How often the mistake is made that all the public expect for outside appearance is a blaze of light. The wise picture theatre manager knows this is far from the case, and will see that the embellishments and adornments are neither garish nor glaring.

Nothing short of eighteen feet should be devoted to the lobby. Nor is this waste space, for it enables an advertising display to be made to advantage, and the passer-by who stops to read the program boards or day bill is well against the pay box before he or she realises that their curiosity has already got him or her almost inside the theatre.

The floor should be of tile or cement, and care must be taken to see that it is swept and washed at least once, if not twice a day. Greater variety of material is permitted in walls and ceiling. As a general thing, plaster casting is to be preferred to imitation marble ; and if tastefully done, finished in white and gold, and kept always fresh by the plentiful use of white paint and gold foil as required, such plaster casting will have a very good effect indeed.

The lighting should be brilliant, but not dazzling, and plants and shrubs—which should be carefully tended and watered, and full of life—not faded and dead, to convey the impression that the show is also half-dead—should be placed in suitable positions out of the way of the traffic.

The many excellent frames, easels, and advertising devices put on the market by such firms as the Tress Company, the Tyler Apparatus Company, Walturdaw Company, and many others, make it possible for the manager to give an interesting and attractive display in an unobtrusive fashion. The gaudy, bloodthirsty posters issued by some of the Continental and American makers are to be avoided in the better-class neighbourhoods, and the manager must see that his announcements are not an exaggeration of his program, or disappointment will invariably "kill off" those who might become regular patrons.

The pay box—that important feature of the lobby—like the announcements, must not be too obtrusive. People must be attracted inside the lobby and incidentally pay their entrance money before they know they are off the pavement. At this latter and most important department, the manager must adopt a careful system of money taking, and when adopted, see that it is carried out in every detail. If a ticket-issuing machine is used, it must be frequently examined and checked, and the manager should constantly pop in and see that his instructions are being minutely carried out. The weekly statement sheets published at the offices of the KINEMATOGRAPH WEEKLY give a comprehensive scheme of account adjustment, and if used in combination with the Harper Ticket Issuing and Recording Machine, or some other suitable check issuer, they make this part of the manager's task easy—if only he religiously adheres to the work of attending to them at a fixed time each morning.

In too many of the theatres, spectators are treated to currents of cold air falling on their shoulders and making them so uncomfortable as to discourage them from returning. A waiting room, however, obviates this, and it should be adjoining the lobby. Also with the present system of continuous performance and of allowing anyone to enter or leave the auditorium while the picture is on the screen, many devotees deeply interested in a scene have either to move to allow someone to pass in front of them, or to have some newcomer masking the view while looking for a seat. A waiting or ante-room again proves a genuine remedy to this drawback, as the ushers would allow no one either to enter or leave the auditorium while a picture is on the screen.

And now, having passed through the entrance and waiting room, we enter

THE AUDITORIUM.

The brilliancy of the outside and lobby here gives way to a somewhat dark and sombre interior. But even though in many existing halls the colouring of the walls and upholstery may be rather grave, perhaps almost to depression, there is no reason why the hall should not be suitably and artistically decorated, so that when the lights are up the audience are impressed with their surroundings.

In a light coloured theatre, the light of the machine naturally reflects on the cream coloured walls, and from them back on the curtain, and many exhibitors not acquainted with this fact blame the operator for a bad light. An experienced operator may suggest some colour effects that would suit a particular house better than our present general suggestions, but at least we can say avoid glaring contrasts of colours and vivid hues, and kill the man who wants to put a couple of pounds of gold leaf on the walls. Light greens, blues or pinks, with a deeper tint in the shadow, would work well, as will a French grey worked up with a very little white. Two shades of the same colour are to be preferred to contrasting colours, but the great requirement for a moving picture theatre is that the paint shall be flat. It is not enough that it is said by the makers to be flat. If there is the slightest gloss it will cause cross reflections. Have the walls sand-papered.

A light tint that will economise lighting current and an 8 c.p. lamp will be as effective as your 16 c.p. in an auditorium done in deep red or brown. In some cases, tinted globes to match the colour scheme will be striking, and for present purposes the tinting had better be done at home. If you are careful not to get the colour on too thick the diminution of light will not be excessive. You can obtain electric lamp globe lacquering solution of almost any colour. In most cases, the solution should be used far thinner than the directions indicate, since you merely wish to tint your light, not to use the lamps for direct display.

A good plan for a dark colour scheme is to have the panels in a rich red border, with a border of a still darker shade, and have all the plastic ornaments painted imitation walnut or mahogany. You will then have one of the richest interiors that you can wish. When you use green for your colours and borders, you can have the plastic ornaments in either walnut or ebony colour. With brown coloured walls, the plastic ornaments may well be imitation old gold or old oxidised silver ; this combination would produce a rich and tasteful interior.

For floor covering, it is becoming increasingly universal to use a good carpeting instead of linoleum. There is something in the feel of a velvet pile that sub-consciously suggests and conveys the impression of luxury. It is hard to keep clean on muddy days, but it is worth the care, and if you can afford it, it will pay. If carpet is too expensive for the character of the house, use linoleum in solid colours for the aisles, and have the rest of the floor of bare hardwood, well waxed, but not to the point of slipperiness. Keeping the floor clean will then be a comparatively easy matter.

THE SEATING AND FITTINGS.

There is only one form of seating that is worthy of consideration, and that is the tip-up ; but there are tip-ups and tip-ups ! The market has been flooded with a kind of gaspipe arrangement which sells at four shillings, but beware of these and go to a reputable firm who will supply seats which will stand the wear and tear, and you will gain in the end. Among the many firms specialising in suitable seating are Messrs. J. S. Lyon and Company, Lazarus and Company, Hampton and Company, Maple and Company, Whiting and Bosisto, the Premier Seating and Electrical Company, City Wholesale Cabinet Works, Duffield and Company, A. R. Dean, Ltd., etc., etc.

It is well to have a centre, as well as two side aisles where floor area permits. The sides can be used for entrance and the centre for exits. Give as much space as possible between the rows of seats, from 2ft. 6in. to 3ft. is a fair distance. The number of seats in a row is, of course, dependent on the width of the hall.

The upholstery should be in keeping with the other decorations, and a point should be made of having the seats and hangings carefully brushed each morning before the hall is swept out.

HEATING AND VENTILATION.

These are two important points which many a manager overlooks. If hot water pipes—the acme of perfect heating—are too expensive. an excellent substitute will be found in the gas steam radiators now so much in evidence at our places of amusement. They have the preliminary advantage of a good reputation, being much in use and very effective in their results. A big mistake is made in having the hall too hot. People get sleepy and languid, lose interest in the pictures and refuse to budge. You don't want them to occupy a comfortable seat for the whole evening, and you don't wish them to say the pictures (for it is always the pictures which get the blame) gave them a fearful headache.

With regard to ventilation, too, many a manager thinks that by creating a draught with a fan he is ventilating the hall, but he is really only stirring up dust and other trouble. The best plan is to go to a firm specialising in ventilation and let them handle the problem in a systematic and professional manner. Such firms as the British Westinghouse Company, the Sturtevant Engineering Company, the General Electric Company, etc., specialise in ventilation systems for buildings.   Now we have the hall, the lobby and fittings, the seating, ventilation, heating, and naturally the next item of importance is

The Screen and Proscenium.

Time and again have we been asked to advise as to the best material for the former important fitting of the hall, and, of course, we have been solicited to give an opinion on patented screens, which would be difficult to touch upon in this work.   No screen at all is wanted if you have a good, solid even wall, properly treated and kept clean, but if you do have a screen, mind you get one of even texture, and see that it is hung tautly.   Many firms specialise in screens, including the Tyler Apparatus Company, the Walturdaw Company, Bulman and Partners, New Things, Ltd., Wilmot, Barnard and Company, etc.

A screen, however, which is in front of the people all the time must be something more than the bare white material on which the films are to be presented.   It should have an ornamental and artistic bordering or curtain, with a row of plants at the foot, or grouped artistically at each side.   The best plan is to fix upon the amount you can spend on plants for this and the lobby, and let the local florists tell you the best they can provide at this figure.   Of course, if you can get them to do it in exchange for an advertisement in your program or notices, saying " the Plants and Floral Decorations are provided by——" so much the better.

It is incumbent on the manager to get the best terms on his fire policies, and to do this he should instal some of the approved automatic fire sprinklers, hand grenades and fire buckets.   Not only does he effect economy on his insurance by so doing, but the public are impressed by the precautions taken on their behalf.

Disinfecting the Theatre

Another feature which must not be lost sight of is the thorough daily sweeping and cleansing of the theatre and its fittings.   Very much depends on this, and also upon the use of disinfectants.   For removing dust, nothing is better than one of the forms of vacuum cleaner now on the market.   Then, too, there are patent circular brush brooms, as instance the " Bissell," and many others.

With regard to disinfectants, do not allow the use of strong smelling, over-advertised materials, but use those which are really capable of killing the bacteria and obnoxious putrefactive organisms always deposited where people most do congregate.

The frequent spraying, too, of some of the scented disinfecting essences not only helps in purifying the air, but the audience prefers the flavour to the moist, perspiring odour only too frequently found in our theatres.   Among the devices for spraying may be mentioned the vaporizer of the Tyler Apparatus Company.   Some excellent essences are manufactured for the purpose by F. J. Hyam, of Finsbury Pavement.

How to Advertise.

Our remarks here must, of necessity, be of a limited nature, for the field of possibilities can only be covered by an entire work on the subject. The tactful and economic manager may be content with a brilliant front and his personality to assist in making regular friends and patrons of those who may be attracted inside by the exterior show. But more than this is needed now that competition is so keen, and halls are continually opened within a stone's throw of each other. Local advertising is always more or less of a gamble, and before advertising in the local press, posting the hoardings, or putting out sandwich men, the wise manager will weigh up every argument for and against each means of making his theatre known, and only indulge in those likely to bring results to the box office. If he is advertising in the local press, he should get all the news pars, puffs and write-ups it is possible to obtain ; if posting bills on the hoardings, he should not be content with the billposters' display, but see that only the best positions are utilised for his announcements and if sandwich men are employed, give them definite stations to be found at—not too near the public houses, for unless looked after carefully, more than half the time of these individuals will be spent at the bar.

One suggestion we make which, as the result of practical experience should be of value to those managers who have not adopted it. This is, that every now and then, say once a month, an exceptional film subject should be boomed as a special attraction. No matter who supplies the film service, or on what basis it is arranged, some presumably rather extraordinary film of the startling kind now so often announced in the Kinematograph Weekly should be made much of, and it should be presented with special music and effects, and featured as a star attraction. This is a fine paying advertising instrument, when carried out with proper preparations and announcement.

Another excellent method of keeping the public anxious to patronise the show is occasionally to present some sort of souvenir, which thus forms a permanent advertisement. Novelties which are shown to friends because of their ingenuity ; illustrated booklets which are taken home, and though inexpensive, are too good to throw away ; picture postcards, and many other souvenirs are sprats to capture shoals of mackerel, and the wise manager will ever be on the *qui vive* to discover attractions in this direction.

Programs, Sweets and Teas.

A program may cause a manager a good deal of work, but it should not only become a paying proposition but a useful advertiser if made attractive enough for the patron to take away with him. Brief synopses of the films, taken from the Kinematograph Weekly, make excellent reading, and materially help the story of the pictures, and add to the attractiveness of the program. Photographs of the actors, too, can now be obtained from the film makers, and if used in a program create a lively interest in the pictures.

The sale of chocolates and sweets is a profitable addition to the returns if properly managed, and the inducement of a cup of *good* tea leads many to visit the show who would not enter for the pictures alone.

THE STAFF AND OFFICIALS.

Great discretion should be used by the manager in engaging those who are to assist him in running the hall, and a careful and comprehensive agreement—not of too legal a nature—is essential if matters are to run smoothly.

We start first with that important, dignified and conspicuous individual, the doorman, generally a huge commanding specimen of manhood, resplendent in, say, blue and gold, who in stentorian tones announces the "special" now showing, and in grandiose manner directs his "captures" to the ticket office. A good man on the door is one of the greatest acquisitions to the hall, and his duties do not end at the entrance, for in the morning he takes his share in the cleaning up, and as the last to leave at night, it is he that sees everything is O.K. before finally locking the front door. His salary is anything from 25s. to 50s. weekly, including uniform.

The cashier or pay box attendant is generally a lady of more or less fascinating appearance and businesslike methods. She must be quick at handling the cash, on the watch for bad coins, and able to fill up the cash forms and slips at the end of each day. Her weekly wages run from 12s. 6d. to £1, and considering the many cases where she handles quite a goodly sum, her salary is not too remunerative.

Then at the door of the auditorium we run across the check taker, chucker-out, messenger and general utility man. He is also in uniform of a more subdued nature than our friend, the doorman, however. He must be courteous and responsive to the many questions continually thrust at him by those entering or leaving the theatre, and 25s. is his average weekly wage.

Once inside, the seat attendants, with their electric torches, conduct us to our places, and their neat costumes and smart appearance do much to keep up the prestige of the house. They must be sufficiently attractive to be in keeping with the general style of the show, but not so attractive as to warrant flirtation with every youth who enters into conversation with them. If love making is allowed to start it seems contagious, and the manager will find all his work cut out to prevent every member of the staff giving more attention to the pastime than to the work they were engaged for.

In many halls, the attendants sell programs and sweets, and add to their 10s. or 15s. weekly wage by a commision given on their sales.

It will be seen from this chapter that the manager's job is no sinecure. He must be ever on the spot, at the beck and call of his assistants ; ever on the alert for improvements in the performance ; ever courteous to his numerous patrons, and ever in possession of a manner calculated to surmount the many difficulties which continually crop up, even in the best regulated picture show.

CHAPTER VI.

SELF-PRESERVATION IN THE TRADE.

A WORD OF WARNING.

Those who have traced the devious paths in which the kinematograph trade has trod during the past ten years must have stood aghast at the snares and pitfalls which have ever beset the honest, straightforward dealer who desired to become acquainted with a new profession. It is, therefore, but right that in such a Handbook as the present, space should be devoted to making known certain dangers to be avoided by those who seek to enter the profession.

The kinematograph trade is somewhat of a mushroom growth, and consequently during its brief existence has had many drawbacks caused by want of organisation and cohesion among its members. This has been particularly noticeable in our own country, and if one looks back to the records of 1905 it will be found the fact was already being recognised, for this year saw the first suggestion of amalgamation among kinematographers, with the object of correcting the want of solidity in the business. This took the form of a Lantern Operators' Guild, whose objects were :—(1) To see that the interests of operators were secured with regard to salary, hours and health ; (2) To determine the status of operators by a qualifying examination, and thus raise the status of this branch of the profession ; (3) To give the various branches of the trade a means of exchanging ideas and establishing a centre where trade disputes could be adjusted. But in this year the question of the operator was not the only one needing consideration, for the grievance of duplicating film subjects was much discussed, and the advocacy of registering and copyrighting films gave the manufacturers a chance of getting together to safeguard their interests. In France, which was the centre of the industry at that date, the question of co-operation was also in evidence, and a " General Cinematographical Association " was formed (1) to bind the trade closer together, (2) to hold competitions and a congress for the International Exposition of Cinematography, and (3) to form a school to grant diplomas to practical cinematographers.

About this date, Mr. R. W. Paul, who worked so hard in the initial stages of the business, threw energy into an association to preserve the rights of manufacturers, and from this was formed the Kinematograph Manufacturers' Association.

Later, we have had a Defence League to protect the showmen's interests, and a Renters' Association to bind in closer harmony the members of this important branch of the industry. But even were these organisations in working order, there are many phases of wrong doing which the unwary are likely to be the victims of unless put upon their guard. Sharks abound in all directions, and the uninitiated will find slippery places where least they are to be expected.

GRIEVANCES OF THE MANUFACTURER.

We will first deal with the manufacturer, as the most important unit. He has suffered in many ways. Bogus companies with flashy stationery, insinuating, well-dressed and plausible representatives and sumptuous offices have ordered films lavishly, have paid splendidly at first, and have obtained unlimited credit, only finally to let the manufacturer in for a big sum. The moral is that greater care should be taken to obtain regular and prompt payment, instead of allowing the accounts to drag on.

Then, again, manufacturers have sent films on approval, and in some cases allowed over a week to elapse before their return, to find that the subjects are sent back badly scratched and worn, with a letter stating that the applicant finds them unsuitable for his requirements. Here, again, there is a remedy, and that is to forward an invoice with the goods, which states in clear terms that unless returned within a certain number of *hours* (not days) the films will be treated as having been purchased.

In a measure, the law previous to the passing of the Copyright Act, 1911, was favorable to the wrong-doer, and in no case was it so evident as in that of the duplication of subjects. What was easier to a man with a knowledge of the business and the necessary apparatus than to obtain a subject which cost hundreds of pounds originally to produce and whip off duplicated copies for sale in other countries? But individuals who were guilty of this bare-faced robbery soon over-reached themselves. They obtained "on approval copies," duplicated them, and sold these "dupes" before the makers' release dates ; they were not content with selling in foreign lands, but pushed them into certain renting concerns as second-hand goods. Luckily this was discovered, and the agreement between the makers and renters and the passing of the Act, put a stop to the nefarious practice.

There are firms and individuals who sell " sole rights " to photograph topicals, and who take no precautions to keep out unauthorised photographers, or to safeguard the interests of those whose money they have accepted.

The long credit demanded and taken by the renter is disastrous to the manufacturer with small capital. Some of the larger firms have taken advantage of this fact, and they have ultimately suffered from bad debts. The system of giving long credit should at once be discontinued.

Another disadvantage the manufacturer has is in having to sell all films at 4d. per foot irrespective of the cost of production and the pretensions of the subject. It seems ridiculous that a subject which has cost a thousand pounds to produce should be sold at the same price as a scenic—for which there was necessarily no expensive preparation.

There are many other grievances from which the makers suffer, but want of space will not allow us to deal further with the subject.

Gulling the Hiring Concern.

The chief troubles experienced by those who hire films to exhibitors are those of incurring bad debts, and of having reels badly treated. With regard to the former, much of the loss is richly deserved, owing its existence to careless and lackadaisical methods of account keeping on the part of many renting houses. But not only are they in fault in bookkeeping, but price cutting and long credit are also too often used to snatch business from competitors, while, needless to say, many clients are found only too ready to take full advantage and finally to make this fatal system recoil on the heads of those who adopt it.

Bad treatment of the films is only too frequently evident to those who have occasion to see films returned after a week's hire. In all cases, it is up to the renter to loan his goods under a definite agreement, and to see that the terms of it are enforced.

The renter certainly has a grievance against many of the manufacturers and selling agents, for in many cases he is invited to see a film run through only to find on arrival at the specified time that preparations are not complete, the operator is at lunch, the film is out elsewhere on approval, or else he is kept waiting for others to turn up. Even the renter's time is money, although the manufacturers class him with the small fry, and make him wait their pleasure.

But this question of the value of time is also ignored by many a renter who breaks faith with the exhibitor by not despatching his reels to the promised time and throwing the blame on the carrier. A little more consideration is needed by both parties.

Here is a case which recently came to our notice. A certain so called but unregistered company obtained its films from a renter, and for some time all went well. But presently the company sold its picture theatre for a mere song, and still week by week the films were sent and used. After eight weeks of this state of things, the first purchaser again sold the show to another man, without telling him of the two months' arrears of film rental by now accumulated. The renters all along thought they were treating with the original owners till they suddenly learned the truth, and at the same time found they had no redress, as they could not find the individual who owned the show for the two months between the original company and the last man, while from the latter they could only recover the amount for the films he had actually used.

The loss sustained in damage to film by the carelessness of the exhibitor's employees is well known. Pieces cut out and bad joins, perforations ripped through, scratching through dirty gates, the bending or folding of the film, and many other results of rough usage can only be realised by those who go through the reels when returned from the shows. Then there is the difficulty of attaching blame for the damaged films in the proper quarter, more especially where the transfer system is in vogue. Some method is badly needed to stop this disastrous ill-use of other people's goods.

Owing to over-production, the life even of good films is a very short one, so that taking all these considerations together, the renter does not have the rosiest time in making things pan out profitably. But notwithstanding all these troubles there is now going on a reckless reduction in the charge for hire service, and each renter seems anxious to get his competitors' customers, whether the rental may be profitable or not.

How the Exhibitor Suffers.

The renter may find some small satisfaction in knowing that the showman also has his troubles, and we will now deal with a few which have come to our notice.

First, there are the unfair tactics of competitors, who issue misleading advertisements and stoop to every device to attract clients from the opposition show. Perhaps the following will better prove what we mean. When Barker's " Henry VIII." film was being boomed a certain theatre paid a big price for the rights. Next day a hall four doors from it had in tremendous letters across the front, " Henry VIII. now showing." This proved to be an old film of the Eclipse Company, and, of course, those who expected to see Sir Beerbohm Tree's Company were disappointed, and the enterprising "sole right" man suffered by the underhand business.

Many an exhibitor objects to the system of giving exclusive rights, as being adapted to squeeze his purse still further.

Then, too, the new agreement between the manufacturer and renter is causing the showman to shout. It is suggested that it gives to the renters who are on the joint committee (if they are showmen as well as renters) an unfair advantage over other showmen in towns where they themselves possess theatres, by preventing the outside showman from buying films, and compelling him to hire instead at the renters' own figure.

Obtaining Goods and Cash by Fraud.

Too frequently has our attention been called to the loss of films and apparatus which have been forwarded in response to an apparently satisfactory " want " advertisement. The advertiser will have given what reads as a genuine enough address for the goods to be sent to.

Take one case. An advertisement appears something after the style of the following :—" To be sold after Tuesday to first person sending 20s., only used two nights (here followed the title of a subject much in request, and the value of which was quite £5). Send P.O.— Jackson, Theatre Royal, Margate." Many postal orders were sent by persons anxious to secure so great a bargain, and in due time Mr.

Jackson—or whatever his name was—called at the Theatre Royal for letters, informing the door-keeper such had been "intended for the Electric Theatre, Margate." He then scooted with the contents. The same sort of game is also played the other way round, and certain second-class films, etc., are advertised for, and exceptional cash value is offered on receipt of them. The big price tempts the owner to send along his films or apparatus, but his frequent applications for cash are returned "Not known." In both cases the lesson is taught that it is unwise to part with goods or cash to an advertiser at a distance unless his *bona fides* are known to be beyond reproach.

Here's another case :—A kinematograph operator was charged on warrant with unlawfully pawning on two dates 2,000 feet of film, and a lamp, value £23 10s., the property of a picture hall proprietor. The prosecutor stated that he advertised kinematograph supplies and the prisoner had dealings with him, receiving a number of films and a projector. Witness identified two spools of films and the lamp produced at a pawnbroker's ! The prisoner's solicitor explained that his client was formerly employed as a manager of a picture theatre which was being wound up. £10 was due to him for wages, and he pawned the films, thinking he would be able to redeem them when he got his wages.

The above instances are of a painful character, but we can cite another which is even more outrageously dishonest. A well-dressed individual asked to be allowed entry to a certain hall, with the idea of renting it for a picture show. The caretaker was instructed to allow him access at all times, so that he might plan out his arrangements. Meanwhile, the applicant for the hall advertised for a manager, door-keeper, cash taker and operator. They were to apply personally on certain days and hours, and he plausibly held out possibilities that each applicant was just the man he wanted, took their addresses, and the day following their visit, each received a letter saying that he had decided to employ them, but each must deposit a certain sum (fixed according to what he thought they were worth) as security. Five of them (unbeknown to each other), glad to get so promising a job with such an excellent salary, scraped together the sums named, and after other correspondence, called at the hall, signed and took away a copy of agreement, and parted with their cash. Only after the bird had flown from his address did they learn from the caretaker that the " gent " had not really taken the hall but was considering the advisability of so doing, and although the matter was left with the police, nothing further was heard of the individual.

Then, again, there is the advertiser for " an operator with own machine and films," to give a week's show in a remote town or village. A man is out of engagement, borrows apparatus and films, pays his railway fare and goes on spec., to find at the end of his run a man of straw, unable either to continue the show, or pay his expenses.

"Dusting Down" the Investor.

How many of the directors and promotors of the hundreds of motion picture companies registered during the past three years have failed to carry out the schemes or give the results so lavishly promised in their prospectuses ? How many of these schemes have been of the wild cat order, floated solely for the purpose of obtaining from the public promoters' plunder ? For enticing reading, the prospectuses are enough to draw blood from a stone, and their far-reaching results have done much to frighten the investing public from further supporting the industry. It is to be hoped that the process of time has done much to weed out this element of danger which, till recently, beset the industry, but even yet new companies are sprung on the public by men outside the legitimate business, and channels have to be found for the watered stock.

Companies have been formed with glowing prospects, but bad management kills the profits, and finally a friend of the directors manages to buy for a mere trifle what has originally cost thousands.

The shareholder is trotted round the theatre, he sees the crowd guided up to the pay-box, and is told that every sixpence paid represents threepence profit to be used in paying dividends. The air of prosperity and the wiles of the managing director have such an effect on him that he not only buys more shares himself, but persuades his friends to do the same. Meanwhile, those in the know are busy unloading their own stock, and perhaps to make matters more favorable, a dividend is declared, which naturally gives further credence to the game. But there comes the evil day. Debentures are issued, reconstruction follows, and it's good-bye to much hard-earned wealth as far as the shareholders are concerned.

Much more in similar strain could be written in connection with kinematograph financial matters, but like the other features of this chapter, we have had to curtail our remarks on the subject as being somewhat subsidiary to the real purpose of the Handbook.

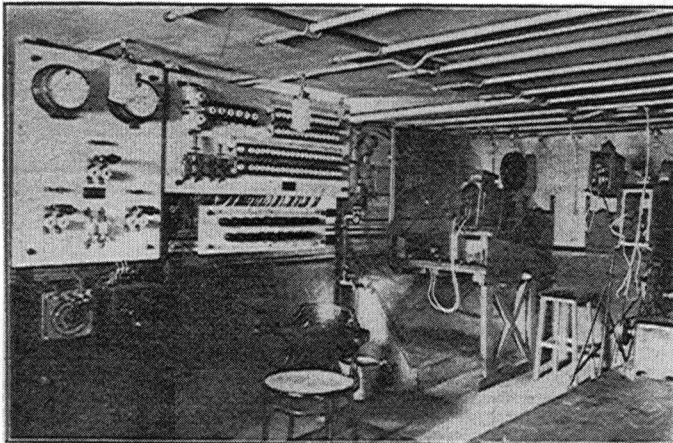

Fig. 229. A Roomy Continental Operating Box.

CHAPTER VII.

THE LAW AND THE KINEMATOGRAPH.

Until the passing of the Cinematograph Act in 1909, which came into operation January 1st, 1910, the picture showman had a fairly free hand in the conduct of his performances, but the powers which this act gave to the various councils caused very stringent regulations to be put into force, which, as circumstances and necessities have arisen, have been materially added to and altered. In the following pages we have not attempted to deal *in extenso* with the Act itself, but have condensed the most important and essential points.

WHAT IS THE CINEMATOGRAPH ACT, 1909 ?

The Act primarily is to make better provision for securing safety at kinematograph exhibitions, and first *provides against any motion picture exhibition for which inflammable films are used, elsewhere than in licensed premises*, and unless the regulations of the Secretary of State for securing safety are complied with.

It gives power to the county councils to *grant yearly licenses* for that object, and to *transfer such licenses*. The applicant for the license or transfer must give seven days' notice in writing to the county council or chief police officer. The county council may grant, or renew transfer, and may fix their charges at an amount not exceeding £1 for a year, or in the case of a grant or renewal for any less period, 5s. for every month for which it is granted.

THE PENALTIES.

The penalty if the owners use or allow to be used (or if the occupier of any premises allows to be used) the premises contrary to the provision of the Act, is a fine not exceeding £20, and in the case of continuing the offence, a further penalty of £5 each day, and the license may be revoked.

INSPECTION OF PREMISES.

The Act gives power to an officer appointed for the purpose to enter the premises at reasonable times to see that the provisions of the Act are complied with.

DELEGATION OF POWERS TO OTHER AUTHORITIES.

The council may delegate its powers to justices sitting in petty sessions.

No License for Occasional Use.

It is not necessary to obtain a license for premises used only six days in a year for a kinematograph show, but notices of such occasional shows must be given to the county council or chief police officer, and these shows must conform with the regulations.

Licensing Travelling Showmen.

Performances may be given in movable structures without a license from the council of the county in which the performance is to take place, as long as a license in respect of that building has been obtained from the council of the county in which the owner ordinarily resides, but two days' notice must be given to the council or chief police officer, and the regulations must be complied with.

The Regulations of the Secretary of State.

Thus, the Act vested the Secretary of State with powers to make and enforce regulations to provide for safety in kinematograph exhibitions. The first set of regulations was issued from the Home Office on December 20th, 1909, but these were amended and repealed on February 18th, 1910, and these latter we give *in extenso*.

General.

1. In these regulations the word " building " shall be deemed to include any booth, tent, or similar structure.

2. No building shall be used for kinematograph or other similar exhibitions to which the Act applies, unless it be provided with an adequate number of clearly indicated exits so placed and maintained as readily to afford the audience ample means of safe egress.

The seating in the building shall be so arranged as not to interfere with free access to the exits ; and the gangways and the staircases, and the passages leading to the exits shall, during the presence of the public in the building, be kept clear of obstructions.

3. The kinematograph operator and all persons responsible for or employed in or in connection with the exhibition shall take all due precautions for the prevention of accidents, and shall abstain from any act whatever which tends to cause fire and is not reasonably necessary for the purpose of the exhibition.

Fire Appliances.

4. Fire appliances adequate for the protection of the building shall be provided, and shall include at least the following, namely, a damp blanket, two buckets of water, and a bucket of dry sand. In a building used habitually for the purpose of kinematograph or other similar exhibitions they shall also include a sufficient number of hand grenades or other portable fire-extinguishers.

The fire appliances shall be so disposed that there shall be sufficient means of dealing with fire readily available for use within the enclosure. Before the commencement of each performance, the kinematograph operator shall satisfy himself that the fire appliances intended for use within the enclosure are in working order, and during the performance, such appliances shall be in the charge of some person specially nominated for that purpose who shall see that they are kept constantly available for use.

Enclosures.

Regulations applying in all cases and to all classes of buildings.

5.—(1) (*a*.) The kinematograph apparatus shall be placed in an enclosure of substantial construction made of or lined internally with fire-resisting material and of sufficient dimensions to allow the operator to work freely.

(*b.*) The entrance to the enclosure shall be suitably placed and shall be fitted with a self-closing close-fitted door constructed of fire-resisting material.

(*c.*) The openings through which the necessary pipes and cables pass into the enclosure shall be efficiently bushed.

(*d.*) The openings in the front face of the enclosure shall not be larger than is necessary for effective projection, and shall not exceed two for each lantern. Each such opening shall be fitted with a screen of fire-resisting material, which can be released both inside and outside the enclosure so that it automatically closes with a close-fitting joint.

(*e.*) The door of the enclosure and all openings, bushes and joints shall be so constructed and maintained as to prevent, so far as possible, the escape of any smoke into the auditorium. If means of ventilation are provided, they shall not be allowed to communicate direct with the auditorium.

(*f.*) If the enclosure is inside the auditorium, either a suitable barrier shall be placed round the enclosure at a distance of not less than two feet from it, or other effectual means shall be taken to prevent the public from coming into contact with the enclosure.

(*g.*) No unauthorised person shall go into the enclosure or be allowed to be within the barrier.

(*h.*) No smoking shall at any time be permitted within the barrier or enclosure.

(*i.*) No inflammable article shall unnecessarily be taken into or allowed to remain in the enclosure.

Regulations applying only to specified classes of buildings.

(2) In the case of buildings used habitually for kinematograph or other similar exhibitions, the enclosure shall be placed outside the auditorium ; and in the case of permanent buildings used habitually as aforesaid the enclosure shall also be permanent.

Provided, with regard to the foregoing requirements, that, if the licensing authority is of opinion that compliance with either or both of them is impracticable or in the circumstances unnecessary for securing safety and shall have stated such opinion by express words in the license, the requirement or requirements so specified shall not apply.

LANTERNS, PROJECTORS AND FILMS.

6. Lanterns shall be placed on firm supports constructed of fire-resisting material, and shall be provided with a metal shutter which can be readily inserted between the source of light and the film-gate.

The film-gate shall be of massive construction and shall be provided with ample heat-radiating surface. The passage for the film shall be sufficiently narrow to prevent flame travelling upwards or downwards from the light-opening.

7. Kinematograph projectors shall be fitted with two metal film-boxes of substantial construction, and not more than fourteen inches in diameter, inside measurement, and to and from these the film shall be made to travel. The film-boxes shall be made to close in such a manner, and shall be fitted with a film-slot so constructed, as to prevent the passage of flame to the interior of the box.

8. Spools shall be chain or gear driven and films shall be wound upon spools so that the wound film shall not at any time reach or project beyond the edges of the flange of the spool.

9. During the exhibition all films when not in use shall be kept in closed metal boxes.

LIGHTING.

10. Where the general lighting of the auditorium and exits can be controlled from within the enclosure, there shall be also separate and independent means of control outside and away from the enclosure.

11. No illuminant other than electric light or limelight shall be used within the lantern.

Electric Light.

12.—(*a.*) Within the enclosure the insulating material of all electric cables, including " leads " to lamps, shall be covered with fire-resisting material.

(*b.*) There shall be no unnecessary slack electric cable within the enclosure. The " leads " to the kinematograph lamp shall, unless conveyed within a metal pipe or other suitable casing, be kept well apart both within and without the enclosure, and shall run so that the course of each may be readily traced.

(*c.*) Cables for kinematograph lamps shall be taken as separate circuits from the source of supply and from the supply side of the main fuses in the general lighting circuit, and there shall be efficient switches and fuses inserted at the point where the supply is taken, and in addition, an efficient double-pole switch shall be fitted in the kinematograph lamp circuit inside the enclosure. When the kinematograph lamp is working, the pressure of the current across the terminals of the double-pole switch inside the enclosure shall not exceed 110 volts.

(*d.*) Resistances shall be made entirely of fire-resisting material, and shall be so constructed and maintained that no coil or other part shall at any time become unduly heated.* All resistances, with the exception of a resistance for regulating purposes, shall be placed outside the enclosure, and if reasonably practicable, outside the auditorium. If inside the auditorium, they shall be adequately protected by a wire guard or other efficient means of preventing accidental contact.

The operator shall satisfy himself before the commencement of each performance that all cables, leads, connections and resistances are in proper working order. The resistances, if not under constant observation, shall be inspected at least once during each performance. If any fault is detected, the current shall be immediately switched off, and shall remain switched off until the fault has been remedied.

Limelight.

13.—(*a.*) If limelight be used in the lantern, the gas cylinders shall be tested and filled in conformity with the requirements set out in the Appendix hereto. The tubing shall be of sufficient strength to resist pressure from without, and shall be properly connected up.

(*b.*) No gas shall be stored or used save in containers constructed in accordance with the requirements contained in the Appendix.

LICENSES.

14. Every license granted under the Act shall contain specific conditions for the carrying out of regulations 2 and 5 (1) (*a*), (*b*), (*c*), (*d*), (*e*), (*f*) in the building for which the license is granted, and may in accordance with the regulation 5 (2), contain an expression of opinion on the matters referred to in the proviso thereto.

15. Subject to the provisions of No. 16 of these regulations, every license granted under the Act shall contain a clause providing for its lapse, or, alternatively, by its revocation by the licensing authority, if any alteration is made in the building or the enclosure without the sanction of the said authority.

16. Where a license has been granted under the Act in respect of a moveable building, a plan and description of the building, certified with the approval of the licensing authority, shall be attached to the license. Such a license may provide that any of the conditions or restrictions contained therein may be modified either by the licensing authority or by the licensing authority of the district where an exhibition is about to be given. The license and plan and description or any of them shall be produced on demand to any police constable or to any person authorised by the licensing authority or by the authority in whose district the building is being or is about to be used for the purpose of an exhibition.

17. The regulations dated December 20th, 1909, made under the Cinematograph Act, 1909, are hereby repealed, provided, nevertheless, that any license granted prior to such repeal shall remain valid for the period for which it was granted without the imposition of any more stringent condition than may have been imposed at the time of the grant.

*e.g., they shall not become so heated that a piece of newspaper placed in contact with any part of the resistance would readily ignite.

APPENDIX.

LIMELIGHT.

The gas cylinders shall be tested and filled in conformity with the requirements set out below, which follow the recommendations of the Departmental Committee of the Home Office on the Manufacture of Compressed Gas Cylinders (C. 7952 of 1896.) :—

Cylinders of Compressed Gas (Oxygen, Hydrogen or Coal Gas.)

(a) *Lap-welded wrought iron.*—Greatest working pressure, 120 atmospheres, or 1,800 lbs. per square inch.

Stress due to working pressure not to exceed $6\frac{1}{2}$ tons per square inch.

Proof pressure in hydraulic test, after annealing, 224 atmospheres or 3,360 lbs. per square inch.

Permanent stretch in hydraulic test not to exceed 10 per cent. of the elastic stretch.

One cylinder in fifty to be subjected to a statical bending test, and to stand crushing nearly flat between two rounded knife-edges without cracking.

(b) *Lap-welded or seamless steel.*—Greatest working pressure, 120 atmospheres, or 1,800 lbs. per square inch.

Stress due to working pressure not to exceed $7\frac{1}{2}$ tons per square inch in lap-welded, or 8 tons per square inch in seamless cylinders.

Carbon in steel not to exceed 0.25 per cent. or iron to be less than 99 per cent.

Tenacity of steel not to be less than 26 or more than 33 tons per square inch. Ultimate elongation not less than 1.2 inches in 8 inches. Test bar to be cut from finished annealed cylinder.

Proof pressure in hydraulic test, after annealing, 224 atmospheres, or 3,360 lbs. per square inch.

Permanent stretch shown by water jacket not to exceed 10 per cent. of elastic stretch.

One cylinder in fifty to be subjected to a statical bending test, and to stand crushing nearly flat between rounded knife-edges without cracking.

Regulations applicable to all Cylinders.

Cylinders to be marked with a rotation number, a manufacturer's or owner's mark, an annealing mark with date, a test mark with date. The marks to be permanent and easily visible.

Testing to be repeated at least every two years, and annealing at least every four years.

A record to be kept of all tests.

Cylinders which fail in testing to be destroyed or rendered useless.

Hydrogen and coal gas cylinders to have left-handed threads for attaching connections and to be painted red.

The compressing apparatus to have two pressure gauges, and an automatic arrangement for preventing overcharging. The compressing apparatus for oxygen to be wholly distinct and unconnected with the compressing apparatus for hydrogen and coal gas.

Cylinders not to be refilled till they have been emptied.

If cylinders are sent out unpacked the valve fittings should be protected by a steel cap.

A minimum weight to be fixed for each size of cylinder in accordance with its required thickness. Cylinders of less weight to be rejected.

NON-INFLAMMABLE FILMS.

It will be seen, therefore, that where non-inflammable film is used, the Act and Regulations in no way apply; and in several cases this point has been tested, but the results have not been entirely satisfactory, as the onus of proving that the film was *in no way inflammable* was fixed on the user, who, in several instances, failed to prove conclusively to the magistrates that the film *would not burn*.

APPLICATIONS FOR LICENSES.

The following is the form used in applying for a license

ADMINISTRATIVE COUNTY OF LONDON.

CINEMATOGRAPH ACT, 1909 (9 Edw. VII., Ch. 39).

APPLICATION FOR LICENSE

....19......

(a) *Insert Christian name and surname of applicant.*

(b) *Insert place of residence.*

*(c) *State whether applicant is occupier of the premises or owner of apparatus.*

(d) *Insert letter of Police Division.*

I, the undersigned, (a)......................................

residing at (b)..

(c)..

hereby give notice that at the expiration of seven days I intend to apply for a License for a Kinematograph Exhibition to be carried on within the premises called or known as..

and situated at...

in the Metropolitan Borough of...........................

and in the Metropolitan Police District of (d)...........

The Exhibition to be held for a period of...............

commencing on...................................

....

Signature of Applicant.

To

The Clerk of the London County Council,
          County Hall,
                    Spring Gardens, S.W.

*Except in the case of an occasional license the application must be made by the occupier of the premises. Where the premises are in the occupation of a company or syndicate the application should be made by the Secretary or Manager and the address of the registered offices of the company should be stated.

NOTE.—*Notice should be given to the Commissioner of Police of the Metropolis, New Scotland Yard, S.W., or if the premises sought to be licensed are situated within the City of London, to the Commissioner of Police for the City of London, 26, Old Jewry, E.C.*

We give hereunder the form in which the license is granted :—

ADMINISTRATIVE COUNTY OF LONDON.

Cinematograph Act, 1909 (9 *Edw. VII., Ch.* 30.)

WHEREAS...

of..

has duly given the notices prescribed by sub-section 4 of section 2 of the Cinematograph Act, 1909, the London County Council, in pursuance of the provisions of section 2 of the said Act, hereby grants this Licence to the said.................

....to use the premises called or known as...................

....and situated at.............................
for the exhibition of pictures or other optical effects by means of a kinematograph
or other similar apparatus for the purposes of which inflammable films are used.
Such exhibition to be subject to the regulations of the Secretary of State for
securing safety and on the terms and conditions and under the restrictions following, viz.—

1.   That the period during which such license shall remain in force
shall be............................from the...............................day of
........................, 19..., unless previously revoked in pursuance of the
provisions of the above-mentioned Act.

2.   That the premises be not opened on Sundays, Christmas Day or
Good Friday for kinematograph entertainments.

3.   That in the event of any alteration being made in the building or
enclosure without the sanction of the Council having been first obtained
the license will be liable to be revoked by the Council.

4.   That all the exits be indicated by notices clearly painted to the
satisfaction of the Council over the doors or openings at a height of at least
6 feet nine inches above the floor.

5.   That each exit door or opening do have a distinct light fitted
over it to illuminate the exit notice, and that such light be on a different
system from the main lighting of the building, and be maintained throughout the performance.

6.   That all exitways, corridors, passages and staircases affording
means of egress from the premises be efficiently lighted by two independent
systems of lighting during the whole time the public are on the premises.

7.   That all exit doors, if fastened during the time the public are in
the building, be secured during such time by automatic bolts only of a
pattern and in a position to be approved by the Council, and do have a
notice clearly painted on them indicating the method of opening.

8.   That the management do allow the public to leave by all exit and
entrance doors, which must open outwards.

9.   That the seating be set out so that there shall be a space of at least
1 foot in depth between the front of one seat and the back of the next
measured between perpendiculars and that where chairs are used they be
battened together in lengths of not less than 4 or more than 12 chairs.

10.   That all curtains covering doors or in passages be hung on sliding
rings and so as not to trail on the ground, and be parted in the centre.

11.   That persons be not permitted to stand or sit in any of the inter-
secting gangways, and, if standing be permitted in the gangways at the
sides and rear of the seating, sufficient room be left for persons to pass
easily to and fro.

PICTURE SHOWS ON SUNDAY.

The London County Council, having been given power to enforce
these Regulations of the Secretary of State, were bold enough to take
full advantage of Clause 2 of the Act, which states that they " may
grant licenses to such persons as they think fit to use the premises
specified in the license for the purposes aforesaid *on such terms and
conditions and under such restrictions* as, subject to regulations of the
Secretary of State, the Council may by the respective licenses determine."

Sunday was one of the most profitable days the showman had,
and representations were made and much discussion took place until
finally the London County Council issued the following manifesto,
which naturally sets the precedent for other licensing bodies to follow.

LONDON COUNTY COUNCIL.

SUNDAY CINEMATOGRAPH ENTERTAINMENTS.

The Council on 11th April, 1911, considered the question of Sunday entertainments at premises licensed by it for cinematograph exhibitions, and decided that applications for permission to use premises licensed by the Council under the Cinematograph Act, 1909, for Cinematograph Entertainments on Sunday or other days prohibited by the license, be considered only when the entertainments will be given by recognised societies or organisations unconnected with the premises concerned, and only when accompanied by a copy of the agreement between the licensee and the society or organisation proposing to give the entertainments, and by a joint undertaking, signed by the licensee and by a responsible officer of the society or organisation in question, to the effect that :—

1. The entertainments will be of a healthy and elevating character, and properly conducted and not for private gain or by way of trade.

2. The name of the society or organisation giving the entertainments will be exhibited in a conspicuous position outside the premises.

3. No performance shall begin before 6 p.m., or finish later than 11 p.m.

4. The licensee or his servants will have nothing to do with the arrangements for the entertainments, (*e.g.*, the engagement of operators or employees) beyond being responsible to the Council for the observance of its regulations.

5. No person shall be employed on Sunday who has been employed in connection with the cinematograph entertainments for each of the previous six days.

6. The society or organisation will by its duly appointed representative pay to each employee his or her wages for the Sunday, and such representative shall not be the licensee or any of his employees, or any person officially connected with the licensed premises.

7. The signature of each employee will be obtained each Sunday by the duly appointed representative of the society or organisation giving the entertainments to a wages sheet containing the following particulars : names and addresses of the employees, the capacity in which each serves, the wages for the week, excluding Sunday, the agreed wages for the Sunday, and a statement that each employee works voluntarily on the Sunday and without pressure from the management and such wages sheet must be signed when completed by the representative of the society or organisation.

8. An audited balance sheet giving full details of the receipts and expenditure for each Sunday will be submitted to the Council by the representative of the society or organisation giving the entertainments at the end of each four weeks, and there shall be forwarded with the balance sheets the wages sheets referred to in condition (7).

9. The rules required to be observed on week days for securing the safety of the audience will be complied with.

10. The licensee and the heads of the society or organisation will hold themselves responsible for seeing that the undertaking given to the Council is adhered to.

In any case in which it appears from the agreement that the sum proposed to be paid for the hire of the hall is greater than is necessary to cover one-seventh of the weekly expenditure for rent, rates, taxes, etc., and the actual out-of-pocket expenses, such as cost of lighting and heating the premises, damage and depreciation to building, hire of films, etc., the application will be refused on the grounds that the proposal is inconsistent with the condition that the entertainments shall not be for private gain or by way of trade.

In order, therefore, to enable the Council to come to a decision on an application, there should be forwarded with the copy of the agreement referred to above, a statement of the annual expenditure on rent, rates and taxes, on the lighting and heating of the premises, and on any other items covered by the payment to be made for the use of the premises.

MUSIC IN PICTURE THEATRES.

Under an act of George II.—The Disorderly Houses Act—no musical entertainment can be given unless the premises have been duly licensed for that purpose.

Pictures require the enlivening influence of music to increase their attractiveness, and many showmen, on the plea that a piano or gramophone was a subsidiary part of the performance, introduced automatic musical instruments, only to find that the law quickly stepped in and prohibited their use. There is still a doubt as to the legal position, and the exhibitors who desire to keep clear of the " myrmidons of the law " would do well to save the expense of ultimate legislation, and apply to the licensing authorities for the license.

The form issued by the London County Council is as follows :—

ADMINISTRATIVE COUNTY OF LONDON.

MUSIC, MUSIC AND DANCING, AND STAGE PLAYS LICENSES.

APPLICATION FOR LICENSE.

(a) *Insert " Music " or " Music and Dancing," or" Stage Plays".*

FOR A (a)...LICENSE

...............................191

(b) *Insert Christian and Surname of applicant.*

I, the undersigned, (b)...

of (c)..

hereby give notice that I intend to apply, under the provisions of the Statutes 25 Geo. II., chap 36, or 6 and 7 Vict., chap. 68, and 51 and 52 Vict., chap. 41, to the London County Council for a License for (a)...........................

(c) *Insert place of residence.*

...........................to be carried on within the house or premises, situated at.......................................

and known as the...in

(d) *In the cases of the City of London and the City of Westminster, strike out the words "Metropolitan Borough " and insert the word " City."*

the Metropolitan Borough of (d)...............................

in the London County Council Electoral Division of.........

and in the Metropolitan Police Division (e).................

and now in my occupation ; and I further give notice that such application will be made at a meeting of the Theatres and Music Halls Committee of the said Council, to be held on or about the 11th day of November next.

(e) *Insert letter of Police Division.*

....

Signature of Applicant.

N.B.—The Council does not recognise any special agent or other intermediary in regard to applications made for licenses or the transfer of licenses. No charge is made by the Council in respect of any such application.

The license when granted, reads as follows :—

ADMINISTRATIVE COUNTY OF LONDON.

WE, THE LONDON COUNTY COUNCIL, at a Meeting holden in and for the said Administrative County of London, on the Twenty-fifth day of November, 1910, Do, by Virtue of the Power given us by the " Disorderly Houses Act, 1751 " (as amended by the " Public Entertainments Act, 1875 ") and " The Local Government Act, 1888 " HEREBY license.. (hereinafter called the " Licensee ") to keep a certain House or Place called .... in the said County for public MUSIC...to the end of the Meetings of the said Council, sitting for the purpose of granting and refusing Licenses, in the ensuing year of 1911. The Licensee to take care, as far as in h... lies, that no disorders be committed within the said House or Place, and that nothing contrary to Sobriety, Decency and Good Manners be exhibited, represented or transacted therein ; and that...he do not suffer any of the aforesaid Entertainments after midnight ; and that ...he do not open the said House or Place on the Lord's Day (commonly called Sunday), nor on Christmas Day, Good Friday, nor on any day of Solemn Fast and Humiliation which now is or hereafter shall be by lawful authority appointed ; and ...he do in all things conduct the said House or Place decently, soberly, and orderly, according to the true Intent and Meaning of this License, and of the said Acts of Parliament. PROVIDED NEVERTHELESS that the Licensee, in order to give public Notice that the Said House or Place is so licensed as aforesaid, Do affix and keep up in some Notorious Place over the Door or Entrance thereof, an Inscription in Large Capital Letters in the words following :—" LICENSED PURSUANT TO ACT OF PARLIAMENT OF THE TWENTY-FIFTH OF KING GEORGE THE SECOND." AND provided LIKEWISE that the said House or Place so licensed as aforesaid shall not be opened for any of the said purposes on any Day whatever, before the hour of noon.

GIVEN under the Seal of the said Council at the said Meeting on the said Twenty-fifth Day of November, 1910.

....
Clerk of the Council.

By the Second Section of the " Disorderly Houses Act, 1751," it is directed that no Fee or Reward shall be taken for this License.

This License shall remain in force from its date to the end of the Meetings of the London County Council, sitting for the purpose of granting and refusing Licenses, in the next ensuing year of 1911.

Subject to the undertaking which I hereby give :—

AN AGREEMENT WITH THE MANAGER.

It is always advisable for all parties concerned that proprietors should have definite and concise agreements with managers, operators, and other employees. To use a stereotyped form of agreement is unwise, as the local requirements and individual needs in each case should be dealt with by a specially drawn agreement. As some guide to the form used, we give hereunder a form used by many companies:—

MANAGER'S AGREEMENT.

AN AGREEMENT made the...............................day of....................191 between...of............................. (hereinafter called " the Company ") of the one part and............................. ....of.................................(hereinafter called " the Manager ") of the other part WHEREBY it is agreed as follows :—

1. The Company shall employ the Manager and the Manager shall serve the Company as working Manager of the Company's business carried on at ....for a period of....................calendar months from the......... day of............. and the Manager's employment may be determined on the ....day of..............next by either the Company or Manager giving to the other one calendar month's previous notice in writing. The Manager's remuneration shall be ....per week payable weekly, the first payment to be made on the.................day of..............and the Manager shall also be entitled to a bonus of Five per centum of the net profits of the business divisible as dividends earned by the said Company in each month, and such bonus shall be paid within 5 days of the end of each month and the Certificate of the Company's auditor shall be conclusive evidence of the amount of such net profits and of the proportion thereof to which the Manager is entitled. The Manager shall be entitled to a proportional part of such bonus at the termination of his employment.

2. If at any time during his employment the Manager shall be guilty of misconduct or in any way whatever pledge the credit of the Company or shall neglect to give adequate time and personal attention to the said business or shall neglect to open punctually and carry on efficiently the entertainments to be given by the Company or shall fail to maintain good order and discipline amongst the staff and to keep the premises clean and in good order or shall neglect or disobey any lawful orders or directions of the directors then the directors may determine his employment without notice and without being liable for any claim for compensation by reason of such determination.

3. The Manager shall so far as possible personally attend to the said business at all times during the usual business hours and shall also personally exhibit as far as possible all pictures and films and shall give such attention to the working of the engine and other apparatus as is consistent with the efficient projection of the pictures.

4. Subject to such orders and directions as may from time to time be given to him by the directors through their Secretary (all which orders and directions the Manager shall promptly and faithfully obey observe and comply with) the Manager shall have the general control and management of the said business, and of all persons employed in and about the same and shall use all proper means in his power to protect and further the interests of the Company PRO-VIDED THAT :—

(*a*) The Manager shall not engage any employee without the sanction of the Directors.

(*b*) No goods shall be ordered for or in the name of the said Company except upon the Company's printed order form countersigned by the Secretary and no goods shall be paid for by the Manager except such as may be authorised by the directors to be paid for out of petty cash.

5. Upon the determination from whatever cause of his employment the Manager will not at any time or for any purpose use the name of the Company or any information concerning the Company to its detriment or so as to in any way injure the business of the Company.

6. In case the Manager is prevented by illness or personal accident from performing his duties and shall furnish the directors with such evidence thereof as may be satisfactory to them he shall receive his salary in full for the first two weeks and half his salary for the two succeeding weeks during such incapacity and if he is incapacitated for longer than four weeks the directors shall have power to determine his employment and he shall not be entitled to claim any compensation from the Company in respect of such determination.

AS WITNESS, etc.

Is a License Needed for an Open-Air Show?

In the Regulations, the definition of the term "building" is given as including "a booth, tent, or similar structure," therefore we thought it advisable in the interests of the trade to take counsel's opinion as to whether the word "premises" could be made to include land in the sense of an open field. We regret to find that it does so and print below counsel's opinion to this effect.

> "In our opinion the Act is clear. A kinematograph exhibition may not (when inflammable films are used) be given elsewhere than in premises licensed for the purpose. The popular meaning of the word 'premises' includes land, and if it did not an exhibition given on unlicensed land would certainly be given 'elsewhere than in premises licensed.' The fact that the regulations framed under the Act deal wholly, or, as we should say, chiefly with buildings, cannot qualify the Act. The requirements in the case of an open air exhibition may be merely nominal, but the need for the license is not dispensed with."

THE WORKMEN'S COMPENSATION ACT.

Showmen are responsible for accidents to employees who do not receive more than £250 per annum. This does not apply to casual workers, but it would apply to a woman who was engaged to clean windows, say, every Friday, because, being employed *every* Friday, the work is not casual. Further, the Act treats certain diseases arising in the course of employment as accidents. Fortunately, a very easy, and all things considered, economical solution is at hand in the form of insurance of employees.

THE CHILDREN'S ACT, 1908.

There is only one section applying to showmen, and it is due, without doubt, to the fact that an accident happened from the faulty construction of a staircase. The section applying is 121, and is wedged into the statute. But it only applies where the majority of the audience are children, at which some, at least, reach their seats by way of a staircase, and even then the children are to exceed one hundred in number, when three attendants should be provided for each hundred.

IS LAVATORY ACCOMMODATION COMPULSORY?

Section 36 of the Public Health Act allows the local authority to require that the occupier or owner of a house which has not sufficient lavatory accommodation in the shape of water closets, shall provide such water closets. But the question is, what does the section mean by the term "house"? Section 4 defines house to include schools, factories and other buildings *in which persons are employed*. One of the best text books states "it is presumed that the term would signify any building in which persons are employed." It is quite certain that persons are employed in places of entertainment, and the proprietors are bound to supply sanitary conveniences for such persons and also for artistes whom they may employ.

SHOWMEN LIABLE FOR ACCIDENT TO PATRONS.

A showman is compelled to take every precaution for the care and safety of those visiting his show, but still accidents continue to happen. Here is a case which came recently to our notice :—A person, a woman, had been visiting a show, and upon leaving, stumbled over a step and fractured a leg. This step was in a side passage, and the passage was fairly well lighted. She stated it was not lighted at all ! She brought an action claiming £40 for injuries and £16 special damages ; four weeks at seaside, £10 ; new dress, £4 ; special nourishment, wine, beef tea, chicken, etc., £2. In all £56. Most motion picture shows are given in the dark, and the question is, under the circumstances, did the woman willingly expose herself to the risk of walking along a dark passage ? If she knew of the danger and ran into it of her own accord, she cannot recover. But this case is somewhat wider. The woman fell in a fairly well-lit passage. Moderate lighting is a wise precaution, because if too well lit, a person coming out of the show into a sudden glare cannot see at all—is really more or lese blind for a few moments. Accidents often happen from such causes. Before she could recover she must prove that the showman was negligent. If the case went for trial, the showman's possible negligence would be that he did not station an attendant at the top or near the step to call out : " Mind the step.''

HOW LONG MAY FILMS BE RETAINED ON APPROVAL.

Manufacturers of film subjects have had many abuses played upon them by unscrupulous showmen. One of the worst is obtaining films on approval, making use of them for show purposes and returning them in three or four days as not suitable for their requirements. This treatment has caused several County Court actions, and in these the general opinion has been expressed that films retained for more than twenty-four hours have been purchased. Judge Woodfall, however, stopped a case in February, 1910, brought by the Nordisk Films Company against the New Film Hiring Company, Limited. He considered the case rested on two alternative grounds : whether the film sent on the Saturday and not returned on the Monday constituted a sale, or whether there was a clear case of sale at any time. He admitted the sending back of certain films was in the plaintiff's favour, but as the managers of the defendant company had both denied buying, he must assume the other alternative, viz., the acceptance by the time the film was kept. To that His Honour contended no evidence had been given to prove that such a custom prevailed, and that *the twenty-four hours' approval limit was not binding without an individual contract being entered into* and was honoured as much in the breach as in observance.

DOES A PICTURE SHOW CONSTITUTE A FACTORY?

Several summonses have been taken against showmen under the Factory and Workshops Act. In one case at Burnley, a visitor entered the room where the proprietors generate their own electric supply, and became entangled in the machinery with fatal results. The summons was brought under the Factory and Workshops Act, the prosecution contending that the premises came within the scope of that measure on account of the arc lamps overhanging the streets. The Home Office inspector explained that an engine used to generate electricity for the purpose of lighting a public place, street, or thoroughfare, came within the meaning of the Act. The company denied that on the night the accident happened, the arcs were lit, and eventually the case was dismissed on payment of costs. As a matter of fact, there is no doubt that where generating sets are used, the Factory Act applies. In the case of shows where motor generators (or transformers) are installed, however, we have thought it worth while to be at some considerable trouble to get the authoritative opinion of the Home Office as to how such shows stood with regard to the Factory Act.

In the end and after the customary delay and red tape which was to be expected in a direct appeal to the head authority, we have been successful in our efforts. Moreover, the true state of the case as regards showmen installing motor generators turns out to be particularly interesting. It is this :—

Where the convertor is used for transforming down for the kinematograph arc only it does not place the show under the Factory Act.

Where used for general hall or show front lighting in addition to supplying current for the projection arc, a rotary convertor does bring the showman under the factory regulations.

FIG. 230.   POSING FOR THE CAMERA IN EAST AFRICA.

CHAPTER VIII.

THE COPYRIGHT ACT OF 1911 AND KINEMATOGRAPHY.

Since the last issue of our Handbook, the Copyright Bill of 1911 has made a difference to the law as far as kinematograph films are concerned.

Previously these films for all purposes of copyright came under the heading of " photographs," and it was only under the heading of the Fine Arts Copyright Act of 1862 that the owner could register the copyright. This Act provided for the separate registration of each photograph of a film, and this being impossible from the manufacturer's point of view, he was contented with registering a picture here and there throughout his film, in the hope that he might be able to catch the " duper." It was financially absurd to copyright each small photograph of, say, a 3,000 ft. subject of 16 pictures to the foot—48,000 registrations for one series would be ridiculous.

The whole thing was more or less a farce until the Act of 1911 came into force. By virtue of this Act the films are now recognised by distinct titles as such in respect to copyright, and now only one registration is necessary to preserve the rights to the maker.

This is in accordance with Article 14 of the Berlin Convention. This article provides that " authors of literary, scientific or artistic works shall have the exclusive right of authorising the reproduction and public representation of their works by kinematography." Kinematography for reproductions shall be protected as literary or artistic works, if by the arrangement of the acting, form, or the combination of the incidents represented, the author has given the work a personal and original character.

Without prejudice to the rights of the author of the original work, the reproduction by kinematography of a literary, scientific or artistic work shall be protected as an original work.

The Copyright Act of 1911 deals with films and their protection in the following manner :—

By Section 1 (1) it is provided that " Subject to the provisions of this Act, copyright shall subsist throughout the parts of His Majesty's dominions to which this Act extends for the term hereinafter mentioned in every original literary, dramatic, musical and artistic work, if (a) in the case of a published work, the work was first published within such parts of His Majesty's dominions aforesaid, and (b) in the case of an unpublished work the author was at the date of making the work a British subject, or resident within such parts of His Majesty's dominions as aforesaid ; and by Section 1 (2) 'copyright' is defined as the sole right to produce the work or any substantial part thereof in any material form whatsoever, to perform, or in the case of a lecture, to deliver, the work or any substantial part thereof in public, and if the work is unpublished, to publish the work or any substantial part thereof ; and shall include the sole right . . . . . (d) in the case of a literary, dramatic or musical work, to make any record, perforated roll, kinematograph film, or other contrivance by means of which the work may be mechanically performed or delivered, and to authorise such acts as aforesaid."

Section 21 is very emphatic in its meaning, and gives protection to the kinematograph film in two distinct ways.

"The term for which copyright shall subsist in photographs shall be fifty years from the making of the original negative from which the photograph was directly or indirectly derived, and the person who was owner of such negative at the time when such negative was made shall be deemed to be the author of the work, and, where such owner is a body corporate, the body corporate shall be deemed for the purposes of this Act to reside within the parts of His Majesty's dominions to which this Act extends if [it has established a place of business within such parts."

Then in Section 35 appears the following :—

"In this Act, unless the context otherwise requires, ... (1) 'Dramatic work' includes any piece of recitation, choreographic work or entertainment in dumb show, the scenic arrangement or acting form of which is fixed in writing or otherwise, and any kinematograph production where the arrangement or acting form or the combination of incidents represented give the work an original character.

". . . . 'Photograph' includes photo-lithograph and any work produced by any process analogous to photography ;

"'Kinematograph' includes any work produced by any process analogous to kinematography ;

". . . . 'Infringing,' when applied to a copy of a work in which copyright subsists, means any copy, including any colourable imitation made, or imported in contravention of the provisions of this Act.

"'Performance' means any acoustic representation of a work and any visual representation of any dramatic action in a work, including such a representation made by means of any mechanical instrument ;

"'Delivery,' in relation to a lecture, includes delivery by means of any mechanical instrument ;

"(2) For the purposes of this Act (other than those relating to infringements of copyright), a work shall not be deemed to be published or performed in public, and a lecture shall not be deemed to be delivered in public, if published, performed in public, or delivered in public, without the consent or acquiescence of the author, his executors, administrators or assigns.

"(3) For the purposes of this Act, a work shall be deemed to be first published within the parts of His Majesty's dominions to which this Act extends, notwithstanding that it has been published simultaneously in some other place, unless the publication in such parts of His Majesty's dominions as aforesaid is colourable only, and is not intended to satisfy the reasonable requirements of the public, and a work shall be deemed to be published simultaneously in two places if the time between the publication in one such place and the publication in the other place does not exceed fourteen days, or such longer period as may, for the time being, be fixed by Order in Council.

"(4) Where, in the case of an unpublished work, the making of a work has extended over a considerable period, the conditions of this Act conferring copyright shall be deemed to have been complied with, if the author was, during any substantial part of that period, a British subject or a resident within the parts of His Majesty's dominions to which this Act extends.

"(5) For the purposes of the provisions of this Act, as to residence, an author of a work shall be deemed to be a resident in the parts of His Majesty's dominions to which this Act extends if he is domiciled within any such part."

It will therefore be seen from the above digest of the Copyright Act of 1911 that the original owner of a kinematograph subject is amply protected, and it is to be hoped that the trade will never again be troubled with that wily individual, the "film duper."

Fig. 231. A Battle with Live Fish.

THE FILM CENSORSHIP.

As we go to press the terms under which the newly appointed Film Censor grants permits for the exhibition of subjects comes to hand, and we are enabled to briefly outline them.

Publishers of films will enter into an undertaking to submit to the Board all films to be released except "Topicals" and "Locals," and a fee will be paid for each subject at the rate of one shilling per hundred feet, with a minimum fee of five shillings. When a film has been passed by the Board, a certificate, in one of the two forms which appear in facsimile on this page, will be issued, and a photographic reproduction must be attached to each copy immediately after the main title. The publisher further agrees not to make any alteration in the film without re-submitting it to the Board, and also undertakes not to publish any film which has been rejected.

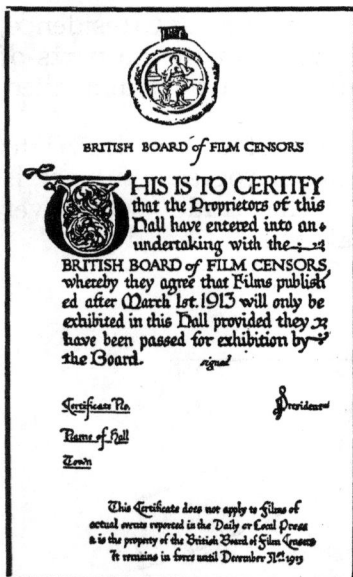

FIG. 232.
EXHIBITOR'S CERTIFICATE.

FIG. 233.
THE MANUFACTURER'S CERTIFICATES.

The object of the two certificates is to differentiate between films for public exhibition and "Universals"—specially for children's matinees.

Proprietors and managers will also play an important part in making the Censorship effective. They are to undertake not to exhibit any film released on or after March 1st unless it has been passed by the Board and bears a photographic reproduction of the official certificate. Each proprietor will pay the sum of five shillings, when a certificate will be issued for exhibition in their theatre. This is liable to be cancelled if there be any breach of the conditions under which it is issued, and it is understood that it does not apply to the exhibition of "topicals" or "locals."

Williamson House.

Est. 1886.

WILLIAMSON MACHINERY.

Cameras- -   - - Known

Printers -   - - - Used

and   and

Perforators   Appreciated

Throughout the World

SYNOPSIS OF CHAPTERS.

CONTENTS.

426

The

Original

THE CINFONIUM

The first Orchestral Piano to be introduced, is still far in advance of anything of the kind on the market. The only instrument with a 16 foot organ stop. It combines piano, organ, bells, zither, harp, banjo, etc., and is fitted with Venetian swell.

CALL AND HEAR IT. BOOKLET FREE.

The INDOMITABLE

A projector superior to all others in its massive construction, scientific design and hard wearing capacities. It is BUILT TO ENDURE, has the highest light efficiency and the most perfect optical system. Don't purchase until you have inspected it. Booklet free.

CALL, OR SEND FOR BOOKLET.

The TYLER APPARATUS Co.

LIMITED,

11 CHARING CROSS RD., (Near Trafalgar Square,) LONDON, W.

BLOCKS & DIAGRAMS.

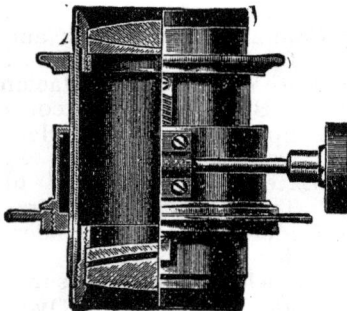

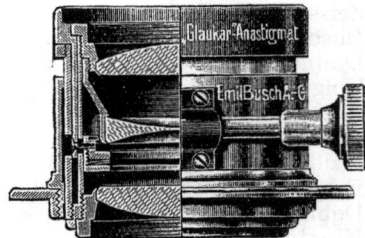

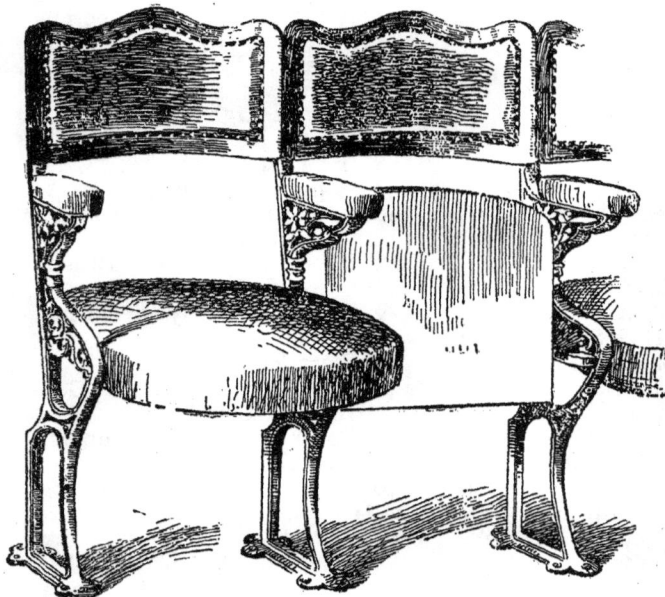

440